Alphabet to Internet

What Greek philosopher thought writing would harm a student's memory? Was the poet Byron's daughter the first computer programmer? Who plays more video games, women over 18 or teenage boys?

In *Alphabet to Internet: Media in Our Lives*, Irving Fang looks at each medium of communication through the centuries, asking not only, "What happened?" but also, "How did society change because of this new communication medium?" and "How are we different as a result?"

Examining the impact of different media upon a broad, historical scale—among them mass printing, the telegraph, film, the Internet, and advertising—*Alphabet to Internet* takes us from the first scratches of writing and the origins of mail to today's video games, the widespread and daily use of smartphones, and the impact of social media in political uprisings across the globe. A timeline at the end of each chapter places events in perspective and allows students to pinpoint key moments in media history.

Now in its third edition, *Alphabet to Internet* presents a lively, thoughtful, and accessible introduction to media history.

Irving Fang has been a journalist, teacher, author, and publisher. His career has included the *Daily Times* of Nigeria, Reuters, ABC News, and the University of Minnesota. He has served as a visiting professor in Singapore and as a Fulbright professor in the Philippines. He wrote the first book about television news skills and possibly the first doctoral dissertation ever printed by computer. He lives in Cambridge, Massachusetts.

Alphabet to Internet

Media in Our Lives

Third Edition

Irving Fang

Routledge
Taylor & Francis Group

NEW YORK AND LONDON

Editor: Erica Wetter
Editorial Assistant: Simon Jacobs
Production Editor: Reanna Young
Text Design: Apex CoVantage
Copyeditor: Andrea Service
Indexer: Kristin Harley
Cover Design: Gareth Toye

Third edition published 2015
by Routledge
711 Third Avenue, New York, NY 10017

and by Routledge
2 Park Square, Milton Park, Abingdon, Oxon OX14 4RN

Routledge is an imprint of the Taylor & Francis Group, an informa business

First and second editions published
by Rada Press 2008, 2012

Trademark notice: Product or corporate names may be trademarks or registered trademarks, and are used only for identification and explanation without intent to infringe.

Library of Congress Cataloging-in-Publication Data
Fang, Irving E.
    Alphabet to Internet : media in our lives / Irving Fang.
        pages cm
    Includes bibliographical references and index.
    1. Mass media—History.   I. Title.
    P90.F264 2014
    302.2309—dc23
    2014019078

ISBN: 978-1-138-80584-2 (hbk)
ISBN: 978-1-138-80585-9 (pbk)
ISBN: 978-1-315-75195-5 (ebk)

Typeset in Warnock Pro
by Apex CoVantage, LLC

Printed and bound in the United States of America by Sheridan Books, Inc. (a Sheridan Group Company).

To Oscar, Ruby, Max, Annika, and Lucy
who will navigate through a life of media

Contents

Introduction: Adapting to Our
Media Environment　　　　　　　　　　1

▶ 1　Writing: Gathering Thought　　　　13

▶ 2　Early Printing: Reaching More of Us　　37

▶ 3　Mass Printing: Reaching Still More　　59

▶ 4　Mail: The Snail that Could　　　　87

▶ 5　Telegraph: Uniting the United States　　111

▶ 6　Telephone: Reaching without
Touching　　　　　　　　　　　　125

▶ 7　Recording: Beyoncé Sings Better
than Our Sister　　　　　　　　　147

▶ 8　Photography: Personal and
So Much More　　　　　　　　　163

▶ 9　Silent Film: The Audience Waits　　183

▶ 10　A Movie Century: Moving Us　　203

▶ **11 Radio: Helping Us through the Rough Years**   **225**

▶ **12 Television: Pictures in Our Parlors**   **251**

▶ **13 Computers: Beyond Calculation**   **277**

▶ **14 The Internet: The World at Our Fingertips**   **293**

▶ **15 Video Games: Leaning Forward**   **315**

▶ **16 Persuasion: The Push Never Stops**   **335**

▶ **17 Media Matter: Entwined in Human Life**   **351**

Further Reading   355
Image Credits   373
Index   375

Introduction: Adapting to Our Media Environment

A 2012 survey of 19,271 respondents taken in 25 countries reported that more than one person in five (22 percent) would rather give up sex than a mobile phone.[1]

By marital status, 17 percent of the married and 26 percent of others would give up sex before surrendering their mobile phones, and 18 percent of the employed compared with 26 percent of the unemployed. No difference was reported for level of education.

Percentage Preferring the Cell

	Worldwide	United States
Women	30	30
Men	13	11
Under 35	23	25
Ages 35–49	19	18
Ages 50–64	24	18

A different survey found that more people would rather leave home without their wallet than their smartphone.[2]

These results may end up as tidbits to brighten party conversations, but— even allowing for some skepticism —they tell us something important about what is going on where cellphones are used, and that is almost everywhere in the world. For significant numbers of people, mediated communication— using a device that connects with someone else at some distance—matters more than one of the most fundamental elements of life, and arguably the most intense. Mobile phones are preferred to sex by quite a few of the young, whose levels of testosterone and estrogen are at their peak, as well as by the old, whose hormonal fires have dimmed.

'What's wrong? You've hardly touched your phone.'

By K. J. Lamb. Courtesy of *The Spectator*.

Our love affair (an apt phrase) with a medium of communication extends beyond the mobile phone. How often has a couple after going to bed delayed turning out the light and turning to each other until someone finishes a magazine article? Or until a television program has ended? First things first. (An Italian study found that couples who kept a television set in their bedroom had sex half as often as those who did not.[3]) How often has a couple interrupted the most intimate of moments to attend to a ringing telephone? The title of a *Time* article about social media reinforces the statistics: "The Friendship Trap: Are Our Social Lives Sabotaging Our Love Lives?"[4]

To prefer a tool of communication to sex could even raise questions about the continuation of the human species. Never mind the puzzled look from Sigmund Freud. What would Charles Darwin make of this?

▶ WHAT HAS SUDDENLY HAPPENED?

So, let us ask: What has suddenly happened to bring about this preference by one in four or one in five people in the world who were queried?

The answer is that nothing has *suddenly* happened. Media *use* and accompanying media *dependence* have been growing for centuries. Looking at the media-obsessed "Millennial" generation (born between 1980 and 2000), columnist Joel Stein observed that "millennials' self-involvement is more a continuation of a trend than a revolutionary break from previous generations. They're not a new species; they've just mutated to adapt to their environment."[5]

So it has always been. We adapt. Now we have adapted to a media-suffused environment. Mediated communication began more than 5,000 years ago with the first scratches on clay tablets. From a useful tool, dependence on media has grown over the centuries. The pace has quickened and it is recorded. Depending upon how eager each of us is for information, we know more than any previous generation knew, or at least we have the potential to know more and to know it sooner, no matter where in the world anything is happening. Frightening or laughable, it is all a finger tap away.

For any invention or new method of doing something to succeed, it must find a social use. As the number of users spreads, the world adapts itself to accommodate what is new, so that the invention or method affects even those who do not personally use it. Consider the automobile. Those who do not drive are still affected in dozens of ways, from road traffic and auto pollution to cheap and varied food and other goods brought by truck. Or consider the sewing machine. People who do not sew and have never owned a sewing machine benefit from the variety of inexpensive clothing that machines make possible, but may also feel a need to protest the wages and working conditions in the textile factories of poorer countries. Consider the disadvantaged lives of non-literates who cannot use the alphabet or printing. Or consider the limitations on people who are unable to communicate by telephone when nearly everyone else does. Now consider the efforts to give inexpensive computers to children to aid their education.

Arguing that introducing a new technology has wider implications, media theorist Neil Postman used the analogy of caterpillars: "If you remove the caterpillars from a given habitat, you are not left with the same environment minus caterpillars; you have a new environment . . . the same is true if you add caterpillars to an environment that has had none."[6] Postman used the term *media ecology* to identify the study of the role that media play in human affairs. According to the Media Ecology Association, media ecology "looks into the matter of how media of communication affects human perception, understanding, feeling, and value, as well as how our interaction with media facilitates or impedes our chances of survival. The word ecology implies the study of environments: their structure, content, and impact on people."[7]

Marshall McLuhan divided history into communication eras: Tribal Era, Literate Era, Print Era, and Electronic Era. He identified *communication technology* as the primary cause of social change and also of transition into new eras. Not the only cause, of course, but primary.

▶ MASS AND PERSONAL

Each new medium has penetrated the lives of individuals and societies. To say that communication media have been a factor in the course of history is not a deterministic point of view, for wars, disease, conquests, exploration, and other factors have also played their part. Technology is not the sole driver of the development of a society. The point made in these pages is that mediated communication has been a *significant* and, today, an expanding element of historic change.

Mediated communication can be defined as both *mass* and *personal* information exchange using a physical medium. In fact, because mass and personal media use the same tools and sometimes have the same goals, their distinctions have eroded. The inclusive term is not *mass* communication. It is *mediated* communication. Because so much of our daily life is spent with it, we should know how it affects us. Besides asking what mediated communication does *for* us, we should also ask what mediated communication does *to* us.

Mediated communication—using external means to carry information—has been part of human life since the start of recorded history. By definition, recorded history requires media and itself uses such media as alphabets and paper. The term "mediated communication" includes every means of communication listed in this book's table of contents, and more. The communication can be as broad as showing the world humans' first moon landing or as personal as helping a family member to reach a decision. Modern technology has enmeshed as never before what is mass and what is personal.

In 2011 Japanese were informing relatives and friends around the world via Facebook, Twitter, and a special Google service that they had survived the 9.0 earthquake and tsunami. As images of the horrors filled YouTube and flowed onto television, social media removed at least some of the pain of not knowing. Reporters interviewed both victims and experts via a video telephone service, Skype. The mass communication ability to inform on a global scale and the personal communication ability of one person to connect to another at a global reach became intertwined through the Internet, a network of networks.

Social networks are both mass and personal communication. So is email. Postal services have enabled both mass and personal communication at least since Benjamin Franklin mailed out his first catalog for scientific and academic books in 1744. Today when disaster strikes, CNN trawls for witnesses who took pictures.

▶ A SHIFT TO ISOLATION

For the many centuries during which most of the world was illiterate, people received their information from each other, from travelers, and from their local priests. Entertainment came from one another in the form of singing, dancing, and story-telling. The shared element was community. Each other. Media brought isolation. This was not *always* true, for certainly a literate parent could read to a child from a book, and in the age of recording, broadcasting and motion pictures, absorbing media was often a shared experience. However, the dominant behavioral factor has been that media are usually received alone, marked by separation from others.

For all those centuries, learning for most people did not require media. A boy learned as apprentice to a master. A girl learned tasks from her mother. Everyone learned from one another, from one generation to the next, and from keeping a keen eye for what nature taught. As formal education took hold, people figured out how to use media tools, starting with the alphabet. The more educated a person became, the more the elements of media were needed, depended upon, and substituted for the community. The scholar required isolation.

When mediated entertainment took hold during the 20th century, some of it was received communally at first, such as the weekly night out at the downtown movie palace or the neighborhood cinema; but it has increasingly become a solitary activity. People listen to mediated music through earphones. News is received over car radios by drivers commuting alone. So are audio books. Movies and television programs are downloaded to computers and handheld devices for solitary enjoyment. Youths congregate with cellphones pressed to their ears, their attention to someone not in sight. Beachgoers ignore the beach, the water, and those around them to focus on iPads and Kindles.

Besides the recent electronic inventions that make all this isolation possible, there is an exponential growth of content choice. Thousands of movies and novels and songs can be downloaded and even stored in improbably smaller devices. The cornucopia of the Internet is one button push away. With so many choices, community is more fragmented than ever. The village may be global, but it is hardly a communal village these days.

In the 21st century many of us are media *creators* as well as media *receivers*. Social media sites such as Vine, Instagram, and YouTube, plus the easy-to-use digital tools allowing for desktop publishing and desktop video and the popularity of Twitter and audio mash-ups, as well as the blogosphere and "lean-forward" interactive, multiplayer games, all add up to active involvement that could hardly have been imagined in the mass communication world of the 20th century. Yet what was available in the 20th century could hardly have been imagined by the dwellers of the 19th century, and what was invented in the 19th century—photography, recording, the telegraph and telephone, the rotary press, paper from trees, point-to-point wireless—would have astonished even the doughty 18th-century inventor Benjamin Franklin. Today's expansion of the available tools of communication is a continuation of what has gone before at what appears to be an exponential pace.

▶ NEEDING MEDIA

Have you heard any of these excuses? Each carries a whiff of dependence, of *needing* media:

> "I can't tonight. I'm binge-watching season 3."
> "My soap is coming on. I have to watch."

"This is my favorite (video) game. I'll join you later."
"This is my favorite (ball) game. I'll join you later."
"I'm never without my cell. It's like my right arm."
"I have a call. Sorry. I've got to take it."

Buyers add to their credit card debt not only for cellphones and smart-phones, but for all means of receiving media, and go deeper into debt to replace a perfectly useable working device with one that is bigger (TV, desk computer) or smaller (mobile phone) or thinner (laptop), or has more features, memory, or apps, whether or not the buyer will ever use them. When a new device is rolled out, banner headlines carry the news. Thousands of the hardier members of the human species will wait in line through a cold night to acquire the device. Would they do so for anything else?

It should be obvious that these means of connecting us matter intensely to our times. Mediated communication keeps ties with distant family members, reignites connections with friends, brings valuable information to our fingertips that we cannot otherwise acquire, and provides a measure of companionship to those who are alone. Life increasingly revolves around media for work, study, leisure, information, entertainment, and contacts. At least one clothing company designs its coats around as many as two dozen pockets for holding mostly devices for communicating. Even its boxer shorts have a pocket for an iPhone. Other companies are building communication devices into wearables. Google Glass is just one example of what is coming.[8]

More is at work here than *using* media. It is *needing* media. A *dependency* on the tools and content of mediated communication is greater than it has ever been and shows no sign of diminishing. In 2013 the Bradford Regional Medical Center in Pennsylvania began an inpatient treatment program for Internet addiction. Dependency is fed by endless advertising campaigns that would, both overtly and subtly, add more time spent with media. To cite just one example, a commercial for DISH Network has a family sitting down in front of the TV, saying they now receive Blockbuster movies with thousands of choices via satellite: "So we can all watch what we want when we want." A commercial for Hulu makes the same promise in almost the same words. *Entertainment Weekly* asked, "Who needs human interaction? All the friends, secret crushes, and family drama you'll ever need are on your small screen of choice this fall." Perhaps the question of who needs human interaction was asked sarcastically. Perhaps not.[9]

If we are welcome to watch whatever and whenever, we are being invited to spend even *more* time in this enjoyable activity than we spent before. We are certainly not being invited to spend *less* time. As Robert Putnam observed in his now famous study, *Bowling Alone*, Americans instead are spending less time in such communal gatherings as Parent–Teacher Association meetings and bowling leagues.[10] Faith Popcorn called the preference for curling up at home in the evening "cocooning" and predicted much more of it.[11]

Futurist Neil Postman and others have written extensively about Americans choosing to stay home with mediated amusement.[12] Popcorn and

Postman wrote before mobile devices made cocooning an activity that would often be done alone. One result of cocooning has been that the downtown streets of many American cities are "rolled up" in the evening. Few people dare to go downtown to look in shop windows and mingle with others. The others aren't there either. It is a perverse mark of progress that we find the pleasure of an evening stroll in the company of strangers or to sit outside and chat with neighbors mostly in poorer cities of developing nations.

AN EXAMPLE OF DEPENDENCE

In 1979, the Minneapolis–St. Paul television station WCCO-TV offered people phoned at random U.S.$500 if they agreed to live without television for one month. Of 45 people called, 27 refused. Elderly people living alone said television was their only friend. Several who refused said they risked divorce without television. Those who agreed were first given diaries to log how much time they actually spent watching TV, and were surprised by how much they underestimated their actual viewing. Five families were chosen, with each member of the household promising not to watch any television whatsoever for one month. The station said the families were a representative segment of the audience. Family members found other activities to occupy them, but not without difficulty and stress. One participant, Patricia Gessner, recalled that the biggest gift she got from the experiment was "hearing myself think again. I remember that fall, we spent more time outdoors, and more time indoors being creative. I built a cardboard kitchen for Ben, and we did a lot more reading. I didn't have too much in the way of withdrawal; it was more the experience of discovery." But the moment the month's experiment ended, her TV set went back on. One man said that being without television was "like a death in the family. It really is."[13]

The experiment was done long before the Internet and video games offered their alternate mediated attractions. Even in stringent times, $500 may not be enough to convince five families to turn off all their screens for a month.

▶ THE SOURCES OF OUR VALUES

Mediated communication has a push–pull effect, pushing us apart but keeping us tethered to family and friends, to home and sometimes to workplace. It helps us to stay in contact with one another while also contributing to our physical separation. The Internet is just one of the latest catalysts for our new reality. Soldiers serving in Afghanistan can receive digital pictures daily from their families and friends using camera phones, or can talk to the family via Skype or FaceTime. When children travel they stuff DVD movies and portable gaming systems into their carry-on backpacks. If they move to another country their parents now have nightly podcasts of American radio and television newscasts to keep them up to date about events at home.

At some level, humans have had media for centuries to accompany life's changes. Communication media are so tangled up in our existence that we give little thought to these connections or to living without them. Yet societies are both subtly and profoundly affected by media. So is individual behavior. Values and culture once came entirely through the family, the church, the community, the school. Values came from people you knew and saw. This changed when the Industrial Revolution brought mass media. Advertising, newspapers, magazines, and the novel introduced the standards of people who lived far away. Immigration, driven in part by communication, has led to cities bulging with the signs and sights of many cultures. Personal advice now also comes from the newspaper column and the television screen.

With the integration of each new medium, life became different for those who used the medium. Because you are reading these words it is likely that you will spend more time today with mediated communication—in some of its many forms—than doing anything else, including sleeping. If you decide to test this, you can use a stopwatch or the stopwatch feature of your smart-phone. Click it if you wake to a clock radio or turn on the TV. Click it at the breakfast table if you read a newspaper or the back of the cereal box. Click for the car radio and the billboards you glance at. Click for phone calls. Click for the letter you are writing, because mediated communication runs in both directions and you will be using the technology of an alphabet and the postal service. Continue to click as warranted throughout the day until you finally turn out the light. Add up the times tomorrow.

Much of our use of media is routine and habitual, baked into our lives. If you read a morning newspaper, do you read it at breakfast, always starting at the same section, such as the sports page, the comics, or the obits? When you flip your car's ignition switch, does your radio come on, always tuned to the same station? When you arrive at work, do you start with the same blogs or news reports as you did yesterday? How about your television view-ing? You may know it's Tuesday because your favorite show is on tonight; on Tuesdays if you don't have a digital video recorder (DVR) you stay home for it. If a popular news anchor changes her hairstyle, she can be sure some viewers will complain, for the change has intruded into *their* expectations, *their* routine.

However, Marshall McLuhan famously told us that the *medium* is the message, not the *content* it brings. He saw media tools as extensions of our senses and our limbs. He could be scathing: "Our conventional response to all media, namely that it is how they are used that counts, is the numb stance of the technological idiot."[14] A theory that reportedly guided CBS network programmers was that viewers watched television, not programs, so they will watch whatever bores them or bothers them least.

▶ ADAPTING TO OUR MEDIA ENVIRONMENT

A perception exists that to succeed in romance or business today we must use the latest tools of mediated communication, or at least be able to talk about them with familiarity. We adapt ourselves to media imperatives. We carry devices everywhere. We respond to the ringing tones wherever and whenever. We sometimes watch what our friends watch just so that we can talk about it. We learn the jargon. We adjust. Not to put too fine a point on it, we as a society create mediated communication that alters how we spend our days, how we live our lives, how we relate to others. That way, we may succeed. Darwin never taught a clearer lesson.

History has repeatedly demonstrated the capacity that communication media have to affect our lives. Each new medium has brought in its wake a pattern of change distinct to that medium. Yet many media encountered opposition along the way to general acceptance, a grudging recognition that change was not always welcome. While certain elements of change are common to several media—such as separating us from our immediate surroundings—each medium creates its own pattern, its own signature of human behavior.

An area of communication research known as "uses and gratifications theory" examines ways that all of us use media to meet specific needs. At a basic level we use weather reports to decide if a child should wear mittens to school. We listen to a favorite radio commentator to reinforce our political views. The theory is based on the premise that readers, listeners, and viewers are not simply passive vessels to be filled with whatever media sends our way. Instead, we are active consumers who use media for specific purposes. We, the audience, are aware of what we are doing.

▶ CHANGES THAT MEDIA BROUGHT

The chapters that follow examine how our lives have been affected by the adoption of new means of communication. These are just some of the changes that have made the deepest impact. They should be obvious to us, but it doesn't hurt to remind ourselves of them. Here is a look at the chapters that follow.

Writing stores most of mankind's knowledge and allows that knowledge to be unlimited by memory. Writing carries thought across the centuries and across the lands and oceans. It makes progress and our civilization possible. Nations with significant illiterate populations are at a disadvantage. The scattered tribes that cling to an oral culture eke out a bare existence.

Printing broadens the spread of information and provides the pleasure to be found in reading. It makes mass education and democracy possible. Printing has expanded science and medicine and every other field of knowledge. It has also expanded commerce, the rule of law, and almost every human activity.

The **mails** for centuries have carried information, bringing us both personal and commercial messages. Where postal services are weak, the spread of information is stunted. Where they are strong, nations benefit.

The **telegraph** stitched together distant communities and connected individuals with information that they could share and that arrived almost instantly. It made railroads safer. Its role has diminished only because it is the parent of the telephone, radio, and the other ways we transmit messages.

The **telephone** brings familiar voices and emotions even to people who are separated by events that have altered their lives. Much of what makes loved ones special flies through the wires, and now through the air. The telephone saves lives by giving us a means to summon help. Because it makes life safer and more pleasant, many of us keep a telephone by our side day and night. Yet the same phone that can keep us physically independent from others, like parents, can also, if we want, pull us into a flash mob that overwhelms police efforts at control. Phones that snap and twitter images of violence have sent crowds into inflamed, destructive riots.

Recording brings us entertainment of a quality we could not otherwise encounter. It holds the music that is an expression of every culture. It retains memories that delight us as the years roll by, connecting us to distant times and places and people who mattered to us.

Photography enriches our memories and our awareness and has shown us scenes that we could not personally witness. Although photographs today can be altered, most photos for most people still fit the saying that seeing is believing. Photos also remind us of past times, and that is important. When people are forced to flee a home because of fire or flood, what they may clutch in their hands is a photo album.

Movies give people everywhere the realities and stories that have become part of our lives. To see a film, literacy doesn't matter. Today it is not only easier to own movies but it is also easier to make them. We recognize movie stars much more readily than those who govern us. To appreciate the impact of the motion picture, we have only to consider the nature and direction of censorship.

Radio, immediately within reach, keeps us company with information and entertainment no matter where we are. It can be a companion from the moment we wake, through each day's commute, and as we fall asleep. In remote places where no other communication is available, radio remains a dependable servant. Before broadcasting, radio was known for its wireless capacity to connect ships and distant places.

Television keeps us company with news and a variety of entertainment so compelling that people all over the world spend hours with TV each day. More television sets than people reside in the average American home. Visitors may enter our homes or leave, events may occur that demand attention, but for many viewers the TV stays on. Yet the technology is shifting in ways that will affect us.

The **computer** as a tool of communication assists our work and our studies. It extends our reach in every direction and reduces our need for transportation. It stores data and calculates far better than our minds can. It helps us to publish books and produce films. It provides the physical underpinning of the Internet and email. Yet here too the technology is shifting.

The **Internet** opens up as much of the world to us as we want. It leads us into new areas of knowledge at the touch of a button. The more educated you are, the more likely to use the Internet. The unfolding social networks are a part of the astonishing communication revolution that is now under way.

Video games are the new way that we entertain and challenge ourselves. Many people, especially but not only younger people, never tire of such a challenge. The games allow us to interact with a means of professionally created entertainment. They reflect human values and human desires, not all of which are matters of pride.

Persuading others to a point of view or to take an action has always been part of life, and certainly of communication. Advertising and propaganda are ever with us. They take many forms, overt or subtle, including public relations. Persuasion via mediated communication has a considerable role in modern warfare and in both political and religious conflict.

The tools of communication have accompanied us in our journey across the centuries. Year by year the amount of mediated communication in our lives increases both in what we are able to send and what we receive. In all these ways and in many others we are different because of our means of communication. Let us examine the specific changes that each brought to human life. We start with writing.

▶ NOTES

1 Countries in the Asia–Pacific region are most likely to say they would give up sex over giving up their mobile phones. nearly half of those in Japan (47%) would do so, followed by Hong Kong (42%), South Korea (38%), Indonesia (33%), and India (31%). Brazilians are least likely to say they would give up sex (8%) instead of giving up their phones, followed by Argentina (9%), Spain (10%), Italy (11%) and Canada (12%). These are some of the findings of an Ipsos Global @dvisor poll conducted between January 5 and January 16, 2012. Ipsos is a global marketing research firm. The survey instrument was conducted in 25 countries: Argentina, Australia, Belgium, Brazil, Canada, China, France, Germany, Great Britain, Hong Kong, Hungary, India, Indonesia, Italy, Japan, Mexico, Poland, Russia, Saudi Arabia, South Africa, South Korea, Spain, Sweden, Turkey and the United States. An international sample of 19,271 adults aged 18–64 in the United States and Canada, and aged 16–64 in all other countries, were interviewed. Approximately 1,000+ individuals participated on a country-by-country basis with the exception of Argentina, Indonesia, Mexico, Poland, Saudi Arabia, South Africa, South Korea, Sweden, Russia, and Turkey, where each had a sample 500+. Weighting was then employed to balance demographics and ensure that the sample's composition reflected that of the adult population according to the most recent country census data and to provide results intended to approximate the sample universe. A survey with an unweighted probability sample of this size and a 100% response rate would have an estimated margin of error of +/−3.1 percentage points for a sample of 1,000 and an estimated margin of error of +/−4.5 percentage points for a sample of 500 19 times out of 20 per country of what the results would have been had the entire population of the specifically aged adults in that country been polled. A separate study of 2,000 participants, ages 18 to 91 equally divided by gender, in Britain, found that certain pieces of recorded music created a similar reaction to what happens when people have an emotional or sexual stimulus. For 40% of the respondents the music recording evoked a greater response than actual touch. That study, reported on October 24, 2012, was commissioned by Spotify and conducted by music psychologist Daniel Müllensiefen of Goldsmiths, University of London. For further information, go to http://www.ipsos-na.com/news-polls/pressrelease.aspx?id=5647.

2   McKinsey Global Institute, "Disruptive Technologies: Advances that Will Transform Life, Business, and the Global Economy": 29.

3   "TV in Bedroom, Problems for Your Sex Life," ABC, January 17, 2006, http://abclocal.go.com/kabc/story?section=news/health&id=3806654.

4   *Time*, February 24, 2014: 52.

5   *Time*, May 20, 2013: 31.

6   Neil Postman, *Technopoly: The Surrender of Culture to Technology* (New York: Knopf, 1992) 18.

7   "What Is Media Ecology," *Media Ecology Association*, 2008. Postman founded the Association.

8   Bill Wasik, "Try It On," *Wired*, January 2014: 90. Examples of "Technology Enabled Clothing" can be found at http://www.scottevest.com.

9   *Entertainment Weekly*, September 27, 2013: 47.

10 Robert Putnam, *Bowling Alone: The Collapse and Revival of American Community* (New York: Simon & Schuster, 2000).

11 Faith Popcorn, *The Popcorn Report: The Future of Your Company, Your World, Your Life* (New York: Doubleday, 1991).

12 Neil Postman, *Amusing Ourselves to Death* (New York: Viking Penguin, 1985).

13 A report on the effects of television viewing, from 1979. Accessible at http://tcmedianow.com/video/wcco-tv-dave-moore-report-death-in-the-family-a-report-on-the-effects-of-television-viewing-from-1979/.

14 Marshall McLuhan, *Understanding Media: The Extensions of Man* (Toronto, University of Toronto Press, 1964) 18.

1

Writing: Gathering Thought

In most conflicts pitting an oral culture against a written culture, the literates win a lopsided victory. Non-literates are sometimes credited with a more romanticized culture, such as the Native Americans who encountered the arriving European immigrants, but time and again, they ended up enslaved or dead. The Vikings, who made limited use of runes, and Mongols did well in their day, but the peoples who left writing behind them have influenced the future far more than the efficient warriors who once shook worlds.

Media historian Harold Innis credits writing with the establishment of ancient empires: "The written record signed, sealed, and swiftly transmitted was essential to military power and the extension of government. Small communities were written into large states and states were consolidated into empire. The monarchies of Egypt and Persia, the Roman empire, and the city-states were essentially products of writing."[1]

Today, in literate societies, individuals who lack literacy in the language of their community are disadvantaged. The remaining non-literate communities in remote corners of the world have no more power than the literate world grants them. The few pockets of oral culture that survive do so by the sufferance of the literate. They manage well enough without writing as long as they are left alone by the always more powerful possessors of writing.

Writing, the use of symbols to express thought and set information down, is as old as recorded history because, of course, that is how history was recorded. Speech and gesture preceded writing, but distance limited their reach. Cave paintings preceded writing, as did engraved marks on bones and antlers, but the meaning of their messages is mostly lost to us today. Native American smoke signals were limited. African drums—the original telegraph—may have preceded writing, but, remarkable as they could be, what they transmitted and how far they could send a message were also limited. However, the scratches on Sumerian jars, Babylonian clay tablets, Egyptian stone and papyrus, Chinese silk and Indonesian lontar leaves started a process that continues with the public library, the newspaper on your doorstep, Internet blogs, tweets, and what's on TV tonight.

A few people, Socrates among them, disparaged literacy. Still others would control what the public should be allowed to read. Yet writing continues to be our principal form of communication beyond the range of conversation.

Of writing's many advantages, a few stand out:

- Writing stores much of humankind's transmittable knowledge. Humans, of course, are the only animals able to store knowledge outside the body.
- Knowledge no longer needs to be limited to memory. With stored writing, our potential knowledge has no limits.
- Written information in a fixed form can travel across any distance. It can be organized thoughtfully and shared widely.
- Written information can travel from generation to generation for centuries without change. We can and do build upon what we already know.
- The literate own an immensely powerful tool—or weapon—denied to individual illiterates and to oral societies.[2]

▶ ORAL CULTURES

Writing and reading usually are done alone, solitary and silent activities, but in an oral culture, to communicate means to be in the presence of a listener, an audience. Oral cultures pull their members together to communicate information. To communicate by writing, no listener is present. The listener is imagined and is separated from the writer. Writing splits thought from action, as Marshall McLuhan noted.[3] Without writing, the literate mind could not think as it does, said Walter Ong, a Jesuit priest and one of the foremost authorities on oral and print cultures: "More than any other single invention, writing has transformed human consciousness."[4] When introduced into an oral society, Ong wrote, writing alters much of that society, including its culture, economics, politics, and social behavior. Once again, humankind adapts to its communication tools.

Media historian Elizabeth Eisenstein wrote, "By its very nature, a reading public was not only more dispersed; it was also more atomistic and individualistic than a hearing one. Insofar as a traditional sense of community entailed frequent gathering together to receive a given message, this sense was probably weakened by the duplication of identical messages which brought the solitary reader to the fore."[5]

To move comfortably in a world of abstractions is one of writing's gifts to us, but only at a cost. Did we pay for that gift with the coin of memory as Socrates predicted? Bards and other members of oral cultures have a tradition of memory that astounds those of us who learn to memorize from written text. It was said that medieval minstrels could hear an hour's recitation just once before repeating it verbatim. Yet today, having the gifts of paper and printing, indeed having computer flash memory encased in a bit of plastic, we don't care.

Knowledge in an oral culture is handed down to the next generation by parents and storytellers. Wisdom is passed to the younger generation by the elders. An oral culture bases itself upon two-way, restricted information. It has a human dimension, a human limitation. Members speak of a "hammer" or a "saw," not of the more abstract "tool."[6]

Writing began the shift away from the wise old elders, who could not possibly tell all that writing has stored. What we have instead is a written culture so extensive that no human being can absorb its totality. Who can, for example, recall every scrap of information in an encyclopedia or, for that matter, in a textbook for a college introductory course? No one is expected to, because the book is there. (Today we can add "or *was* there," for fewer readers need a book printed on paper if an online source is there.)

Written language undergirds most of civilization, yet there have always been societies without writing. Most of the ancient world remained illiterate. And oral cultures continued to serve people. In considering the advantages of a written culture, we should remember that the praise that always accompanies literacy comes from the literate. A degree of self-satisfaction should not be overlooked.

The European religious upheaval marking the Reformation spread Gutenberg's invention of printing through a largely illiterate population. According to one estimate, German-speaking regions in Martin Luther's day had as many as 90 percent illiterates and semi-literates.[7] However, the printed word could still reach them by being read aloud by the literate few. Oral learning continues today as part of the literate world. In places where most people are illiterate, a literate priest or teacher can read aloud. Learning what is written by rote recitation, such as at many Muslim madrassas for young pupils, has old roots.

▶ THE BEGINNINGS

Symbols date back to cave paintings drawn well before foragers became farmers. The Chauvet Cave in southern France holds drawings of animals that are 30,000 years old. But writing did not start in caves. The more recent alphabetic markings that Western cultures identify as writing are different than drawings because they led to the phonetic system of representing *sounds* that are spoken language.

Instead of marks on a surface, writing may have begun as physical tokens representing numbers and goods. The history of producing and storing information in the form of molded clay objects began about 8000 BCE in Sumer, possibly in towns along the Euphrates River.[8] One theory, which is not accepted by all scholars, holds that, over many centuries, small triangles, spheres, cones, and other tokens were molded to represent sheep, measures of grain, jars of oil, and other possessions. These tokens kept track of goods for the purpose of pooling and redistributing a community's resources.[9]

Cuneiform script on a clay cone, circa 18th century BCE.

As settled communities grew, fed by local agriculture and trade, their need for records expanded. About 5,000 years ago, numbers broke away from other information. Mathematics was born. The symbols for sheep or jars of oil came to differ from the symbols for their quantity. Tokens were placed in round sealed clay envelopes. The need to identify an envelope's contents led to scratching or pressing a representation of the tokens on the surface of the envelope. It could not have taken long to figure out that with the scratches on the outside, the tokens were no longer needed. The clay envelope itself was flattened into a tablet.

About this time the first logograms emerged, those written symbols that each represented a spoken word. These scratches were true writing, the representation of what someone might say.

Pictograms, the picture symbols representing objects and concepts, and ideograms, the symbols representing ideas, would in future become Egyptian hieroglyphics, Babylonian cuneiform, and Chinese characters. Centuries later, independently, the Mayans developed a script. Even later, so did the Aztecs. The Incas used dyed yarns attached in specific patterns to convey messages.

▶ THE ROLE OF PRIESTS

Recognizing the value of marks on clay or papyrus, people would eventually control them and punish anyone who intruded into their mysteries. Writing became sacred. The priests of many religions, the keepers of the mysteries of the gods, found writing to be a natural fit for themselves. By keeping records, they could inventory food stocks in the nation's granaries, predict weather cycles and the rising of the Nile or the Yangtze. They guarded the skill, aware of how it conferred authority. And all societies had their gods, with a priestly class to interpret the gods' mysterious behavior and to intercede for frail mankind. Each priesthood in societies as remote as Easter Island in the Pacific Ocean has needed ways to separate itself. Those who could write stood apart and above the illiterate mass of their fellows. As the priests were often the healers as well as the guides to the afterlife, it was to them that the common folk had to appeal, at times receiving charms to ward off illness and danger, as in ancient China and Japan. What will men and women not pay for health and salvation?

In society after society, priests chose the task of teaching selected youths. Scribal cultures developed. Priests educated boys in temple schools denied to outsiders. From the ranks of students came an aristocratic class, public administrators, and new priests. Literacy and education, the outpourings of mediated communication, gave them an indisputable advantage. A surviving papyrus says, "It is only the learned man who rules himself."[10]

One reason that empires held together for centuries was the capacity of a central government to write and transmit messages to governors of outlying provinces. Writing became central to societies as trade grew more complex. As writing moved out of the Fertile Crescent, it was transmitted from one culture to another. In Egypt, hieroglyphics, that most visually beautiful of written forms, were used on monuments and tomb walls. Egyptians created hieratic (the later Greek word for "priestly"), a cursive version of hieroglyphics with about 400 signs, a mix of pictograms and consonants. It became the written language of rulers and priests, used for their documents and letters. A simplified secular version, demotic (the later Greek word for "popular"), was used for record keeping and letters, useful for merchants and craftsmen and the slaves lucky enough to become scribes. Just as it is true today for mathematicians, doctors, and musicians, those who could make sense of certain symbols held the key to a specialized knowledge that set them apart, giving them something denied to others.

▶ STONE OR PAPYRUS

According to Innis, the increased use of a cursive hieratic writing on papyrus in Egypt instead of priestly hieroglyphic carving in stone and the growth of writing and reading made government more efficient and produced an organized civil service peopled by an army of scribes. With this came more secular writing, thought, and activity.

McLuhan agreed with Innis: "Engraving in stone is for the priests; they have an affinity for spanning eras. But soldiers are no-nonsense managers. They need to deal with the here and now. The alphabet and paper created armies, or rather the bureaucracies which run armies. Paper creates self-contained kingdoms at a distance."[11]

An example of Egyptian hieroglyphics, found on a temple wall at the Medinet Habu Site.

This shift from dependence on stone to dependence on papyrus and the changes in political and religious institutions imposed a strain on Egyptian civilization. Egypt quickly succumbed to invasion from peoples equipped with new instruments of attack.[12]

▶ WHO INVENTED THE ALPHABET?

Who developed the first true alphabet, in which a written letter represented a spoken sound (a phoneme) rather than an object or concept? Hieroglyphics and demotic script had some alphabetic characters. The Akkadians in Mesopotamia also had alphabetic symbols in their writing, but not a full alphabet.

The first true alphabet may have emerged about 4,000 years ago from managers at copper and turquoise mines in the Sinai Desert, a Semitic territory of the Egyptian empire, or it may have been born in a remote outpost in central Egypt manned by Semitic mercenaries on duty in the Egyptian army.[13] Or it may have been the inspiration of merchants living in that remote community. No one knows for sure. But why did it happen in such a place? Why would one of the most important advances in all of human history come out of a relatively unlettered corner of the Near East? Why not a center of culture like Thebes?

One may guess that a rigid, centralized education system of the Egyptian empire would not be inclined to change in this way. Why would those ancient priests and scribes see any need for a simplification that would spread literacy? Rather, would they not think that a series of *sound* symbols was an absurd substitute for a logogram, a single *word* symbol? They would have no reason to make writing simple or to educate the illiterate masses. Quite the contrary. Mystery and complexity served them well. Linguist Amalia Gnanadesikan called the early alphabet "a dumbed-down version of writing for the illiterate."[14] Someone even suggested—perhaps as a joke, perhaps not—that the idea of an alphabet might have come from a child in northern Syria who was fed up with having to learn cuneiform and got the idea from Egyptian writing that he put in his own Semitic language.[15]

The most recent theory, based on a discovery in the Egyptian desert northwest of Thebes, dates alphabetic writing to about 2000 BCE in writing possibly by a scribe traveling with a group of foreign mercenary soldiers, or a mine foreman or a military captain, quite possibly Semitic.[16] If that is the original source, then the alphabet might have started as Egyptian hieroglyphs lifted by semi-literate Semites in Egypt, and applied to the Semitic language. A definitive answer is not possible at present.

Copper mine managers or military officers who did not dream of entering the restricted doors of temple schools could learn an alphabet. Literature could hardly have interested them, but a more practical way to keep records and to communicate with symbols to match the words they spoke would be as welcome as a more practical way to do anything. The alphabet's ease enabled them to figure out how to use it.[17] A simple phonetic alphabet, first developed in a remote corner of the civilized world, would nicely serve mercantile or military needs for semi-literate users.

Egypt's hieroglyphic system had an entire alphabet of phonemes embedded within its daunting list of 700 images, each alphabetic picture denoting one consonant sound. Language scholar David Sacks takes the guessing from there: "Evidently someone among the Semites, a lone genius or a group, became inspired by this alphabetic principle in Egyptian writing. A purely alphabetic system was envisioned, to be adjusted to Semitic speech."[18]

It traveled, and as it traveled the shape of the letters changed and so did the languages they supported. An alphabet can support any spoken language, any dialect. That is its genius. For traders moving among a variety of languages, a phonetic alphabet was a useful and flexible tool even if the traders did not remember everything just as they had learned it. Traders are not linguistics scholars concerned with the exactness of orthography or the niceties of definitions. Copies of texts contained mistakes. Ears tuned to local dialects misheard pronunciations as this borrowing of alphabetic letters from language to language went from the Semitic mercenaries (or miners) to the Phœnician (also Semites) sea traders, to the Greeks, to the Etruscans, to the Romans, and on to the extensive Roman Empire, and so to the world.

The Greeks added vowels to the list of consonants. Results were not always efficient. The English alphabet has 26 letters. Russia's cyrillic alphabet has 33 letters. Because it has a "K" and an "S," English doesn't need a "C" for most uses and doesn't need a "Q" at all, but might earn the gratitude of schoolchildren and immigrants if "long" and "short" vowels were distinguished.

GOD'S WORD

Beneath an organized religion that was founded upon written scriptures, an oral culture breathed. Israelites in Egypt were likely to be illiterate, as were most Egyptians. Writing itself may have been unknown to them. According to the Bible, Moses brought down from Mount Sinai more than commands for righteous conduct. He brought the very words of God.

Yet they were in a form unfamiliar to the people gathered below. According to media ecologist Robert K. Logan, the manner of presentation was unique, "written with the finger of God."[19] If one believes that the sight of God's speech given as marks on tablets convinced idol worshippers to reform their ways, Logan's theory would seem to be early evidence of the potential of media to effect change.

▶ THE GREEKS

We speak of the "Phœnician" alphabet, but Phœnicians did not invent it, just as we speak of "Arabic" numerals that actually originated in India. "The Phœnicians did not create the alphabet," said historian Will Durant. "They marketed it."[20] This Semitic seafaring people trading across the Mediterranean established colonies in Greece and at Carthage on the North African coast. It is probable that the Phœnicians gradually brought the alphabet to the Hellenic world along with the dispersal of written magic charms. As the alphabet spread over the centuries, local communities changed and improved it to fit their own spoken language. The Greeks not only added vowels but also democratized the alphabet by simplifying it still further. They added much, much more, using the basic blocks of communication media to move the world in new directions.

With the alphabetic script and the availability of papyrus,[21] the Iliad and the Odyssey, the epic poems of Homer, based on tales that evidently had been repeated orally for the previous three or four centuries by storytellers or sung by bards, were written down, probably during the eighth century BCE. Writing enabled the tellers of tales to separate themselves from their memories. It allowed them to leave those memories and come back to them, for it also allowed them to forget.

What followed was totally new in the history of the world, an outpouring of intellectual, artistic and political ideas, an intellectual revolution conveyed by literacy. From this ferment arose the concept of the individual. According to classics scholar Eric Havelock, "This amounts to accepting the premise that there is a 'me,' a 'self,' a 'soul,' a consciousness which is self-governing . . . the counterpart of the rejection of the oral culture."[22] Among most Greeks, the oral tradition remained. Nevertheless, during ancient Greece's classical age (about 480–320 BCE), the era of Socrates, Plato, and Aristotle, the Greeks developed the literate basis of modern thinking.[23] Far more than simple pictures on walls or a tally of accounts, they created a means of surviving their own life span by leaving a legacy of their thoughts, satisfying the human desire to be remembered. Egyptian and Mesopotamian kings had done this in self-praising monuments, but not ordinary people. With supplies of papyrus and parchment and the employment of educated slaves as copyists, readers, and librarians, books were produced by the Greeks on an unprecedented scale. Greek city-states provided a large reading public.[24]

Yet Innis concluded that the spread of writing contributed to the collapse of Greek civilization by widening the gap between the city-states. In powerful Sparta, the oral tradition continued. Spartan subjects were subjected to an aristocratic military system while Athens practiced democracy, a new form of government in the world. And Athens lost to Sparta in the Peloponnesian wars.

▶ SOCRATES

In Plato's *Phaedrus*, Socrates relates a conversation between the Egyptian god Theuth, the inventor of writing, and the god Thamos, who disagreed about the benefits of writing, saying, "this discovery of yours will create forgetfulness in the learners' souls, because they will not use their memories . . .

you give your disciples not truth but only the semblance of truth; they will be hearers of many things and will have learned nothing."

Unless you believe in old Egyptian gods, Socrates was the first to observe how media change us.[25] According to Plato, Socrates, who wrote nothing, opposed the teaching of writing, the first significant medium of communication beyond the body. He called writing "inhuman," for when confronted with a contrary point of view, text is mute. Socrates was right in saying that the use of letters would encourage forgetfulness, but this did not discourage the spread of literacy. Socrates did not prevail.

Writing has proved more powerful and more arguably human than any medium that followed. It led to the greatest changes in human life. Just to imagine any of the sciences or medicine or law or commerce without writing is to sense this immediately. As for oral culture being more human, if Socrates was correct that some humanity is lacking in writing, consider that the oral stories that have come down to us, such as Homer's epics, have relatively flat characters. Well-rounded, fully human characters seem to have emerged out of written culture.

ARISTOTLE

During the fourth century BCE, Aristotle set about gathering and classifying the available body of knowledge and creating libraries. He could not have done so without a written language and the papyrus to hold it, giving him a permanent record on a storable medium. Because of Aristotle, education in the Greek world would be based on reading, not simply listening to lectures. His library and other ancient storehouses of written information began the collections that would carry information from generation to generation down the ages. Oral transmission could not begin to match it. With Aristotle, the Greek world took steps from oral instruction to the habit of reading.[26]

Mathematics, medicine, physics, Earth sciences, and biology advanced because of ideas, conclusions, and reports of experiments written and stored by Aristotle on the transportable medium of papyrus. He himself wrote about philosophy, music, politics, linguistics, theater, ethics, logic, rhetoric, and more.

▶ GREEK ACCOMPLISHMENTS

The Greek adoption of literacy, said Havelock, accompanied "the ascent of man through education from the life of the senses towards the life of the reasoned intelligence . . . How did the Greeks ever wake up? The fundamental answer must lie in the changing technology of communication. Refreshment of memory through written signs enabled a reader to dispense with most of that emotional identification by which alone the acoustic record was sure of recall."[27] The Greeks separated mankind and human accomplishments from the world around them, regarding nature as a separate entity worthy of study. Greek scholars wrote of philosophy, metaphysics, history, science, and politics. They wrote plays both comic and tragic. They wrote to explain the nature of truth and beauty. Their scholars had a genius for abstract thought, rational thought, and plain common sense. They invented democracy, and writing helped the Greeks to govern themselves. It allowed the Greeks to conceive of objectivity, separating the knower from what is known. It was the gateway to the scientific method, to logic and analysis.

Scrolls carrying fresh ideas not only circulated in the cities, but also reached isolated scholars thanks to the trading ships plying the Mediterranean, truly the world's first information highway. Poetry, plays, and essays in addition to philosophy and mathematics traveled not only horizontally but vertically through the generations. More than any previous civilization, the Greeks used written language to create different kinds of expertise. The Greeks for centuries became the teachers, the source of much of the Mediterranean world's culture, knowledge, and education. Aristotle is credited with showing the Egyptians how to set up proper libraries instead of mere collections of books. The Greek-controlled port city of Alexandria became the leading center of book publishing. The Alexandrian Library was the greatest of the ancient world. Greek knowledge and ideas would travel the world in phonetic letters on papyrus and, later, the treated animal skins of parchment and vellum.

Thanks to the influence of Greek teachers and Greek thought, a growing literacy enriched the Roman Empire. The first daily news reports, the *Acta Diurna* (*Daily Acts*), on waxed wood tablets were posted in the Roman Forum to let its citizens know what the Senate was doing and the announcements of public holidays, an ancient form of government press releases. "Diurna" is the root Latin word for "journal" and "journalism." By the fourth century CE, the city of Rome itself had at least 28 libraries with 20,000 or more papyrus rolls each. Throughout the empire there were city and private libraries and book collections. According to Seneca, private libraries became as common as baths.

▶ SCRIBES

The world's first formal educational system involved the training of scribes, those programmers of the ancient world. Slaves fortunate enough to be scribes probably considered themselves more intelligent than other slaves, an illusion of the literate that survives the centuries. Indeed, reading and writing were skills often beyond the capacity of masters who could only stare dumbly at the marks on clay or papyrus.

In ancient Egypt, a scribe might be a government bureaucrat, and exempt from heavy manual labor, taxes, and military service. To a household slave, literacy was the path to a better—and longer—life than anything else available. The household scribe kept the accounts, recorded tributes to tax collectors and priests, noted what was bought, what was sold, and how much was paid. He read and wrote contracts, oversaw commercial dealings, and engaged in exchanges of diplomatic notes. In doing all this, he achieved a measure of influence rare for slaves. The clerical, scribal skills also appealed to many of the freeborn.

Yet, as it was everywhere, most people in the ancient empires remained illiterate. Except for the scribe, a literate peasant or slave would have been a stench in the nostrils of an illiterate nobleman. Not many people had ever heard of such a thing as a book. Communication was by word of mouth.

SACRED DUTY

With the collapse of Roman rule European civilization entered the Dark Ages. Learning and communication suffered. The pursuit of knowledge shrank into the pinpoints of lighted candles in remote monasteries. Monks, especially Benedictines, took up the scribe's pen to transfer the writing on the crumbling, old papyrus manuscripts onto parchment that was prepared in or near the monasteries. They huddled over their painstaking illuminations of the Bible, religious commentaries, and, in some orders, copies of works from classical Greece or Rome.

In chilly and drafty rooms, their fingers stiff and their backs aching, the monks sat hunched over their desktops in scriptoria, in their own cells, or in recesses in the monastery cloister as they hand lettered and painted magnificent copies of books for libraries and cathedrals.

Scriptoria may have been cold and grim, but they were not silent, for monks customarily mumbled or read aloud as they worked, or they listened to readings accompanying the scratching of their pens on parchment.

To be a scribe was no longer a mean calling fit for slaves. It was to do God's work.

▶ THE MIDDLE AGES

When universities arose in Europe starting in the 12th century, Latin was the language of scholars. Out in the towns and the countryside, people spoke a babble of vernacular languages made all the more separate because the network of Roman roads had fallen into decay, but all the scholarly books were written in Latin. Literacy during the Dark Ages meant knowledge at least of Latin, to which scholars could add Greek and Hebrew, and this knowledge set them apart from the rest of humanity.

The monopoly of the monasteries over book production and distribution ended with the founding of universities in Western Europe, starting in Bologna in 1158. In the back shops of stationers in university towns, scriveners copied books by hand that were still too expensive for poor students to buy, but students could rent the books and perhaps copy the copies to share among themselves. Not until the printing press did education significantly change.

England in the 12th century allowed defendants who could read Psalm 51 to be tried before an ecclesiastical court where sentences were likely to

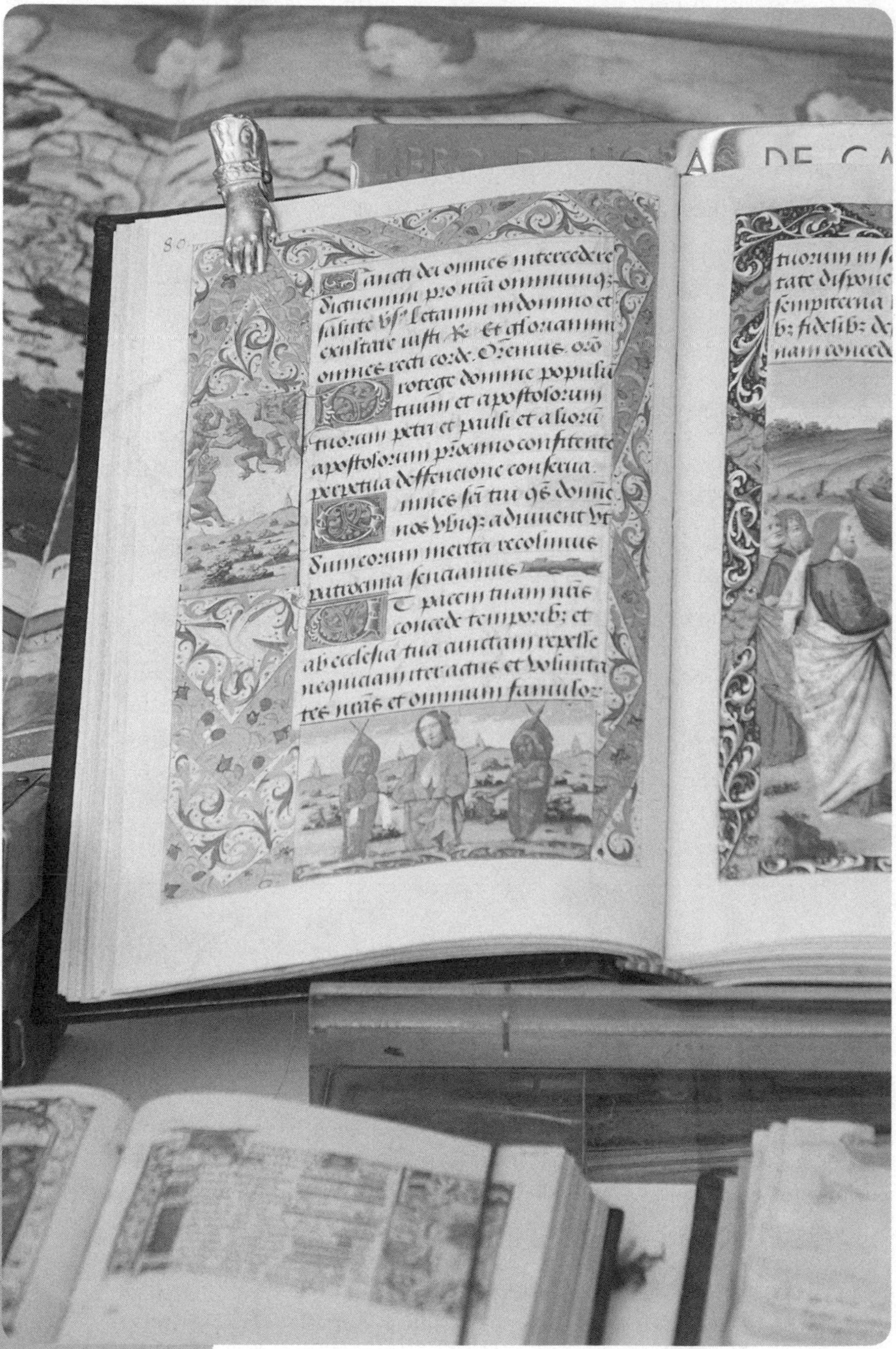

A page of an ornately illustrated medieval manuscript.

be milder than in common law courts. That would encourage literacy for, as Samuel Johnson later observed, the prospect of hanging concentrates the mind wonderfully.[28]

In medieval Europe before printing, it was expected that the clergy could read and ordinary folk could not. Neither could many knights nor even lords. Except for a few who were high-born, medieval women were illiterate. Yet as Europe entered the modern age, the ability to read at some level became a means to social advancement, despite the occasional protest that feudal distinctions should predominate.[29] Societies' elites erected and guarded the literacy barriers from commoners, convinced that only they had any need to know the intelligence contained in books and news reports. Specialists developed and protected what Innis has called "monopolies of knowledge."[30] Parchment, limited and expensive, supported the Church and the monasteries' monopoly of knowledge. The spreading use of paper, cheaper and more plentiful, weakened monastic monopoly as it supported the growth of trade, of cities, and of education outside monastic control. Paper also supported literature written in the vernacular, and the vernacular hastened the growth of nationalism in Europe, for if you could read in, say, French, you were more likely to agree that being French carried its own distinction.[31]

Education was still mostly for the wealthy, but a teaching scholar occasionally accepted the promising son of a poor family. Lucky families eagerly and gratefully sent off their sons for such schooling, the way for him to a better life. As illiterate marauders gained power and became kings or dukes, they absorbed the culture along with the treasure of those they conquered. They opened schools or hired tutors for their own children to make sure they were taught to read and write.

▶ A GROWING LITERACY

Toward the end of the 17th century, Sweden required reading literacy of all of its citizens, but not writing literacy. Elsewhere, writing masters advertised their skill at teaching different levels of penmanship. At the bottom level was handwriting for business. A letter might be written in a "secretary hand" to show that it had been dictated, then signed in the "fine Italian hand" of its high-born author. To perversely show scorn for plebes who had learned the "mechanical" art of penmanship, some English and French aristocrats cultivated an illegible scrawl as a sign of their breeding.[32]

As societies became more complex, the need for writing grew. Far from Europe, other civilizations advanced in their own ways, with their own oral and written languages. Despite little formal contact, similar approaches developed in unconnected cultures for the role of written language. Writing everywhere emerged as a tool of the classes of priests and aristocrats. Everywhere it marked authority and conferred power. Everywhere it was rationed.

Where reading was taught to girls, as in colonial America, the goal was to read scripture, not to write anything and not to read handwriting.[33] When girls were taught penmanship in 19th-century schools, it was a shrunken style suitable for private correspondence, not the generous "mercantile running hand" that their brothers learned.[34]

Today, penmanship is being phased out of school curricula. Students type and text and tweet.

▶ CHINESE AND KOREAN WRITING

The Chinese written language consists of ideographs, the representations of images, but ideographic writing is no friend to simple literacy. You have to work at it. The complexity of its language supported a rigid imperial hierarchy. Nevertheless, China developed written civil service examinations and a large, literate bureaucracy.[35]

An 18th-century Chinese dictionary listed 40,545 characters, far more than any scholar could ever memorize. This is as elitist as language gets. Efforts to simplify Chinese writing can be traced back for 2,000 years, but they always ran into opposition from conservative scholars. The most recent efforts came under Mao Tse Tung in 1955, with a simplified Chinese script, and in 1958, with a Latin script, Pinyin.

Scholars across East Asia used Chinese ideographs. One of the great coincidences of history is that Johannes Gutenberg in Germany lived contemporaneously with the Korean king, Sejong the Great, who is credited with a major advance in literacy. In 1443, when Gutenberg was starting to print, Sejong created *hangul* (or "*hang' ul*"), a simple phonetic alphabet for commoners, with 17 consonants and 11 vowels.[36] It may be the world's most efficient script for reproducing human speech, an alphabet based on Sanskrit. A document of the day praised the ease of learning the characters: "A wise man can acquaint himself with them before the morning is over; a stupid man can learn them in the space of ten days."[37] Kings of the medieval Chosun dynasty believed in the Confucian ideal that reading books would "satisfy reason and reform men's evil nature."[38]

Nevertheless, most Koreans remained illiterate, and only aristocrats and officials had ready access to books. Here too aristocrats argued against giving commoners access to writing. Historian Amalia Gnanadesikan noted, "Fierce objection to Sejong's work surfaced almost immediately . . . [It was argued that] by lowering standards of literacy, the new alphabet would lead to rampant cultural illiteracy as people would neglect the study of Classical Chinese and of high culture."[39] Commoners were entitled to read, but as schools were for the most part restricted to the children of the aristocracy, education was limited.

For many centuries, China was to Korea and Japan as Greece was to Rome: its principal fount of culture, religion, technology, and education. Confucian thought came from China and Buddhist faith arrived with strong Chinese influence, although Korea battled frequently with the Chinese just as it did with the Japanese and Mongols.

Korea followed China in starting a national competitive civil service exam that was open to commoners. Unlike Europe's contemporaneous medieval nobles who sometimes boasted of their illiteracy, Korea's feudal aristocrats saw themselves as scholars. The degree of literacy among Koreans has long been a point of national pride. Printed books were closely related not only to scholarly education, but also to the national examinations that led to preferment for government jobs. Their content affected the mindset of students, the future government officials, by standardizing knowledge and creating uniform interpretations of a moral life."[40] Today, Korean students are among the top scorers in annual international competitions, following one of history's better traditions. For example, South Korean students ranked second in a 2012 international competition in problem solving. (Singapore ranked first; the United States ranked eighteenth.)[41]

QUIPU

A sample of the quipu recording system.

Of all the writing systems that humans devised to communicate information, the strangest may be the *quipu* of the Incas in Peru. Unlike the Aztecs and the Maya, the Incas had no script. Instead, they tied knots in cords. The kind of knot and its location on a cord allowed the Incas to keep track of the movement of goods.[42]

This is proto-writing, a primitive, early stage of writing, and it is not alone in the history of writing. Bones full of carved notches have been discovered dating to the Ice Age. In Europe during the Middle Ages, customs officers used tally sticks during the collection of duties on wine. The British Treasury used tally sticks with notches to identify a sum of money until 1834.

SEQUOYAH

We deeply admire the illiterate native American chieftain Sequoyah, who recognized the power of the black scratches on the white men's papers. He created a written language for his people, the much abused Cherokee nation.[43]

In the presence of many communication tools, we may take writing for granted, but Sequoyah did not. He produced a *syllabary* of 86 characters, the first writing system in modern history made by an illiterate people themselves. Each character represented a syllable, not a single sound. The Cherokee people who adopted it quickly surpassed the literacy rate of the European Americans who lived nearby.[44] His biographer, Jane Shumate, summed up his achievement, "Sequoyah achieved a feat rare in history."[45]

▶ AMERICAN LITERACY

By the start of the American Revolution, 90 percent of New Englanders were functionally literate. This means they read well enough for daily life. Other northern colonies were about 80 percent literate, but this was not the situation throughout the colonies. In some new colonial settlements, illiterates served as part-time county justices because nobody else was available. Within narrow limits girls were taught to read. Boys could go on if the money could be found. Blacks had almost no chance.[46]

Literate when they arrived, many New Englanders brought books that their children would inherit. Reading the Bible for themselves was central to the faith of the religious dissidents who were early settlers. Pilgrims had hardly landed at Plymouth Rock when they began primary schools. Several were operating in Massachusetts by 1635. Many children were schooled at home.

For the lower classes, sending a child to school—which wasn't free—or going oneself offered a path to new occupational skills and maybe even to upward social mobility. Parents who were considered unfit to educate their children might see their sons put out as apprentices to local craftsmen to learn a useful trade, to acquire the functional literacy needed to read the Bible and to participate in the rural commerce.

Not everyone was keen on education. Remote villages sometimes paid a fine to the colonial government because that was cheaper than building a school.[47] Many colonists were indifferent to literacy. Where low taxes competed with literacy, illiteracy often won out. The governor of the Virginia colony in 1671 gave thanks for the lack of free schools or printing, "for learning has brought disobedience and heresy and sects into the world, and printing has divulged them."[48]

An examination of wills and other records in colonial America showed literacy among adult white males ranging from 44 to 93 percent. Generally, two out of three white men were literate at some level. Marriage registries

The Reader (2008) stars Kate Winslet as a woman who has managed to keep her illiteracy hidden for decades. Her former lover (Michael Berg) reveals it at her trial for war crimes.

and other documents in Western Europe from the 17th to the 19th centuries showed similar percentages among adult males, and a growing literacy during the advancing decades.[49]

▶ EXTENDING LITERACY IN MODERN TIMES

By the start of the 19th century nearly all men and most women in the northeastern United States were literate. By the middle of the century, nine out of ten white people throughout the expanding nation had at least a basic reading skill. Out in the expanding west, pioneers wanted to keep in touch with events in the rest of the world, particularly in the places they had come from, and newspapers and letters were treasured.[50] When slavery was still in existence in the South, blacks were usually prevented, sometimes violently, from learning to read.

The Industrial Revolution saw significant literacy advances in both Western Europe and North America. For all its ills, the Industrial Revolution was midwife to a rise in functional literacy among the middle and working classes. For the first time in history, nations adopted policies of universal education. In theory, everyone, not just the sons of the wealthy, would be given at least a rudimentary education. In practice it did not quite work out that way. Many parents saw no need for educated children. Many factory owners pressed to keep all hands, large and small, at labor.[51]

We read today about American high school diplomas handed out to functional illiterates. How well can someone get by in the digital age barely reading? Could you get by only with common sense? If learning can occur with just the most meager literacy, then the labor to become fully literate has diminished value. This is painful for teachers whose efforts are challenged by the popularity of television, video games, movies, and recorded music. A survey by the National Endowment for the Arts in 2002 reported that fewer than half of all American adults had read any fiction in the preceding year, but 57 percent had read at least one non-fiction book.[52]

At national and international levels the distinctions of the "knowledge gap" and the "digital divide" have brought to our attention the disadvantages of a lack of information. The "knowledge gap" argues that each new medium of communication increases the distance between the information rich and the information poor.[53] As mass media information increases, the higher socioeconomic communities tend to acquire it faster, increasing the gap in knowledge. The "digital divide" refers to the gap between populations who have access to computers and the Internet, and those who do not.

Controlling access to literacy has always been a way to keep an uneven social order. To withhold literacy was a way to hold serfs and slaves in their place. It was a policy during the American Civil War era. Everywhere and at all times up to the present, it has been a way to control women. Even in recent days headlines have told of the destruction of schools for girls in Afghanistan and horrific reports of acid hurled into the faces of girl students. According to a report, al Qaeda in Iraq sought illiterate women to serve as suicide bombers.[54]

With the first decade of the 21st century behind us, mediated communication is perversely giving us the tools for illiteracy. Yet it is fair to note that Stanford University professor Andrea Lunsford concluded after a five-year study that media technology is actually reviving writing and pushing it in new directions: "I think we're in the midst of a literacy revolution the likes of which we haven't seen since Greek civilization."[55] Examining thousands of college student writing samples, she did not encounter a single instance of texting speech in a paper that was handed in for a grade. Instead, students used what ancient Greek rhetoricians called *kairos*, which meant adapting their style to their audience.

▶ SUMMING UP

Armed with the gift of writing, human beings have built soaring edifices of thought. As the centuries passed, writing has led to new means of education and to libraries. The human mind is no longer restricted by memory's limitations. Writing has enabled its users to hold thinking and memory outside the brain, sharing their inferences and deductions with other people in other places. Literate people have reflected upon the writings of others, added to them, and packaged knowledge for future generations. Readers were the first people to learn from contemporaries they did not see. In culture after culture, writing has contained and communicated information, along with myths, prejudices, observations, and the gathered knowledge derived from all of these.

▶ TIMELINE

BCE (many dates are estimates)

10,000	Notches in bones found in the Near East presumed to be a lunar calendar.
8000	In Sumer, clay tokens appear; may symbolize goods like sheep or jars of oil.
3100	Sumerians cuneiform numerals are separated from symbols of goods.
3000	Egypt develops hieroglyphic writing.
2600	In Egypt, scribes employ hieratic writing, a condensed, cursive hieroglyphic.
2200	Oldest extant writing on papyrus.
2100	In Sumer, tokens representing goods are placed in clay ball envelopes.
1700	The written law code of Hammurabi, in Babylonia, carved on a stone pillar.
1650	Alphabetic symbols derived from hieroglyphs found in Sinai inscriptions.
1500	In India, sacred Hindu hymns of the Rig Veda are written in Sanskrit.
1200	The Phoenician alphabet, 22 letters, all consonants.
	Chinese writing.
950	The oldest books of the Bible are written.
900	Phonetic alphabet spreads across the Mediterranean.
	Olmecs, a pre-Mayan people, invent first writing system in Americas.
	Oldest extant Hebrew text: schoolboy's clay tablet listing months of the year.
800	Greeks improve Phoenician alphabet by adding vowels; capital letters only.
750	The *Iliad* and the *Odyssey*, written about 400 years after the Trojan War.

600   Mediterranean cultures agree on left-to-right writing.

         First appearance of Latin.

213   China's Ch'in emperor, Shihuang, orders destruction of all books.

179   The Rosetta Stone in Greek, Demotic, and Hieroglyphics.

59   Julius Caesar orders postings of a daily gazette, the Acta Diurna.

47   Alexandrian Library survives fire set by Julius Caesar's troops; many books lost.

CE

65   Mark writes the first Gospel.

105   Chinese imperial eunuch Ts'ai Lun is officially credited with inventing paper.

391   Alexandrian Library destroyed; said to have been ordered by Archbishop of Antioch.

520   The start of Western monasticism; will keep learning alive in Christian Europe.

1002   Murasaki Shikabu's *The Tale of Genji*, the world's first novel.

1200   Books are copied and sold for profit by stationers, usually at universities.

1333   Petrarch's discovery of classical manuscripts helps bring on the Renaissance.

1370   The Bible is translated into English.

▶ NOTES

1   Harold A. Innis, *Empire and Communication* (Toronto: Dundurn Press, 2007) 30.

2   For a thoroughgoing comparison of chirographic (writing-based) and oral societies, see Walter J. Ong, *Orality and Literacy: The Technologizing of the Word* (London: Methuen, 1982).

3   Marshall McLuhan, *The Gutenberg Galaxy: The Making of Typographic Man* (Toronto: University of Toronto Press, 1962) 22.

4   Ong, 78.

5   Elizabeth Eisenstein, *The Printing Press as an Agent of Change*, vol. 1 (Cambridge, UK: Cambridge University Press, 1979) 132.

6   Ong, 51, describing research by Aleksander Luria, *Cognitive Development: Its Cultural and Social Foundatons* (Cambridge, MA: Harvard University Press, 1976).

7 Robert Scribner, "Oral Culture and the Diffusion of the Reformation," in Harvey J. Graff, *Literacy and Historical Development* (Carbondale: Southern Illinois University Press, 2007) 161.

8 Denise Schmandt-Besserat, *Before Writing* (Austin: University of Texas Press, 1992) 1.

9 Schmandt-Besserat, 178ff.

10 Adolf Erman, *Life in Ancient Egypt* (London, 1894) 328, mentioned in Will Durant, *Our Oriental Heritage* (New York: Simon & Schuster, 1936) 170.

11 Marshall McLuhan and Bruce R. Powers, *The Global Village: Transformations in World Life and Media in the 21st Century* (New York: Oxford University Press, 1989) 136.

12 Innis, 36–39.

13 Amalia E. Gnanadesikan, *The Writing Revolution: Cuneiform to the Internet* (Oxford: Wiley-Blackwell, 2009) 143.

14 Gnanadesikan, 144–145.

15 Andrew Robinson, *The Story of Writing* (London: Thames & Hudson, 2007) 159.

16 Robinson, 223–224.

17 Jack Goody, *Literacy in Traditional Societies* (Cambridge, UK: Cambridge University Press, 1968) 3.

18 David Sacks, *Letter Perfect: The Marvelous History of Our Alphabet from A to Z* (New York: Broadway Books, 2003) 25.

19 Robert K. Logan, *The Alphabet Effect: The Impact of the Phonetic Alphabet on the Development of Western Civilization* (New York: William Morrow and Co., 1986) 82.

20 Durant, 106.

21 Henri Jean Martin, *The History and Power of Writing* (Chicago: University of Chicago Press, 1994) 46.

22 Eric Havelock, *A Preface to Plato* (Cambridge, MA: Belknap Press of Harvard University Press, 1963) 41.

23 Havelock, 200.

24 Innis, 116, 120.

25 Socrates relates a conversation between two Egyptian gods, Theuth, the inventor of letters, and Thamos, the ruler of Egypt. When Theuth said the use of letters would make Egyptians wiser and give them better memories, Thamos replied, "this discovery of yours will create forgetfulness in the learners' souls, because they will not use their memories; they will trust to the external written characters

and not remember of themselves. The specific which you have discovered is an aid not to memory, but to reminiscence, and you give your disciples not truth, but only the semblance of truth; they will be hearers of many things and will have learned nothing; they will appear to be omniscient and will generally know nothing; they will be tiresome company, having the show of wisdom without the reality." *Phaedrus*, trans. C.J. Rowe, 2nd (corrected) ed. (Warminster, UK: Aris & Rowe, 1988).

26 Frederick G. Kenyon, *Books and Readers in Ancient Greece and Rome* (Oxford: Clarendon Press, 1937) 25.

27 Havelock, 205, 208.

28 James Boswell, *Life of Johnson*. Quote found at http://www.samueljohnson.com/mortalit.html#383.

29 A letter from a 16th-century English gentleman declared, "I swear by God's body I'd rather that my son should hang than study letters. For it becomes the sons of gentlemen to blow the horn nicely, to hunt skillfully and elegantly, carry and train a hawk. But the study of letters should be left to the sons of rustics." In Lawrence Stone, "The Thirst for Learning," in Norman Canton and Michael Werthman, *The History of Popular Culture* (New York: Macmillan, 1968) 279.

30 Innis, 162. The subject is discussed extensively in his *The Bias of Communication* (Toronto: University of Toronto Press, 1951).

31 Innis, *Empire and Communication*, 158–159.

32 Tamara Plakins Thornton, *Handwriting in America: A Cultural History* (New Haven: Yale University Press, 1996) 13–14.

33 Thornton, 4–12.

34 Thornton, 56.

35 Ian Morris writes of "more effective organization and widespread literacy" before 200 BCE: *Why the West Rules—For Now* (New York: Farrar, Straus and Giroux, 2010) 279.

36 Hangul now uses 14 consonants and 10 vowels.

37 *Hunmin Jeongeum Haerye*, postface of Jeong Inji, p27a, translation from Gari K. Ledyard, *The Korean Language Reform of 1446*, 258.

38 National History Publication Committee, *The Political Structure of Early Chosun: Korean History*, vol. XXVII (Seoul: Tamgudang, 1994) 15.

39 Gnanadesikan, 203.

40 C. Choe, "A Comparative Study of the Socio-Cultural Backgrounds of the Printing in Korea and Germany," in *Report of the International Symposium on Printing History in East and West*. (Chungju, Korea: Chungju Ancient Art Museum) 303.

41 PISA 2012 Results: Creative Problem Solving, http://www.oecd.org/pisa/key-findings/pisa-2012-results-volume-V.pdf.

42 Robinson, 55.

43 Gnanadesikan, 133–142.

44 John Noble Wilford, "Carvings from Cherokee Script's Dawn, *New York Times*, June 23, 2009.

45 Jane Shumate, *Sequoyah: Inventor of the Cherokee Alphabet*, North American Indians of Achievement (New York: Chelsea House Publications, 1993).

46 For a comparative study of colonial literacy rates and those in Europe, see Farley Grubb, "Growth of Literacy in Colonial America: Longitudinal Patterns, Economic Models, and the Direction of Future Research," in Harvey J. Graff, *Literacy and Historical Development* (Carbondale: Southern Illinois University Press, 2007) 272–298.

47 Ronald E. Seavoy, *An Economic History of the United States: From 1607 to the Present* (New York: Routledge, 2006) 48.

48 Seavoy, 28.

49 Grubb, 274–277.

50 Lucien Febvre and Henri-Jean Martin, *The Coming of the Book: The Impact of Printing 1450–1800* (London: Verso Editions, 1984) 210–211.

51 Seavoy (115) notes that a few heartless mill owners who employed fathers and children threatened to fire them all if one of the children was removed to attend school.

52 Reported in Susan Jacoby, *The Age of American Unreason* (New York: Pantheon Books, 2008) xviii.

53 The knowledge gap theory was first proposed in 1970 by Philip Tichenor, George Donohue, and Clarice Olien, University of Minnesota.

54 Umm Badr, "Obstacles in the Path of the Jihad Warrior Woman," cited in Katharina von Knop, "The Female Jihad: AlQaeda's Women," in *Studies in Conflict & Terrorism*, 30:397–414, 2007. Also, see CNN's report at: http://edition.cnn.com/2008/WORLD/meast/06/22/iraq.main/index.html?eref=edition.

55 See Clive Thompson, "The New Literacy," *Wired*, September 2009, 48.

2

Early Printing: Reaching More of Us

The story of written communication dates back 5,000 years to marks on clay. For most of the subsequent centuries, most people still got their information through word of mouth in the usual way of the old telling the young and the powerful telling the powerless, or at fairs, or from the balladeers, who earned their bread by chanting the news from town to village, the occasional traveling morality play, and, of course, gossip.

Writing spread knowledge across ancient civilizations, but in a limited way because literacy was limited. Few people had even heard of a book. Printing changed it all. It enabled mass education. It began mass communication. Publication created a sense of "the public," for no "reading public" had existed in the modern sense. Authors had no public any more than a scientist today has a public.

Marshall McLuhan called typography—printing with movable type—not only "the technology of individualism" but also "a natural resource or staple, like cotton or timber or radio." Printers ran the first assembly line and started mass production. Typography was also the first time a handicraft was mechanized.[1]

Printing that began in the mid-15th century set the Reformation ablaze in the 16th century, although most of Europe remained illiterate and most people depended on the local priest to read the printed sheet. In fact, for the centuries before printing, "reading" meant reading aloud, or listening, and prose was oral rather than visual. Through books and newssheets printing also spread the Florentine Renaissance, that awakening of intellectual life based upon ancient Greek and Roman texts.

Printing began for such purposes as providing books for daily prayers and liturgical ceremonies, but soon went far beyond religion. It introduced humanistic thought to a widening population. It aided the commerce that would replace a millennium of feudalism. For those who were already educated, printing added to their knowledge and expanded what they believed. Elizabeth Eisenstein summed up, "It brought about the most radical transformation in the conditions of intellectual life in the history of western civilization. Its effects were sooner or later felt in every department of human life."[2]

The seemingly modest accomplishment of Johannes Gutenberg in the mid-15th century and printers who followed him would help transform the political and economic structures of Europe from feudalism to mercantile capitalism and encourage the growth of cities. As feudalism declined and printers churned out books in the vernacular of country after country, nationalism rose. A world of knights could not withstand the onslaught of the printers, for printed books led to the growth of a genuine middle class of merchants and artisans, and a shift of power away from the feudal baronies that had dominated Europe for 1,000 years. Among the readers of the new vernacular literature were women of the developing middle class.

Printing would later undergird the Enlightenment that substituted reason and scientific inquiry for tradition and doctrine. It would lead to declarations of human rights and to governments based on laws and constitutions. Could any of this have been imagined in the Mainz goldsmith's shop where Johannes Gutenberg crafted a new way to produce books? The exact date that he started using movable type is not known but it was about 1440. In 1455 he sold copies of his beautiful folio Bible.

Printing today is so deeply embedded into our lives that some mental effort is needed to imagine the world without it. We might conclude that, by providing the means for spreading information to a broad segment of the population, printing set the basis for democracy in all the nations that now enjoy it. True, but printing also exists in dictatorships. Wherever printing has gone it has been followed by censorship and propaganda. As far back as 1486 censorship of the printed word can be traced to Archbishop Berthold von Henneberg in the same German city of Mainz where Gutenberg had his printing shop.[3]

▶ A CHINESE INVENTION

Gutenberg did not invent printing. Centuries before him, people were carving images or text into blocks of wood or clay, then smearing ink on what they had done and applying it to some sort of surface. Gutenberg did not invent the printing press either. He made use of a press that was commonly used for crushing olives or smoothing clothes. Gutenberg was not even the first person to use typography. That had been done in China and Korea, Buddhist lands where the repetitive act of making impressions was in keeping with religious practice. Yet it is the German goldsmith who is credited with one of the world's most important inventions, a superior printing system that used hard metal punches to make soft lead type of a precise height and an oil-based ink that stuck to the type. It was Gutenberg who began the process that moved the world into the Modern Age. Printing led Europe there, and Europe led the rest of the world. What Gutenberg invented was a remarkable, efficient *printing system*. And he did it in a time and place ready for the change it brought.

McLuhan said, with a touch of humor, "The purpose of printing among the Chinese was not the creation of uniform repeatable products for a market and a price system. Print was an alternative to their prayer-wheels and was a visual means of multiplying incantatory spells, much like advertising in our age."[4]

What did Europeans know of Asian printing? Did Gutenberg, the German goldsmith and mirror maker, know? Maybe not, but even if he had never heard of Cathay, did he know of the printing that had been done there for centuries? A few clues indicate that Gutenberg ought to have known something of block printing, if not of movable type. Europeans knew that paper money was printed in China and Persia because travelers, including Marco Polo, reported it.[5] Missionaries and other travelers who returned to Europe with news of the Chinese invention of paper may have reported that a great number of books were printed in China. A papal envoy to China, John of Plano Carpini, returned with a letter sealed in the Chinese style, ink printed upon paper. "Europeans could not know nothing about it," Chinese historian Pan Jixing concluded.[6]

Europe at the time was not a nation or even an idea. It was a diffusion of kingdoms and baronies. Yet decade by decade in towns and cities, no matter what else happened, merchants still looked for trade and bureaucrats demanded records. Into this ferment came printing, the first efficient way to spread information and opinion beyond the range of the human voice to large numbers of people. No human endeavor had ever reached so many people in so short a time. Organized mail services began to take root. Universities, limited at first to the studies of theology and law, were established in several countries. Students sought books that came not only from monasteries but also from the shops of stationers, and on an increasing range of topics.

▶ THE INVENTION OF PAPER

If printing was the engine for the Modern Age, another Chinese invention supplied the fuel. The papermaker's art as much as the printer's art led to our modern world. The availability of printed books, made possible by the paper mills of Europe, allowed a broader growth of literacy. Literacy in turn increased the demand for books, pamphlets, broadsides. It should come as no surprise that dictatorships control the paper supply in their nations.[7]

Its technology a guarded government secret, paper was used in China alone for five centuries until Buddhist priests carried it east to Korea and Japan, and west to the outposts of the Chinese empire. The Islamic conquest of the city of Samarkand in 751 turned up some Chinese papermakers, who were taken west as prisoners. Learning the art of fabricating paper, the Arabs set up paper mills in Baghdad and Damascus. The following centuries saw the height of Muslim culture, expressed by a love of learning and great libraries established from Baghdad to Córdoba.

According to one report, a crusader prisoner named Jean Montgolfier escaped from Damascus, where he had been a slave in a paper mill. Finding his way home to France, he set up the first paper mill in Christian Europe. Although more fragile than parchment, the superiority of paper in taking ink and its lower cost soon led to paper mills springing up across Europe. Merchants, bureaucrats, clergy, and scholars benefited from paper production. Letter writing increased.[8]

The supply of rags to make paper was far greater than the supply of sheepskins for parchment and vellum, which continued to be used for luxury editions and for the missals and breviaries that monks were copying. The superiority of paper over parchment was evident in the printing of the Gutenberg Bible. Thirty of the 210 copies were printed on parchment, each requiring the skins of 300 sheep. By the end of the 15th century, parchment was seldom used to print books.

Yet paper has been less durable than parchment. Among those who worried about the loss of precious documents was Thomas Jefferson. He wrote, "What means will be the most effectual for preserving these remains from future loss? All the care I can take of them will not preserve

An 19th-century engraving of Gutenberg taking the first proof from his printing press.

them from the worm, from the natural decay of the paper, from the accident of fire, of those of removal when it is necessary for any public purpose."[9]

▶ STARTING THE MODERN AGE

It does not take away from the significance of printing to identify other catalysts of the modern world. Change came to medieval Europe from every direction. The bubonic plague—the Black Death—first arrived a century before printing in three waves, probably by ships from India or China, and killed one European of every three. More misery came from starvation caused by an ice age. As feudal rulers huddled in their castles, bandits roamed; bands of knights were the *ronin* of Europe. Fanaticism and revolts pocked the era. The fear of the Mongols to the east and of Arabs ranging from Jerusalem to Spain added to European life's unease. Constantinople, for centuries the heart of Christendom, fell to Islam and the Ottoman Turks.

Before Gutenberg began printing, most books in Europe were written in Latin and were unavailable to an illiterate public. Newspapers and magazines did not exist in this oral world. Stained glass church windows carried the only history most people ever knew or cared about. It would not be the last time that a story was told in pictures. If something written needed to be revealed, one person could read aloud to many. That person was likely to be the local priest. In monastery scriptoria, monks toiled over manuscripts. In the 1,000 years from the fall of Rome to Gutenberg's press, what book production existed in Europe was copied by hand, line after line after line.

According to McLuhan, the manuscript culture in existence *before* the invention of printing continued *long after* because it deeply affected "the manner of composing and writing, [and] it meant that writing, reading, and oratory remained inseparable until well after printing."[10]

Monks gave no thought to making books available to ordinary people. The concept would have seemed absurd. Most people during the Middle Ages managed to live their lives well enough without reading, let alone writing. They knew where the butcher's shop was without reading a sign saying "Butcher," and even if they could not see the sausages hanging, a sign with a drawing of a pig informed them.

▶ PRINTING AND LITERACY

A mark of the Modern Age, distinguishing it from the Middle Ages, was the growth of literacy. Printing and literacy were two hands washing each other. *The more printing, the more literacy.* The presence of books in the vernacular language that ordinary people spoke on the street stirred a desire to understand what was written. *The more literacy, the more printing.* Readers wanted books. And printers could provide them more cheaply than scriveners who copied texts by hand.

As printers learned their craft and carried their tools to set up shop in cities throughout Europe, they published books on a variety of topics both religious and secular, including stories written to entertain as well as to inform and inculcate. Many were illustrated by wood-block engravings. The demand for books increased as schools multiplied and vernacular literacy rose. Compared with hand-written manuscripts, the easier-to-read printed texts promoted silent and quicker reading. With cheap books coming off the presses, a reading public grew. Printed books were smaller than manuscript texts, and could be carried around. Spectacles first appeared in Europe in the 13th century. The invention of the chimney, which heated private rooms, may have increased book reading among the nobility because printing encouraged silent reading, privacy, and separation from other people. When a printed book could be read in privacy, reading aloud was pointless, but that did not happen immediately for most people.[11]

More and more, merchants and artisans learned to read for themselves. A merchant class—a genuine middle class—arose to claim its place in society. For them literacy provided a useful business tool. As historian De Lamar Jensen noted, "It was long after the invention of printing before more than a fraction of the population could read or write. Yet print technology did have an inexorable impact on people's lives from that moment on."[12]

As feudalism lost its grip in the Middle Ages, noble birth mattered less and the ability to read and write mattered more to the burghers who sat in city governments where they wielded real power. They could improve lives blocked by the rigid feudal system that allocated an unchangeable fate to man from the day he was born. The nobility, who had insisted that their authority was a right bestowed by God, read the new writing on the wall. Nobles began to make sure their sons became educated.[13] Burghers of the new middle class took their sons to school and stayed to learn themselves.

▶ SPECIALIZED BOOKS

Gutenberg's invention soon splintered knowledge into specialties. Having an entire shelf of books on a single subject, such as medicine, was possible. Books organized what was known about a subject. As specialized books encouraged monopoly of knowledge, expertise, and separation from those who did not share the same esoteric knowledge, mediated communication demonstrated its force to alter society. Guilds hoarded knowledge, but information still managed to spread. Monopoly led to higher prices for manuscripts, but it brought out competition that lowered prices.[14] Artisans, mechanics, and mariners who had mastered the alphabet not only read the technical books they could find, but contributed to learning and the cross-fertilization of ideas in new books. They made significant contributions to early modern science in an era of alchemy and the search for the philosopher's stone.[15]

Some scholars who already had access to learning denounced printing as a disrespectful vulgarization.[16] Mediated communication is jealously guarded by those who would deny it to others. During the Middle Ages, such scientists as Francis Bacon and Galileo were as eager to have ideas spread by printing as Copernicus and Newton were reluctant.[17]

With printing, book learning was no longer limited to old men and monks. For the fortunate few, it became the focus of daily life starting with childhood. Education was transformed from "learning by doing" to "learning by reading." ABC books, Latin grammars, law books lined the school's path to adulthood. Schools that now required the student to sit and read during daylight hours became much stricter to enforce the necessary discipline.[18]

Before the 18th century, few books for children's pleasure were published. One exception, the bestiaries, moral fables with woodcut drawings about real or mythical animals, were available for pleasure and children's nightmares. As with much medieval writing, they made points about vice and virtue, of Christ and the Devil. By the 19th century, despite the growing number of published books, in many homes the Bible and an almanac were the only books to be found. Both also helped to advance the desire to read.[19]

WOMEN WERE NOT ENCOURAGED

Women, as usual through much of history, were not encouraged to read, for the skill was considered both unnecessary for women and potentially harmful. For centuries it was widely felt by literate men that reading romantic fiction was especially risky for women. Some men responded to novel reading by women, according to one writer, "claiming that women's novels were sexually corruptive, dangerously distracting, and hopelessly unrealistic, or even damaging to women's mental health. (One 19th-century doctor, faced with a novel-reading woman, prescribed a book on beekeeping instead.) Male authors adapted by publishing helpful advice for women targeted at keeping them in their place."[20] Reading was regarded as pointless for the working class. Among lower class women, literacy barely existed.

▶ THE REFORMATION

Before Gutenberg, books were costly. Copying was weary work and often careless. Libraries were small and private. Before Gutenberg, the Church controlled nearly all education and from the beginning the printing presses were tools for promulgating faith. Inevitably with printing, more than one religious point of view would be inked and distributed.

The pivotal religious movement was the Protestant Reformation. Beginning in the 16th century in an effort to reform the dominant Roman Catholic Church, Martin Luther made effective use of Gutenberg's invention. What followed was a campaign of posters, pamphlets, and caricature drawings, first across Germany and then across the rest of Europe. Printers could hardly keep up. It was ironic that the printing trade was in the forefront of the attack on the sale of indulgences, the remission of punishment for sins. After all, who but the printers printed the indulgences that roused Luther's ire?

Luther was not the first churchman to attack the practices of the Roman Catholic Church. The Wycliffite and Waldensian heresies preceded him, but Lutheranism was the first to use the printing press. That made all the difference, for hundreds of thousands of copies of Luther's writing were distributed across Europe. Protestantism was the first movement to exploit the potential of the printing press as a mass medium. It was also the first movement of any kind, religious or secular, to use the new presses for overt propaganda and agitation against an established institution.[21]

Aided by his followers, Luther translated the New Testament into the German vernacular so that ordinary people could understand it for themselves. His Old Testament translation followed. Luther also wrote a mass in German intended for his countrymen who did not understand Latin. In the nearly 70 years between Gutenberg's printing of the Bible and the printing of Luther's translation of the New Testament, about 20 translations of the Bible in the German vernacular appeared.

In Switzerland, John Calvin and Ulrich Zwingli became leaders of the Reformation, though they did not fully agree with each other on the various points of doctrine. By the end of the 16th century many Christians had separated from the established Church. This was especially so in northern Europe. The Reformation led to new Protestant faiths throughout Europe as the Bible was translated into a number of vernacular languages.

The Church, of course, was aware of the power of the printing press, although not all churchmen were. A Catholic reformation to bring internal reforms and to institute more rigorous training of the clergy, as well as the Catholic Counter-Reformation to respond to the Protestant movements, made considerable use of the printing presses that were being set up in cities across Western Europe. In fact, the Church itself provided a large market for the printing industry because poor priests needed books. [22]

The availability of Bibles did not mean that lay readers were always encouraged to read them. In England the Act of 1543 during the reign of Henry VIII prohibited any unlicensed person to read or discuss in a public assembly any annotated Bible. After Elizabeth took the throne, restrictions on Bible reading were eased. Under her successor, James I, the King James Version of the Bible and the issue reached, in Elizabeth Eisenstein's phrase, "a triumphant conclusion."[23]

▶ THE RENAISSANCE

A second great movement arose at about the same time as the Reformation. Besides the art and architecture for which it is justly famous, the Renaissance introduced the classical literature of Greece and Rome to a Western Europe that had been largely unaware of the ancient books. Constantinople, the capital of the Christian Byzantine Empire, fell to the Muslim Ottoman Empire in 1453. Greek scholars fled westward with their libraries. An increasingly literate population thirsted to read the books. The copyists in the back shops of the booksellers and stationers could not have met the demand. The printers obliged. The spread of secular books and humanism led to a new division from the Church, quite different from the Reformation. Access to such books stimulated individual scholarship. Inductive reasoning, ancient literature, secular moral thinking and political awareness of classical Greece further demarcated the Modern Age from the Middle Ages.

At the same time, explorers voyaged to Asia, Africa and the New World, where for good or ill, they set down roots. In this era of global exploration, printers produced engraved maps and geography texts. Written tales of the voyages of discovery stirred the kind of excitement that space exploration has generated in our lifetime. Armchair readers eagerly learned of new continents and descriptions of the peoples who inhabited them. The maps encouraged commerce and further exploration, and reassured investors.

Crusaders and merchants had returned from the Near East during the Middle Ages. Some brought back a new knowledge of astronomy, geography, medicine, mathematics, and philosophy acquired from a Muslim world that religious hostility had shut away. These works were eagerly translated and copied in European humanist circles. Technologies newly invented or discovered from distant lands were described: the water wheel for driving forge hammers, flour mills and mechanical saws, the crane, the wood plane, the weight-regulated clock, the rudder, the compass, gunpowder, and paper.[24]

Medieval alchemy reluctantly gave way to authentic scientific inquiry. The intellectual ferment would lead in the 17th and 18th centuries to the Enlightenment, a revolution in human thought with a focus on the here, not the hereafter. Through the expansion of literacy and printing, ordinary Europeans would learn to think rationally and to conclude that change was both possible and desirable. The classical texts of Ptolemy, Galen, and Aristotle that had been accepted as true since ancient times were newly scrutinized by scientists who questioned their facts and discovered their errors. By allowing "natural philosophers" and scholars to publish their own observations and absorb the observations and conclusions of others, printing would make the Scientific Revolution possible. Ptolemy on geography, Aristotle on astronomy and physics, Galen on medicine, and others whose faulty opinions were unquestioned for nearly 2,000 years finally were discarded.

MOST LITERATE OCCUPATIONS

By the end of the 16th century in Europe, certain occupations could boast of members' literacy. A survey in the French city of Lyon reported that the most literate professions were printers (of course), surgeons, and medicine dispensers. Painters, musicians, tavern owners, goldsmiths, and metal workers were also likely to be literate. Next on the scale were furriers, leatherworkers, and people in the clothing trades. Least likely to be literate were workers in construction trades, food occupations, gardeners, and unskilled day workers.[25]

▶ PRINTING AND LANGUAGES

Another change brought about by printing was a sense of nationalism. The Holy Roman Empire, an attempt to recreate the Roman Empire in a Christian world, gave way to nation states. Unlike Latin, the vernacular languages spoken in each region had not been considered fit for texts until printing codified them by making them a basis for written as well as spoken communication. McLuhan identifies the arrival of printing not only as a cause of nationalism, but as its counterpoint: opposition to government.[26]

Within nations a variety of languages and dialects spoken by a minority gave way to consolidation of language. If you read in English, you shared that skill with everyone else who read in English. That made you different from those who read in French or German. The English language, like the other vernaculars, identified a population that had a territory and boundaries and a distinctive speech.[27] These languages had existed before printing, but now they were fixed with structures. Medieval Latin remained a borderless international language for scholars.

Grammar and eventually spelling became boundaries of both inclusion and separation. The resident of Spain who never thought of himself as a Spaniard took pride in his new status. In the age of the divine right of kings, the kings were not slow to see the benefits of the new national spirit raised by printing and the codified national language where Latin had once ruled.

Since the invention of printing, communication media have been an element of all wars.[28] Innis makes a strong point of arguing that the savage religious wars of the 16th and 17th centuries can be laid at the door of the printing shop. And if you factor in other media, so were the vicious conflicts of the 20th century.[29] McLuhan agreed, even saying that his book, *The Gutenberg Galaxy*, "might be regarded as a gloss on [that] single text."[30]

MUSIC

Musicologist Alfred Einstein pointed out that printing of music notation, starting around 1500, created a music revolution. A visual representation of melody became the basis of notation.[31]

▶ CENSORSHIP

Before the invention of printing, the Roman Catholic Church from time to time found heresy in books. When Gnostics in the second century preached salvation through study and self-knowledge, their books were burned by Church authorities who demanded that only the Bible could be the source of knowledge and only the Church hierarchy were permitted access to it. However, during the thousand years of the Dark and Middle Ages, when few but Church scholars were literate or had access to books, the authorities thought little about heresy in books. The Church considered books to be the tools of scholars, who were relatively free to express themselves as long as the common people were not disturbed. One of the principal concerns of the Church had less to do with access to books by the common people, most of whom were illiterate anyhow, than with priests and monks who might be won over to heresy. They worried over what preachers might say to the masses in the common language.[32] Medieval bishops actually supported civil illiteracy.

Typography was a bomb thrown into that world. The rapid spread of vernacular printing undercut Church and State. The Church's response was to print for its own purposes and to censor but not totally stop what others did. Church leaders ultimately concluded they could not stop printing, nor was it necessary to do so. They could deal with it.

After Gutenberg, the Inquisition to root out heresy consigned offending books to public bonfires. In 1502, the Church issued a papal bull ordering the burning of all books that questioned ecclesiastic authority. This was followed in 1516 by a directive banning printing that lacked Church approval, followed further in 1559 by the Index of Prohibited Books. The burning of unapproved Bibles, other books, and pamphlets limited but did not stop the printing and secret distribution of banned works. The pages of the centuries are studded with such well-known book burners as Savonarola, the priest in Florence who damned the Renaissance, which was born in Florence. A Dominican friar and a fiery political radical in his day, Savonarola and his followers publicly burned thousands of books, art objects, and even cosmetics deemed "occasions of sin" in a "Bonfire of the Vanities."

One of the few havens for printers and writers was Holland after it won its freedom from Spain in the 17th century. Dissidents who found their way into Holland not only continued publishing but also smuggled their works back into their home countries.

ANTHONY COMSTOCK

In the 19th century a private individual, Anthony Comstock, took it upon himself to clean up the mails. Comstock founded the New York Society for the Suppression of Vice and convinced Congress to pass what became known as the Comstock Law, prohibiting the transportation or delivery of pornography. This included birth control information and anatomy textbooks for medical students. Wrangling an appointment as an unpaid postal inspector with the right to carry a weapon, he began a one-man, anti-porn crusade. Using a New York anti-obscenity law as his weapon, Comstock cracked down on medical and sociological articles that offended his sensibility, regarding anything he disapproved of as filth. He boasted that he was responsible for 3,000 arrests, the destruction of 1,500 tons of books, untold numbers of printing plates and nearly 4 million pictures.

Fiction has always been vulnerable to controversy. The popular colonial preacher Jonathan Edwards, known for his fiery sermons, said reading novels was an indulgence leading to a moral decline. Not untypical was this warning, couched in an epistolary novel, from another minister: "The free access which many young people have to romances, novels, and plays has poisoned the mind and corrupted the morals of many a promising youth."[33]

▶ MEDIA IN THE AMERICAN COLONIES

Starting in Boston in 1721, James Franklin gave readers of *The New England Courant* lively news and commentary plus essays of literary quality. His newspaper was a challenge to government and religious authority, for which he was jailed for one month and the *Courant* suppressed.

His younger brother, Benjamin, carried that attitude into his own newspaper in Philadelphia. Franklin's *Pennsylvania Gazette* was what readers wanted. Advertisers followed. Ben Franklin took risks but was also cautious enough not to seriously offend Crown authorities. He said, "If all printers were determined not to print anything till they were sure it would offend nobody, there would be very little printed."[34] Franklin's extensive contributions to mediated communication included improving the Crown's postal service. After the Crown dismissed him because of his revolutionary activities, he helped to set up a separate postal service for the new nation. He also helped to found the first college free of religious domination, the University of Pennsylvania. In Philadelphia in 1727, at the age of 21, Franklin established the first privately supported circulating library in the colonies. By 1776, about 50 public libraries and collections existed.

With their witty essays, the Franklins went beyond the dry recitations of facts that were the stuff of newspaper articles. They pointed to the future of newspapers as carriers not only of facts and advertisements but also of human interest that the entire family could enjoy and read aloud to one another. Benjamin Franklin's book filled with pithy sayings, *Poor Richard's Almanac*, was widely read in the colonies and in Europe, as well, a bestseller averaging 10,000 copies a year.[35]

Benjamin Franklin wanted to be the first American to publish a magazine, but his rival Andrew Bradford beat him in 1741 by three days with the monthly *American Magazine*. It survived for just three months. Franklin's *General Magazine* lasted six months. By the end of the century, about 100 magazines had been published, however briefly, offering entertaining essays, fiction, information, and moral guidance. A few carried engraved illustrations, foreshadowing the picture magazine of the 19th century.

Benjamin Franklin became both a publisher and a postmaster, a joint arrangement that spread widely because post offices and newspapers went well together. Many newspapers were mailed postage free at the postmaster's choosing before the Revolution. Postal acts following the Revolution set cheap rates for delivering newspapers. Postal carriers sometimes provided the service of collecting for subscriptions and for identifying subscribers who had moved away or died.

The first issue of Benjamin Franklin's *General Magazine*.

▶ THE REVOLUTIONARY PRESS

As the colonies grew, new businesses and industries started that competed with established business and industry in the mother country. The frictions between them were codified as laws and tariffs of Britain's mercantile system, favoring those who had the ear of Parliament. Limits on westward expansion into new territories also created friction. It did not help that the members of Parliament and the royal governors sent from London to rule the colonies were far too often greedy and incompetent men who cared little for the welfare of the colonists. In 1735, the printer John Peter Zenger was put on trial in New York, charged with seditious libel. Defended by the brilliant lawyer Andrew Hamilton, who argued that truth is a defense against libel, Zenger was declared innocent.

Better-educated colonists read the ideas of English and French philosophers who argued that citizens had an implied social contract with their governments. They bristled at taxation without representation and the standing military contingents that they had to support, soldiers who came to look less like protectors and more like an army of occupation. From the British point of view, the army of redcoats guarded colonists from the Indians and the French, so the colonists should help defray the costs of their own defense. Opinions on all of this were hand-cranked on printing presses that turned out newspaper essays, pamphlets, and leaflets that further polarized a divided colonial populace.

The Stamp Act of 1765 required that newspapers, magazines, and legal documents must be printed on paper from London that carried a revenue stamp. Printers, editors, and lawyers were directly affected by this tax, but everyone was bothered to some degree. Fierce objection arose to the Stamp Act, voted by an English Parliament that had no colonial members. To escape the financial burden of the Stamp Act, some printers stopped publishing newspapers. Others continued publishing but dropped the masthead that identified them, and a few risked publishing without the stamp.

Parliament revoked the act a year later, but the damage had been done. Taxes on tea and molasses led to street demonstrations and organized violence such as the famed Boston Tea Party. Sons of Liberty rebel groups arose. Colonists were reminded that many of them had come to the colonies to escape the tyranny and neglect of the British government that now seemed to be pursuing them.

The best paper available came from English mills. When that source was shut off during the Revolution, the colonial paper mills did their best with available cloth rags, but with paper made from trees still a century away, even rags were in short supply. Paper was needed not only for newspapers but also for the cartridges in muzzle-loading guns. The records of the Massachusetts House of Representatives for February 16, 1776 stated, "the inhabitants of this Colony are hereby desired to be very careful in saving even the smallest quantity of rags proper for making Paper, which will be a further evidence of their disposition to promote the publick good."[36]

Not all printers and editors supported revolutionary sentiment. Conservative businessmen such as Benjamin Franklin's own son, William, were outspoken Tories, known as Loyalists. The rebels—known as Patriots—did not hesitate to criticize, threaten, and even raid Tory newspapers, and forced most of them to cease publication. Newspaper essays, often signed with anonymous Roman names like Cato and Cicero, reflected both the colonial discontent and the pro-British arguments of the Loyalists. Readers torn by conflicting arguments and by self-interest could be swayed to one side or another, giving newspapers a pivotal role in the years leading up to the Revolutionary War.

Political radicals calling for independence published their opinions in newspapers. The leading Patriot writers lived in Massachusetts. Samuel Adams, Thomas Paine, and Isaiah Thomas combined essays with reporting of events. A Pennsylvania Quaker farmer who was not an editor, John Dickinson, wrote a series of influential letters published by the *Pennsylvania Chronicle* that upheld the values of the propertied class. He argued that change was indeed necessary, but wanted something short of independence. His moderate views were especially impressive to merchants and property

THE AREOPAGITICA

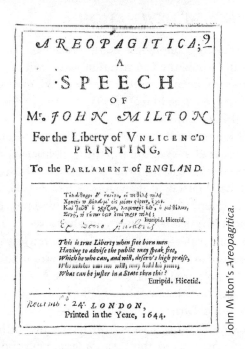

John Milton's *Areopagitica*.

In 1644 the poet John Milton published the *Areopagitica*, with its famous plea for freedom of expression, "Let her (truth) and falsehood grapple; who ever knew truth put to the worse in a free and open encounter?" Milton pleaded before a Protestant-dominated English Parliament, his political allies, for an end to censorship. Most of the Roundheads then in power were not impressed. More than a century would pass before his peculiar notion of freedom of speech would be picked up an ocean away, and would lead to the First Amendment to the US Constitution.

THE FIRST AMENDMENT

> Congress shall make no law respecting an establishment of religion, or prohibiting the free exercise thereof; or abridging the freedom of speech, or of the press; or the right of the people peaceably to assemble, and to petition the Government for a redress of grievances.

owners. Other leading writers who contributed their voices in this period were the poet Philip Freneau, a Patriot, and James Rivington of New York, a Loyalist editor whose home and press were attacked by a mob. (However, after war broke out he became a spy for General George Washington.[37])

Paine's pamphlet, *Common Sense*, and his *Crisis* papers kept the revolutionary spirit breathing during its bleakest years among common men who passed the printed sheets from hand to hand. His writing was simple and had the style of oratory. He spoke to ordinary people as one of them. His pamphlet, *The American Crisis*, begins: "These are the times that try men's souls."[38]

▶ INFORMING THE NEW NATION

In the new United States, among the compromises reached by Federalists and Democrats in drafting the Constitution was a Bill of Rights. The very first of its original ten amendments called for freedom of the press, along with freedom of religion, freedom of speech, the right to assemble, and the right to petition the government.

The years that followed the Revolution in the United States were marked by agitated newspaper attacks against opposing politicians, as the press and its news columns were used as the principal tools of persuasion in resolving the many issues that confronted the vigorous new nation. The aristocratic Federalist faction around Alexander Hamilton argued for a strong federal government. Anti-Federalist factions, especially those around Thomas Jefferson, saw the small farmer as an ideal and supported less government.

The First Amendment took the rare step of permitting freedom of the press, but in 1798 a polarized Congress passed the Alien and Sedition Acts, threatening two years imprisonment and a then forbidding U.S.$2,000 fine for anyone who would "write, print, utter, or publish . . . any false, scandalous, and malicious writing" against the government, the president, or Congress. A partial reversal of the First Amendment, the Acts did allow truth as a defense, an echo of the John Peter Zenger trial, and did not forbid criticism of government, only false and malicious criticism.

The Sedition Act was generally supported by the Federalists and opposed by Jeffersonian Democrats. Media theorist Neil Postman concluded, "There is not a single line written by Jefferson, Adams, Paine, Hamilton, or Franklin that does not take for granted that when information is made available to citizens they are capable of managing it."[39] Jefferson never abandoned the principle of a free press, although in the years to come, he clearly grew sick of the "lying and calumniating" of the Federalist press that opposed him. The acts expired two years after they were passed, but not before eight convictions affected newspapers, and fear of speaking out cast a wider net. The acts would not be replaced for more than a century at American entry into World War I.

The growth of cities in the United States saw weekly newspapers increase their circulation. Some turned into dailies. The nation expanded westward into the Louisiana Purchase lands, towns formed, and newspapers met their needs, supported by legal notices, paid circulation, and advertising.

Frontier newspapers were one of the few means that pioneers had of keeping connection with the world they had left behind, but they were also a connection with one's neighbors. News, as usual, was eagerly read despite being full of misinformation and frequently nasty opinions.

Despite the increase of city populations in the decades before the Civil War, nine out of ten Americans lived on farms, in villages, and in small towns; but the nation was changing, industrializing. Coal dug from new mines was carried by river and new railroads to factories in the northern states. Unions formed to include unskilled workers and to express a willingness to strike, and labor newspapers were published, an effort to match the commercial Whig newspapers supporting the business class. Andrew Jackson never lost his back-country roots, and his new Democratic Party built in opposition to the business-oriented Whigs found strong support among workers in the cities, the Irish, and other arriving immigrants.

Alexis de Toqueville travelled across America with a discerning eye for the newspapers that were so different from newspapers in France. "To suppose that they only serve to protect freedom would be to diminish their importance: they maintain civilization. I shall not deny that in democratic countries newspapers frequently lead the citizens to launch together into very ill-digested schemes; but if there were no newspapers there would be no common activity. The evil which they produce is therefore much less than that which they cure."[40]

A Hungarian visitor, Sandor Bölöni Farkas, a free-thinker seeking to meet fellow Unitarians, saw "magic" at work in just how quickly American society changed: "That magic at work in America is the printing of newspapers. For instance, stagecoaches regularly carry newspapers, whose delivery in the wilderness delighted and surprised me. No matter how remote from civilization or poor the settler, he reads the newspaper."[41]

A famous visitor, Charles Dickens, would be much less kind in his waspish portrayal of America. On the subject of newspapers, he wrote: "What are the fifty newspapers, which those precocious urchins are bawling down the street . . . what are they but amusements? . . . To those who are accustomed to the leading English journals, or to the respectable journals of the Continent of Europe; to those who are accustomed to anything else in print and paper; it would be impossible, without an amount of extract for which I have neither space nor inclination, to convey an adequate idea of this frightful engine in America. But if any man desire confirmation of my statement on this head, let him repair to any place in this city of London, where scattered numbers of these publications are to be found; and there, let him form his own opinion."[42]

The press continued to serve as a vigorous partner in the growth and political development of the nation as it expanded westward across the continent, built up its industry, and divided into two bitter, warring camps, North and South.

During the antebellum era, the decades before the Civil War, patronage aided newspapers with the right connections as political fortunes changed hands. Fees for legal notices, government printing contracts, and sometimes money to start newspapers were handed out selectively to supporters of the party that gained power. Andrew Jackson rewarded several dozen journalists with jobs in his administration. But the press itself was changing as technology, literacy, and the thrust of democracy resonated across political life.

▶ TIMELINE

105   Papermaking invented in China.

550   Chinese develop xylography, printing from carved wooden blocks.

740   A newspaper is printed in China.

751   Paper moves west when Muslims capture Chinese workers in Samarkand.

868   *The Diamond Sutra*, Chinese block-printed book; it's the oldest existing book.

1048   Pi Sheng, a Chinese commoner, fabricates movable type using clay.

1234   Koreans use movable metal type.

1276   At Fabriano, Italy, the first paper mill is built in Christian Europe.

1295   Marco Polo tells of paper money in China. Few Europeans believe such nonsense.

1423   Europeans use xylography to produce books.

1440   Possible date of Johannes Gutenberg's first printing effort.

1456   Gutenberg's 42-line Bible is illuminated and bound.

1486   In Gutenberg's town of Mainz, the first censorship of printing.

1490   Books are widely printed across Europe.

1498   In Venice, the printer Aldus Manutius publishes a book catalogue with prices.

1500   England sees the growth of middle class literacy.

1522   Martin Luther publishes a German translation of the New Testament.

1559   Pope Paul IV creates Index of Prohibited Books; bans books by humanist Erasmus.

1584   Printing is introduced to the New World in Peru.

1605   In Antwerp (now in Belgium), the first regularly published weekly newspaper.

1611   The King James Version of the Bible is published.

1650   In Leipzig, Germany, a daily newspaper is published.

1702   The first daily newspaper in the English language appears, the *Daily Courant*.

1704   Daniel Defoe publishes the first weekly periodical, *The Review*.

1735   Trial of John Peter Zenger.

1783   Pennsylvania's *Evening Post*, the first daily newspaper in America, is published.

1791   Congress passes the First Amendment to the Bill of Rights.

1798   Alien and Sedition Acts; will last for two years.

1835   First volume published of Alexis de Tocqueville's *Democracy in America*.

▶ NOTES

1 See Marshall McLuhan, *The Gutenberg Galaxy* (Toronto, University of Toronto Press, 1962) 124.

2 Elizabeth Eisenstein, *The Printing Press as an Agent of Change*, vol. 1. (Cambridge, UK: Cambridge University Press, 1979) 159.

3 *New Advent Encyclopedia*, citation for Berthold of Henneberg, http://www.newadvent.org/cathen/02520b.htm.

4 McLuhan, 34

5 Thomas F. Carter, *The Invention of Printing in China and Its Spread Westward*, 2nd ed. (New York: Ronald Press, 1955) 112.

6 Jixing, Pan, *History of Chinese Science and Technology: Papermaking and Printing* (Beijing: Kexue, 1998) 22–23.

7 Philip N. Howard, *The Digital Origins of Dictatorship and Democracy: Information Technology and Political Islam* (New York: Oxford University Press, 2010) 104.

8 Eisenstein, 47.

9 Letter to George Wythe, reported in Eisenstein, 115.

10 McLuhan, 90.

11 McLuhan, 82, 125, 132, 136, 158, 164.

12 De Lamar Jensen, *Renaissance Europe: Age of Recovery and Reconciliation*, 2nd ed. (Lexington, MA: D. C. Heath and Company, 1992) 222.

13 Lawrence Stone, "The Thirst for Learning," in Norman Cantor and Michael Werthman, *The History of Popular Culture* (London: Macmillan, 1968) 279.

14 Harold A. Innis, *The Bias of Communication* (Toronto: University of Toronto Press, 1951, 2007) 164.

15 Eisenstein, 422.

16 Jensen, 423.

17 Eisenstein, 273.

18 Philippe Ariès, *Centuries of Childhood: A Social History of Family Life* (New York: Random House, 1962) 145, 413.

19 Adam Nicolson, *God's Secretaries: The Making of the King James Bible* (New York: HarperCollins, 2003) 236–237.

20 Amanda Hess, "A Brief History of the Beef against Women Reading," *Slate* October 11, 2012.

21 Eisenstein, 303–304.

22 Eisenstein, 314, 317.

23 Eisenstein, 358.

24 Albert Kapr, *Johannes Gutenberg: The Man and His Invention*, tr. by Douglas Martin (Aldershot, UK: Scolar Press, 1996) 15.

25 Natalie Zemon Davis, "Printing and the People: Early Modern France," in Harvey J. Graff, *Literacy and Historical Development* (Carbondale: Southern Illinois University Press, 2007) 142.

26 McLuhan, 235.

27 Benedict Anderson, *Imagined Communities: Reflections on the Origin and Spread of Nationalism* (London: Verso, 1991) 44.

28 For a discussion of this point, see Asa Briggs and Peter Burke, *A Social History of the Media: from Gutenberg to the Internet* (Cambridge, UK: Polity Press, 2002) 85 ff.

29 Innis, 24–29.

30 McLuhan, 216.

31 Alfred Einstein, *Short History of Music* (New York: Vintage Books, 1954) 20, 45.

32 Henri-Jean Martin, *The History and Power of Writing*. Trans. Lydia G. Cochrane (Chicago: University of Chicago Press, 1994) 266.

33 Reverend Enos Hitchcock, *Memoirs of the Bloomsgrove Family* (Boston: Thomas and Andrews, 1790).

34 Carl Van Doren, *Benjamin Franklin* (New York: Viking, 1938) 100.

35 From "This Day in History, December 19, 1732," http://www.history.com/this-day-in-history/poor-richards-almanack-is-published.

36 Eugenie Andruss Leonard, "Paper as a Critical Commodity During the American Revolution," https://ojs.libraries.psu.edu/index.php/pmhb/article/viewFile/30757/30512.

37 Kara Pierce, "A Revolutionary Masquerade: The Chronicles of James Rivington," Journal of History, Binghamton University, http://www2.binghamton.edu/history/resources/journal-of-history/chronicles-of-james-rivington.html.

38 Published December 23, 1776.

39 Neil Postman, *Technopoly: The Surrender of Culture to Technology* (New York: Knopf, 1992) 67.

40 Alexis de Tocqueville, *Democracy in America*, 1831 (New York: Penguin Books, 2003) Chapter VI.

41 Sandor Bölöni Farkas, *Journey in North America*. Based on travels in 1831. First published in 1834 in Hungarian. Trans. by Theodore and Helen Schoenman (Philadelphia: American Philosophical Society, 1977).

42 Charles Dickens, *American Notes for General Circulation*, 1842.

Mass Printing: Reaching Still More

At the start of the 19th century, communication media meant print. Printers still inked one page of type at a time and placed a rag-based sheet of paper over it before lowering a platen to make the impression. The result of a day's work was a tired arm and a product that was expensive compared to what later years would bring. With their small flatbed presses and single sheets of paper, printing shops would not have looked strange to Johannes Gutenberg 350 years earlier. From a demand that could not be satisfied with the old wooden screw press came such improvements as the iron press and the lever press. A demand for paper came from the increase in its principal use, printing. The availability of paper in rolls led to the development of rotary printing presses that took advantage of them.

By the end of the same century, photographs appeared in bigger newspapers printed by huge rotary presses onto rolls of paper manufactured from trees. Their pages were filled with advertising agency layouts. Wire service news reports were banged out on typewriters instead of hand written. They were sent via telegraph across the nation, and undersea cable connected major cities around the world.

The newspaper was the primary tool that the public used to learn of current events, as well as one of its primary sources of education and entertainment. Steam presses accommodated daily newspaper print runs of 1 million or more copies. There was more. By the end of the century, middle-class families preserved memories with their own cheap, easy-to-use cameras. People in cities and increasingly in rural areas talked to each other over the telephone. They enjoyed recorded music and they read articles about the invention of pictures that moved, and about an Italian youth named Marconi who figured out how to send messages without wires. By the end of the century the public learned about radio's dots and dashes, plus the start of motion pictures. Experiments began that would lead to radio broadcasting, computers, television, and tape recording.

To this list we may add compulsory free public education, at least at a basic level to enable factory workers to recognize letters and numbers. Also add public libraries, mass advertising, cheap books and periodicals, and international postal agreements that encouraged communication. Educated adults abandoned quills for the new fountain pen. Children's fingers grasped mass-produced pencils. Bookstores, museums, theaters, and even opera houses and art galleries opened in cities to meet the desire for culture by a rising middle class. In the evenings, Americans were reading by illumination from electric light bulbs.

The educational reformer John Dewey thought that mass printing had taken schools too far in a wrong direction. He worked to restore education to something approaching its pre-print phase. According to McLuhan, Dewey wanted to get the student out of the passive role of consumer of uniformly packaged learning.[1] Modern communication technology has taken education far from the "Gutenberg Galaxy" that McLuhan believed was now being replaced by the "electric galaxy."[2]

▶ THE CIVIL WAR

As the nation grew, prospered, and expanded westward, sectional divisions sharpened. Economic policies that suited the industrial Northeast did not suit the cotton and tobacco South, the agrarian Midwest, or the frontier Western territories. Slavery was the most contentious issue, but not the only one.

Newspapers reflected the divisions. Horace Greeley's *Tribune* took the strongest anti-slavery stance among large circulation newspapers. From Boston, William Lloyd Garrison's *The Liberator* devoted itself entirely to the abolition of slavery. When copies of *The Liberator* were sent by mail to southern states, postmasters threw them away. In Alton, Illinois, abolitionist publisher Elijah Lovejoy was attacked by a mob and killed. Southern newspapers calling themselves "fire eaters" were just as strident for states' rights and the Confederate cause. *The Charleston Mercury* led the fight for secession.

Literacy made some slaveholders uneasy when they reflected that the slaves might acquire enough knowledge to be dangerous. They sensed the danger of literate slaves, for literacy, the ability to both read and write, conferred power on those who possessed it; illiteracy has always been a weakness. During the colonial period in the South, it had been a common practice for slaves to carry the mail from one plantation to another. A federal law in 1802 forbade anyone except a free white man to carry the mail, fearing organized slave uprisings, but the practice of using slaves to carry the mail continued. Slaveholders were correct to be worried. From 1835, Northern abolitionists flooded the mails going to the South with abolitionist pamphlets. In parts of the South, postmasters themselves destroyed abolitionist mail.[3] Literate slaves reading the abolitionist mail could be moved to attack their overseers and to encourage other slaves to join them.

An issue of William Lloyd Garrison's *The Liberator.*

By the start of the Civil War more than a half million free blacks lived in the United States. In 1827 the first newspaper published by African Americans, *Freedom's Journal*, was printed. Others followed, notably *The North Star*, edited by Frederick Douglass.

The war itself was reported in considerable depth to publics on both the Union and Confederate sides hungry for news. Reporters on both sides enjoyed considerable freedom to travel to battlefields, and their news stories reflecting on heroism and glory revealed how close they came to the actual fighting. They knew that families of the soldiers engaged in the fight would read their reports.

▶ POST-CIVIL WAR

A boom in railroad construction supported by government subsidies and huge land grants followed the Civil War. Factories and shipping docks were built. It was too much, too fast. Railroad companies, banks, lumber companies, and other businesses went bankrupt. Among the speculators in unsecured bonds were ordinary people who invested their life savings. An international economic depression, the Panic of 1873, lasted six years. In Washington tight money policies hurt debtors, especially farmers in the Midwest, the South, and the Plains States who normally carried debt loads. They were also squeezed by high railroad transport rates. In 1877 railroad workers went on strike; President Rutherford B. Hayes sent in federal troops, leading to fights that left more than 100 dead and many more injured.

Among the political issues that filled newspaper pages were reform of the banks and the money supply, interest rates, and railroad regulation. A number of leading editors who supported reforms cheered the candidacy of *Tribune* publisher Greeley for president in 1872, but he fared badly at the polls.

Newspapers continued to reflect their communities. In the North, the *New York Times* remained a voice of thoughtful reason. In the South, Henry Grady, editor of the *Atlanta Constitution*, envisioned a "New South" to build up industry and helped to reintegrate Southern states into the Union but did not abandon his views of white superiority. Grady's New South efforts were also helped by associate editor Joel Chandler Harris, who wrote down many of the oral stories he had heard from blacks as Uncle Remus and Brer Rabbit tales. Judged by the standards of today, these tales would be considered racist, but by the standards of his own time, Chandler was a folklorist who persuaded African Americans to share the tales of their heritage. A more extreme white supremacist novelist, Thomas Dixon, wrote *The Clansman*. D. W. Griffith later filmed it as *The Birth of a Nation*.

▶ THE INDUSTRIAL REVOLUTION

The story of *mass* communication dates back less than 200 years, an effort to reach broad masses of people that began during the Industrial Revolution. Mass marketing with advertising in magazines, newspapers, and catalogs increased the demands leading to the mass consumption that supported the mass production of goods coming out of the factories. The Industrial Revolution created mass society. It brought much to improve life: cheap cotton for clothing, cheap pottery for dishes and a variety of food to ladle onto them, mass-produced furniture instead of handmade, cheap coal to fuel factories, cheap transportation for people and goods.

Working-class children were sent to school, where they learned the basic "3 Rs" of Reading, wRiting, and 'Rithmetic, although little more than that. Importantly, education that reached everyone depended on the availability of printed materials. The Industrial Revolution led to books and magazines shelved in new city libraries, and newspapers filled with the kind of stories and advertising that appealed to ordinary people. Books had a long history, but readership had been limited until books became affordable and accessible.

However, the Industrial Revolution also brought the misery of grueling labor for long hours, the breakup of families, machinery accidents, job insecurity, sudden spurts in food prices, and the lack of support for illness and old age. Cities dumped untreated sewage into rivers to flow alongside the chemicals dumped by factories. In some cities of the United States and Europe, the smoke was so thick that midday appeared like dusk. It was a world that Dickens wrote about in novels, sometimes serialized in magazines, and read as eagerly by Americans as by his fellow Britons. The Industrial Revolution brought labor unions into Northern factory towns where workers, men and women, toiled in 12-hour shifts, child labor was a fact of life, and open sewers ran past slum housing. Strikes to improve conditions were violently put down by police and strikebreakers. In many ways newspapers were a defining element of this economic and social upheaval.

For all its ills, the Industrial Revolution saw a rise in literacy among the middle and working classes. Compulsory free education and lending libraries increased an interest in books, though the curse of child labor continued to deprive the children of poor families of a chance for meaningful education. Still, mass production and literacy put cheap books into the roughened hands of people who otherwise could not afford them. A public appetite for inexpensive, easy-to-read novels filled with action, adventure, and romance led in the 19th century to the dime novel, printed on the cheap new wood-pulp paper and glued to lurid color covers.

New universities added to the store of knowledge and culture, so wealthy young Americans did not need to travel to European universities to complete their education. The Morrill Act of 1862, signed by Abraham Lincoln in the midst of the Civil War, allocated land to create state colleges to teach agriculture, engineering, and military tactics. These land-grant colleges led to the great American public state universities, centers of teaching and research.

▶ NEW TECHNOLOGY

In France, an inventive paper mill manager, Nicholas Louis Robert, in 1798 produced paper in a continuous roll. With improvements, his invention of a continuous rotating web to pick up the wet pulp, instead of workers spreading the pulp on a flat mesh screen, delivered as much paper in two days as hand labor did in three months. Better-designed presses made of iron instead of wood printed words on that paper. It would not be long before steam-powered rotary presses printed on the rolls of paper.

The rotary press arrived early in the 19th century, but the flat page of lead type was unsuited to it. Because of the risk that pieces of type might burst their bonds and spill all over the floor, the makeup of a page was limited to single columns tightly bound by column rules, giving the appearance known as a "tombstone" layout because of the heavy, black, single-column headlines sitting above the type. The stereotyping method solved this problem. An impression of a flat page of lead type was made on a pliable cardboard-like mat, which was then put into a semi-circular mold. Molten lead was poured into it, and the lead hardened and cooled to give the printer an image of the page that could be fitted onto the rotary press—a stereotype (Today when we talk about stereotypes we usually mean standardized but over-simplified mental pictures about people, places, and ideas.) The process, stereotyping, also fixed an image, in this case the image of the page. And it freed the pieces of type in the original page for reuse.

By the 19th century's close a typesetting machine had replaced the slow process of hand-setting the type. Named for the rows of lead it spat out, the Linotype would be the noisy centerpiece of newspaper production well past the middle of the 20th century. Technology in the 20th century added offset lithography, phototypesetting, and the computer.

Paper and bindings are part of technology currently in flux, but they no longer determine what a book is. Consider Google's effort to place all books into a vast electronic database, a controversial project that led to several international lawsuits. Now add the emergence of Apple's iBook and e-book tablets such as the iPad, Kindle, and Nook, plus the popularity of audio books. They all add up to the conclusion that the book will endure for the foreseeable future no matter in what form it reaches us because it has proven to be a practical and desirable way to package knowledge and entertainment.

▶ THE PENNY PRESS

The first daily newspapers were published in Europe in the early 17th century. With the addition of other inventions of the Industrial Revolution, the modern newspaper took form. In the early part of the 19th century, most newspapers had either promoted the issues of a political party or were meant for people in commerce. A newspaper's price of 6 cents was suited to a middle-class purse. Some newspaper publishers required an annual subscription of as much as U.S.$10 for a product that was of little interest to the working class and, in any case, did not support their interests. A popular press did not exist. Gossip was swapped in coffee houses.

Change came in England starting in 1832, when *The Penny Magazine* was published especially for the working class. It developed an American readership also. In New York on January 1, 1833, Horatio Shepard published a daily newspaper that workers could afford, the *New York Morning Post*, hawked on the streets for a penny. The *Post* was followed later that year by another New York penny newspaper, the *Sun*, published by a young printing shop owner, Benjamin Day, who had no previous experience in journalism. He changed the dynamic by reaching out to the large segment of the population who had little interest in business or national politics, but had a thirst for gossip, sensation, and local news. Day filled his small paper with lightweight local news of scandal and crime written in a lively manner. Before long he was selling more papers than anyone else and had plenty of advertising. Day was not above stretching the truth for a good story, such as a six-article series in 1835 about a colony of people living on the moon, with the articles accompanied by lithographs of humans with wings. Some readers took it seriously. Circulation rose. The *Sun* never issued a retraction.

Here was mass communication, something new in the world, a business of funneling information to large numbers of people from a limited number of providers. Supported heavily by mass advertising, the penny papers satisfied that thirst for sensation. The newspapers were enjoyed by Americans coming out of a public school system that taught them to read but did not necessarily equip them with a burning thirst for knowledge.

News came to have value as a commodity instead of merely supplying the basis for political partisanship. Like a bushel of oats or a yard of silk, in a newspaper, ink upon paper, news had the means to be packaged, to become a product. Certain stories had more value than others. Local news had more value than distant news of a similar event. Sensational news had more value than dry reports. Readers thirsted for stories of crime, adventure, and the exotic. Reports of battles mattered, the closer the better. What also mattered was political news that might affect the reader's life. The popularity of the penny press in New York led to similar newspapers in other cities.

Sharing the pages of the penny newspapers were advertisements addressed to a mass audience. The penny press ads were an integral part of the Industrial Revolution through which its readers were living, for the manufacture of consumer goods required their purchase, and that meant informing and convincing buyers. Newspapers grew fat with advertising. Advertising agencies went into business.

The penny press did not really compete with the more expensive traditional commercial or political newspapers for the reader's penny, but rather competed for the working man's coin against the small cakes and apples also sold on the street. The penny newspapers depended upon these street sales by news hawkers, not subscriptions. Building up large circulations, the *Sun* and its rivals, notably James Gordon Bennett's *New York Herald*, tapped a vein of public curiosity involving scandal and other "human interest" news. The *Herald* crossed over to appeal to the middle classes with business news, society news, sports reports, critical reviews, and religious news that offended the established clergy. It added national and international news, and doubled the price of a copy to two cents. The penny press was maturing from its salacious beginnings as other newspapers followed Bennett's lead.

The penny press was not all sensationalism. Most notable for early political commentary was the *New York Tribune*'s editor Horace Greeley. He preferred political news and became a leader in the abolitionist struggle to end slavery. Greeley barred from the *Tribune*'s pages the salacious news that the *Sun* thrived on. Along with his eye-openers he supported the working man and the formation of unions, equal pay, and, unusual for the day, full civil rights for women, temperance, agrarian reform, a greater share of material wealth for common people, the abolition of imprisonment for debt, and the abolition of slavery.

The *New York Times*, begun in 1851, also sold for a penny, but its pages were not filled with the sensationalism of the *Sun*, nor did it stray into extreme political positions or odd causes such as spiritualism that Greeley believed in. Instead, it expressed moderate political views and thoughtful news reports.

Before the penny press, newspapers employed few, if any, reporters to dig out news stories. News gathering had always been done by editors. Pages were filled with the editors' own reports of local events, their opinions, or letters from readers, clippings from other newspapers containing news and opinions, legal notices, poetry, and advertisements. News from afar arrived by mail. With more money coming in, newspapers were able to hire their own reporters.

Then as now, news reports were regarded with a special stamp of authenticity when the reporter at the scene of events told of personal observation and added interviews with the important players of each drama, such as statesmen and battlefield generals. The practice of active investigation soon followed, as did a rise in the circulation of newspapers willing to pursue news actively. In response—or self-defense—organizations from police to government to private business learned myriad ways to cope with an interviewer's questions. A public relations industry developed. Some organizations actually improved the ways they were behaving.

Recognizing the value of newspapers to bind the nation, Congress gave newspapers favored mailing rates, postage-free exchanges of newspapers, and free in-county delivery. Large urban newspapers did employ reporters to cover the Senate and the House of Representatives and other government offices, or they used a Washington news service. International news arriving by clipper ship was contained in foreign newspapers and in dispatches from foreign correspondents. By mid-century, steamships were replacing the slower sailing ships on the Atlantic run, so they were delivering foreign news sooner.

▶ YELLOW JOURNALISM

The late 19th and early 20th centuries brought "yellow journalism," named for the yellow coat a child cartoon character wore, and identified newspapers that featured sensational crime and scandal. Publishers Joseph Pulitzer of the *New York World* and William Randolph Hearst, whose newspaper empire included the *New York Journal*, built huge circulations through yellow journalism. By 1935, its peak year, the Hearst empire owned 26 daily newspapers in 19 cities, plus magazines, radio stations, movie companies, and both wire and photo news services. In his early years Hearst championed a number of progressive reforms such as labor union rights, but his later years would be marked by reactionary views, such as isolationism and opposition to the United Nations. An early supporter of the New Deal, he would turn bitterly against it and against pro-union legislation.

Hearst and Pulitzer engaged in a circulation war that reached its peak during the last decade of the 19th century. Pulitzer hired dozens of reporters, including women, and combined sensationalism with solid political reporting and comment. Hearst's newspapers outdid Pulitzer for sensational headlines not much different from current tabloid magazine headlines at the supermarket checkout counters. Hearst's *San Francisco Examiner* headlined a story of a hotel fire: HUNGRY, FRANTIC FLAMES, with the lede: "They Leap Madly Upon the Splendid Pleasure Palace by the Bay of Monterey, Encircling Del Monte in Their Ravenous Embrace From Pinnacle to Foundation."[4] What distinguished Pulitzer's *World* and sent circulation soaring was narrative and color. Beyond providing dry information, his reporters told stories. It should have come as no surprise that the public loved stories.

In 1889 Pulitzer sent young reporter "Nellie Bly" (a pseudonym for Elizabeth Cochrane) racing around the world in a successful stunt to sell papers, but he also crusaded for a number of serious liberal causes, particularly for taxing large incomes and against business monopolies. An immigrant himself, Pulitzer reached New York's large immigrant community with simple writing, photographs, and reports about the tenements and sweatshops where immigrants spent their lives. He created the Pulitzer Prizes and the School of Journalism at Columbia University, and he influenced the creation of the Missouri School of Journalism, two of the best in the world.

NELLIE BLY

Elizabeth Cochrane/Nellie Bly spent ten days in an insane asylum to reveal its shameful conditions. Of the meals fed to women inmates, she wrote, "The hungry and even famishing women made an attempt to eat the horrible messes . . . The most insane refused to swallow the food and were threatened with punishment. In our short walks we passed the kitchen where food was prepared for the nurses and doctors. There we got glimpses of melons and grapes and all kinds of fruits, beautiful white bread and nice meats, and the hungered feeling would be increased tenfold."[5] As a result of her first-hand account, conditions improved considerably, the most brutal nurses were transferred, and the city allocated more money for its hospitals.

By the end of the 19th century, the days of major newspapers depending on clipped editorial matter had passed. A new kind of journalism was based on staffs of competent reporters and editors aided by American and European news wire services. Telegraph lines crisscrossed the United States. The Atlantic cable was laid and other cable links stretched into Asia.

▶ MANIFEST DESTINY

The 19th century was the era of "manifest destiny," the conviction widely held by Americans that their nation was divinely favored. It was America's destiny, based on religious and racial superiority, to spread its influence and power across the continent and, after that, to native peoples across the world. The natives would be civilized and, in return, Americans would benefit by exploiting the mineral and agricultural riches of their lands. It was, in a word, imperialism. Not all Americans favored it, but those who advocated manifest destiny looked at the colonial empires of Britain, France, Portugal, Germany, and Spain and saw no reason why America should not project its power across the Pacific. Americans encouraged by newspapers cast covetous eyes on China, a sorely troubled nation being forced to grant concessions to colonial powers.

Among the most strident advocates of manifest destiny were publishers, with William Randolph Hearst in the forefront. Hearst beat the war drum for action against Spain's colonies in Cuba and the Philippines, where rebel groups struggled for independence. According to a famous and much disputed tale, artist Frederic Remington, sent to cover the pending war in Cuba, cabled back that there would be no war, and received Hearst's reply, "You furnish the pictures and I'll furnish the war." Hearst was by no means alone in his drum beating for manifest destiny. Supporters of what was called "jingoism" got their way. The United States annexed Puerto Rico, Guam, and the kingdom of Hawaii, as well as Cuba and the Philippines.

The era of the "press barons" like Hearst and Pulitzer continued well into the 20th century. "Colonel" Robert McCormick owned and published the *Chicago Tribune*, a bastion of conservative journalism that led the opposition to the New Deal of President Franklin Delano Roosevelt. An isolationist, McCormick also led crusades against the League of Nations, United States entry into World War II, and the United Nations. McCormick's cousin Joseph Medill Patterson founded the *New York Daily News*, the nation's first tabloid-size newspaper.

▶ MUCKRAKERS

President Theodore Roosevelt called investigative journalists "muckrakers," meant as an insult. Roosevelt took the term from the 17th-century book *Pilgrim's Progress* by John Bunyon, who wrote of "the Man with the Muckrake, the man who could look no way but downward . . . but continued to rake to himself the filth of the floor." Actually, Roosevelt also emphasized the benefits of some investigative reporting and counted reporters among his friends. Offended and shamed at first, the investigative reporters in time would consider it a badge of honor. The power of muckrakers, expressed through magazines or books, could be formidable. They published serious, factual exposé articles in magazines, especially in *McClure's Magazine*, and in newspapers and books. They wrote about sweatshop factories, abuses in insane asylums, corruption within the Standard Oil Company and railroads, and the mistreatment of Native Americans and African Americans.

McClure's Magazine hired a staff of writers to investigate and write the exposés that made the magazine famous. They included some of the most notable writers of the period, among them Lincoln Steffens, Willa Cather, Stephen Crane, and William Allen White. Ida Tarbell's exposé of John D. Rockefeller's Standard Oil tactics solidified her reputation as the nation's leading investigative journalist.

Strong competition came from *Harper's Magazine*, which began in 1950, and published influential reports by John Muir, Jack London, and Theodore Dreiser. *Leslie's Weekly*, founded in 1852, was also a strong competitor with patriotic themes and heroic battle stories.[6]

Upton Sinclair's 1906 book *The Jungle* exposed filthy conditions in the meat-packing industry. He found that simply carrying a dinner pail allowed him to wander around slaughterhouses without interference. "There would be meat that had tumbled out on the floor, in the dirt and sawdust, where the workers had tramped and spit uncounted billions of consumption germs. There would be meat stored in great piles in rooms; and the water from leaky roofs would drip over it, and thousands of rats would race about on it. It was too dark in these storage places to see well, but a man could run his hand over these piles of meat and sweep off handfuls of the dried dung of rats. These rats were nuisances, and the packers would put poisoned bread out for them; they would die, and then rats, bread, and meat would go into the hoppers together."[7] Federal meat inspection legislation followed. It also created a lot of vegetarians.

An exposé of patent medicines that were made up of either useless or harmful ingredients led to the Pure Food and Drug Act. Danish immigrant Jacob Riis, a police reporter in New York, took photographs of the squalid conditions of immigrants that were published in his books, *How the Other Half Lives* (1890) and *Children of the Poor* (1892).

In the 20th century other exposés revealed the organized maltreatment of Native Americans, intentional government neglect of black men suffering syphilis in Tuskegee, Alabama, the inadequate response to the onset of the AIDS epidemic in the 1980s, and dozens of other examples of corruption and malfeasance.

What has mattered throughout history is that media exposure can bring about change. As editors Judith and William Serrin note, "Reporters have caused the reform or closing of mental hospitals, the cleaning up of municipal water supplies, new rules for ferry boat operators in San Francisco, and efforts to aid federal workers exposed to plutonium . . . Journalists helped bring safer use of fireworks, safer automobiles and meat, and urban renewal . . . Journalism helped reduce child labor, exposed the unnecessary high costs of the American funeral industry, brought to light the dangers of the use of DDT and other pesticides, and led to the recall of automobiles and automobile and truck tires."[8]

A government printing office, early 20th century.

▶ THE GREAT AGE OF NEWSPAPERS

In the years just before World War I, more newspapers were published in the United States than ever before or since. The census of 1910 reported 2,600 daily publications of all types, of which 2,200 were English-language newspapers, and approximately 14,000 weekly newspapers.[9]

If the average American was becoming more interested in national and international news, some credit goes to the news services. The Associated Press (AP) began as a news gathering cooperative of New York newspapers in 1849, five years after Samuel Morse introduced his telegraph. Members agreed to exchange news and share costs. Other news associations were formed to compete with them, notably United Press (UP) and William Randolph Hearst's International News Service (INS), which one day would combine into UPI. The British news service Reuters got a foothold in the United States in 1865 when its report of the assassination of President Abraham Lincoln was the first to reach Europe. The news services mailed out still photographs to client newspapers, then added a facsimile photo service and television news coverage starting in the 1950s.

World War I was followed by more than a decade of high-flying confidence in America's future. Newspapers published a lot of photographs, headlines screamed sensational stories of hot romances, and some big-city newspapers were printed tabloid size, easier to read while holding on to a streetcar, bus, or subway strap. You could even read the small print that reported the rising prices of the stock you bought on margin. Broadway audiences in 1928 laughed at *The Front Page*, a play about a cocky reporter who hides a fugitive inside a roll-top desk to score a front-page byline scoop.

The newspaper was the way to learn what was happening at home and in the world, but new kinds of mediated communication were popular in the Jazz Age. Radio broadcasting took hold. Movies added sound. In 1928 Walt Disney introduced Mickey Mouse. An early version of the jukebox played recorded music for couples who wanted to dance in places where they drank illicit booze. The Depression was coming and a new world war. The day of the newspaper was waning, even if no one recognized it. People did not need to be literate to benefit from mediated communication that brought them entertainment and information in new ways. They could just sit back and watch or listen.

One kind of information to the American public was particularly suspect during the first half of the 20th century. Many Americans, especially those whose relatives came from Germany, were convinced that British propagandists, sending a stream of news of alleged German atrocities, duped the United States into entering World War I. Capitalists seeking war profits were considered complicit in what was the start of the public relations industry. Circus owner P. T. Barnum had pulled some stunts decades earlier, for example, when he displayed and got publicity for a "genuine" mermaid and a 161-year-old former nanny to George Washington. But the occupation of public relations really spread after turn-of-the-century muckraking articles about greedy capitalists. Publicity offices went into operation to defend against these attacks. Ivy Lee, the best known of the early publicists, argued that industry was best served by a policy of openness and frankness, not by trying to hide news of damaging events. Political columnist Walter

Lippmann and publicist Edward Bernays wrote widely circulated books about how public opinion is formed.[10]

▶ SOMETHING FOR EVERYONE

News, opinions framed in editorials, and advertising were not the only products a newspaper had to offer as the decades went by, nor were they the only means to shape attitudes toward political issues. Political columns, political cartoons, photographs, and advice columns have all done their bit to persuade. So have comics, ranging across the political spectrum from the conservative Orphan Annie to the liberal Doonesbury. The line between information and entertainment was frequently crossed in the never-ending quest for more readership. Horoscopes, household hints, and dozens of other features crowded the printed pages.

What the newspaper did was not only to connect readers to their community but also to the world beyond the horizon. For many generations the newspaper was the primary or indeed the only medium of mass communication. That is no longer the case. For the public, particularly the young public, a loss of interest in newspapers reflects the changing times.

Historically, most news has been transmitted mouth-to-ear. Radio and television newscasts are basically extensions of such communication. Newspapers struggled for decades to compete with each other and with broadcasting, and now wrestle with challenges from the Internet. Charging for content by erecting "paywalls" for premium access has been one answer.

Another is the tablet news app like Zite and Flipboard. News goes to tablets such as the iPad, not only constantly updated but also customized from many sources to the user's choice of topic. It is news-on-demand in your pocket. But newspapers have had a history of change ever since the world's first newspaper appeared 500 years ago.

▶ THE ALTERNATIVE PRESS

The international depression that began in 1873 left many European countries impoverished. In the decades immediately after the Civil War, Irish, German, and Scandinavian immigrants poured into the United States. Chinese men were brought in as contract laborers until Congress passed the Asian Exclusion Act that sharply limited the practice. By the close of the 19th century large numbers of Italians and Eastern European Jews were arriving. Some states began to pass their own immigration bans until the US Supreme Court ruled in 1875 that this was a federal matter. Opposition to the newcomers came, of course, from earlier arrivals and their descendants. The fiercest opposition came from nativist groups such as the anti-Catholic, anti-immigrant, anti-black, anti-Semitic Know Nothings movement that flourished in mid-19th century before dissolving. They had minor success at the ballot box, but little if any significant media support.

The mainstream press by no means met all the concerns of the nation. A vigorous alternative press presented other voices. A Socialist Party press supported unions and backed Eugene V. Debs, who ran for president five times. The women's suffrage movement had mainstream support as well as its own weekly newspaper, *Woman's Journal*.

African American newspapers and magazines have been published ever since *Freedom's Journal* printed in 1827. Today, a number of cities have their own African American newspaper, such as the *Chicago Defender* and the *Pittsburgh Courier*. Magazines such as *Ebony, Jet*, and *Essence* have international circulation. Journalists such as Ida B. Wells gave a voice to African American terrorized into silence by lynchings.

Foreign-language newspapers served the large immigrant communities. Among them: the German-language *New Yorker Staats-Zeitung*, *Il Progresso Italo-Americano* for Italian immigrants, and a considerable number of publications for Jewish immigrants in English, Hebrew, and Yiddish. Hispanic, Chinese, Japanese, and Arabic immigrant communities had their own newspapers. The foreign-language press continues today to serve their specialized communities, such as *Hmong Today*. For all immigrant communities, their periodicals helped them to keep in touch with one another and with their countries of origin, at the same time giving them a sense of pride in their heritage and assistance in adapting to their new country.

▶ MAGAZINES

The magazine was born in England in the 18th century as a weekly periodical. The remarkable and busy Daniel Defoe, author of *Robinson Crusoe* and *Moll Flanders*, founded the *Review* and filled it with essays, some of which he himself wrote.[11] Defoe also wrote the first modern newspaper editorial. He is considered a founder of the English novel and, because of his interviews, the founder of modern journalism. And he was a spy for an English government minister.

In England, *The Tatler* and *The Spectator* followed the *Review*. In 1741 the Philadelphia printer Andrew Bradford published the first magazine in the American colonies. Other colonial printers tried publishing magazines, but most failed, even though newspapers and magazines accepted goods for ad space and subscriptions, such as the Massachusetts publisher willing to barter subscriptions for butter and groceries.[12]

Without advertising or the postal considerations given to newspapers, magazine survival was difficult. Lack of illustrations, except for the occasional woodcut, limited their attraction, as did their high cost plus the poor quality of paper and presses. Yet the growth of the new United States was matched by an increase in the number of weekly, monthly, and quarterly periodicals, including magazines for genteel middle- and upper-class women starting with *The Lady's Magazine* in 1770 with literary and fashion articles plus embroidery patterns. In England *The Penny Magazine* was written for literate workmen. Religious magazines and those aimed at the working class were early examples of the fragmentation that specialized magazines brought to a community.

A few magazine publishers continued to appeal to a well-educated readership, but success depended on a broader audience. Congress extended low-cost mailing privileges to magazines in 1879. The end of the 19th century also saw several dozen illustrated mass circulation national magazines heavily supported by advertising. Cyrus Curtis published *The Saturday Evening Post* and *The Ladies Home Journal* based on the concept that large circulation magazines could profit more from advertising than subscriptions. His policies allowed him to pay top dollar for the best writing and art. He saw editorial content as incidental to advertising.

Curtis once asked an audience of advertisers, "Do you know why we publish *The Ladies Home Journal*? The editor thinks it is for the benefit of American women. That is an illusion, but a very proper one for him to have. But I will tell you the real reason, the publisher's reason, is to give you people who advertise things that American women want and buy a chance to tell them about your products."[13]

Popular taste magazines reached out to all members of the family with articles on the latest trends, sentimental romance fiction, pictures, and exposés. In 1893, depending upon advertising dollars, publishers Frank Munsey and S. S. McClure and *Cosmopolitan* editor John Walker engaged in a circulation war that dropped the price of their magazines below production costs. In doing so, they contributed to a societal movement for change in America. Creating the first *national* mass audience, their magazines built large circulations that commanded high ad rates for the mass-produced goods their magazines advertised. One reason why *McClure's Magazine*, one of the most interesting and respected magazines of the age, was able to sell copies cheaply, 15 cents instead of the 35 cents that similar magazines charged, was the new process of photoengraving. The usual process of creating wood engravings from drawings was considerably more expensive than creating an engraved image directly from a photograph.

By the middle of the 20th century, thousands of trade and specialty magazines were published for targeted readerships. They fared better than the mass circulation *Life, Look, Coronet* and *The Saturday Evening Post*, magazines that lost the struggle.[14] Mass circulation popular taste magazines succumbed to assaults by the new medium of television, which also appealed to popular tastes. A few mass circulation magazines, notably *Reader's Digest*, continued to thrive, but for most magazines, targeted readerships and targeted advertising provided the greater profits. During World War II, homesick soldiers who received special editions without advertising complained that the ads told them more about home than the editorial content.[15]

News magazines, notably *Time*, bedeviled by the need to compete with daily television newscasts for timely reports, fought back; but in 2012 *Newsweek* gave up its printed edition, although it started again in 2014. To speed the process of getting news into readers' hands, magazines sent pages via communication satellite to regional printing plants from which copies with imprinted addresses were flown or trucked to local distribution points to be mailed. National newspapers such as *The Wall Street Journal* thrown on doorsteps chose similar solutions to reach their far-flung readers.

While most newspapers address a geographic community, most magazines connect shared interests. It may be in politics, religion, occupation, social life, or hobbies. It is an endless list that includes city magazines (shared geography) too. A few general-interest magazines are sold, but millions of readers prefer magazines that address their preferences, and most of the 19,000 magazines published in the United States do that. People tend to go where they can get specifically what they want. The specialized magazines also give us a nationwide or even worldwide sense of community for each of our special interests, sending readers to find connections at a distance.

If a common theme can be found in the history of the magazine, it is that targeting a specific readership succeeds better than trying to reach the most diverse audience possible. In the world of printing, desktop publishing and e-readers are changing book and magazine publishing. Anyone who wants to imagine the future of television or any other medium of communication might do well to browse magazine racks for the growth of specialization.

PULP FICTION

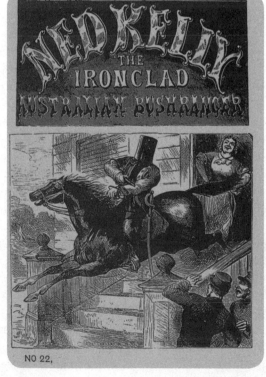

An 1880s penny dreadful, *Ned Kelly the Ironclad.*

Morality has been a recurring theme in books. In 19th-century America, the popular *McGuffey Readers* promoted hard work, study, good behavior, kindness, and honesty. They encouraged not only children but also their parents to acquire the skill of figuring out the message on the printed page in front of them. They emphasized oral techniques such as reading aloud passages from speeches, accompanied by pronunciation and breathing drills. More than 100 million of William McGuffey's *Readers* were sold. Another Victorian, Horatio Alger, repeatedly wrote of poor boys who succeeded by following the path of virtue. His books also sold in the millions. They served as guides for generations of youth growing up in America. Their influence lingers.

A reaction to uplifting tales was inevitable. Public appetite for inexpensive, easy-to-read novels filled with action, adventure, and romance led in the 19th century to the dime novel. A survey showed that most readers of this cross between a book and a magazine were working-class men with a grade school education.[16]

The books were nicknamed "pulp fiction" because of the rough wood-pulp paper they were printed on. They were sometimes called "blood and thunders" because of their content. (English boys bought the similar "penny dreadfuls.") By the 20th century their shiny covers in bright colors often featured drawings of scantily clad women and men in violent action. Priced from a nickel to a quarter, they contained up to 130 pages of short stories that bore little connection to the garish covers. They carried advertising for physical or mental self-improvement such as correspondence courses and muscle building. *Penny Dreadful* is the title of a new series on Showtime that evokes those over-the-top horror tales.

▶ BOOKS

The public learned to love novels. England, France, Germany, and Russia developed rich traditions of literary fiction in the 18th and 19th centuries. The novel was still an unusual literary form in 1719 when Daniel Defoe wrote of his shipwrecked mariner Robinson Crusoe, and Samuel Richardson told his readers about Pamela, whose virtue was rewarded, albeit sorely tested.

Written with middle-class sensibilities for middle-class readers about matters that concerned them, like social pretensions and the desire to improve one's status in a class-conscious society, the English novel set new standards for literature. Popular novels such as those by Charles Dickens were serialized in magazines. To keep the readers buying new issues, writers ended chapters on a note of suspense. This may also explain the large number of chapters. The important point is that these novels influenced behavior. They set standards of conduct. They created heroes and heroines whom readers regarded as models.

You may have heard stories of traditional parents who oppose advanced education for a daughter or, in fewer cases, a son. The parents fear that books will take their children away from them. They may be right, but if you fear change, books are not the only media you should fear. All media change us. They inform, educate, entertain, channel, and disengage us, separating us from what is near, connecting us to what is distant, different, strange.

Every type of mediated communication becomes more egalitarian with the passage of time, although media empires continue to build. This has been true of books since the invention of printing, but never truer than in the run-up to the Great Depression of the 1930s and the years since. The Book-of-the-Month Club and The Literary Guild, both started in 1926, became a new way to sell books to middle-class readers, or a "middle-brow culture," as some would have it. By the end of the 1920s several more book clubs joined them. Buying books in bulk, printing cheap editions, and peddling subscriptions, the clubs sold hundreds of thousands of novels, non-fiction titles, and reference books at prices that bookstores could not match. Department stores advertised popular titles at bargain prices to woo customers into their stores.

During the Depression, when the book business was hurting, publishers dropped the price of new novels. They still could not match the price of *Little Blue Books*, a "university in print." Three hundred million of the small, stapled booklets were sold between 1919 and 1949 at prices ranging from 10 cents to U.S.$1. Fitting into a worker's shirt pocket, the booklets aimed at getting literature and a range of ideas to as wide an audience as possible. Paperbacks followed what was by now a tradition of affordable reading. Because many titles still sold at regular prices, book buyers might have been confused and angry at the cost of books. An indignant *New York Times* editorial worried that prices might rise enough to cause "abandonment of the reading habit."[17]

As computers were inserted into the publishing process during the latter decades of the century, it became easier and cheaper to produce books of passable quality. Today, print-on-demand books occupy a small but growing segment of publishing. For university presses, small presses and self-publishers, printing a few copies at a time in response to a customer's order makes practical sense. No big investment is needed, the price-per-copy method is affordable, and no copies are sitting in warehouses waiting to be either sold or destroyed. Inevitably, more producers and more readers emerge for a wider range of material. New machines and companies have arisen to do business here.[18] The suspect, old-line vanity presses have both more opportunity and more competition.

In the 21st century, despite the competition from other media, books still sell well, although Borders and some smaller bookstores have not survived. Book chain stores feature coffee shops and encourage browsing. Amazon.com and Barnes & Noble do a brisk book business online. The most popular books boast sales of more than 1 million copies each. Meanwhile, books extend their reach through non-print media, particularly audio books that entertain drivers on the daily commute.

Each year e-book devices come closer to the reading experience of holding a book in your hands. Several dozen manufacturers such as Apple and Amazon have competed at bringing devices to market. Hundreds of thousands of titles are for sale at sharply lower prices than printed books. Quite a few may be freely downloaded through Project Gutenberg. Clearwater High School in Tampa Bay, Florida, in 2014 planned to give each student a Kindle e-reader loaded with the entire year's textbooks assignments for that student. A similar experiment in seven colleges, however, ended in disappointment.[19]

And what can be downloaded can be uploaded, giving self-publishing authors instant access to readers through gateways such as the Amazon Digital Text Platform. Magazines and newspapers are available as well. Online libraries may one day consign the bookcase to join the buggy whip.

The fragmentation and recombination of readers into narrow but national and even international interest groups also expresses itself in news-letters. Once mimeographed and stapled, modern newsletters are either slick products that draw on desktop publishing techniques or are sold for online delivery that requires no paper at all.

The ranks of newsletter publishers have risen exponentially because of the minimal costs of online publication. Among them are "zines," published on such personal subjects as the publisher's music tastes, a paper version of Internet blogs. Many of them have circulations of less than 100, turned out on copiers. The creators' motives are almost always self-expression, not profit.

▶ THE TYPEWRITER

Importantly, the typewriter deserves some credit for a social change of last-ing effect: the emancipation of women from their financial dependence on fathers and brothers. It was a daring step in the 19th-century Victorian Age to go out to work as a receptionist in an office full of men to whom they were not related. Nevertheless, many women refused to be dictated to. They went out to become stenographers and even entrepreneurs. News stories and romantic fiction about young women who broke the restrictions of the traditional home inspired other women to take risks.

The typewriter, which produced so many words for more than a cen-tury, deserves mention for still more. Today these machines gather dust in the antique shops of the cities of the industrialized world, but they may still be found, sometimes in developing countries, doing their job of generating information along the mediated communication trail leading from someone's brain to everyone's eyes. Even in the computer-rich West, a battered type-writer might be found at the fingertips of a self-professed Luddite who will have nothing to do with digital media. (During the Industrial Revolution, the followers of Ned Ludd destroyed textile machinery that was replacing them, one more example of the responses people have had to technological change.)

The idea of a writing machine may have originated with an English engineer, Henry Mill, who received a patent in 1714 but did not construct a machine. Typewriters constructed during the 19th century were built in Austria, Switzerland, France, and Italy. One goal for such a machine was to emboss letters on paper so that the blind could read, an enterprise perhaps motivated by the example of a French youth, Valentin Haüy, who started a school for the blind. A French youth who had gone blind, Louis Braille, attended the school, where he improved on Haüy's book-embossing code. Another impetus for a writing machine came from the new telegraph industry. Skilled telegraphers could understand messages as fast as the clicks arrived, but could not write them down by hand fast enough.

Patents flew thick and fast in several countries as imaginative citizens thought up machine designs that resembled everything from a small piano to an oversized pin cushion. The 52nd typewriter patent issued by the US Patent Office in 1868 went to Christopher Sholes of Milwaukee, a printer who joined friends to design a workable machine that sent keys moving *up* to a print point. Because each key fell back slowly, pulled just by the force of gravity, it was easy for an ascending key to block a descending key; hence the "scientific" design of the keyboard to reduce the number of jams. Incremental improvements by Sholes and his friends were speeded up when the Remington Company, maker of guns and sewing machines, took on the new business. The sewing machine foot treadle was adapted as a carriage return. Of the dozens of companies that later manufactured typewriters, International Business Machines (IBM) made the most changes with its line of electric typewriters, notably the Selectric typing ball.

The computer keyboard maintains the anachronistic QWERTY keyboard designed for mechanical typewriters to minimize jamming the keys at the print point by positioning the common letters "a" and "s" under the weak fingers and the uncommon "j" under the strongest finger, an arrangement that also separated the most frequent pairs of letters so that they are struck by alternate hands. The rationale for QWERTY disappeared with the electric typewriter and certainly does us no favors in the electronic world. Yet each generation learns this keyboard arrangement only because the previous generation is accustomed to it, rather than learning a more efficient arrangement such as the Dvorak system, which places all the vowels on the home row under the left hand and the most frequently used consonants on the home row under the right hand. The goal is less finger motion, a faster typing speed, and fewer errors. This keyboard is an option offered by Microsoft Windows, Mac OSX, and Linux operating systems.

The concept of the typewriter, a personal writing machine that would replace a pen that cost a penny, did not catch on immediately. Before the typewriter, offices did not have machinery, but the advantages of mechanization ultimately became apparent. Typewriters were followed by dictaphones, mimeographs, adding machines, bookkeeping machines, envelope addressers, check writers, and postal meters.

▶ HYPERLOCAL NEWS

Unfortunately for admirers of the printed page, although the second half of the 20th century brought improved printing technology through computerization, newspaper readership has declined as more people turned to competing communication technologies. News could be delivered by radio and later by television. When the 21st century began, the Internet allowed what may prove to be, for printed newspapers, devastating competition. Readers, especially youth, turned away from the daily newspaper but not from news. They liked Internet news and entertainment, they liked the opinions of bloggers, and they liked it all free.

Once again, communication media affected the general society, this time in the disturbing direction of inadequately informed or grossly misinformed opinions based on the skimpy information of bloggers with a political agenda. Nothing new here. The first newspaper printers had done much the same. Yet it was not long before "hyperlocal" news blogs brought improved standards to online local news sites. For example, AOL has targeted dozens of mostly small affluent communities as "Patch" sites, where local news is gathered by trained journalists and presented along with local advertising. AOL seeks to make them online versions of community newspapers without the costs of newsprint, ink, and delivery.[20]

In the digital age, journalism is no longer limited to journalists, but trained journalists bring reporting, editing and layout skills that bloggers may lack. Taking advantage of Internet and digital technology, hyperlocal blogs are easy and cheap to produce and access. And they attract advertising from the local shops and classified ads that are the bread-and-butter of the free urban community newspaper "shoppers" and the newspaper advertising inserts that land on doorsteps. With such competition, the days of the free shopper may be numbered, driven out of business by news blogs that compete without paper.

Hyperlocal news may pull in participants who are everyday neighbors and, in fact, anyone with a digital camera. The addition of parking spaces to a local strip mall can be "front page" news. The real concern need not be for the survival of ink-on-paper, but rather for a news delivery structure with the virtues of professional preparation: honest, accurate, thoughtful, balanced, interesting, informative, engaging.

▶ ADVERTISING

Mass advertising began during the Industrial Revolution. Factories turned out goods and needed customers. Workers received cash wages. As mass production of a variety of goods grew, accompanied by mass distribution, it was inevitable that mass marketing would follow, for the goods had to be sold. Beyond notices to *meet* demand, advertising was needed to *create* it. From the beginning of the 20th century, the national magazine presented itself as the vehicle for the advertising of factory goods. Soon, entrepreneurs were buying space in bulk from both magazines and newspapers, and then selling it retail to the manufacturers (for a more thorough explanation of this early spread of advertising, see Chapter 16).

However, newspapers and magazines were not the only printed media that carried advertisements. In the cities and along the sides of the roads, billboards appeared. Signs advertising tobacco and patent medicine went up on fences, barns, bridges, large rocks, and even curbstones. Vacation destinations, roads, and railroad pathways have been favored locations for billboards, to the point that a few communities have passed laws limiting such signage; later, some laws faced First Amendment challenges. Serial signs along highways, notably the Burma Shave rhymes, became part of the American culture, changing the look of the landscape. These appeared on highways across the nation, a series of five signs easily read by drivers as they cruised by at 40 mph or so. Typical: "Train approaching / Whistle squealing / Stop / Avoid that run-down feeling / Burma Shave."

With its jingles, slogans, theme songs, comedians' jokes, and the natural appeal of a voice, radio humanized the products that were advertised. The commercials were often the target of radio humor, but the product was always presented seriously. Television commercials would join the effort. At the very start of commercial television in 1941, an ad for Bulova watches ran for 10 seconds during a baseball game televised in New York.[21]

Radio broadcasting added slogans and singing commercials to rattle around inside people's heads. Hearing a jingle sung innumerable times led some people to sing or hum it themselves at odd times. Anglo-Saxon males dominated ad agencies from the start, a condition recalled by the *Mad Men* television series. It was reflected in advertising images that too often showed women as appendages to men, and almost never featured people of color or those without conventional Anglo-Saxon features.

All of advertising has formed the basis of the consumer culture that is so pervasive in American society and has spread to cultures around the world, based on the dubious premises that buying something solves emotional problems and that worth can be measured by ownership.

▶ THE CONTEXT OF TEXTBOOKS

Fueled by propaganda in newspapers and magazines of German military atrocities, anti-German feelings during World War I before America entered the war led to the passage of the Espionage Act. American entry into the war was quickly accompanied by a government information office to feed war news and by a voluntary censorship code for newspapers. Isolationist newspapers came around immediately when war was finally declared by the United States in 1917. To emphasize loyalty, cheap newspaper mailing rates were denied to German-language and socialist newspapers. Some were banned from the mails. The Sedition Act of 1918 extended the Espionage Act, giving teeth to government controls over what was regarded as the Bolshevik menace.

Censorship was re-established during World War II with an Office of Censorship and the Office of War Information, which fed news and propaganda to media outlets. At the same time, journalists had virtually unrestricted access to soldiers at the front, as Ernie Pyle did when the much loved correspondent reported the war in infantry foxholes, and were permitted such advantages as flying on bombing raids, as Edward R. Murrow did. However, military censors checked stories before they went out to guard against reporting classified information.

Censorship is happening today in, of all places, our K-12 schools, and it is not being imposed by governments. Movement away from mass communication to individualized, on-demand content has taken hold in textbooks. Censorship concerns both textbooks and curricula, with censors arguing such religious and political questions as whether evolution should be taught without also teaching creationism.

Efforts to limit what children can read in school come from both liberal and conservative sources. Among the many topics to be avoided in modern textbooks are abortion, unpleasant creatures like rats and cockroaches, death, disease, disrespectful or criminal behavior, evolution, magic, witchcraft, people's height and weight, politics, religion, child abuse, animal abuse, addiction, unemployment, weapons, and violence.[22] Textbooks dealing with such unavoidable subjects as literature, history, and biology are minefields. Self-appointed experts hold fast to their familiar staked-out positions on issue after issue. Renowned authors and famed literary works are not spared the wrath of those intent on protecting children from what these textbook content advocates deem harmful.

The quarrels bubble up from individuals using government levers to limit what can be printed or shown. They want to protect children, the targets of all this concern. A fight over K-12 textbooks has been focused on test questions, because they guide what publishers put in their textbooks. The terrain has been further focused on Texas and California because smaller states frequently follow the lead of these two large states that adopt books on a statewide basis. It takes only a few persistent voices in those two states to have an outsized influence on what is included or excluded from what millions of children are permitted to learn.

An observer of the battle in Texas commented, "It became clear that the list of historical figures deemed worthy of inclusion in civics textbooks was up for discussion: at various points, Thurgood Marshall and Cesar Chavez were among those on the chopping block, while the inventor of the yo-yo (I'm not making this up) was cheerfully inserted and the laundering of Joseph McCarthy's reputation was contemplated. Aesop's fables were found wanting, as was a discussion of the separation of church and state. There was also a problem of race and ethnicity—or lack thereof. Board members not allied with the conservative bloc complained that the non-Anglo history of the state was getting increasingly short shrift—despite the demographic makeup of the Alamo battlefield, or the fact that Texas will soon be majority Hispanic."[23]

In this textbook battle, government does not instigate the censorship. It acquiesces. Caught in the middle, publishers who want to stay in business are desperate not to offend anyone. Children are, not unsurprisingly, bored by what their teachers assign. The kids find their natural desire for mental stimulation in video games, television, comic books and other non-school outlets.[24]

▶ A BROADER PERSPECTIVE

It may be cynical fun to examine ideologue complaints about Aesop's fable "The Fox and the Crow" for gender bias (the clever male fox flatters the vain female crow) or to wonder why the faces on Mount Rushmore cannot be discussed in a history class (the Lakota Indians don't want the sculptures there), or to reflect on how dinosaurs got along with humans living side by side.

But the textbooks that are adjusted to raise the fewest hackles are mass printed for millions of children and they are a central part of mass communication. So let us take a broader perspective. Take a step back from specific examples to consider that a bottom-up wish to censor, coming from ordinary citizens rather than the government, is as natural to a free-wheeling democracy as the wish to persuade. Media control is now potentially within everyone's reach. In this case it is K-12 textbooks. It could be any medium at any level. Aware that they can exert enough force at educational pressure points to change content to suit their opinions, some people are doing just that: changing what other people may be allowed to learn.

Considering the long history of top-down censorship, bottom-up censorship is remarkable, if no less questionably motivated. However, in the world of modern communication, nothing is certain except change, a lesson the Greek philosopher Heraclitus taught.

Along with people who want to convince you of something are people who want to prevent you from learning something else. Often, they are the same people. Those able to restrict the communication choices of others—by any method, subtle or coerced—guard their authority, legally acquired or not.

The urge to control all mass communication media remains vigorous both in and out of government. The last few years have seen all too many reports of journalists killed in Russia, Mexico, and Colombia, of imprisonment in Egypt, Turkey, and Iran, and of writers, journalists, newspaper and television executives harassed in many countries. Reporters Sans Frontières (RSF), based in Paris, compiles an annual index of such attacks. China is a leading example of how far a government will go to control mass information. Their principal target, the Internet, continues to be a stubborn example of how a communication technology—overcoming opposition—expands the numbers of people who send and receive information. Messages continue to trickle through the most imposing censorship dams. The battle between wanting to know and wanting to block knowing never ends.

▶ TIMELINE

1800   Iron presses permit printing on large sheets of paper with thicker fonts.

1819   In England David Napier's rotary printing press; two-sided impressions.

1829   Louis Braille invents embossed printing.

1833   The penny press, especially the *New York Sun*, opens a mass market.

1840   German paper makers experiment with wood pulp.

1846   Richard Hoe's cylinder press produces 8,000 sheets an hour.

1851   Post Office offers a cheap newspaper mailing rate.

1856   A full-page newspaper ad is printed by the *New York Ledger*.

1860   *New York Herald* starts an information archive, a "morgue."

1867   Christopher Sholes of Wisconsin constructs a Type-Writer.

1869   Newspaper circulation figures are made public.

1870   Wood pulp widely used to make paper.

1878   Photogravure printing.

1880   A halftone photograph, "Shantytown," appears in a newspaper.

1886   Ottmar Mergenthaler's Linotype at the *New York Tribune* replaces handset type.

1890   Mimeograph machines bring printing to the small office.

1892   Four-color rotary presses.

1903   The first tabloid-style newspaper, the *New York Daily Mirror*.

1904   Offset lithography becomes a commercial reality.

         Comic books are published.

1917   Photocomposition begins.

1933   Newspaper publishers try to limit radio news, but fail.

1955   Newspapers start using teletypesetting.

1947   Phototypesetting spreads, replacing hot lead letterpress.

1961   Xerox introduces photocopying.

1967   The switch to computers begins.

1971   Offset printing is common.

1985   Desktop publishing becomes familiar: PageMaker, laser printers.

1996   Traditional newspapers add online versions.

1998   Google improves information retrieval.

2000   People read e-books.

2004   Google begins scanning millions of books for online searches.

2007   Number of US daily newspapers drops to 1,456.

2009   Newspapers are hurting as advertising revenue plummets.

▶ **NOTES**

1 Marshall McLuhan, *The Gutenberg Galaxy* (Toronto: University of Toronto Press, 1962) 144.

2 McLuhan, 278.

3 Siva Vaidhyanathan, *The Anarchist in the Library* (New York: Basic Books, 2004) 102.

4 David Nasaw, *The Chief: The Life of William Randolph Hearst* (New York: Houghton Mifflin, 2000) 75.

5 Nellie Bly, "Ten Days in a Mad-House," *New York World*, October 16, 1887.

6 It was first called *Frank Leslie's Illustrated Newspaper*.

7 Upton Sinclair, *The Jungle* (New York: Doubleday, Page & Co., 1906) Chapter xiv. Project Gutenberg, http://www.gutenberg.org/files/140/140-h/140-h.htm#link2 HCH0019.

8 Judith and William Serrin, eds., *Muckraking: The Journalism That Changed America.* (New York: The New Press, 2002) xx.

9 Michael Emery, Edwin Emery, and Nancy Roberts, *The Press and America: An Interpretive History of the Mass Media*, 9th ed. (Boston: Allyn and Bacon, 2000) 288.

10 Walter Lippmann, *Public Opinion* (New York: Harcourt, Brace and Company, 1922). Edward L. Bernays, *Public Relations* (Boston: Bellman, 1945).

11 It was first called *A Weekly Review of the Affairs of France*.

12 *Worcester Magazine*, III, 181 (first week, July 1787).

13 James Playsted Wood, *The Story of Advertising* (New York: Ronald Press, 1958) 211.

14 *Life* ended weekly publication in 1972, but struggled on with special editions until 1978, then as a monthly until 2000. Since then it has been a newspaper supplement and a website: life.time.com.

15 Wood, 444.

16 William Gray and Ruth Munroe, *The Reading Interests and Habits of Adults* (New York: Macmillan, 1929) 149.

17 Ann Haugland, "Edward L. Bernay's 1930 Campaign Against Dollar Books," in Ezra Greenspan and Jonathan Rose, eds., *Book History*, vol. 3 (University Park: Pennsylvania State University Press, 2000) 233.

18 *The Economist*, 27 February 2010, 72–73.

19 *Tampa Bay Times*, April 3, 2014, http://www.tampabay.com/news/education/k12/clearwater-high-prepares-to-hand-out-kindle-e-readers-to-its-2100-plus/1120428.

20 *Tech & Learning*, July 2011, http://www.techlearning.com/editorblogs/404-08.

21 "History of TV Ads," http://www.qualitylogoproducts.com/lib/history-of-tv-ads.htm.

22 Diane Ravitch, *The Language Police: How Pressure Groups Restrict What Students Learn* (New York: Alfred Knopf, 2003).

23 See, for example, Evan Smith, "The Texas Curriculum Massacre," *Newsweek*, April 26, 2010, 34–35.

24 The argument and eye-opening examples of excess zeal are offered by Ravitch in *The Language Police*.

4 Mail: The Snail that Could

The days are long gone when almost the only way to send a message to a distant person was to drop it in a mailbox. Yet, it was not so long ago that most families lived isolated lives, their principal links to the outside coming through the local post office. Ralph Waldo Emerson called mail delivery "a fine meter of civilization."[1]

Compare the postal service with radio or television. Each has had a considerable impact upon our world. Each brings information, entertainment, and advertising to our homes. Each depends upon international agreements, national standards, and some government supervision. Each is built upon broad communication technologies. Most obvious for the postal service is its dependence on paper and printing.

The postal service and broadcasting are alike in having competition in what they do. Federal Express, United Parcel Service, DHL, Amazon, and the U.S. Postal Service compete heavily. The mail carrier also competes in the message delivery business with fax machines, cellphones, instant messaging, email, electronic banking, automated bill payments, and even inserts in newspapers.

Because Netflix uses the postal service to deliver movies, the mail carrier is partly competing with the cable television provider. Of course, distinctions exist. The postal service provides personal, point-to-point communication. Radio and television provide the physical reality of the machine in the living room. Mail dates to the dawn of history. Both the postal service and broadcasting in most countries are fully or partly government run, though not broadcasting in the United States. A closer analogy can be drawn by comparing the postal service with the telephone, the telegraph, the communication satellite, and the Internet.

▶ ANCIENT POSTS

Postal beginnings are lost in antiquity. Like language itself, messages went out in a hundred disorganized oral and written ways over the centuries.[2] Their oral delivery obviously came before writing, but it was writing that led to the organized postal services. The mail carrier followed two trails, the path of the government and the path of the private citizen and the merchant. In some places at some times the two paths were one, but only in the last few centuries, a fraction of postal history, have they merged. Yet, because of necessity and suspicion, some governments still kept separate channels.

Moving the mail was never a simple matter. Delivery has included carrier pigeons, human runners, fast ponies, slow donkeys and camels, dog sleds, stagecoaches, as well as all manner of boats, trains, trucks, and airplanes.

Postal service is the handmaiden of central government, essential to retaining power. Kings knew that if they wanted to control their land, they had to control communication. The Chinese Empire had an official postal service in the tenth century BCE. By the 13th century CE, Kublai Khan had the world's best courier system. A network of 1,400 post houses and relay stations for an estimated 50,000 horses were on duty throughout his empire. Boats waited for mail at river and lake crossings. Camels and carriages hauled ordinary mail as well as passengers. First-class mail, limited to royal and military mail, always went by pony express in relays. A rider who didn't meet his schedule faced a whipping. Marco Polo was sufficiently impressed to include a description in his reflections.[3]

Government postal services in China until recent centuries were meant only for government departments, just as they were in other countries, but merchants also used the system, and no doubt love letters sneaked in. To the east the Japanese postal system was officially limited to government use until a private courier service began in the 17th century.

The New World had no horses until European invaders introduced them, so Aztecs, Incas, and Mayas employed relay stations of human runners. Certain Native American tribes notched or painted sticks to convey messages. Incas in South America stored and conveyed information on knotted colored cords that the Spanish invaders called *quipu*. Such media had limited advantage aside from being easily carried. Aztec couriers also delivered freshly caught fish to inland villages, an early parcel post service.

The Old and New Testaments mention letters. King David's letter to the battlefield sealed the fate of Bathsheba's unlucky husband. Dispatches are mentioned in the Book of Esther. Job lamented, "My days are swifter than the post." Paul sent many letters to Judea and Macedonia.

The first record of a written message stamped with a seal and apparently delivered by a courier dates to King Sargon of Babylon, about 2300 BCE. The Egyptians had a relay system that helped to maintain central control of their empire. An ancient Egyptian papyrus scroll carries the request, "Write to me by the letter carrier." In the third century BCE, Ptolemy II introduced the camel into Egypt and organized a camel post to carry government and commercial messages to the south. Under the rulers Cyrus, Darius, and Xerxes, Persians built roads and established pony express relay stations throughout the empire. To interfere with the mails was punishable by death.

Observing that messages could travel 200 miles in a day, the Greek historian Herodotus wrote, "Nothing mortal travels so fast as these Persian messengers . . . And neither snow nor rain nor heat nor gloom of night stays these couriers from the swift completion of their appointed rounds."[4] That inscription is carved into the stone of the New York City Post Office.

Ancient Greece, lacking a central government, had no known postal service, but several tales of running messengers have come down to us. In Homer's day communication was by messenger or by signal fires from mountaintop to mountaintop. The most famous Greek messenger we know of, Pheidippides, ran so hard to report the victory at Marathon that he collapsed and died uttering the message *Nike!*" ("Victory!"). Marathon races honor his achievement, be it fact or myth. So do running shoes.

▶ THE ROMANS

The large Roman postal system, the *cursus publicus*, stretched across the Empire from Egypt to Britain. It was so fast that no postal organization matched its speed for nearly 1,900 years.[5]

One reason for those famous Roman roads was the wish to improve the mails. Like Persia, the Roman Empire established relay stations with post houses that the dwellers of nearby villages reluctantly maintained but were not allowed to use themselves. To reach its distant colonies, Rome also organized the world's first sea post. It is likely that the English word "post" is derived from the Latin word for relay station, "*posita.*" We use it in "postal," "post office," and, of course, "postage."

In the Philippics of 44 BCE, Cicero railed against spying on private letters, but this bureaucratic addiction has proved durable over the centuries. By the fourth century CE, the emperor Diocletian placed the Roman postal system under an imperial secret service that included officials called *curiosi.* Their duties included government spying and catching mail fraud. No doubt they opened letters. More than 1,500 years after Cicero, Martin Luther had the same complaint as that Roman senator.

Ordinary citizens of the Roman Empire, forbidden to use the government *cursus publicus*, devised their own means of long distance communication, but contact remained sparse between Rome and the aristocrats who preferred to live on their country estates. Some of the best and brightest citizens did not participate in government as long as they were out of the city, but they still received messages.

Over short distances, servants, usually slaves, carried letters. It was not the softest of jobs, for a slave could be killed if his master's enemies caught him, but if he failed to deliver the letters promptly, his irritated master might slay him. The phrase "to kill the messenger" recalls the ancient tendency to punish the bearer of bad tidings.

▶ MEDIEVAL POSTAL SERVICE

Message delivery changed over time, with the distinction of backsliding during the Dark and Middle Ages. When the Roman Empire collapsed, so did the efficient Roman postal system. Illiterate peasants certainly had no need of a postal service. Hardly anyone else did either. The roads were no longer safe for post riders, nor were they as necessary during the Dark Ages that followed the fall of the Roman Empire because of illiteracy and the isolation of communities.

A mailed letter was probably less secure then than an Assyrian or Persian letter 4,000 years earlier. Walled towns flourished when literacy and writing were at their lowest point. Marshall McLuhan noted that a simple alphabet written on easily transportable papyrus and parchment encouraged communication, which was later discouraged by the walled towns and city-states that rose as Rome fell.[6]

During the Dark Ages, postal service could be of little value even for nobles where illiteracy was the norm for all but a few. Independent thought had as little meaning as the notion of freedom to choose a government or a religion. You were what you were told that God intended.

Four centuries after the fall of Rome came Charlemagne, the first of the Holy Roman Emperors, who dreamed of reviving the glory of Rome under the mantle of Christianity. He restored a rudimentary postal system using the old, deteriorating Roman roads. Postal routes and stations were established.

By the 12th century, monasteries had established regular links with their distant brethren. Written information was borne in the *rotula*, a round-robin newsletter. The abbot of a monastery would report monastic events on a parchment scroll, such as who had died during the previous year. At the next monastery the abbot might add a fresh item or two about other events, plus such entries as "Common report has it that the Antichrist has been born at Babylon."[7]

Craft guilds and merchant guilds set up their own mail operations. Service by service, the illiterate feudal age of Europe was giving way to the mercantile age, to literacy, and to the desire to gain knowledge.

The advent of universities, the expansion of towns, and the needs of trade increased the amount of written communication. Peddlers, pilgrims, merchants, and crusaders carried news and private messages across Europe and the Near East. During the 13th century at the University of Paris the foundation of a truly national postal service began in France under the umbrella of the Roman Catholic Church. It came about because university teachers and students were regarded as ecclesiastics. The messengers received the same royal guarantees and exemptions that faculty and students enjoyed, such as safe conduct when they traveled and exemption from military duty and taxes. In other words, the postal carriers had some of the same privileges as priests. As a result of this generous gesture the job of carrying messages became coveted. To put it more precisely, the franchise to employ messengers was hugely valuable. As the years passed, despite restrictions, the messengers added to their income by carrying outside mail.

Just as the absence of mail was a mark of the decline of Roman civilization into the Dark Ages, so a growth of mail marked a renewal of civilization into the Middle Ages. The spreading mercantile interests of cities and towns led to arrangements to protect their trade with the outside world, particularly against bandits and feudal lords who taxed and sometimes seized goods crossing their lands.

During the 14th and 15th centuries, the Italian Della Torres family ran a private courier service that over the years spread across Europe. Rich and powerful, and operating under charters of the Holy Roman Empire, the firm built a swift and dependable postal system across Central Europe. After some marriages to nobility, the firm took on the name Thurn and Taxis. The latter name is used the world over to identify a vehicle for public use. It was then a kind of pony express, at first serving emperors and military officers. Inevitably, it served merchants as well.

The few literate people who could not take advantage of an existing postal system might have sought out a guild or Church courier willing to carry an extra letter for a coin. In time, such a side business was openly incorporated into the organization and became part of the courier's duty. By 1500, letter

PIGEON POST

During the Dark Ages the Arabs established pigeon courier services. According to one tale, a caliph in North Africa satisfied his taste for Lebanese cherries by having pigeons fly them in. Each carried one cherry inside a silk bag, the first parcel post. Reportedly, a prize pair of carrier pigeons could be sold for as much as 1,000 gold pieces.

Pigeon post was the world's fastest communication system for all the centuries of the Dark and Middle Ages, and remained so until Samuel Morse's invention of the telegraph in 1844. Stockbrokers and bankers continued to rely on pigeons through much of the 19th century. In 1840 the European news agency Havas ran a London-to-Paris pigeon news service with the promised flying time of six hours. In the Franco–Prussian War of 1870–1871, a gap existed in telegraph lines between France and Germany. Julius Reuter bridged it with pigeons and made the fortune that he used to found what is now Reuters, one of the world's great news agencies.

Even in modern times, pigeons have been postal couriers. In 1981, Lockheed engineers in California needed to send photographic negatives on a regular basis to a test station. The birds covered the distance in half the time and at less than 1 percent of the cost of a car delivery. Other means of communication have replaced the cooing messengers, but here and there they can still be found doing the useful work that made them the email of the Middle Ages. And they work for . . . pigeon feed.

routes were open to the public across Europe. Postal fees were based on what the public could bear and could be heavy. If a letter would cause financial damage to the receiver, the person wishing to write might have second thoughts about it.

Some news arrived in disorganized ways. Gossip of distant events was borne on the lips of traveling minstrels. It was said that they could repeat without error a rhyming ballad of 1,000 lines heard only once. The rhymes, sometimes accompanied by a lute, aided the memory.

▶ ROYAL MAIL SERVICE

In 15th-century France, Louis XI revived a national postal service strictly for government use, the first national service since Charlemagne. The king ordered 200 couriers to be stationed in towns across France to convey royal messages. The king declared that anyone who dared to inject private letters into the service was doomed to Hell. That was serious, for the Middle Ages acknowledged the divine right of kings. Louis, after all, communicated with God!

Fear of Hell did not stop all private communication when a coin or two might change hands. In 1600, the Spanish ruler of The Netherlands, the viceroy Cardinal Duke Albrecht VII, legalized what had been a crime openly practiced. He gave the Taxis service officials permission to charge for private letters. William Shakespeare mentioned the post in several plays, sometimes in the phrase "post haste." Actual letters, written on parchment and sealed with wax, sometimes bore this request for urgency: "Haste, Post, Haste, for Thye Lyfe, for Thye Lyfe, Haste." Maybe it helped.[8]

A postal service depended upon the king's permission for a price. A king appointed a postmaster the way a city today grants a franchise to a cable television company. The franchisee paid for an exclusive right to pursue a profitable enterprise called a "farm." The postal "farmer" paid rent to the king or the government for the privilege of managing the posts. The farmer "harvested money" from those who used the service. Starting in 1627 most of the British government's postal service and private operations merged into a single State Post, but additional private services continued as early versions of UPS and Federal Express.

Where rival postal systems sprang up, overly zealous competition led to highway ambushes and royal court intrigues. During the English civil war of the 17th century, in a battle over who had the franchise for delivering the mail, the Earl of Warwick's men stopped a mail carrier on a rural road and seized his mail. They had not ridden far when another group of men seized the earl's men.

Most letters were not sent inside envelopes prior to the invention of postage stamps. Instead, letters were folded to put the writing inside and show the blank side out for the address, seal, and indication of payment. The widespread preference for envelopes separate from their contents began in France about 1845.

THE POST-BOY

For centuries the "post-boy" with his mail pouch was a familiar sight in Europe, sometimes on foot, sometimes poking along on a swayback horse, if artists of the period can be believed. On his back he slung his post-horn, which he blew to announce to villagers that he had arrived with the mail. He was an easy target for highwaymen.

▶ THE NEW WORLD

In 1639, less than 20 years after the Pilgrims landed on Plymouth Rock, a post office was set up in the tavern and home of Richard Fairbanks of Boston, following the European practice of using taverns and coffeehouses for mail drops. Arriving ship captains delivered their mail packets and picked up those bound for Europe. As the New World's first postmaster, Fairbanks was allotted one penny per letter.

For the most part, letters and packages were carried by friends or trusted strangers, or they might be entrusted to a magistrate or religious minister.[9] Dependable regular delivery inland waited until postal routes were planned through the wilderness. Even then, the trails of the colonial letter carrier on foot or horseback were little more than footpaths used by local Native American tribes.

The first private post boxes might consist of a row of old boots nailed against a wall at a river steamboat landing. Each bore a settler's name. The mail sat in the boot until the settler came to town. A letter at a remote outpost could sit for six months or more before the settler picked it up. Someone else might open a letter just to learn the most recent news from back East.

In colonial days, the Atlantic crossing was safer, surer, and cheaper than the inland roads. From Boston it cost only 2 pence to send a letter to England, but 15 pence to the closer parts of Pennsylvania and New Jersey. From Boston to New York it cost 9 pence to have a letter delivered. Going the other way cost 12 pence.[10]

A struggling printer and newspaper publisher in Philadelphia, Benjamin Franklin was appointed postmaster of Philadelphia in 1737 when he was 31. The Crown's colonial postal service was a financial mess, yet it had advantages for a publisher. Postal officials had the power to order newspapers to pay letter rates or pay on the basis of an agreement between postmaster and publisher. By contrast, when they were one and the same, the postmaster–publisher could reach such an agreement with himself while shaving. Many colonial newspapers were mailed postage free at the postmaster's choosing.

The former postmaster did not allow his post riders to carry Franklin's newspaper. Franklin had to bribe them until he became the postmaster, but he proved fair in dealing with other publishers. In 1753, having grown wealthy, Franklin was again promoted by the Crown, this time to be deputy postmaster general for all North American colonies. He improved service and showed the first surplus in the colonial postal service budget, but Franklin believed that running the postal system only to make money was a ruinous policy. Putting service first, he felt, would ultimately produce a profit through greater use of the mails. His arguments fell on deaf ears back in England. During his tenure, Franklin established post roads from Canada to Florida and set up a regular schedule between the colonies and England. He organized auditing procedures and ordered land surveys that shortened several routes. Under Franklin, the Philadelphia–New York delivery time was cut in half. He also started the modern postal inspection service. Riders started hauling mail at night.

However, no angel, Franklin engaged in the nepotism common in his day. He appointed his brother John as postmaster in Boston. When John died, Franklin chose John's widow to succeed him. Mrs. John Franklin became the first woman postmaster (or postmistress) in America, the first woman to hold public office in America.[11]

▶ SERVING THE REVOLUTION

The Crown mail service added to the colonists' complaints that led to the American Revolution. The British government had never abandoned the idea of squeezing out a profit from its postal service. The colonists grew more convinced that the Crown's colonial post was just another way to tax them, and taxes on newspapers in both England and the colonies were denounced as "taxes on knowledge." The British Parliament might well have expected an uproar when it passed the Stamp Act in 1765, taxing newspapers and documents as a means of raising revenue. In England it more than doubled the price of the *Times*. The public outcry "No taxation without representation" echoed across the colonies. The British Parliament rescinded it the following year. Nevertheless, the Stamp Act was one of the causes of discontent that led to the American Revolution and one of the arguments for putting freedom of the press in the First Amendment.

As a protest, the colonists ignored the postal laws and sent letters outside the official mails, depriving the Crown of income. To refuse to use the royal postal service was considered not only the morally right thing to do, but it also saved money. By the end of 1775 so few letters were passing through the royal postal service that it was shut down. A patriot postal service, the Constitutional Post, had all the business.

By assigning postmasters to collect newspaper postage and newspaper subscription fees, Franklin in effect turned postmasters into publishers' agents. He arranged for the free exchange of newspapers among editors. His policies made the American colonial post office the most progressive in the world, well ahead of those in England.

At a time when few letters carried prepaid postage, post riders earned extra money by carrying postage due mail and pocketing what they collected. Stagecoach drivers employed a sly trick that allowed them to swear their coaches did not *contain* mail that they profited from. They hung a pole outside the stagecoach, from which a bag of letters dangled. Therefore, the mail was technically not *in* the coach, so the coach did not *contain* the mail. Franklin eliminated some of these sharp practices.

Crown authorities censored the mail and, despite what Franklin had accomplished, they dismissed him in 1774 because of his revolutionary activities. A year later, with the colonies breaking away from Britain, the newly formed Continental Congress met to create an independent government. Close to the top of the agenda was how to deal with mail. The Second Continental Congress chose Franklin to set up a separate postal system, the best way to get word to colonists who wanted independence. Franklin was the new nation's first postmaster general. He served for 16 months.

▶ WORKING WITH NEWSPAPERS

In combination, newspapers and the postal service were the most important means of informing the public at the time of the birth of the United States. Vestiges of their fruitful collaboration lie in the number of newspapers today that have the word "post" in their names. Both the Federalists and their political opponents, the Jeffersonian Republicans, supported postal subsidies for newspapers in a new nation as thinly populated, as spread out, and as diverse as the various regions of the United States of America. Together, newspapers and the postal service were much needed glue to bind the nation.

The American Constitution authorized a national postal operation with the sentence, "The Congress shall have power . . . to establish Post Offices and post Roads." The new Congress set up the General Post Office, but only on an annual basis and for only five years. The postmaster general reported to the Secretary of the Treasury. He and his postal service would not be subject to control by the individual states. In the years to come, the postal service would have an integral role in supporting the provision calling for freedom of the press in the First Amendment.

At the time the constitution was being adopted, a letter traveling along the main post road from Georgia to Maine might take three weeks to arrive. And it still wasn't cheap. A one-page letter going up to 30 miles cost 6 cents, which was a penny more than the cost of a dozen eggs. (The cost of a first-class postage stamp today roughly equals the cost of three eggs.) The same one-page letter going more than 450 miles cost 25 cents. To avoid paying for a second sheet, letter writers not only wrote small on both sides of the page, but filled up the margins by writing up and down the sides of the page. Postal receipts for the entire nation in 1790 were U.S.$37,935 against expenses of $32,140. The United States had 75 post offices. Five years later, it had 453.[12]

Interrupting the U.S. mail was a grave matter. As in many other countries since the Middle Ages, only one penalty existed for interfering with the mails:

death. However, the United States had trial by jury and jurors hesitated to inflict such a sentence. At first, Congress voted flogging as punishment for a first offense, death for a second. Later, prison sentences were substituted. Until 1872, however, mail robbery could still bring the death penalty.

"There is an astonishing circulation of letters and newspapers among these savage woods," wrote the French aristocrat Alexis de Tocqueville as he traveled across the new country and recorded his observations of the American people with a shrewd, admiring eye. To de Tocqueville, that heralded better economic conditions. "I only know of one means of increasing the prosperity of a people . . . communication," he wrote in *Democracy in America*. "In Michigan forests there is not a cabin so isolated, not a valley so wild, that it does not receive letters and newspapers at least once a week; we saw it ourselves."

Press and post grew side by side, each affecting the other. Thanks to newspapers and mail reaching the cabins scattered across the huge, new land, settlers figured out that they belonged to the national community that was taking shape. They also gradually understood that what the government decided affected their lives.

▶ CARRYING THE MAIL

Pioneers blazing trails through the wilderness, crossing mountains, and clearing forests for farms did not ask much of the government back east. They did ask for mail service, post offices, and post roads. Mail service struggled to keep up with the growing nation. By 1820, the young United States had more post offices and newspapers per capita than any nation in the world.[13]

As communication between cities increased, a better means of transporting mail was needed than a man on a horse. The stagecoach was the answer, but was not without problems. Roads, even highways, were usually unpaved, rutted, and full of potholes. Bridges washed out. Streams had to be forded. When rain fell, a coach-and-four (horses) or a coach-and-six was needed to drag its heavy load through the mud. Some roads were so bad that no wheeled traffic ever used them. A guard often sat next to the driver because of the danger of highwaymen insufficiently troubled by thoughts of the noose.

As the stagecoaches bounced over the rutted roads, the heavy mailbags shifted as if fighting the passengers for seats. Postal couriers sometimes refused the added weight of newspapers, so they piled up at loading points. As for magazines, postmasters had the authority to exclude them from delivery if facilities were inadequate. Newspapers and magazines lying on the ground were likely to be pilfered by otherwise honest citizens eager to catch up on events. If they were not stolen and were eventually delivered, they might be handed over wet and dirty. When a stagecoach arrived, people gathered around as the driver called out the names of those for whom he had newspapers, not unlike a modern summer camp or military mail call.

STEAMBOATS

Steamboats went into passenger service beginning when Robert Fulton steered the Clermont up the Hudson River in 1807. Six years later, steamboats were carrying mail under contract. On inland navigable waters, designated as post roads by Congress in 1823, steamboats were a familiar sight hauling mail along with passengers and freight up and down America's rivers. Mail was also carried on towpaths alongside canals. It was slow, but mules or draft horses pulled barges carrying mail free of the mud that stagecoaches dealt with. The steamboats were also free of highway robbers.

A steamboat landing in Vicksburg, Mississippi, early 20th century.

▶ SORTING MAIL ON A MOVING TRAIN

The Puffing Billy—a nickname for early trains—replaced slow coaches jouncing over bad roads. Chugging at unaccustomed speed over long distances, the iron horses carried all the letters that anyone cared to write, plus all the newspapers and magazines, with no threat to throw them off at the next station to make room for passengers. Mail delivery by rail began in 1829 in Pennsylvania. The westward expansion of the railroad solved most of the problems of irregular and unsure newspaper and magazine distribution.

By 1930, more than 10,000 trains carried mail to every hamlet in the nation that rail lines served.[14] Railroad postal service ended as a result of the Transportation Act of 1958, which favored airmail. A dozen years later, almost no first-class mail was carried by train. The last railway post office, running between New York and Washington, DC, was shunted to a side track in 1977.

▶ **MAIL BY SEA**

Sending mail by ship was chancy. Schedules were erratic. Sailing ships needed favorable winds, of course; but a ship owner's wish to sail with a full load could send a ship from port to port gathering cargo while letters sat in the mail packet. The solution was the small, fast packet ship that carried passengers and goods, but was foremost a ship to carry the mail and to follow a schedule for doing so.

Mail was sometimes handled in imaginative ways. Ship captains docking to take on casks of freshwater at Cape Town (then known as "Table Bay") on the southern tip of Africa knew that bags of mail waited near a freshwater stream in a hole at the foot of Table Mountain. A stone over the hole had a painted sign, "Hereunder look for letters."

Eastbound letters were picked up by eastbound ships, which deposited westbound letters under the stone. This post office served ports as far away as Batavia, in the present Indonesia. The English and Dutch were often at each other's throats in the competition for colonies, but they forwarded each other's mail.

PONY EXPRESS

The Overland Pony Express (1867), from a painting by George M. Ottinger.

The Pony Express advertised that it could get telegraph messages from San Francisco to New York in 8 days and letters in 12 days. Riders galloped through alkali deserts, mountain passes deep in snow, and rocky ravines where a stumbling horse could mean death. "Road agents" lay in wait to snatch money sent by mail. Native American war parties lay in wait. Hungry riders sometimes resorted to eating wolf meat. It was no job for the faint of heart. "Orphans preferred" read the job ads.

The Pony Express lasted only 18 months during 1860 and 1861, unable to match the new technology of the telegraph. The Pony Express had carried a total of nearly 35,000 letters. Today it is part of American lore.

▶ BEFORE POSTAGE STAMPS

Let us cross the Atlantic to look inside the General Post Office in London in the 1830s, the years before postal reform introduced postage stamps. A postman, who collected letters by walking through the streets ringing his bell, arrives. The room he enters is dark and windowless, so that postal clerks working in the gloom must hold each envelope up to a candle to see how many items are enclosed. If there is one enclosure besides a single sheet, double postage is charged. Two enclosures, triple postage.

Is money in the envelope? A mistake by someone too trusting. The letter is furtively slipped into a trouser pocket. The clerks keep busy weighing letters and writing information. They record each letter onto a form so that the cost of sending it can be debited against the postmaster of the town to which it will be sent.

When a letter finally is delivered to a cottage in the country, the postman will knock. Whoever answers will be asked to pay for the letter before it is handed over. That may lead to an argument because the postage will not be cheap. Although methods vary from country to country, it is the custom for addressees to pay for receiving mail, just as the buyer of potatoes pays for the potatoes. One mail carrier complained that it took him more than five minutes to deliver a single letter. But what if the addressee refuses? Sometimes the addressee is unwilling to pay, unwilling to receive what may be bad news.

With this cumbersome system, the British Post Office lost money year after year. Another reason the British Post Office lost money was that members of Parliament and certain state officials had franking privileges, which meant they sent mail postage free. The word "frank" or "free" next to a seal with a unique mark was all that was needed. The officials' idea of "mail" included 30 dogs sent to Rome, two laundresses sent to an ambassador, a cow that accompanied a doctor on a trip, and a parcel of lace sent to a duke's regiment.[15]

The government tried to limit the worst misuses, but the members of Parliament and the lords—often the same people—used every loophole they could to keep this privilege. The British Post Office in the 19th century, a victim of so many abuses, faced bankruptcy.

▶ ROWLAND HILL'S PLAN

Postal reformer Rowland Hill saved it. He calculated that the cost to the Post Office of delivering a letter bore no relation to the distance it traveled within Britain. The real cost, said Hill, was in the complex handling of a letter so that the addressee would pay. He said this in one of the most famous pamphlets ever written, *Post Office Reform: Its Importance and Practicability.* Instead of raising postage rates once again, Hill recommended lowering them sharply so that even poor people could afford letters. At the time it was estimated that the postage on an ordinary letter cost half a day's wages for a factory worker or shop clerk. Obviously, working-class people wrote few letters.[16]

Hill proposed a uniform rate based on the weight of a letter regardless of the number of sheets of paper, with a 1 penny minimum for a half-ounce letter irrespective of the distance the letter traveled within Britain. Increasing the weight of the letter, not the number of enclosures, would increase the postage. He suggested that senders should be required to mail letters in wrappers or "little bags called envelopes" with markings showing that postage had been paid.

Hill also proposed abolishing the franking privilege and charging newspapers postage. Most important, he proposed that postal charges should be collected in advance from the sender of a letter. That the letter was prepaid would be noted by "a bit of paper just large enough to bear the stamp and covered at the back with a glutinous wash."[17] And so, in 1840, after the government recovered from the shock of these radical proposals, was born the postage stamp.

▶ SUPPORT AND OPPOSITION

Merchants supported the plan to lower postal rates and use postage stamps. So did a number of newspapers and a public-spirited citizenry. Reform supporters argued that to increase revenue the Post Office should charge less so that more people would use the mails. Yet, even such a slight blurring of class distinctions as postal reform had its opponents. They responded that to increase postal revenue, it made sense to charge more.

In class-conscious England, the notion that the poor would write letters if mailing costs were reduced to a penny not only failed to move the opposition to reform, it was an argument against reform. Stamps dented the wall of privilege. One opponent argued that the Post Office would be overrun with mail if this reform took effect. A few of the rich expressed snobbish displeasure that just anyone could now use the mails. Lord Lichfield, the Postmaster General, called postal reform "the most extravagant of all the wild and visionary schemes" he ever heard of.[18] "The walls of the Post Office would burst," he said.[19] Of course, that was the idea.

As Hill predicted, letter writing rose sharply and the poor benefited. Within 20 years most of the world had adopted Hill's reforms. Postcards at a halfpenny each were particularly popular. Hill received many proofs of what his work had meant to the poor and humble. On a journey in Scotland, he once gave his coat for mending to a journeyman tailor in a little village. On learning who Hill was, the man refused payment.

Letter carriers must have enjoyed some easing of their stressful lives with payment now severed from delivery. The mail carrier no longer had to seek out someone at each home, no longer had to cajole someone into buying a letter, no longer had to wait or to trudge back to the station with unwanted letters. The postage stamp also aided business. The flow of information by this means of mediated communication soared. In 1839, 76 million pieces of mail went through the British Post Office. In 1850, the number jumped to 350 million and continued to climb.[20] People who had never received a letter were now sending and receiving them even if the writing was difficult and the reading was slow. Many letters still had to be written by surrogates and read aloud when they arrived, but literacy climbed. The mail carrier became the partner of the schoolteacher.

Rowland Hill died in 1879, filled with honors. His system of cheap prepaid postage had spread across the world. Nations everywhere adopted his reforms because they produced a service that was at once profitable to the government and a delight to people all over the world who were getting dependable and speedy delivery of personal letters and public information at modest cost. It was all based on a tiny bit of gummed paper stuck on the outside of an envelope dropped into any corner mailbox day or night. This was truly a revolution.[21]

In 1847, the United States followed Britain's lead in selling adhesive-backed postage stamps, followed five years later by stamped envelopes. However, for eight more years the use of prepaid postage stamps was voluntary and most mail went collect-on-delivery. Nevertheless, as in Britain, stamps and other reforms led to a huge increase in mail.

A CLEVER RUSE

Some Britons managed a ruse to get a mailed message without paying.

A frequently told tale tells of a man walking in the Lake District one day when he saw the postman stop outside a mean cottage. An elderly woman came out, took a letter from the postman, turned it over in her hands, and then gave it back. It was from her son, she said, but she did not have the money to pay for it. The observer, moved with pity, offered to pay the fee, but the woman refused with warm thanks.

When the postman left, she confessed that the letter would have contained no writing. Her son regularly sent such letters. The way he spaced and wrote the address told her how he was getting on. It seems likely that the postman knew all about the little ruse but sympathized with his poor client. Such use of codes in addressing letters grew common. Had she paid, the Post Office would not have known unless the postman told them, for it was not unusual for postmen to pocket postal fees.

▶ FREE DELIVERY

The U.S. Post Office Department was not tasked with putting letters into home mailboxes. It just had the responsibility of hauling mail from one post office to another. Before free home delivery, a city or town resident normally took mail to the post office. The addressee went to another post office to get it, saving the penny or two for voluntary delivery.

In 1855, the law in the United States was altered so that the sender had no choice but to buy a stamp, but still went to the post office to mail the letter. That changed in 1858 with the appearance on New York City streets of mailboxes, a French invention. Those proved so popular that they were installed in every city. At the other end, the addressees still paid extra to have a mail carrier deliver the mail, though they could trudge to the local post office to get their mail without paying. Some newspapers routinely listed people who had letters waiting, an early form of "You've got mail."

In 1863 Cleveland's assistant postmaster, Joseph Briggs, adopted the idea of free city home delivery because he "was appalled at the sight of anxious wives, children and relatives waiting in long lines at the local post office for letters from soldiers off fighting the Civil War."[22] By coincidence on July 1, 1863, the first day of the Battle of Gettysburg, free home delivery began in 49 cities. Before the century ended, post offices were offering free delivery to homes in cities throughout the nation.

▶ INTERNATIONAL MAIL

During the 19th century the postal services in several nations were a mess, with their own rules, their own rate scales, and their own suspicions of foreign mail, all adding up to a maze of conflicting regulations. A letter crossing several borders added charges by each country. From the United States to Japan, a letter could cost anywhere from a dime to 60 cents in postage, based upon five routes and five rates. Nations negotiated separate treaties with each country. Strong nations served as transit points to weaker nations not only for the postage income but to exert influence over their neighbor. Nor did possibilities for spying escape notice.

In 1863, in the midst of the Civil War, United States Postmaster General Montgomery Blair called an international conference. Delegates from 15 nations met in Paris and agreed to use the metric system to calculate distance and weight. Eleven years later, 22 nations met in Berne, Switzerland, for the first International Postal Congress, which created the General Postal Union. The Treaty of Berne, signed on October 9, 1874, is now observed as World Post Day. In 1878, because membership grew so fast, the name was changed to the Universal Postal Union, the world's first truly international organization. UPU members agreed on a single rate for foreign mail, with no difference in the treatment of domestic and foreign mail. Each nation would keep the money from its sale of stamps, but it would not charge to deliver foreign mail.

The delivery of letters would no longer be part of international scheming for power. It was no longer necessary to add postage stamps of every country that a letter or package passed through. However, some payments to the receiving countries still exist. The Universal Postal Congress still meets every five years. It has added such services as money orders, registered mail, parcel post, and reply cards. Each country issues its own stamps.

▶ RURAL FREE DELIVERY

If you lived in the American countryside in the 19th century, you still went to town for your mail. Of course, you combined that trip in your buggy with shopping in the general store and visits to the doctor or the blacksmith. A trip to town could occupy most of your day. Actually, the post office was as likely as not to be set up in the general store. When a weekly trip to the village post office was the farmer's only way of receiving mail, there was little reason to subscribe to a daily newspaper. The country weeklies best served the farmer's needs.[23]

Country folks, outnumbering their city cousins by four to one, might have envied city free home delivery, but it wasn't until 1890 that free delivery was offered to rural areas. Postmaster General John Wanamaker had been pushing for rural free delivery for some time. Opposition came from small-town postmasters who correctly saw that rural free delivery would shut down the smaller post offices. The small town tavern owner was especially upset. So was the owner of the country general store where the fourth-class rural post office had been situated until postal routes came along. Storekeepers knew that when Mr. and Mrs. Farmer came to town for mail, they often stopped to buy something. If they didn't have to come to town, they might prefer to order from the mail order catalogues that advertised their wishes and dreams. Aaron Montgomery Ward of Chicago started printing catalogues in 1872 with a one-page price list.

Wanamaker's supporters for rural free delivery included the urban newspapers that saw the possibility of getting a daily newspaper into farmers' hands. Effects on advertising rates could be substantial. Farmers wanted daily newspapers not only for the news and general reading pleasures but also in these pre-radio days for weather and crop market reports. And, very important, by having mail delivered, the farmer saved the time it took to ride into town to the post office.

Congress voted funds for a test of rural free delivery (RFD) in 1893. Opponents in Washington called RFD a foolish expenditure, believing that sending a mail carrier out summer and winter over bad roads or no roads at all to every home in every hollow was a waste of money. That was not the opinion of people in the country. They craved mail service. Men, women, and children who lived along rural roads waited patiently beside their mailboxes for the postman. In the years before radio and rural telephones, a chance to read the latest happenings in letters and newspapers eased their isolation. The new free rural delivery service was made permanent nationwide in 1902.

Rural free delivery helped to expand the American network of roads and bridges. The mail carrier who trundled down the road stopping at the rural mailboxes needed a better road to trundle down, or at least a road without deep ruts that would be under water in the spring and under ice in the winter. The U.S. Post Office Department rejected hundreds of applications for RFD service after inspecting the roads. It required that roads be passable all year. Heeding the frustrations of farmers, local governments raised the revenue needed to gravel roads, repair bridges, and construct culverts. As the years went by, the gray, tunnel-shaped rural letterbox with its red flag popped up on fences and posts along dirt roads across the country, replacing the lard pails and soapboxes that were used at first. Circulation of daily newspapers skyrocketed.

Mail and parcel post bringing newspapers and magazines as well as goods are two means of mediated communication that have made country living less isolated and more desirable. In a curious way, the Internet has joined RFD in encouraging a return to village and rural life. The Internet makes it possible for many professions and businesses to function from anywhere, including deep in the countryside. Various jobs are performed via high-speed connections. Education is available through the Internet and so is entertainment by means of television and DVD as well as the Internet.

▶ PARCEL POST

Fat catalogues sent to millions of households became a principal means of shopping, thanks to RFD. Bulk mailings could be enormous. Catalogue stores were the amazon.com of their day. The 540-page catalogue mailed out by Montgomery Ward in 1887 listed 24,000 items for sale. Sears Roebuck matched it with a catalogue of more than 500 pages in 1894. Sears in 1897 mailed out 318,000 catalogues, about 2 million in 1904, and 6 million in 1907.[24]

A mailman empties a mailbox, early 20th century.

The introduction of parcel post was a political minefield, an issue that brought the federal government into competition with private express services and small town shopkeepers. Like rural free delivery, it was a boon to farm families but a bane to the fellow who ran the general store in town. Unhappy local merchants put pressure on their newspapers to fight the "Mail Order Trust" by refusing to advertise. Coupled with catalogues, parcel post doomed their businesses. The small town general store, which once thrived, survives mostly as American folklore. Today, online shopping, based on an even newer means of communication, has in its turn seriously hurt catalogue sales.

▶ MODERNIZING

Directed by the Espionage Act passed by Congress during World War I, the Post Office suppressed newspapers, magazines, and other printed matter that were considered subversive. The publications came from socialists, pacifists, and labor unions, plus some whose only offense was that they were written in German, the language of the enemy. Postal authorities backed away from this kind of suppression during World War II and after.

Meanwhile, the Post Office's money problems did not go away. Postal policies changed over the years, sometimes to save money, sometimes in the cause of efficiency. During World War II, V-mail ("V" for "Victory") became the way to correspond with military personnel and others overseas. The lightweight pale blue sheets were photographed, reduced in size and weight, flown overseas, then recreated. V-mail arrived quicker and took up less space on cargo planes.

In 1950, home delivery was cut from twice daily to once. When President Dwight Eisenhower's choice for postmaster general, businessman Arthur Summerfield, began his new job in 1952, unpleasant surprises greeted him. Summerfield's inspections uncovered a massive, creaking 19th-century bureaucracy. Equipment and facilities were outdated. Shopworn equipment was housed in run-down, overcrowded, poorly lighted postal buildings. Wages were low. Despite all this, the Post Office Department was bleeding the U.S. Treasury of millions of dollars a day. Summerfield began a modernization program that successive postmasters general have carried on.

The 1960s witnessed a steep rise in the amount of mail, especially business mail. Computers at banks, utility companies, insurance companies, credit card issuers, and department stores were sending bills, receipts, notices, and advertising to their millions of customers. The government mailed truckloads of Social Security checks each month. Yet at post offices thousands of clerks still sorted the mail by hand, throwing letters into bins or sacks, moving them to central locations and then unpacking and sorting them again. The Post Office Department knew its operations had to be mechanized.

In 1963, five-digit ZIP codes were added to addresses. The Zoning Improvement Plan (ZIP) code, built around 85 big city hubs, reduced the congestion especially on busy downtown streets. These hubs became the core of 552 sectional centers. Each center managed from 40 to 150 local post offices. For the next step, each sectional center got a code number. Beyond this, numerical codes were issued to neighborhood post offices. The result was a five-digit code that covered the entire United States. Every home and business address had its five-digit code. The first digit represents a region, from 0 in the Northeast to 9 in the Far West. The next two digits identify cities and sectional centers that fit the U.S. Postal Service (USPS) transportation plan. The last two digits identify individual post offices or urban postal zones.

As it modernized, the Post Office Department automated. Pigeonhole boxes were thrown out when machines could sort the mail, including parcels. Envelope addresses were read by optical character readers. Conveyer belts moved letters along. Vending machines sold stamps, including the popular self-sticking type. Other machines canceled them. Computer scales at the postal clerk's window not only weighed but calculated costs for various classes of mail. Bar codes stamped by mass mailers of national newspapers, magazines, and catalogues hurried them through the system.

The newest generation of automated equipment can read an entire address optically and convert it into a bar code sprayed on the envelope that is read by an electronic sorter that processes nine envelopes a second. Even some hand-written envelopes can be moved along like this. The combination of regional printing plants and bar code addresses puts newspapers and magazines in home mailboxes often within hours of printing.

▶ PRIVATIZATION

As the postwar national mood swung toward privatization of industry, eyes turned toward the postal service. After lengthy negotiations and a strike by postal workers, Congress passed the Postal Reorganization Act in 1970. President Richard Nixon signed it. By its provisions, a year later the Post Office Department became the U.S. Postal Service, an independent organization. The postmaster general's position in the president's cabinet was eliminated.

The USPS would become a self-supporting business corporation wholly owned by the federal government, run by an independent board of governors appointed by the president for nine-year terms with approval by the Senate. A separate five-person Rate Commission would determine the price of postage stamps, and the Postal Service would be fully independent of Congress. Even the postal emblem changed, from a post rider to the national symbol of the bald eagle standing on a block labeled U.S. Mail. In 1977, to compete with Federal Express and UPS, the Postal Service introduced Express Mail.[25]

To honor the Postal Service, the National Postal Museum was opened in Washington, DC, in 1993. A Smithsonian Institution museum, it is housed in the old Post Office Building. It features the artistry that goes into the engraving of stamps. But all is not well, as the rising cost of stamps and services attest. Because the Postal Service runs deeply in the red, its future remains cloudy. It has been hurt by the advent of email and smartphones, but is unlikely to be replaced. In 2012 the USPS cut mail service sharply and that slowed delivery of first-class mail and packages. The mail carrier's bag, lighter than before, is stuffed with junk mail yet continues to carry what we want. In the world of the 21st century, modern communication companies such as Amazon.com and Netflix still depend upon the mails.

▶ SUMMARY

Postal service has mattered to every society that used it and to everyone who has looked forward to getting a letter. Empires depended upon it. So did the growth of business.

The postage stamp belongs in the category of media that changed the world. The simple bit of printed and glued paper and its accompanying reforms added to the rise of both democracy and literacy. Stamps are among the 19th century changes in mediated communication that left a permanent mark on society. Because of them, we all live in a much different and more egalitarian world.

▶ TIMELINE

BCE (dates are estimates)

2350   Mesopotamian king uses homing pigeons.

900   China's Zhou Dynasty sets up a pony express postal service for its government.

500   Persian government also establishes a pony express.

490   Pheidippides dies after bringing to Athens the news of victory at Marathon.

CE

14   Rome sets up network of relay runners carrying messages 50 miles in a day.

650   Muslim caliphs set up a regular pigeon post, the first news service.

1200   The University of Paris is granted its charter, starts mail, messenger service.

Monasteries contact each other by their own postal systems.

1305   Europeans have a private postal service run by the Taxis family.

1464   In France, a government postal system.

1627   French government establishes registered mail as a way to send money.

1639   Boston tavern gets European mail by ship, starts colonial postal service.

1653   Paris gets mailboxes.

1775   Continental Congress establishes a postal service.

1792   New U.S. government passes Postal Act.

1815   U.S. Postal Service expands rapidly; now 3,000 post offices.

1837   Rowland Hill's pamphlet on postal reform is published; will have global influence.

1840   England starts penny post. Stamps are cheap, so people write more letters.

1855   Americans are required to put stamps on letters.

Registered mail.

1858   Some American cities get mailboxes.

1863   Mail is delivered free to some American city homes.

Paris is host to an international postal conference.

1864   Post offices are put in trains to speed mail handling.

1869   From Austria, postcards are introduced.

1873   Penny postcards are sold in the United States.

1874   Germany begins a regular domestic parcel post service.

1887   Postal mass marketing takes off with fat Montgomery Ward catalog.

1896   Rural free delivery (RFD) is inaugurated in the United States.

1911   A U.S. postal savings system offers banking service, a boon for poor people.

1912   Airmail.

1916   Postal detectives solve the last known stagecoach robbery in the United States.

1939   Trans-Atlantic airmail service.

1942   Lightweight V-mail is created, mainly to handle wartime armed forces letters.

1963   Five-digit ZIP codes improve delivery.

1970   Troubled U.S. Postal Service becomes self-supporting.

Express mail service set up to compete with FedEx, UPS.

1983   ZIP codes add four more digits; postal bar codes.

1992   Automatic stamp delivery machines.

1993   The National Postal Museum opens.

1998   Postage stamps downloaded from the Web, then printed, go on sale in United States.

2007   The "forever stamp" is sold to be usable always for first-class mail.

2012   USPS reduces mail service to save costs.

▶ NOTES

1 Ralph Waldo Emerson, "American Civilization," 1862. Reprinted online: http://www.theatlantic.com/magazine/archive/1862/04/american-civilization/306548/.

2 For some opinions on this topic, see Alvin F. Harlow, *Old Post Bags* (New York: D. Appleton, 1938) 7.

3 The Silk Road Foundation website, http://www.silk-road.com/artl/marcopolo. shtml.

4 Herodotus, *The History* 8:98.

5 Wayne E. Fuller, *The American Mail* (Chicago: University of Chicago Press, 1972) 4.

6 Marshall McLuhan, *Understanding Media: The Extensions of Man* (New York: McGraw-Hill, 1964) 100.

7 William Manchester, *A World Lit Only by Fire: the Medieval Mind* (Boston: Little, Brown, 1992) 61.

8 Shakespeare's phrase was used as the title of a postal history, George Walker's *Haste, Post, Haste* (New York: Dodd, Mead & Co., 1939).

9 Alison Gavin, "Hugh Finlay and the Postal System in Colonial America," *Prologue*, Summer 2009, vol. 49, no. 2, http://www.archives.gov/publications/prologue/2009/summer/finlay.html.

10 Rates often changed. For more detail, see the discussion at http://www.tngenweb.org/tnletters/rates/.

11 For a fuller examination of the postal service in the early years of the republic, see Richard R. John, *Spreading the News: The American Postal System from Franklin to Morse* (Cambridge, MA: Harvard University Press, 1995).

12 "Statistics: Pieces and Post Offices," http://about.usps.com/publications/pub100/pub100_075.htm.

13 Richard B. Kielbowicz, "Post Office and the Media," in Margaret Blanchard, ed., *History of Mass Media in the United States* (Chicago: Fitzroy Dearborn Publishers, 1998) 57.

14 "The Post Office Role in U.S. Development," About.com, http://inventors.about.com/library/inventors/blmailus2c.htm.

15 Mauritz Hallgren, *All about Stamps* (New York: Alfred A. Knopf, 1940) 47.

16 The human side of Britain's postal reform is described in Laurin Zilliacus, *Mail for the World* (New York: John Day Co., 1953).

17 Rowland Hill, "Post Office Reform: Its Importance and Practicability," pamphlet, 1836.

18 Richard Menke, *Telegraphic Realism: Victorian Fiction and Other Information Systems* (Stanford: Stanford University Press, 2008) 35.

19 Harlow, 191.

20 "Rowland Hill's postal Reforms," British Postal Museum and Archive, http://www.postalheritage.org.uk/page/rowlandhill.

21 Hill, 37.

22 James H. Bruns, *Mail on the Move* (Polo, IL: Transportation Trails, 1992) 89.

23 Daniel J. Boorstin, *The Americans: The Democratic Experience* (New York: Random House, 1973) 135.

24 Boorstin, 128.

25 Gerald Cullinan, *The United States Postal Service* (New York: Praeger Publishers, 1968) 192–193.

5 Telegraph: Uniting the United States

The most important development in bringing distant news was the invention of the telegraph by Samuel Morse in 1844. It allowed people to communicate instantly with each other beyond the reach of a human voice. It was the first device to use electricity for a practical purpose in a day when no one was quite sure what kind of "fluid" electricity really was or how it worked. The telegraph sped information through society at speeds the Pony Express could not dream of. Overnight that colorful enterprise went out of business.

National politics was sectional. The United States was united mostly in name, and soon enough that would fall apart. By connecting the scattered communities of the vast American nation, the telegraph helped to unite the United States. The telegraph was expected by some enthusiasts to change the world by bringing understanding to all mankind of a shared humanity and world peace. A popular slogan suggested that an effect of the telegraph would be to "make muskets into candlesticks."[1] The telegraph also brought change by connecting cities across the world. However, the hope that the telegraph might lead to world peace was never realized. Instead what followed in the United States was the Civil War.

▶ WHAT THE TELEGRAPH DID

Before the telegraph, no communication could exist further than what was visible; beyond this, communication required transportation, with the limited exceptions of semaphore flags, smoke signals, or homing pigeons. Semaphore was being used for some information transmission in Europe, and from ship to ship or between ship and shore, but it never gained a foothold in the United States. This visual communication system had begun in France in 1790 at the time of the French Revolution. A network of more than 500 stations sent messages between towers with large wooden arms that held flags and could pivot. Their position identified alphabetic letters and numbers. Messages read by telescope were relayed from tower to tower.

The telegraph connected communities and businesses, not families and ordinary individuals, so its effects on us were commercial and political rather than personal and emotional as the telephone would be. It brought about standard time zones. It sharply reduced the time between an event and public awareness of it. Media theorist Postman noted, "In the United States, the telegraph erased state lines, collapsed regions, and, by wrapping the continent in an information grid, created the possibility of a unified nation-state."[2]

John Dewey, a philosopher of the 19th century, commented, "As a result of the locomotive and telegraph, frequent, rapid, and cheap intercommunication by mails and electricity was called into being. Travel has been rendered easy; freedom of movement, with its accompanying exchange of ideas, indefinitely facilitated. The result has been an intellectual revolution."[3]

Historian Marion May Dilts recalled what communication was like in the 19th century for average people: "Ordinary folk did not very often have occasion to communicate at a distance in those days. Our population was only about a third of what it is now,[4] and seventeen postage stamps a year fulfilled the communication requirements of the average person. Most men and women lived their lives, visited and died, within fifty miles of the place where they were born. When they wanted to know how John and Mary were doing, they hitched up and drove over in the buggy, or inquired at the general store when they went there for the mail. They sent telegrams only when something momentous happened; the receipt of one was cause for anxiety."[5]

By giving businesses the ability to learn what customers wanted to buy, the telegraph encouraged mass production by combining with the railroads to create a rational system for moving goods to market.[6] It altered the nation's economy by smoothing out the variation in prices among different regions, for the price of food differed from place to place more than prices do today. It expanded the delivery of a wider variety of foods. With the telegraph, dealers in fish and other perishable foods could gauge market demand more accurately. The messenger who arrived first with news that led to a rise or fall in cotton prices promised large profits for his quick-witted employer.

The last telegraph pole became the new information frontier. By removing the barrier of transmission time, the telegraph altered the look and urgency of news and, to a degree, its very nature. When information could arrive instantly from distant places, the value of news dispatches as a commodity increased because fresh reports are always preferable to old reports. Newly formed organizations such as the Associated Press were dependent upon telegraph dispatches. The AP was created in 1846 by five New York City newspapers to share the cost of transmitting news about the Mexican–American War. Because news services made money by having large numbers of subscribing newspapers, politically neutral, objective reporting took hold.

"The telegraph and the power press and the mass-circulating newspaper brought the same information and the same images to people thousands of miles apart," Daniel Boorstin wrote. "Human experience for millions became more instantaneously similar than had ever been imagined possible."[7]

Freight trains hauled the heavy poles and the telegraph wires that ran alongside the tracks, the nerve beside the spine. Each brought business to the other. The telegraph needed the business the railroad brought. The railroad had so much need of the telegraph to dispatch trains and carry messages that the jobs of railroad station agent and telegrapher were combined, with the railroads paying their salaries. The railroad companies hauled the poles, wires, and other equipment free, and also helped to pay for putting them in place and in good repair.[8] The telegraph made the railroads safer. Dots and dashes alerted switchmen so they could send to a siding any trains heading in opposite directions on the same track. The engineer had less worry about whether the "9:05" was on schedule. Rail operations were more efficient, with lowered freight charges and consequently more goods.

Now it made economic sense for publishers to mail to distant subscribers the daily newspapers and the magazines that too often had been abandoned in soggy piles near a stagecoach stop. The typical flimsy newspapers would not reach their readers if stagecoach drivers dumped them at the roadside to make room for a paying passenger. Delivery of information by horse and stagecoach was quickly forgotten with the dawning of the age of the railroad and telegraph. Their paired growth stimulated another means of communication—the mail system, which required dependable transportation for the growing nation. U.S. stamps went on sale in 1847, three years after American telegraph companies began stringing wire.

▶ A NATIONWIDE GRID

In the decades leading up to the Civil War, most Americans were scattered in small towns and villages or on farms. Cities did not have easy contact with the countryside. Roads were bad. Railroad tracks were just being laid in the East. Boats that chugged along rivers or ran along the nation's coasts carried information in personal letters and newspapers, but news from New York might reach London by clipper ship before it arrived in a Southern port.

The first telegraph line went into service in 1844 between Baltimore and Washington, DC. Year by year, more cities were added to a nationwide grid.

Competing companies fell as Western Union grew, but that growth stopped at the water's edge until a suitable insulation was extracted from the gutta-percha tree gum growing in the British colony of Malaya. Wire was then laid across channels, rivers, seas, and finally the great oceans.

▶ NO SINGLE INVENTOR

No one person really invented the telegraph, just as there was no single inventor of the photograph, the motion picture, or the computer. In 1684 scientist Robert Hooke laid out plans for a visual telegraph, more than a century before electricity came out of the laboratory. The idea of electricity as a means of sending messages was considered before Samuel F. B. Morse thought of it. A Danish scientist, Hans Christian Oersted, discovered electromagnetism in 1820. In 1830, an American scientist, Joseph Henry, rang a bell more than 1,000 feet down an iron wire circuit from an electromagnet hooked to a series of small batteries. Morse, an artist not a scientist, may not have known of most of the previous experiments with this invisible "fluid." According to a frequently told tale, Morse was a passenger on a ship taking him back to America after three years in Europe trying to make a living as an artist. A dinner conversation with other passengers about electromagnetism led him to conclude that an electric telegraph was feasible, saying, "I see no reason why intelligence might not be instantaneously transmitted by electricity to any distance."[9]

An electric telegraph functioned along the Great Western Railway in England in 1839. A renowned physicist, Charles Wheatstone, and a businessman, William Cooke, built this crude but workable system based on an alphabetic code system that required five needles and five wires. Two years later these inventors came up with the first printing telegraph; it sent as many as 15 words a minute. The British public and the government paid little attention until they learned of its role in the capture of a murderer and a pickpocket gang. All of them had tried to escape by train but ran into police who had been alerted by telegraph messages. Such seemingly insignificant news reports helped to establish the telegraph in the minds of government officials as well as newspaper readers. And from the telegraph much of modern communication has evolved.

Assembled by Morse and his assistant Alfred Vail, a more efficient experimental wire reached Baltimore with news of the Republican political nominating convention. Later, at a formal opening of the telegraph, Morse chose as his first public message a quotation from the Book of Numbers: "What hath God wrought?" The pious artist and inventor was convinced that God had chosen him to improve communication on Earth. Not all religious leaders agreed. In Baltimore, ministers expressed the opinion that the telegraph was too much like black magic.[10] Some people assumed that the wires were hollow. Others believed they could transmit physical objects. One woman in Europe wanted to telegraph a dish of sauerkraut to her soldier son.[11]

▶ PRIVATE INDUSTRY

When Congress chose not to buy the patent rights to the experimental line, private news express companies rushed in. Once Morse had shown the way, the technology was simple to copy. Within a few years more than 50 telegraph companies were active. The American telegraph, unlike most of the world's telegraph systems, would be managed as a commercial venture. In years to come, private industry would embark on development of the telephone, radio, and television. Most governments chose the path of government control and often ownership of all these forms of mediated communication.

The Crimean War, during 1854 to 1856, saw the telegraph used both for military orders and reportage. During the American Civil War both armies relied on telegraph communications, but the South suffered from a lack of wire and other supplies. Wires radiating from General Grant's headquarters enabled him to coordinate troop movements across a wide front. President Lincoln was able to keep abreast of military operations without being at the front.

By the end of the Civil War, as a result of mergers and acquisitions, only three fiercely competitive telegraph companies remained. When Western Union bought out its two rivals, the U.S. Telegraph Company and the American Telegraph Company, it became the first major company of any kind in the United States to gain a business monopoly. The main use of the telegraph was for commerce, echoed today by the Internet's "dot. com" enterprises. Speculators thrived on early information. Businesses expanded to open branch offices that could be instantly reached from a head office.

Telegraph banking allowed a merchant to authorize payment in another city. When the funds were handed over, a confirming telegram would release the goods without the need for travel. Location became less important, speed more important. A business journalist of the day said that what once was done in two to four weeks by mail could now be done in one day, and he called that "almost incredible."[12] "During the 1840s and 1850s, with the rapid development of a commercial infrastructure based on railroad and telegraph and the advent of American industrialization, the wholesale jobber completely replaced the traditional mercantile firms that had dominated the world's trade for half a millennium," sociologist James Beniger wrote.[13] The telegraph was prominent among the means that was able "to reassure merchants in their transactions with strangers."[14]

Europeans had entered the news service business even before the Associated Press was created in the United States. In Paris in 1833, the year the penny press began in New York, Charles Havas opened a news agency using the mails and carrier pigeons. In exchange for his news reports, newspapers gave him advertising space that he could sell. The enterprising idea led two of his workers, Bernard Wolff and Paul Julius Reuter, to start

A view of telegraph and telephone wires over New York City, 1887.

their own news agencies. When the telegraph lines went up in Germany and France, Reuter observed that the lines of the two nations were unconnected. Seeing a business opportunity, he covered the gap with carrier pigeons, which he had already employed to report the latest market prices. In time, Reuter moved to England, where he founded the news agency now known as Reuters, one of the world's largest.[15]

▶ TRANSMITTING NEWS

Historian Daniel Boorstin wrote that the telegraph transformed American journalism, because until the coming of the telegraph, "the reporting of political news in the United States was a bitterly partisan business. Newspapers were owned body and soul by one or another political party, and generally speaking, lacked moderation, conscience, or decency . . . It was the telegraph, of course, that made possible the establishment of enterprises such as the wire services selling news to newspapers." He also noted that the volume of advertising in the penny press further encouraged newspapers to assert their political independence.[16]

Newspapers had begun to compete over the speed of news delivery in the late 1820s, when two New York business periodicals, the *Journal of Commerce* and the *Courier and Enquirer*, turned to pony expresses and fast boats that met clipper ships from Europe to get a beat on business and other information. Combining the telegraph with the railroads further transformed commerce. Manufacturers could bypass wholesalers, saving on commissions, by dealing directly with retailers, often undercutting the prices of competitors. With the telegraph, dealers in fresh foods could gauge market demand more accurately. Perishable food moved more easily from farm to table. Wholesalers and retailers alike could keep small inventories when they could reorder quickly.[17]

The telegraph chipped at the barrier of time in transmitting news. Independent "telegraph reporters" tried to get a foothold in the new industry, but newspapers preferred their own system. Several Eastern city newspapers agreed to create something new, the news gathering cooperative. In some cases, competitive newspapers shared the services of the same reporter. The Associated Press arose out of these combines in 1848, formed by six New York dailies that otherwise competed furiously. To a great extent the telegraph changed the American newspaper from being primarily a political party organ to being primarily a purveyor of new [*supplier*] information.[18]

Newspapers and telegraph companies, in a stormy debate over costs, got into a battle of wits concerning what a word was. Because the telegraph companies charged by the word (as much as 50 cents to send ten words between New York and Boston), editors grew creative. Dispatches combined verbs and prepositions into single words that Noah Webster had not identified, never mind the occasional blunders. Telegraph operators also used codes such as "GM" ("good morning") and "SFD" ("stop for dinner"), just as people today tweet "LOL" ("laughing out loud"). Telegraph companies retaliated against newspapers by charging every five letters or even every three letters as a word. A reporter sent a telegram asking the age of actor Cary Grant: HOW OLD CARY GRANT? The actor saw it and supposedly replied: OLD CARY GRANT FINE. HOW YOU?

REPORTERS' ABBREVIATIONS

potus: President of the United States

scotus: Supreme Court of the United States

outpoint: point out

yam: yesterday morning

ogt: on the grounds that

gx: great excitement

American news writing also became more concise. The writing style known as "the inverted pyramid" replaced the opinion-filled narrative style. Journalists altered their writing style to reflect the realities of such telegraph transmission problems as sudden signal failures. The 5-W lead replaced the essay for revealing breaking news events. Within the new style the most significant elements, the 5-Ws (who? what? when? where? why?), were combined in the first sentence. As the story progressed, the writer added information in declining order of importance.

Access to telegraph reports influenced newspaper success. In the delivery of important political and military reports, small town newspapers had no chance to compete against large dailies until the telegraph leveled the playing field. When regional and small town newspapers could get news just as quickly, city newspapers in the American interior could compete on the same footing as the Eastern press. Equal access to news encouraged the growth of dozens of new dailies.[19] Publishers of large Eastern city newspapers did not greet the equalizing effect of the telegraph with unalloyed joy. The manager of *The Times* of London said he wished the telegraph had never been invented.[20]

▶ OBJECTIVITY

A new concept took hold on what news was and how it was to be delivered to the mass audiences who read the penny press newspapers that took root a few years before the telegraph was invented. The concept was objective reporting.[21]

In the mid-19th century, penny press newspapers were sold with the primary goal of entertaining, but dispensing opinion was not far behind. The raffish penny press reached readers who enjoyed the scandal and crime news that filled its columns and were not at first particularly interested in political opinions.

A wire service made money according to how many newspapers it could sign up. Because newspapers did not agree on political issues, a wire service saw a greater value in impartial reports that irritated the fewest number of editors. And so objectivity was born, defined as providing information containing only verifiable assertions and avoiding value judgments that lack clear attribution to source. Overt opinions were confined to the editorial page and the "op-ed" page (the page opposite the editorial page), and there they have remained to this day.

In short, the growth of wire services such as the Associated Press brought objectivity in its wake for sound business reasons rather than as a moral imperative. The AP chose a neutral approach to controversial events because it did not want to alienate its publisher customers, who had widely divergent political views. Over time, some newspapers adopted a timid version of the AP way for their own news stories. Even their editorial pages took neutral stands on issues that mattered, a policy dismissed as "Afghanistan-ism," which meant you could print what you liked about distant events, but don't say anything about our controversial mayor. Today, because Afghani-stan is very much in the news, the term has gone out of use.

During the 20th century, outside of the editorial page and the op-ed page, objectivity became a newspaper standard. *Fairness* in presenting informa-tion was important to build circulation among readers who held a diversity of viewpoints and to impart at least a sense that the news they were read-ing had not been colored to encourage a conclusion even if a political slant crept in.

Nevertheless, the wish to persuade readers to a point of view that would make itself felt at the ballot box continued to influence journalism, although most of those who use media to express political opinions preach to echo-ing choirs. Newspapers with a point of view were joined during the 1930s by radio journalism and commentary, later by television journalism and even television situation comedies. If any single thread runs through the tapestry

A telegraph operator at work in the White House offices, circa 1909.

of television, it may be that persuasion is at its most effective, at least in the United States, when it entertains. Inevitably, attack shifted from the issues themselves to those who expressed opinions.

As for the telegraph's legacy of objectivity, a new standard may be emerging for the 21st century, one that admits that journalists have views no matter how they try to suppress them. It recognizes that a public awash in sources of information is willing to accept opinion so long as accuracy and honesty accompany it. Sources should be fully identified. "Transparency" is the new term.

▶ SPREADING THE TECHNOLOGY

Telegraph wires also spread across Europe, Canada, and parts of South America. However, the Europeans continued to thwart Morse's dream that the telegraph would encourage international understanding and goodwill. For example, Austria and Prussia built their German-language national telegraph services with no direct connection between their political and commercial centers in Vienna and Berlin. Instead, at a shared border office a telegraph clerk from one country physically handed a message to a clerk from the other country for retransmission. This stand-off policy was no accident.

In time, interconnection agreements would be signed, but the telegraph made diplomats nervous, for diplomacy requires patience, not the instantaneous awareness brought by the electric wire. If a message could zip to a national capital in no time at all, troops could be ordered to the frontier more quickly than ever.

A cable under the English Channel allowed British and French merchants to exchange news and prices in just minutes by 1851. After several failures, a permanent transatlantic cable was laid in 1866 between England and Canada by the Great Eastern, a vessel five times the size of any other ship afloat. Australia was connected to the telegraph network in 1902. In 1906 Shanghai became the first point of connection to China.[22]

Laying cables underwater proved a challenge because it was difficult to find a suitable material to cover the wires. Unsheathed iron did no more than stun fish. Rubber cladding failed because it rotted in water. When the problem was solved, Britannia would rule not only the waves, but also the ocean floors where cables were laid. It was Britain's Malayan colony that grew the trees whose gutta-percha gum sheathed the cables as nothing else could.

Thomas Edison made improvements that allowed transmission of two messages at a time in each direction. He was working on further improvements to this "harmonic telegraph" when he stumbled onto a way to record sound, and invented the phonograph. Another inventor trying to improve the telegraph, Alexander Graham Bell, came up with the telephone instead. Radio, television, and the Internet followed, building upon telegraph technology.

SINGING TELEGRAMS AND BAD NEWS

Decades after the telephone was invented and a national network was in place, it was still cheaper to send a telegram than to place a long distance phone call. Telegrams reached a peak of sorts in popular culture between the two World Wars. Radio comedians joked about using the word "stop" in place of periods because punctuation cost extra but "stop" usually went free. They also joked about Western Union messengers delivering off-key versions of "Happy Birthday" singing telegrams. However, during World War II, the laughter was muted. Families feared the sight of a Western Union messenger because the telegram might be from the Department of War reporting that a soldier had been killed.

▶ SHUTTING DOWN

Facsimile (fax) and email eventually overtook the telegram. By 2006, the newer technologies proved too much. Western Union got out of the telegram business. It is still used to transfer money from country to country, allowing foreign workers in Europe and the United States to send wages home.

Meanwhile, the use of fax has been fading for several years under the onslaught of email. One recent failed experiment was the facsimile newspaper. The idea was to transmit news directly to homes and businesses, but the costly fax machines were slow and the output was poor. However, there was a demand for the service itself that is now met by news outlets on the Internet.

Other inventions that grew out of the telegraph included the telex, the teletype, and the teleprinter, which are combinations of printers, typewriters, and telephones that were used mostly during the 20th century by newspapers, government offices, and businesses; the tieline was a direct private line between a telegraph office and a business office. The Telequote and Quotron machines, also derived from the telegraph, provided instant reports on stock market prices. The iPhone has had many ancestors.

▶ TIMELINE

1794   In Revolutionary France, Claude Chappe sets up semaphore signaling system.

1800   Allesandro Volta's battery provides the first long-term source of electricity.

1803   Semaphore code is used on ships.

1814   Under Napoleon, an optical signal system stretches from Belgium to Italy.

1819   In Germany, engineers experiment with an electromagnetic telegraph.

1830   Scientist Joseph Henry sends a signal down a wire using an electromagnet.

1837   Samuel Morse shows a pendulum telegraph, but Alfred Vail invents Morse Code.

1839   Wheatstone-Cooke electric telegraph runs along a railroad line in England.

1843   Congress gives Morse funds to build an experimental telegraph line.

Gutta-percha, a future underwater cable wrap, is found in Malaya.

1844   Samuel Morse constructs a telegraph between Washington and Baltimore.

1846   Printing telegraph is forerunner of ticker tape.

1848   Using the telegraph for news transmission, the Associated Press is created.

1850   Submarine cable briefly connects England and France.

1851   In London, Frederick Bakewell demonstrates fax machine to send pictures.

1854   Telegraph brings out news of the Crimean War.

1858   Atlantic cable built, lasts three weeks.

1859   Telegraph crosses the United States from the Atlantic to the Pacific.

1861   Telegraph brings the Pony Express to an abrupt end.

1861–65 Telegraph helps the Union win the Civil War.

1866   Atlantic cable success ties Europe and the United States for instant communication.

1869   Edison patents stock ticker and printing telegraph.

1870   Telegraph across Europe and Asia connects London with Calcutta, 11,000 kilometres.

1933   Western Union delivers a singing telegram.

1970   Mailgrams.

1974   Mailgrams are bounced off communication satellites.

1980   Money transfer revenue exceeds telegram service revenue.

2006   Western Union gets out of the telegram business.

▶ NOTES

1 Tom Standage, *The Victorian Internet* (New York: Walker Co., 1998) 83.

2 Neil Postman, *Technopoly: The Surrender of Culture to Technology* (New York: Knopf, 1992) 67.

3 Cited in Daniel J. Boorstin, *The Americans: The Democratic Experience* (New York: Random House, 1973) 498–499.

4 Written in 1941, when the U.S. population was just over 130 million.

5 Marion May Dilts, *The Telephone in a Changing World* (New York: Longmans, Green, 1941) 20–21.

6 James Beniger discusses this extensively in *The Control Revolution* (Cambridge, MA: Harvard University Press, 1986).

7 Daniel J. Boorstin, *Hidden History: Exploring Our Secret Past* (New York: Harper & Row, 1987) 307.

8 Alvin F. Harlow, *Old Wires and New Waves: The History of the Telegraph, Telephone, and Wireless* (D. Appleton-Century, 1936) 213–214.

9 George P. Oslin, *The Story of Telecommunications* (Macon, GA: Mercer University Press, 1992) 16.

10 Standage, 52.

11 Standage, 67.

12 Standage, 168.

13 Beniger, 160.

14 Beniger, 130.

15 In the United States, it is known as Reuters, not Reuter, due to the erroneous title of a popular Hollywood movie, *A Dispatch from Reuters*. Life sometimes imitates art.

16 Boorstin, *Hidden History*, 139.

17 Standage, 167.

18 Daniel J. Czitrom, *Media and the American Mind* (Chapel Hill: University of North Carolina Press, 1982) 18.

19 William Sloan, James Stovall, and James Startt, *The Media in America* (Worthington, OH: Publishing Horizons, 1989) 204.

20 Francis Williams, *Transmitting World News* (Paris: UNESCO, 1953) 19.

21 Edward Cornish, "The Coming of an Information Society," *The Futurist*, April 1981: 14.

22 James R. Beniger, *The Control Revolution* (Cambridge, MA: Harvard University Press, 1986) 253.

6 Telephone: Reaching without Touching

To succeed, an invention must find a social use. Those that fare best improve some aspect of life in the society of their time. The telephone was originally envisioned as an aid to business, such as a doctor contacting a pharmacist. That it would find so many more uses took time to evolve, but it did not take long for people to recognize the value of being able to speak directly to someone without traveling to meet face-to-face.

Before the telephone's invention, access to such emergency services as the fire or police departments was slow and often too late. Before the telephone, if you were sick you turned up at the doctor's office or sent someone to fetch the doctor; you could not call ahead. If you needed a policeman in a hurry you were in even more trouble. If you needed a fire wagon in a hurry, too bad. If you lived alone, how would you manage during a sudden illness or after an accident? If you were elderly, to live alone invited problems. If you lived out of town, as most people did, you took a risk to live alone no matter how old you were. By connecting people, the telephone made life safer and more pleasant. It also erased some of the loneliness of living remotely from other people and some of the sadness of being far from loved ones.

Before the telephone, speaking with someone outside your home meant a journey, short or long. When a son or daughter married or moved out of the house to enter a distant school or start a career, your tears were for more than joy, for the child's familiar voice might never again be heard in your home. Such a departure might feel as complete as a death. Before the telephone, people tended to spend their entire lives close to those they knew and loved. It was not unusual to die in the home where you were born. Sigmund Freud took note of this: "If there had been no railway to conquer distances, my child would never have left his native town and I should need no telephone to hear his voice."[1]

Today, with phone calls, emails, messaging, and personal blogs, physical separation no longer means complete separation. Thanks to camera phones and social network sites such as Facebook or Skype, distant communication that includes speaking and seeing eases any decision about going away to take a job, attend school, or spend the winter. The telephone has become such a part of our lives that we use it when we have no need to. We answer a ring regardless of how it intrudes into what is immediately going on around us, intimate or not. It is also such a part of our lives that use it to push people away. Phoning Grandma is so much easier than visiting her.

At the time the telephone was invented, during the height of the Industrial Revolution, business and industry moved at a slower and more cautious pace than they would in the years to come. If, say, you were a wholesaler of fruits and vegetables, how would you know what to load onto a wagon for the grocers you served? Or if you wanted to build a skyscraper, how would the workers at the top communicate with those on the ground? The answer: before the telephone (a time that also preceded the safety elevator and cheap steel), there were no skyscrapers. If you worked in a mine, how would you call for help after a cave-in?

▶ SOMETHING OF A TOY?

The dream of speaking at a distance did not originate with Alexander Graham Bell. "Lovers' telephones" consisting of two cans attached by a wire could carry a voice the length of a football gridiron. Other inventors had tried to create an electric voice carrier. On February 14, 1876, the same day that Bell, a professor of vocal physiology at Boston University, filed his patent (Bell's lawyer did the actual filing), the well-known inventor Elisha Gray (he is also now regarded as the father of the music synthesizer) informed the U.S. Patent Office that he had invented "the art of transmitting vocal sounds or conversations telegraphically through an electric current." Like Bell, Gray had started out to improve the telegraph with harmonic tones. Whether Bell or Gray is the true inventor of the telephone may never be settled to everyone's satisfaction. Historian Alvin Harlow contended that Bell "had not actually produced a workable instrument when he received his patent."[2]

The outcome of a lengthy court battle between them ended in Bell's favor, but the apparatus designed by the 29-year-old Scottish-born teacher of the deaf did not inspire universal confidence.

In London, Bell's demonstration was ridiculed as something of a toy. James Clerk Maxwell, the Scottish scientist whose theory of invisible waves would underlie the invention of radio, concluded that the apparatus could have been "put together by an amateur."[3] The chief engineer of the British Post Office, William Preece, reported to a committee of the House of Commons that Bell's invention might be more useful in America than in Britain,

A portrait of Alexander Graham Bell by Timoléon Marie Lobrichon, 1882.

which enjoyed "a superabundance of messengers, errand boys and things of that kind."[4]

▶ "MY GOD, IT TALKS!"

A famous moment enshrined in telephone lore occurred at the 1876 Philadelphia exposition held to commemorate the centennial of the signing of the Declaration of Independence. Bell went there to demonstrate his telephone, but he attracted little attention until the visiting emperor of Brazil, Dom Pedro II, recognized Bell, the professor who had given a lecture in Boston that Dom Pedro had attended. When Bell demonstrated his device, the emperor allegedly exclaimed, "My God, it talks!"[6] The publicity that followed made Bell's telephone the hit of the exposition.

Alexander Graham Bell and his assistant, Thomas Watson, in working with tonal frequencies to develop a harmonic, multiplexed telegraph signal, recognized that for voices the on-and-off signaling of the telegraph would have to be replaced by a continuous current whose frequency had to be modified. The human voice could be transmitted if a current could be varied to reflect the variations in air pressure as words are spoken, and the voice might be heard with better fidelity if an instrument received the arriving sounds the way an ear does.

That moment famously came on March 10, 1876, when Bell called out from an adjoining room, "Mr. Watson, come here. I want to see you." And the telephone was born.

"JABBERING INTO A DUMBBELL"

We do not blink at seeing someone mumbling aloud while walking down the street, once a sign of insanity. When Cole Younger, a member of Jesse James's outlaw gang, was released from prison, he told a reporter, "It was all I could do to keep my face straight at the spectacle of a fellow jabbering into a dumbbell."[5]

▶ BUSINESS DECISIONS

Bell and his financial backers initially conceived a business model for the telephone, but were delighted when the doctors and merchants who were the first customers ordered telephones for their residences. That inspired the Bell System to rent, not sell, the phones. Its newspaper advertisements soon stressed the telephone as a social tool, offering up such slogans as "Friendship's path often follows the trail of the telephone wire," "No girl wants to be a wallflower," and "Call the folks now!"

Telephones were considered part of an integrated system that included the wires that connected them to a switching network and to the phone operators who were needed to make the connections. Improvements in equipment convinced potential users that what Bell had invented was a tool, not a toy. Within two years of awarding Bell's patent in 1876, some ten thousand Bell telephones were in use.

At first a single megaphone served for both speaking and listening, with the user alternately pressing his ear to the device and turning his head to shout into it. This yielded to a separate transmitter and receiver. The transmitter took a bell shape to focus the sound of the voice. A metal disk substituted for the original skin diaphragm at the receiver. To add to conductivity, copper wire replaced telegraph iron wire.

It was evident from the start that each telephone could not be connected directly to every other telephone. A centralized arrangement was needed. Bell even envisioned a central switching system to connect distant cities so that long distance calling might be possible, even though the existing equipment was not yet up to the task of sending a clear vocal signal between cities. Subscribers who had to shout might have given up. But along came another inventor, Emile Berliner, who was improving the phonograph, to develop a more sensitive transmitter.[7] He is regarded as the inventor of the microphone. His first effort was patched together from a child's drum, a needle, a steel button, and a guitar string.[8]

Western Union executives reached what proved to be a shortsighted conclusion when a Bell partner offered to sell the Bell Telephone Company to them for U.S.$100,000. Western Union turned down the offer. But in 1878 Western Union decided to compete in the telephone business itself, using a receiver designed by Gray and a transmitter designed by Thomas Edison, both superior to the Bell instruments. Western Union had the additional advantage of thousands of miles of telegraph wire already strung along poles.

The newly formed National Bell Telephone Company sued Western Union over patent infringement and won. Western Union gave up its telephone business. National Bell became American Bell and later the American Telephone and Telegraph Company (AT&T), with the goal of establishing phone service around the world. By the end of the 19th century, upon the expiration of the first Bell patent, a number of entrepreneurs went into the telephone business.

To reach all the telephones in town, subscribers frequently had to sign up for both Bell and a competing service. The Bell Company expanded to buy out competing phone companies, to create the phone equipment manufacturing company Western Electric, and to set up a research unit that would become Bell Laboratories. In the future, Bell Labs would be the source of many communications ideas and inventions, including information theory, motion picture sound, transistors, laser beams, optical fibers, the communications satellite, and advances in computers and television.

ROWDY BOYS, CALM WOMEN

The original telephone operators in 1877, teenage boys who did well as telegraph messengers, proved too rowdy in the confined space of a telephone switchboard room. But who could take their place?

It represented a significant social change to replace boys with women because in starchy Victorian times it was unusual and a bit daring for a young woman to take employment outside the home and thereby jeopardize her marriage prospects.

Nevertheless, the chance to get out of the house and earn money of her own to spend as she pleased won over many women. Never mind that the pay packet was light and the headsets were not. Telephone engineers later discovered that the frequency range of a typical woman's voice more closely matched the early frequency transmission band than a man's voice did. Women speaking on the phone were easier to understand.

The president of AT&T testified before a Senate committee in 1874 that he thought very highly of women as telephone operators. In fact, Andrew Carnegie's sister was an operator. An inspector at the Boston telephone office reported that female operators were "much superior to males . . . in civility and general attention to their own tables." But, he added, "The young ladies also appear fond of airing their voices, and sometimes prolong telephonic conversation to talk with their subscribers."[9]

Women telephone operators, early 20th century. A chance to earn a salary of her own.

▶ THE SWITCHBOARD

In 1878, the first commercial telephone exchange was opened in New Haven, Connecticut, with a switchboard of 8 lines and 21 telephones. A year later saw the introduction of telephone numbers, in place of a subscriber asking the operator to place a call based on the operator recognizing a name.

This reportedly followed a measles epidemic outbreak when a physician in Lowell, Massachusetts, feared that if the city's four trained operators came down with the illness, inexperienced substitute operators would throw the phone system into disarray without the simpler use of numbers instead of names. Lowell telephone managers were concerned that the subscribers might bridle at being assigned numbers, but the common sense of the numbering operation prevailed.

All this happened before the automatic dial telephone invented by Almon Strowger in 1891 came into use. A Kansas City undertaker, Strowger, believed that another undertaker had bribed a telephone operator to tell callers that Strowger's line was busy. To protect his business, Strowger invented the forerunners of the dial telephone and the automatic telephone exchange.

The need for several telephones in one location led to the private switchboard, called a Private Branch Exchange, or PBX. Although many are still in use, they have been replaced at large companies by a "local area network," or LAN, to link their telephone systems and computers.

Telephone operators were part of the social revolution that allowed women to work outside the home. Women were hired as store clerks, typists, and, thanks to stories about Florence Nightingale and Clara Barton, as nurses, although middle-class subscribers might regard phone operators—"hello girls"—as household servants. On the other hand, the Chicago Telephone Company found it necessary to instruct operators to query, "Number, please," instead of saying "Hello" or even "What do you want?"

▶ SOCIAL CHANGES

All in all, compared with what they would be after the telephone became a common household fixture, the good old days of the late 19th century were lonely for many, uncertain for most, and pinched. Although it allowed no more than a confined intimacy, for the infirm or the solitary, the telephone was a lifesaver. Despite the old saying, the Englishman's home was no longer his castle when a telephone was installed. The Victorian head of a household may have harrumphed with displeasure at the ringing that interrupted the well-regulated family dinner, but the farmer's wife regarded the telephone as a godsend.[10] The telephone has been—and still is—both irritant and blessing, and it just might be the last means of communication you would willingly part with.[11]

For those you loved, the bittersweet feeling that accompanied separation seemed less bitter, for you could continue personal communication without being there. Daily letter writing took effort, but the telephone easily connected friends or lovers who were physically distant. The traveling businessman, the university student, and the vacationer now stayed in contact with home.

Yet, a phone also keeps us apart by allowing each of us to erect a wall of separation from others. Many people have paid extra for services like Caller ID that filter who gets through. Like most mediated communication, a degree of separation accompanies the telephone, the opposite of the no-touching "Reach Out and Touch Someone." Good for a laugh line on TV is the mother's complaint that the child never calls. The "Reach Out and Touch Someone" contradiction of the telephone manifests itself keenly in achieving such family obligations as an adult child maintaining regular, if sometimes reluctant, contact with an elderly parent. The telephone replaces a little of the need to stop by for a chat and a cup of tea.

▶ STATUS SYMBOL

A Bell advertisement of the times encouraged upper-class sensibilities: "Telephones are rented only to persons of good breeding and refinement. A householder becomes morally responsible for its proper use by all members of his family. There is nothing to be feared from your conversation being overheard. Our subscribers are too well bred to listen to other people's business."[12] A Bell official refused a request by a Mississippi public service commissioner to segregate shared party lines, saying "A customer to us is just a customer, colored or white. We are a public utility."[13]

Snobbish objection was expressed to any widening of access to the Bell system by such additions as coin-operated public telephones or telephone directories available to the general public. One Washington DC hotel proprietor had to go to court to keep his phone service after he allowed guests to use the phone in the lobby. In Leicester, England, a subscriber was criticized for calling the fire brigade about a fire that was not on his property. It took a ruling from the postmaster general to establish that a telephone could be employed in the event of fires and riots. In time, as telephones became as common in homes as the kitchen stove, the telephone took on an egalitarian hue.

Under the leadership of Theodore Vail, a distant relative of Alfred Vail, Morse's assistant in inventing the telegraph, usage spread in the late 19th and early 20th centuries.[14] The American Telephone and Telegraph Company grew to be a communications giant. It proceeded to try to standardize everything possible, even the shape of the black—only black—telephone in every office and home.

As the United States entered the 20th century, more than a million phones were being used.[15] By 1930, that number had jumped to more than 15 million phones.[16] A single, black, party-line phone ringing and interrupting a radio program or the family dinner became quite typical in an American home. Sharing a single telephone line was the primary way that people obtained local telephone service. To distinguish one subscriber from another, operators set a pattern of rings, such as one short ring followed by one long ring. In rural areas, where four- or even eight-party lines were common, people sneakily picked up the ringing phone even though the ring pattern informed them the call was not for them. The occasionally embarrassed listeners-in defended their behavior as making sure there was no emergency that might need their help.

As AT&T bought up all the small telephone companies it could, control of the industry became absolute until government rulings during the late 20th century forced dissolution of AT&T's monopoly and led to greater diversity.

▶ WIRED BROADCASTING

Well before a point-to-point Morse code radio service changed into our present mass communication voice and music broadcasting business, there was *wired broadcasting*. Several European capitals in the 19th century offered a phone service that allowed customers, for a fee, to listen to operas, plays, and concerts picked up by microphones in theaters. In Buckingham Palace, Queen Victoria could hear the opera coming from Covent Garden or the Royal Theater in Drury Lane, while in Paris the Theatrophone Company offered coin-operated headsets at holiday resorts a generation before radio broadcasting.

Several American cities had church services similarly available. One Canadian tavern owner found a judge willing to set a microphone on his bench during a murder trial. A wire carried the testimony to customers who could listen in on one of 20 earphones sets for a fee of 25 cents an hour. The Telefon Hirmondo in Budapest distributed a printed schedule of programs that included music, a calendar of local events, a weekly children's concert, and even commercials, all presented a full generation before regular programming by radio.[17] It tapped into the public's newly discovered desire for information and entertainment on a regular basis, piped into their homes.

The popular desire to be entertained would be more fully met when technology came along in the form of radio broadcasting and all the entertainment media that followed. As for wired broadcasting, it continued, notably in dictatorships. Radio service consisting of one preset station blaring from atop a pole in a village square or on a train to a captive audience, with no competitive broadcasts, is a perfect propaganda tool.

▶ LONG DISTANCE

It was a while before technology caught up with Bell's dream of a nationwide and even an international telephone service. M. I. Pupin's invention in 1900 of the loading coil, Lee de Forest's invention in 1906 of the three-element vacuum tube and H. D. Arnold's vacuum tube amplifier in 1914 added clarity to phone calls and changed a local service into an operation that could comfortably replace the dots and dashes of the telegraph with the human voice. By 1915, AT&T had a transcontinental line running from New York to San Francisco. That year also saw successful testing of the wireless telephone, a boon to the U.S. Navy, which had been trying for years to improve military communication. The government took over all telephone and radio service for a brief time during World War I.

A few years later, AT&T began laying deep-sea cable and providing transoceanic radiophone service. Radiotelephony—combining wireless radio and wired telephone technology—between the New York and London financial centers started in 1927 during the boom of the Roaring Twenties, then was extended to other large European cities and to South America.[18] In 1947, the transistor, an invention out of the Bell Telephone Laboratories, replaced the vacuum tube. Microchips would follow, then microprocessors. A transatlantic telephone cable was laid in 1956. High-speed computer data phone service followed. A fiber optic cable link between California and Japan was laid in 1989. Meanwhile, communication satellites able to carry thousands of calls simultaneously were placed in orbit, starting with Telstar 1 in 1962 that relayed television, telephone and high-speed data communications.[19] How a phone call or an email message reaches its destination is no longer of concern except to engineers. The remark, "You sound as if you are next door," can be heard halfway around the world.

▶ OPENING THE NETWORK

The 1956 Supreme Court Hush-a-Phone decision opened the telephone network to non-Bell equipment. A further change came with the Federal Communication Commission's MCI ruling that opened up the long-distance market. Another FCC ruling in 1968 allowed customers to connect non-Western Electric devices such as their own phones and fax machines to the Bell System. The Carterfone decision in 1978 was over a two-way radio transceiver equipped with an acoustic coupler used for a standard telephone handset. All this was allowed provided the equipment did no harm to the telephone network.

In 1983, AT&T itself was broken into seven regional operating companies. Small companies bought line capacity wholesale, reselling their use retail through telephone cards and special phone numbers. The days of POTS (Plain Old Telephone Service) disappeared as the public snapped up their own telephones in colors and shapes far removed from the AT&T black, rotary dial phone.

Improvements in voice communication were joined by improvements in sending *data* anywhere in the world, from the printing telegraph to the teletypewriter to the teletype to the digital computer data stream, all used by governments, global businesses, wire news services, and even by you and me. In addition to text, images were converted into digital data streams flowing along telephone pathways to be reconstructed as still and motion pictures.

Thousands of inventions have improved the telephone system, including Touch Tone, the coaxial cable, the means to transmit computer data, the conversion from analog to digital signals to improve clarity, microwave, satellite communication, and fiber optics. With Digital Subscriber Line (DSL) technology, the slender telephone line can transmit moving images. You can download *The Wizard of Oz* on a telephone line. These inventions nudge our world into what author Thomas Friedman labels a "flat Earth."[20] Telephone networks with fiber-optic "backbones" are essential elements of globalization, the "flat Earth." Friedman has argued that the world has integrated, in part due to telecommunications and to the global exchange of information and other media content. The peoples of the world are interdependent.

However, technological progress is not always positive, and certainly the telephone has not always been employed to benefit the social order. *Telemarketing* is a case in point, with sales calls buzzing in from "boiler rooms" as far away as India. Adding to a general sense of social disorder is pornography in the form of "adult" phone lines. On the other hand, unlisted

A transcontinental telephone
line is opened, 1927.

numbers, Caller ID, anonymous call rejection, voice messaging, and the answering machine remind us that tools also exist to keep the world at bay.

▶ CELLPHONES

Call it a "mobile" (England, Spain), a "handy" (Germany), a "*sho ji*" (Chinese word for "hand machine"), or "*keitai*" (Japanese for "portable thing"). For anyone in any country, a a personal cellphone matters. So does a private email account, or a Twitter or Facebook connection that is yours alone. For the young, it is a rite of passage in the new millennium. Cellphone technology has improved life for many people in all countries, particularly young adults who expand their social world. In Haiti, where an estimated four out of five residents have cellphones, a "crisis mapping" network helped people in the aftermath of the 2010 earthquake to text for assistance.

Despite complaints and mortality statistics, it hardly seems to matter in much of the world that motorists and pedestrians on cellphones are less aware of their surroundings. Bicycle riders steer with one hand or no hands as they weave through traffic, a cellphone pressed against an ear. Joggers run awkwardly because crooking an elbow throws off their rhythm. A driver still holding his cell sits in a daze surrounded by the wreck that was once his car.

The cellphone has altered the telephone call. Today, nine out of ten Americans own a cellphone and 58 percent own a smartphone.[21] Before the cellphone and earlier mobile phones, a telephone call was directed toward an instrument at a fixed location where, the caller hoped, a specific person would be present. A daughter phoning her mother over a landline, for example, is actually calling her mother's home in the expectation that her mother will be nearby. With an active cellphone in her handbag, her mother will always be nearby, always "home."

▶ FLASH MOBS

Governments in power for decades collapsed at the start of the "Arab Spring." That started in Tunisia in 2010. Their dictators fled. In the streets the young people danced and the old people laughed. Clutched in their fingers were their weapons: mobile phones.

Some observers called these uprisings "social media revolutions," "Facebook revolutions," or "Twitter revolutions." New communication technologies were the magnets that pulled together the dense masses into city squares. At home, viewers have gathered around television sets to watch the street demonstrations in Ukraine and other countries and hear the news of the end of autocrats, seeing events unfold on cross-border programs brought in by satellite dishes. Salma Said, a 26-year-old Egyptian woman activist, said she had been arrested, kicked, groped and pepper-sprayed during the Egyptian uprising in 2011. "Two years ago I just got disappointed in organized groups and left it and discovered this world of Twitter and blogs," she said. "We work with Twitter aggregators, web designers, techno geeks."[22]

We live in an era of "flash mobs." (Like a flash flood it suddenly appears in force.) Rage goes viral and angry people cluster. Information running through social networks and cellphones directs them. In 2011, fueled by Twitter, Facebook, YouTube, email, camera phones and mimeographed leaflets, pent-up fury exploded against government corruption in the Middle East, widespread unemployment, and rising prices. With messages fed into cellphones in every other hand, daily street riots brought down the governments of Egypt, Tunisia, and Yemen. In Syria, scattered rebel groups communicated with each other and the rest of the world through cellphones, stirring world anger by sending out images of the atrocities after the government used poison gas.

Governments control choke points—the ISPs through which electronic messages pass. When the Egyptian government shut down the Internet and cellphone links for five days, ordinary Egyptians turned to the plentiful television satellite dishes, dial-up modems and landlines to reach ISPs in other countries. Security police could confiscate their mobiles but the video was already on its way around the world.[23] *Seeing* what others were watching informed the protestors. *Knowing* that others watched cheered them and drove them on.

Enemies of democracy also network. After a fanatic Florida pastor oversaw the burning of a Koran and was involved in producing a movie vilifying Islam, *Innocence of Muslims*, in 2012, the news that raced across the Muslim world led to deadly anti-American riots.

Pictures of the 2009 Tehran demonstrations that turned bloody were fed to the outside world by phones despite efforts by the Iranian government. A cellphone captured the street death of 26-year-old Neda Agha-Soltan, the student whose picture as she lay dying became an icon for protest.

Mobile media have been in the thick of things at home as well as abroad. The Occupy Wall Street movement in 2011, spreading to cities across the United States and to other countries, had its own media center. It funneled images snapped on camera phones of Occupy movements worldwide to social network sites Tumblr, YouTube, Facebook, and Twitter, as well as to television media. At the same time Facebook and Twitter messages urged worldwide demonstrations. The 2011 urban riots in England and the French urban riots of 2005 were strung together by cellphones, texting, and the Internet. The combination of street organization and cheap technology proved so efficient that the French government and police in 2005 hardly knew what hit them or how to stop it. During the global disputes about the Iraq War that started in 2003, armies of antiwar protesters were summoned to the streets of Western capitals by email and cellphone instant messaging.

News racing from city to city and to journalists who have immediate access to the outer world overwhelms governments trying to control the information. Starting at Macy's department store in Manhattan in 2003, the United States saw flash mobs in several of its own cities looting stores, and causing havoc. However, in London, ordinary citizens organizing via Twitter to protect their neighborhoods followed days of Twitter-fueled riots and looting. Historically, protesters have been weaker than government forces. Perhaps no longer. Cellphones to some extent level the field. The days of workers starting

Thousands of protesters flocked to Cairo's Tahrir Square, Egypt, November 22, 2011. Cellphones played a significant role in assembling Arab Spring crowds.

revolutions by taking over factories are long gone. So are the days of seizing radio stations and, in the immediate post-Soviet Union days, television stations. Today the messages pour out through many avenues.

If we look back across the centuries we find other examples of how media have influenced political action. Tom Paine's pamphlet *Common Sense* and Harriet Beecher Stowe's novel *Uncle Tom's Cabin* spring to mind.

► CONTACT WITHOUT CONTACT

We telephone not to "reach out and touch someone," but because we cannot actually reach out and touch someone. Cellphones have made it easier to have communication with physical separation. The smartphone with Twitter texting makes it still easier. Tweets promise a kind of intimacy—the sharing among friends of momentary emotions, fragmentary thoughts without visibility or proximity, let alone touching. Tweets let anyone in a Twitter network know, for instance, that the sender is at the mall. The total number of tweets—messages limited to 140 characters—is well up into the billions.

In 2006, *Newsweek* columnist Anna Quindlen noted, "The BlackBerry device alone makes it seem as though we're living in a '50s futuristic film. The paradox is that all this nominal communication has led to detachment from what is nearby, with people hunched over handhelds or staring into the screen of the computer. There is the illusion of keeping in touch, but always at arm's length. Sometimes it seems that what people want most is the one thing they no longer have: human contact."[24]

Users are likely to keep phones within reach all day and all night, as much a part of their garb as their shoes. Some people relish a constant connection, but not everyone does. For the employee whose boss wants to reach him at any time, there is no certain time off. An unwanted cellphone has been compared to a slave collar and its ringing to a dog whistle. Calls too often are received or initiated on highways, in restaurants, cinemas, bathrooms, and buses. A ringing backpack in a classroom is not unusual. Concert halls and movie theaters post signs to remind patrons to turn off their communication devices.

Multitasking does not have to include a cellphone, but it usually does, offering another example of focusing on what is far away at the expense of what is around us. Being unaware of what is around you, sometimes referred to as "inattentional blindness," can kill you, as we are told but few of us hear. A study at Western Washington University reported that three out of four test subjects who were on their cells while crossing the campus failed to notice a clown on a unicycle passing by.[25]

► A SHORT HISTORY OF THE CELLPHONE

The cellphone has a short, explosive history. Invented in the United States in 1938, its predecessor, the walkie-talkie, saw extensive military use during

World War II. Mobile radio systems connected to the telephone network were developed in Sweden after the war, expanded to the United States, and gradually shifted from calls placed through an operator to direct dial. Among the early users of these radiophones were police cars, fire trucks, and television news crews who raced to where the police and firemen were headed. Low-powered walkie-talkies were even sold as toys.

The modern cellphone, a version of two-way radio invented in 1973 by Martin Cooper of Motorola, transfers calls from a relay station as a user travels. Portable phones found a ready market in Japan, where many people have been quick to adopt innovations in personal technology. By 1979 the Japanese had the first cellphone network up and running. The FCC did not authorize full commercial cellphone service in the United States until 1982.

In the blink of an eye, modern life *needed* the cellphone. Not even the fear of brain cancer has dissuaded users. As phone size shrank with every new model, a rumor started that sending radio waves into and out of devices pressed against the side of the head damaged brains because the phones were basically low-powered microwave ovens without walls. The accusation was neither confirmed nor fully refuted.[26] Sales continued to soar. Cellphone signals have also been accused of killing honeybees by sending electromagnetic signals that confuse worker bees.[27] Cellphone towers are accused of killing birds.

Because cellphone use spread rapidly in parts of the world where telephone landlines were scarce, instant messaging (IM or "IMing," also called SMS for Short Message Service) got an early foothold in developing countries. In the United States, teens and even pre-teens IM'd friends the instant the closing school bell rang. In addition, IM could connect a group as well as two people for business or personal exchanges in real time.

▶ NEW MOBILE PRODUCTS

New products continued to tumble out. The telephone, the camera, and wireless technology came together in the camera phone, a pocket digital cellular phone that could take and email pictures or post them online.[28] In 2007 the iPhone created excitement with a cellphone that combined an iPod music player with email, Web access and a clever touch-screen that featured hundreds of independently created applications—"apps."

The newest smartphones offer 3D-like viewing of images, music, and image storage, access to the Internet and other computer functions. Smartphones became the coolest, must-have accessory for the fashion conscious. Manufacturers, quick to seize upon trends, turned them out in a variety of styles. Samsung and Android smartphone apps offered health-related features, such as a heart-rate monitor and a menstrual cycle calculator.[29] What is happening is *convergence*, as technologies evolve to come together in a small instrument that can do it all, and telecommunications providers can offer it all.

In Minnesota, a shopper surfs the Internet from a supermarket to pull down a recipe that includes a shopping list. In a McDonald's in Japan, customers point their cellphones at the wrapping around their cheeseburgers to get nutrition data. They point their phones at a magazine to get insurance quotes. If, on the way to the airport, they pass a billboard advertising a movie, pointing their cellphone downloads a trailer. At the airport, pointing their cellphone substitutes for a ticket. In the 21st century, microchips inform microchips as cellphones communicate with airline computers. The wristwatch radiotelephone fantasy of the Dick Tracy comic strip decades ago was almost at hand.

▶ POSTING PICTURES

The little devices have created millions of citizen photojournalists around the world who have the rare opportunity to record history, aided by some encouragement from established media willing to buy newsworthy photographs or videos. This has been more than a nuisance to celebrities. And if no one wants to pay for a cell photo, the video-sharing network YouTube still beckons. When President Obama took office, a Secret Service issue began a national dialogue over whether it was safe for him to use his trusty BlackBerry. He insisted.

But not everything about the camera phone is positive. In the hands of a sexual predator, it creates a frightening invasion of privacy. That problem has yet to be solved. Women have also used them to take pictures of strangers who harassed them, then posted the pictures on websites. School administrators have raised concerns that camera cells could help students cheat on tests.

Despite its smartphone contributions, the United States has not always been in the wireless forefront. Americans have been slower than others to "cut the cord" of an extensive landline system. Look to Europe and East Asia for that. In many of their cities, young people quickly abandoned fixed-lines for mobility in phone calls, chat lines, messaging, and email. Europe and Asia jumped far ahead of the United States for two reasons. First, most cellphone systems were begun by a government-owned and subsidized telephone monopoly that could set standards and run matters as they wished. That could save years of regulatory hearings and competitive wrangling. Second, developing countries had a relatively small—even meager—telephone infrastructure in place, coupled with a huge backlog of requests for telephones. The market for an alternative to landlines was ready and waiting. In poverty-stricken Cambodia in 2003, nine of ten phones reportedly were cellphones.[30] The low cost of wireless technology was a dream come true. It spread like a fire.

▶ HELPING SOCIETIES EVERYWHERE

A researcher in India estimated that a single new phone line in a developing country added an average of U.S.$3,700 to its national wealth. But where roads are bad, travel is dangerous, postal service is slow or corrupted, telephone lines often do not exist. Enter the cellphone. Although computers are scarce, cellphone messages get through. In developing countries a micro-finance program has allowed "telephone ladies" to go into business by purchasing solar-powered cellphones for villages without electricity and selling phone time to other villagers.[31]

Cellphones are being used by election monitors in places where vote counting ranges from shaky to shady. In another example of how mediated communication can enable democracy, *The Economist* reported that a Pakistani bureaucrat required land transfer clerks to send him a list of the cellphone numbers of the people who came to them for document approval. He planned to follow up with the customers to see if the bureaucrats had asked for bribes. Buyers and sellers reported an immediate improvement in honest service.[32]

Using a prepaid billing system is easy in a traditional cash economy. Across the world, in shops along unpaved roads where people hand over cash to "top off" the value of their phone cards, banking services are conducted without banks. No need to waste a day to travel to a bank. No need to risk keeping cash or gold at home. You can deposit money to your account, withdraw it, or send it to someone else by phoning a shopkeeper in your village and reading the code on the card. The shopkeeper ends a transaction by handing money to your family, less a commission.

In Kenya, more than half of the population used a mobile phone banking service, according to a Pew Research Center estimate in 2014.[33] Studies of agricultural marketing in India and Niger have concluded that access to mobile phones made markets more efficient by reducing price variations from one market to another, bringing down consumer prices, and raising the income of food producers.[34] Governments that offered agricultural advice by coaxing farmers to gather at regional locations reached more of them more cheaply by cellphone. News for health workers, weather reports, and information for teachers and local government staffs also flowed more easily.

▶ INTERNET PHONE CALLS

The fast drop in the cost of mobile handsets has naturally made a difference in usage. During the 1990s, a basic handset once cost U.S.$250, a luxury item in much of the world. By 2009 a basic model sold for $20 and a Chinese manufacturer was ready to supply them for $13 apiece.[35] Approximately 7 billion people now live on Earth. In 2012 more than 5 billion mobile phones were in use. By 2013, an estimated 1 billion were smartphones.[36]

The difficulty of Internet phone calls lies in the amount of data that is transmitted. It is the difference between an email transmission that lasts fractions of a second and the voice transmission of a phone call that lasts as long as the call itself. Early efforts to use the Internet for phone calls resulted in poor transmission, but the quality has improved and the cost is hard to beat. Visual calls by a Skype user to any other Skype user anywhere in the world would have been astonishing just ten years ago. Technology has developed that chops voice traffic into digital bits and ships it around the world via the Internet the way that email travels. Cheap Internet telephony known as VOIP (Voice Over Internet Protocol) is already available with good voice quality from Skype and competitors such as Google Talk and iChat. It was only a matter of time after broadband replaced narrow bandwidths that the capacity to make phone calls would bypass local phone companies to go directly out over the Internet.

Inventive users from non-English speaking countries like China are using the VOIP service to contact VOIP users in English-speaking countries at random just to practice their English skills, a kind of audio version of finding a pen pal. Again, we adapt to our media tools.

As it has often done with other kinds of telecommunication in recent decades, Japan has led in using the Internet for voice calling. Companies selling cellphone service and their smartphone descendants do more than expected in many countries. Italy's Telecom Italia rebuilt its entire network around Internet equipment. In Finland, a long-time leader in cellphone technology and manufacturing, the national telephone company TeliaSonera ran radio and newspaper ads in 2002 urging customers to give up their wired telephones for mobile cellphone. TeliaSonera operated DSL connections to the Internet, which can make better use of the 3.2 million copper wires that are the "last mile" to Finland's homes and businesses. This was an effort to do the *Negroponte flip*, the theory that what was wired would become wireless, and vice versa. Nicholas Negrponte, the founder of the MIT Media Lab, predicted in 1993 that limited spectrum would send wireless broadband into cable systems and would be matched by the demand for mobile phone services that would in time replace landline services.[37]

In country after country, newly formed companies have gone into business to sell a variety of communication services. Established national telephone companies have not accepted these changes or this competition quietly but have adapted new technologies themselves. It is much cheaper to set up a cellphone network than to erect telephone poles.

When full mobile satellite service is realized, a portable phone call could be placed between any two spots on Earth. The ultimate goal is to allow any two people anywhere with cellphones to talk to one another and see one another with the clarity that attends digital communication. With the camera phone rapidly being diffused into society, those conversations across continents will undoubtedly someday be routinely accompanied by letting the people who are speaking look at each other, and also see what the other is seeing, another step in the ongoing effort to shrink the globe to a flat Earth.

▶ TIMELINE

1876   "Mr. Watson, come here. I want to see you." Bell invents the telephone.

Elisha Gray files phone patent application the same day Bell does.

1877	Edwin Holmes builds a telephone switchboard.
	Emile Berliner invents the microphone. So does David Hughes.
1878	Thomas Edison invents a better microphone.
	A telephone central exchange is established. Telephone directories are issued.
	Emma Nutt is the first woman hired as a telephone operator.
1879	Starting in Lowell, Massachusetts, telephone numbers replace names.
1888	To make a phone call, drop a coin in a public telephone box.
1891	A mortician, Almon Strowger, develops the dial phone and the switching exchange.
1900	Michael Pupin's loading coil extends the range of long distance calling.
1904	The telephone answering machine.
1907	U.S. Cavalry tests mobile phone; horse's flank provides the ground.
1913	AT&T pledges universal phone service, expands to rural areas.
1915	Americans average 40 phone calls a year.
	Long-distance phone lines connect New York and California.
1919	Automatic switching systems reduce need for phone operators.
1920	Multiplexing allows phone line to carry several simultaneous calls.
1921	Detroit police use mobile radios in their squad cars.
1927	Two-way AT&T radiophone service, United States to London, U.S.$75 for 5 minutes.
1929	Ship telephones can contact telephones ashore.
1935	First telephone call made around the world.
1937	Pulse Code Modulation, a precursor of digital dialing.
1941	Push button phone, Touch Tone dialing, microwave transmission.
1945	St. Louis gets a mobile radio-telephone service, but it's hard to hear.
1946	Area codes join phone numbers.
1947	From Bell Labs comes the transistor, replacing vacuum tubes.
1948	Claude Shannon's information theory; will aid phone communication.
1949	FCC approves radio channels linking mobile and landline phones.
	Model 500 phone combines a ringer and a handset.

1951	Direct (no operator) long distance calling begins.
1956	United States follows Sweden in using car phones that are not car radios.
	First trans-Atlantic telephone cable (Scotland to Nova Scotia).
1962	Telstar 1 launched; carries phone, data, television signals.
	In Illinois, digital transmission replaces the analog system.
1963	Touch-tone phone; ten push buttons replace rotary dial.
1964	Picturephone tested: Disneyland to New York World's Fair.
	Transpacific submarine telephone cable service begins.
	Drivers can dial car phones without need for operators.
1965	Nine of ten U.S. telephones can use direct distance dialing.
1968	911 calls for emergencies, a nationwide service.
1973	Martin Cooper of Motorola invents the personal mobile phone.
1974	Telephone "hot line" set up between the White House and the Kremlin.
	International digital voice transmission.
1975	Fiber optics improve communication; starts with U.S. Navy.
1977	In Chicago, AT&T transmits telephone calls by fiber optics.
1982	Caller ID.
1984	25,000 cellphone subscribers in United States.
1985	Drivers start making (risky) calls on cellphones.
1993	Nokia sends text messages between mobile phones.
	Rumors fly that cellphones cause brain cancer; sales continue to soar.
1994	Phone calls over the Internet: VOIP.
2000	From Japan, the camera-phone.
	Nokia cellphone eliminates external antenna.
	100 million cellphone subscribers in United States.
2001	Cellphone popularity drives Bell South out of pay phone business.
	3G high-speed data network.
2003	Skype lets us see each other.
2004	Survey identifies the cellphone as the chief American love/hate object.

2007   Smartphone iPhone surfs, emails, plays videos and tunes, makes calls, takes pictures.

2010   Portable phones get smarter, add apps.

Google introduces Nexus One smartphone.

▶ NOTES

1 Sigmund Freud, *Civilization and Its Discontents* (New York: W. W. Norton, 1961) 38.

2 Alvin F. Harlow, *Old Wires and New Waves: The History of the Telegraph, Telephone, and Wireless* (New York: D. Appleton-Century, 1936) 363.

3 George Basalla, *The Evolution of Technology* (Cambridge, UK: Cambridge University Press, 1988) 98.

4 Marion May Dilts, *The Telephone in a Changing World* (New York: Longman's Green, 1941) 11.

5 Darrell Ehrlick, *It Happened in Minnesota* (Guilford, CT: Morris Book Publishing, Pequot Press, 2008) 52.

6 Harlow, 365–366.

7 George P. Oslin, *The Story of Telecommunications* (Macon, GA: Mercer University Press, 1992) 227.

8 Harlow, 377.

9 Harlow, 420–421.

10 John Brooks, *Telephone: The First Hundred Years* (New York: Harper & Row, 1976) 94.

11 Before email and Twitter became so widely used, the author asked students to identify the one communication device in the home they would be most reluctant to lose; invariably it was the telephone.

12 Dilts, 15.

13 *Washington Afro-American*, May 1, 1956, http://news.google.com/newspapers?id=h_UlAAAAIBAJ&sjid=qfQFAAAAIBAJ&pg=820,5514413.

14 The website of the Telephony Museum offers a brief overview, and lists books that provide much more information: http://www.telephonymuseum.com/telephone%20history.htm.

15 Brooks, 108.

16 Brooks, 187.

17 James R. Beniger, *The Control Revolution* (Cambridge, MA: Harvard University Press, 1986) 285.

18 Oslin, 281.

19 See NASA's website for a timeline of significant events in the development of satellite communications: http://history.nasa.gov/SP-4217/app-b.htm.

20 Thomas L. Friedman, *The World Is Flat* (New York: Farrar, Straus, and Giroux, 2005).

21 According to a report by the Pew Research Center: http://www.pewinternet.org/files/2014/02/PIP_25th-anniversary-of-the-Web_0227141.pdf.

22 *Newsweek*, March 14, 2011: 71.

23 Clive Thompson, "Watching the Watchers," *Wired*, July 2011: 52.

24 *Newsweek*, March 20, 2006: 80.

25 *The New York Times*, October 22, 2009, http://well.blogs.nytimes.com/2009/10/22/what-clown-on-a-unicycle-studying-cell-phone-distraction/?_php=true&_type=blogs&_r=0.

26 The Mayo Clinic presents one view of the controversy: http://www.mayoclinic.org/healthy-living/adult-health/expert-answers/cell-phones-and-cancer/faq-20057798.

27 Reported on *ZD Net*, May 12, 2011, http://www.zdnet.com/blog/gadgetreviews/can-you-bzzzz-me-now-study-says-cell-phones-are-killing-honey-bees/24673.

28 In 1997, proud father Philippe Kahn sent pictures of his just born daughter from his cellphone to 2,000 relatives, friends, and business associates. It was the start of instant visual communication. The story can be found at *USA Today*, http://usatoday30.usatoday.com/tech/columnist/kevinmaney/2007-01-23-kahn-cellphone-camera_x.htm.

29 For Samsung's heart-rate monitor, see: http://www.health24.com/Medical/Heart/News/Samsung-adds-heart-rate-monitor-to-smartphone-20140225. Nascent Stuff offers a list of the best Android apps for women: http://nascentstuff.com/best-android-apps-for-women/.

30 92% cellphone penetration in 2011, reported in the CIA World Factbook, https://www.cia.gov/library/publications/the-world-factbook/geos/cb.html.

31 For a discussion of these changes, with examples, see *The Economist*, September 26, 2009, special section following page 58.

32 *The Economist*, September 26, 2009, special section, 8.

33 Pew Research Center, "Which Developing Nation Leads on Mobile Payments? Kenya," February 18, 2014, http://www.pewresearch.org/fact-tank/2014/02/18/which-developing-nation-leads-on-mobile-payments-kenya/.

34 *The Economist*, January 9, 2010, 72.

35 *The Economist*, September 26, 2009, special section, 6.

36 According to mobiThinking, http://mobithinking.com/mobile-marketing-tools/latest-mobile-stats/a#subscribers.

37 Joseph N. Pelton, "Overview of Satellite Communications," in Iida, Pelton, and Ashford (eds.), *Satellite Communications in the 21st Century: Trends and Technologies* (Reston: American Institute of Aeronautics and Astronautics, 2003).

7 Recording: Beyoncé Sings Better than Our Sister

Every tribe on Earth responds to music. Melodies from voices and instruments lie at the heart of every culture. Yet, mediated communication has changed the centuries-old custom of listening to the expressions of our own culture, music we create ourselves, indifferent to a throat's rasp or a finger's slip. Instead, we prefer the refined and packaged expressions of many cultures. Professional audio fidelity is at our touch in endless quantity. After all, Beyoncé, One Direction, and Maroon Five do it much better than sister Susie or neighbor Joe.

Hold an iPod in your hand, and any of your thousands of music selections comes flooding into your ears. All of this is improbably stored in a shiny device not much bigger than a pocket comb. Whether anyone needs thousands of songs at the push of a button is not the point. Technology makes them available.

The old-fashioned pleasures can still be found, if we make the effort, in karaoke, the beat-up piano, or impromptu guitar strumming when friends gather, but recordings by professionals set our standards. The clever marketing and immense popularity of the iPod, its competitors, and the iTunes library of music have tapped into a deep love of music in the human spirit. Listeners today may know more *types* of music than our great grandparents knew *tunes*. Do you like classical symphonies? You have them, along with new age music, rock, jazz, reggae, Latin, Christian music, country music, hip-hop, movie soundtracks, Broadway show tunes, grand opera, melodies of any nation, or whatever else suits your fancy. Just turn the dial or push the button.

▶ WHAT IS LOST

Few things come into our lives without a price. Beyond the 99 cents we pay to download a song, we give up listening to Susie warble or Joe pound on the piano. It is the price of a loss of self-expression. The air guitar and the audio mix do not quite compensate for family closeness. In earlier times families might gather in the evening to listen to Mother or Father read aloud or sing. Except for bedtime stories, that practice has gone the way of high-button shoes. Instead, by choosing recorded music over the enthusiastic music we make ourselves, we extend our choices well beyond those of our own culture. The music of other cultures that we hear is of our own choosing, not our tradition.

Until the phonograph was invented, unless you were rich there were no means other than books and magazines to bring mediated professional entertainment into the home. The phonograph led the way, followed by radio, television, cable, audiotape, VCRs, DVDs, and the Internet. Certainly more will come. As the communication theorist Marshall McLuhan put it, the phonograph broke down the walls of the music hall.[1] Other technology broke down the walls of sports arenas, auditoriums, and cinemas. The Walkman family and their i-descendants have drilled further, burrowing into the walls of our homes, our cars, and our pockets.

▶ RECALLING THE PHONOGRAPH

Recording began when age-old dreams of capturing the human voice were realized during the last quarter of the 19th century. As a result, music has crumbled old cultural boundaries and has moved in new directions. Recording brought jazz out of the confines of the African American milieu, just as it carried Irish folk songs beyond their Irish roots, and we have learned to appreciate gypsy tunes, Latin tunes, Arab music, Indian music, Chinese music, and dozens of others.

The first device to deliver recorded sound, Thomas Edison's phonograph, was invented in 1877, about the time of its sister invention, the telephone, extending—for the first time since humans began to speak—the sound of the voice beyond the distance someone could shout. By capturing the voice, recording caught some of the unique personality of the individual.

Both the phonograph and the telephone were results of research into improving the telegraph, with the difference that the telephone was an intended invention. The phonograph came out of an accidental discovery, so unusual that the U.S. Patent Office, looking for connections to other inventions, could find nothing like it. The first invention remotely like the phonograph was Thomas Young's device, built in England in 1807, to trace the amplitude of sound vibrations by means of a stylus on a cylinder blackened with smoke.

In France, a half century after Young's invention, Leon Scott's "phonautograph" used a similar stylus to record the sound of a voice, but could not replicate an actual voice. Again in France, 29 years later, in 1877, the impoverished poet Charles Cros, in a sealed letter left at the Académie

An advertisement for Edison's phonograph, circa 1885.

des Sciences in Paris, described a device that reproduced the voice so that the deaf could hear what was said. This was the country where in 1829 Louis Braille had published his reading system as an aid to the blind. In the same year that Cros left his note, Edison designed a microphone and a voice-recording device, one year after Alexander Graham Bell and Elisha Gray had invented competing voice-transmitting devices.

▶ "WHOOOOO"

In 1877, while trying to adjust the rate of telegraph transmission, Edison heard a musical note at a certain speed. Curious, he pursued the sound by putting a new piece of paper in the revolving disc he was working with and, as he described it, shouted "Whooooo." Sending the paper back through the machine, he heard his voice faintly. He tried it again with some words from a nursery rhyme: "Mary had a little lamb. Its fleece was white as snow." He listened with amazement as the first words ever recorded came back to him.

Always the businessman, Edison thought of recording as a business tool. He made several improvements, but the quality of the tinfoil phonograph he constructed gave no promise of commercial success, so he put it aside to concentrate on the electric light bulb.[2] However, other inventors took up the talking machine, leading Edison a decade later to rethink his dismissal of its commercial possibilities. Increasingly deaf, he did not at first focus on music, but instead considered the potential for dictation, books for the blind, talking dolls, and even a record of someone's dying words that relatives might want to preserve. Edison took out patents for his microphone, a phonograph that played cylinders, and a battery-operated motor.[3] For its potential as a court-recording device, two Supreme Court stenographers were franchised to sell the equipment in Washington, DC, and Maryland. The product did not sell as a business tool, but their company, the Columbia Phonograph Company, would one day become CBS, the Columbia Broadcasting System. Edison took several of his inventions to an exposition in Paris, where he set up listening booths for the phonograph.

When his phonograph cylinders were improved enough to provide entertainment that could return income, Edison placed "automatic phonograph parlors" in stores all over the nation. For a penny or a nickel listeners could put a sound tube against their ears to listen to singers, whistlers, instrumental soloists, and humorists, or that most popular choice of all, a marching band. John Philip Sousa, the brass-band director and composer, saw with some discomfort that the phonograph was creating an appetite for professional music at the expense of what could be produced at home: "With the phonograph, vocal exercises will be out of vogue! Then what of the national throat? Will it not weaken? What of the national chest? Will it not shrink?"[4]

Listeners sat with rapt expressions or burst out laughing at the new entertainment.[5] The well-lit phonograph parlors, with rugs and potted plants providing a homey touch, attracted families, couples who shared listening tubes, and young women whose entertainment choices were limited by Victorian propriety. There were also home versions of the machines on which their owners could record. Columbia's advertising slogan was, "That Baby's Voice in a Columbia Record." Attractive as this feature might be, buyers really wanted the phonograph to play records by professional singers and musicians.

Further improvements came from Emile Berliner, who had invented a microphone and improved Bell's telephone in 1879. For his Gramophone (1887), Berliner used records with lateral grooves instead of the up-and-down "hill and dale" tracks, a coating of fat as its wax, and, most important of all, a flat disc instead of a cylinder. The disc was part of a master system that stamped out records, an efficient and cheap way to produce them. One customer brought his hand-cranked Gramophone to the New Jersey machine shop of Eldridge Johnson, who became so intrigued with the notion of recorded music that he went into the business himself, worked for six years to improve the sound, and joined Berliner to found the successful Victor Talking Machine Company in 1901.[6]

▶ THE PUBLIC WANTS MUSIC

Victor Red Seal records recorded operatic music, a far cry from the turkey-in-the-straw tunes that Edison preferred.[7] This was also the period when Scott Joplin produced some of his best music, such as *The Maple Leaf Rag* (1899), which combined the syncopation of African American folk music with European romanticism. Then came jazz. Increases in sheet music sales reflected a public enthusiasm for playing the music. The recording industry was still quite young when the public indicated their preference for packaged music over homemade. As an observer wrote in 1893, "The home wears a vanishing aspect. Public amusements increase in splendor and frequency, but private joys grow rare and difficult, and even the capacity for them seems to be withering."[8]

The phonograph player, augmented by a large horn, went into lecture halls. A smaller version would find a central place in the home, but might have to be disguised as a kind of furniture to civilize it. When the Victor Company encased its machine in a wooden cabinet and replaced the large external horn with an internal horn, its "Victrola" looked like furniture and truly belonged in the family parlor. Millions would be sold.

A new culture was born. The excitement fueled by recorded music sparked a strong interest in new dances such as the one-step, the turkey trot, and the tango around the time of World War I. To an older generation accustomed to decades of Victorian morality, the American dance craze and the rising popularity of jazz were part of a disturbing pattern of accelerating change.

Machines that delivered sound and machines that one day delivered pictures created at a distance would multiply in different rooms of the home and spread to the family car. In miniature form they would find a place on the body during walks, jogs, and bicycle rides. Family meals would be eaten within earshot of the machines. Conversation would stop. Visitors vied for attention with the radio or television. The food industry produced TV dinners to serve the new mode of living. The notion that people could take media or leave them alone now seems quaint. Nothing indicates that mediated communication can be ignored.

Music recorded electrically went on sale in 1925 during the "flapper" era. It was the start of high fidelity and of public interest in the technology of "hi-fi." Engineers improved every audio element between the microphone and the speaker. They replaced mechanical systems with electronics and added pre-amps and amplifiers. Vacuum tubes would remain in wide use until transistors replaced them after World War II. Bell Labs created stereophonic sound. The public was introduced to "stereo" in Walt Disney's animation film *Fantasia*. First adopters could now listen to music of concert hall quality in their living rooms.[9]

When the public was introduced to high fidelity, the prevailing wisdom in the boardrooms of the radio and recording industries was that the majority of the public would not pay for it. That was challenged by a number of audio engineers whose speakers for the home market set new standards. They included such names as James Lansing, Henry Kloss, Paul Klipsch, and Rudolph Bozak.

Sapphire-tipped needles instead of steel needles, condenser microphones instead of ribbon mikes, and turntables without rumble made a difference, but the scratchy clay-and-shellac 78 rpm (revolutions per minute) recordings limited to five minutes of playing time were still a barrier to listening purists. Peter Goldmark of CBS alleviated the problem in 1948 with the better sound and longer wear of the LP (long playing) record made of plastic, thinner, lighter material that was played at a slower 33 ⅓ rpm and provided 23 minutes of music on each side. RCA responded with the small, cheap 45 rpm disk in a variety of colors, just right for an exciting and controversial new kind of music delivery, one song per side. Young consumers loved it.

NIPPER

The most famous advertising painting ever done was of a dog named Nipper listening with his head cocked to a phonograph record. It was called *His Master's Voice*.

His Master's Voice (Francis Barraud, 1898).

Named because he nipped at visitors' legs, Nipper lived in England and died in 1895. Artist Francis Barraud, who acquired the terrier after his brother died, recalled how puzzled he was to hear a voice from a cylinder recording. Three years after Nipper died, Barraud painted the scene from memory.

He sold the painting to the Gramophone Company on condition that he replace the cylinder machine with a flat disk Gramophone machine. The final painting over the years became the logo for a number of audio recording companies.

▶ MUSIC CHOICES

Choice of music was traditionally influenced by economic class and ethnicity. People listened to what their cultural and family community knew. At the start of the age of recording most people preferred the lively melodies that reflected their own roots. Wealthy patrons of the arts, who shared a European heritage, supported classical music in the grand European tradition, the staid music of drawing rooms, symphony halls, and opera houses, plus their own folk songs and dances.

Finding new types of music and entertainment in recordings, people later tuned their radios to what they liked. Recorded music offered new and enriching choices to multitudes of listeners. All were accommodated by the expanding recording industry.

In Cleveland, disc jockey Alan Freed discovered that white teenagers in large numbers were dancing to the African American music known as "rhythm and blues." He helped to bring it into the mainstream, called it "rock 'n roll" (a phrase from a 1923 song by Trixie Smith) and rejected accusations that he was corrupting a generation. It took white performers, notably Elvis Presley, to broaden the appeal of rock, leading in time to a general acceptance of not only the music but also the performances of African American musicians during the second half of the 20th century.[10] Performer Jackie Wilson said, "A lot of people have accused Elvis of stealing the black man's music when, in fact, every black solo entertainer copies stage mannerisms from Elvis—had always wanted to be like Elvis."[11]

The white teenagers of the 1950s and 1960s who fervently embraced the new music over the objection of their parents would themselves get heartburn a generation later when their own children used a different recorded music genre to identify and separate themselves. Each generation's children adapt to the available media offerings and use them for their own purposes, such as independence.

Recordings can lead to political response. If you can remember the scene in *Casablanca* when French and German nightclub patrons competed in singing patriotic songs, you will recall how they stirred emotions. Tin Pan Alley churned out many recorded songs during World War II, such as "The White Cliffs of Dover" and "Coming in on a Wing and a Prayer." German soldiers had "Lili Marlene" to rake up memories of home.

Emotions were also stirred in 1985 by "We Are the World," which helped to raise U.S.$50 million to buy food and medicine for drought-stricken regions of East Africa, and did so again in 2010 for Haiti. Different emotions were touched by rap, which became a source of identity but was also accused in its early years of demeaning women and spreading hate. There were arguments that some recordings should be labeled "dangerous," like cigarettes. The organization Parents Music Resource Center was formed in 1985 with the stated goal of increasing parental control over the access of children to violent music. Tipper Gore, wife of former vice president Al Gore, was one of its founders.

▶ JUKEBOXES

A 1957 Tin Pan Alley single by Marilyn Fiore.

Phonographs with coin box attachments, invented in 1890, foreshadowed the jukebox. Gaudy, neon-lit jukeboxes made by Wurlitzer and other manufacturers later were featured attractions in bars and restaurants. A nickel offered a popular song from a menu of several dozen selections. The patron watched as a mechanical arm plucked the desired record from its berth, then returned it at the end of play. Still later, smaller versions were installed at tables and along the bar. Prices rose. Patrons danced to the music, listened, or talked over it, but seldom ignored it totally.

Under pressure from the musicians union, the radio networks before World War II banned recorded music, but following the war and the arrival of television, radio needed a new format to survive. Recordings and the disc jockeys who played them came to dominate the radio dial. Radio needed records for programming. The record industry needed radio as sales promotion.[12] One public change that emerged from this was that life became noisier. Once heard only when people actively listened to it, music was now also background to accompany other activities.

Another kind of recorded music was actually intended to be ignored by the conscious mind while it worked to soothe the mood of shoppers. The Muzak company hired arrangers who reworked passages of popular tunes to create melodies that were heard as background music, a pastel environment meant to relax shoppers. Critics derided Muzak and called it "elevator music," but its omnipresence indicated that it did its job. There were even reports of its success in the farmer's barn to soothe cows and chickens as a means of producing more milk and eggs.

▶ AUDIOTAPE

In an 1888 experiment, Oberlin Smith noted that iron filings on a piece of paper rearranged themselves into arcs when a magnet was passed under them. He theorized that permanent magnetic impulses could record sound. Danish inventor Valdemar Poulsen proved it in an experiment with steel wire. Poulsen demonstrated his "Telegraphone" in 1900, expecting that it could become a telephone answering machine or a music recorder and playback device. However, he lacked the funding to accomplish any of this. Success came to another inventor in 1928 in Germany, when Fritz Pfleumer built a prototype of a tape recorder, and the I. G. Farben chemical firm began its long history of manufacturing audiotape.

Magnetophon audiotape recorders that delivered better sound quality than phonograph records were one of the best-kept German secrets of World War II. Allied shortwave listeners who heard music with excellent fidelity from the Berlin Philharmonic in the middle of the night finally realized that the Germans had moved far ahead in sound recording.[13] The Allies had nothing better than steel bands and steel wire as magnetic recording media. American radio journalists using portable wire recorders not only had to endure poor audio quality, but a break in the taut hair-thin steel wire could cause a snarl worse than a fishing line tangle.

As World War II ground to an end, U.S. Army Signal Corps engineer John Mullin discovered audiotape recorder/players at a German radio station. "Liberating" two of them, he brought them to the United States. Mullin was hired by singer Bing Crosby to tape his radio shows for later playback. Mullin would, in a few years, help to invent videotape.[14]

Bing Crosby, among the most popular radio stars at the time, was one of the first to pre-record his show with the new technology.

Tape changed radio news in fundamental ways because listeners could hear taped interviews and ambient sound, everything from artillery to crying babies. Reporters could edit tape with a snip of the scissors and a bit of adhesive tape. The superior sound of audiotape also replaced phonograph turntables, first in radio studios, then in the home. The early tape players were reel-to-reel. These gave way to the endless loop cartridge player, first four-track, later eight-track. They in turn were replaced by the simpler cassette, introduced in 1963.

▶ VIDEOTAPE

Videotape has yielded to digital recording and storage, so it is easy to forget its impact. The explosive growth of television in the 1950s sharpened a demand for recorded programs. In 1951, seeking an electronic solution, engineers at Bing Crosby Enterprises demonstrated a black-and-white videotape recorder that used 1 inch tape running at 100 inches a second. Crosby was driven not only by its business possibilities, but by his wish to play golf without being tied down to live performances. Two years later, RCA engineers fabricated their own recorder, which turned out not only black-and-white, but also color pictures. However, this tape ran past the heads at 360 inches a second, which is more than 20 miles per hour. It was just not possible to produce a stable picture at such a high tape speed.

In 1956 a California firm, Ampex, built a machine on a different principle. Instead of sending the tape racing past a stationary recording head, its engineers spun the recording head. The quality was a tremendous improvement over fuzzy kinescope images. Visiting engineers who saw the first demonstration actually jumped to their feet to applaud. Programs could now be recorded for playback at any time. Stations on the West Coast could delay live East Coast network news and entertainment broadcasts to be aired during evening prime time, when most viewers were home after work and had eaten dinner. A few years later, sports fans could watch instant replay.

One of the engineers on the tape project, Ray M. Dolby, began work on audiotape just after he left high school and later grew famous for his tape noise reduction process.

After videotape recording—VTR—went portable in 1967, news film cameras became obsolescent. Videotape was reusable and was more suited to the television medium than film. Photographers used portable machines in the field to cover news stories that were microwaved back to the station. As the technology improved further, television news editors stopped cutting tape with razor blades and began editing electronically, marking the start of ENG (electronic news gathering). For the audience, this meant more pictures at the scene of news events, more coverage of late breaking news, and live reports combining commentary by a reporter at the scene with videotape of earlier activities.

With broadcasting, educational, and industrial markets in hand, Japanese video companies turned their attention to the vast home market. Sony president Akio Morita asked, "People do not have to read a book when it's delivered. Why should they have to see a TV program when it's delivered?"[15]

Sony introduced its half-inch Betamax machine in 1975. A year later, rival Japanese companies led by JVC brought out VHS (Video Home System) machines, a format incompatible with Betamax. Sony lost the competition. In 1983 the VHS-C camcorder, combining a camera and a recorder, captured the home market. Tapeless camcorders came along in 2003. Unlike film, videotape required no lab processing and was instantly available for viewing. Camcorders were one of the most popular devices ever sold.

After DVD players pushed them aside, it was easy to forget that videocassette recorders had been the fastest-selling domestic appliance in history. DVD players would sell even faster. A *Wall Street Journal* poll reported, not surprisingly, that people most desired those inventions that gave them convenience and control.[16] (See the section on "Renting or Owning" on page 216 for a reference to video rental stores.)

▶ NEW WAYS TO LISTEN

The Sony Walkman, the personal audio cassette player with earphones introduced in 1979, was the first of an enormously popular line of listening devices that changed how people listened to music. It arrived about two decades after the small, battery-operated transistor radio, but worn on the body and using earphones, it was more portable. For the first time people could take their favorite music, a part of their environment, with them anywhere. The Walkman line was expanded to include radio, compact discs, and even television. The unpleasant news that earphones from the

Walkman to the iPod could lead to hearing loss did not seem to deter sales. The portable cocooning that earphones offered, a bubble of privacy amid the urban hubbub, trumped hearing worries. Willing to risk hearing loss, users again adapted to a communication tool.

The closing decades of the 20th century saw rapid changes in audio technology and public acceptance that waxed and waned with each introduction of new home audio equipment. The number of audiophile early adopters sharply increased, spurred by clever marketing.

Not every innovation was snapped up. Quadraphonic sound systems and recordings did not catch on. The compact disc (CD) player, introduced in 1982, was not an immediate hit because of competing, non-compatible formats. Other devices popular in the 1990s included the digital compact cassette (DCC) and the MiniDisc (MD), but they were not compatible with anything else or with each other. Ultimately, the CD won out over other technologies. Its optical pickup head did not make physical contact with the disc, a huge advantage, but it suffered the disadvantage that the home user at first was not able to record.

Digital audiotape (DAT) and tapeless recording angered and frightened the music industry because owners could copy music without losing audio quality. In a precursor to the Napster court battles, music industry spokesmen lobbied for federal legislation to force Japanese manufacturers of DAT players to modify these machines to prevent illegal copying. To no one's amazement, the manufacturers resisted. Copying was, after all, one reason why people bought machines.

At the end of the 20th century, the MP3 software format for compressing and transmitting files was welcomed because of the ease of downloading music from the Internet. The music-downloading Napster was born in 1999, but was soon silenced by court order because of its advocacy of illegal downloads. It was reborn selling downloads legally. In 2001, Apple's iPod MP3 player, which legally downloaded songs for 99 cents each from its iTunes online music store, was immediately and extraordinarily successful. It met the desire for choice, advertised as putting "1,000 songs in your pocket." In 2011 Napster merged with Rhapsody, another company offering music downloads to mobile devices.

Whereas the original Walkman tape player was based on an analog audio format, the iPod was a digital player that could hold several thousand songs. The shuffle feature of random play added to the pleasure of iPod listeners. Dusty attics bore the weight of still shiny but already outdated audio devices and recordings.

Meanwhile, the video iPod was being used to view movies and television programs easily downloaded on computer hard drives. It was one more process to worry entertainment moguls. At the same time, owners of CD collections were transferring them to iPods. In less than a lifetime, the technology has gone from standard 78s to LPs and 45s to reel tape to cartridges to cassettes to CDs to home digital storage, and to digital storage in the cloud.

The growing popularity of audio books met the public's wish for listening choices beyond music. While music has been the dominant product of digital audio technologies for the home market, the public also bought audiotapes and compact discs of spoken content. Audio renditions of novels were sold at bookstores, groceries, gas stations, and convenience stores. The visually impaired have also been appreciative users. For many people, audio books provided an opportunity to listen to a self-help book, a good novel, or a language lesson during a long, humdrum daily commute. They made being stuck in traffic an educational opportunity.

▶ BOOMBOX AND WALKMAN

Music stored on a medium that traveled became more than personal entertainment. It developed into both an irritant that reached into the private space of others and a shield that blocked the outside world from intruding into the user's own private space. Both were uses that their inventors had not considered. Walkman and boombox owners may have been trying to control some acoustical space, but they have affected human interaction in two important yet contradictory ways. First, music pouring out of car radios and hand-carried boombox players at volumes louder than needed for hearing is an expansion of personal space, a challenge to anyone in the listening vicinity. At the same time it is an invitation for a friendly response from those who share those musical tastes. In short, recorded music is a social instrument, even a weapon, and the boombox owner is making a statement.[17]

The opposite effect surrounds an iPod unheard by anyone but the earphoned listener, who tunes out the surrounding sound environment. It helps to make an unbearable job bearable and a monotonous job less so. It is company. Like so many other means of mediated communication, the incoming sound tunes out silence and the thoughts that inevitably accompany silence. Modern music is not a certain accompaniment to contemplation.

Sony founder Akio Morita originally thought the Walkman would offer a way to share music, a mistake he later admitted. "I originally thought it would be considered rude for one person to be listening to his music in isolation . . . We found that everybody seemed to want his or her own."[18] Media writer Steven Levy added, "The Walkman was not about sharing, it was about not sharing. It was a *me* machine, an object of empowerment and liberation."[19]

The now familiar vacant stare into mid-space continues as people listen to MP3 players, iPods, and iPhones as they walk, run, or ride a bicycle. Add drivers with cellphones and you have a community of isolated people occasionally bumping into each other with consequences. A *Washington Post* critic wrote about "the look and sound of the Walkman dead: the head cocked at a slight angle, the mouth gently lolling. The eyes flicker with consciousness but they don't see. They're somewhere else."[20] Author Richard S. Hollander added, "Look at the faces. They are blank. With earphones on, the individual closes out all outside stimuli. He is his own captive audience."[21]

▶ DOWNLOADING

If music delivered by an MP3 player with earphones isolates the listener, shared music does the opposite, at least at a distance through communication media. Exalted status comes from cool music libraries. Some owners of music collections offered them at no cost to their friends or to anyone who wanted to be a friend. Why not? They argued. They had bought the music. Why not share it with everyone everywhere? The distinction between inviting a friend home to listen to a song and sending the song to strangers via download was no big deal, they argued. Having come into their possession, the music and videos were theirs to do with as they wished. Their opinion, not shared by the courts, was reminiscent of the argument that cable signals that crossed your yard should be free for the taking.

Legal action proved difficult because the global nature of communication limits governments from prompt action across frontiers, further evidence of a weakening of nation-states in confrontation with a global community hooked on media, no matter how transitory that community may be. After Napster began downloading on a massive scale, Time Warner CEO Richard Parsons protested, "This isn't about a bunch of kids stealing music. It's about an assault on everything that constitutes the cultural expression of our society. Worst case scenario: The country will end up in sort of a cultural Dark Ages."[22]

The courts put a stop to Napster's free sharing but the desire to use downloading technology to acquire music remained. Along came iTunes in 2005 offering songs for 99 cents. Rdio, MOG, Earbits, Rhapsody, and other services followed with downloads and streaming available free or by subscription depending on the level of service. In 2011 Spotify combined with Facebook to make music sharing a mediated communication social event. Of course, music has been part of social events for many centuries, since humankind first began humming together.

With Spotify, Facebook "friends" can acquire their friends' playlists and listen to what their friends are hearing halfway around the world. Even if the friend lives down the block, it is not necessary to get together in person to share an evening of music listening. Like the telephone, we can reach out without touching. And we can listen on the go with smartphones as well as computers.

Piracy hurt the music industry, and the Internet only made it worse. Purchases of CDs and cassettes have been in long decline. Given the chance to buy a single track, a lot of listeners choose not to pay for an entire album. The 99 cent iTunes option has helped, but sales are still below what the industry was hoping for. Since the introduction of the iTunes Music Store in 2003, music sales in the United States have plummeted.[23]

However, at this writing, new music venues may be turning things around. Subscription services such as Spotify and the European supplier Deezer allow users to stream music either for a monthly fee or free in return for listening to commercials. Online radio services such as Pandora and iTunes Radio and the explosive growth of smartphones have also given musicians something to sing about.

▶ TIMELINE

1821   In England, Charles Wheatstone reproduces sound.

In France, Léon Scott's phonautograph is a forerunner of Edison's phonograph.

1869   John Hyatt's celluloid will lead to phonograph records, telephones.

1877   In France, Charles Cros invents the phonograph. It doesn't matter.

In America, Edison invents the phonograph. It adds to his fame.

1886   Sapphire stylus improves recorded sound.

1887   Emile Berliner's flat "gramophone" disk.

1888   Edison's cylinder phonograph is manufactured for the general public.

Engineer Oberlin Smith conceives of magnetic recording; does not build unit.

1889   Coin-operated phonographs, the first jukeboxes, are placed in bars and arcades.

1898   Artist Francis Barraud paints *His Master's Voice* of Nipper listening.

Valdemar Poulsen of Denmark records magnetic sound on a wire.

1900   Eldridge Johnson produces double-sided phonograph records.

1905   Phonograph records may be 6⅔ inch, 7 inch, 8 inch, 10 inch, 11 inch, 12 inch, 13¾ inch, or 14 inch wide.

1906   The phonograph gets a wooden cabinet; the Victrola is furniture.

1907   Lee De Forest broadcasts music from phonograph records.

1913   *Billboard* magazine publishes its first list of most popular songs.

1919   Americans spend more on records than on books, musical instruments.

1922   Muzak is developed by George Squier.

1925   Music recorded electrically starts high-fidelity popularity.

1928   In Germany, Fritz Pfleumer creates audiotape: magnetic powder on paper, film.

1935   Martin Block's *Make Believe Ballroom* introduces disc jockeys.

1939	The wire recorder is invented in the United States.
1945	Captain John Mullin "liberates" two German tape recorders; starts U.S. industry.
1948	LP (long playing) record: 25 minutes per side; replaces 4 minute records.
1949	RCA challenges the LP record with the one-song 45 rpm record.
1951	Disc jockey Alan Freed introduces the term *rock 'n roll*.
	Videotape experiments supported by Bing Crosby.
1956	Ampex invents a breakthrough videotape machine for networks, TV stations.
1958	Color videotape.
1959	The Grammy Awards, starting with the music of 1958, are presented.
1963	Phillips of Holland invents audiocassettes.
	From Sony: home videotape recorders.
1979	The Sony Walkman tape player, a new way to listen.
1980	Sony introduces the consumer camcorder.
1983	CDs (compact discs, not certificates of deposit) go on sale.
1984	CD-ROM disk holds equivalent of 270,000 typewritten pages.
1986	International standards are set for audio, video, digital recording.
1991	VCRs are the fastest selling domestic appliance ever; 4 billion tape rentals.
1997	DVD players and DVD movies are on the fast track to success.
1999	Napster is created to allow free music downloading.
2001	The iPod holds 1,000 tunes, but fits into a shirt pocket.
	Court ruling ends Napster's free sharing.
2011	Facebook and Spotify make music downloading a social networking tool.

▶ NOTES

1 Marshall McLuhan, *Understanding Media: The Extensions of Man* (Toronto, University of Toronto Press, 1964) 283.

2 George P. Oslin, *The Story of Telecommunications* (Macon, GA: Mercer University Press, 1992) 227.

3 Rutgers offers a complete breakdown of Edison's 1093 patents: http://edison.rutgers.edu/patents.htm.

4 Reported in McLuhan, 275.

5 Daniel Marty, *An Illustrated History of Phonographs* (New York: Dorset Press, 1981) 71.

6 B. L. Aldridge, *The Victor Talking Machine Company* (Camden, NJ: RCA Sales Corp., 1964), 118.

7 Carolyn Marvin, *When Old Technologies Were New* (New York: Oxford University Press, 1988), 203.

8 *Harper's Magazine*, September, 1893: 726.

9 David Lander, "Technology Makes Music," *Invention and Technology*, Spring/Summer, 1990: 63.

10 Christopher H. Sterling and John M. Kittross, *Stay Tuned: A Concise History of American Broadcasting* (Belmont, CA: Wadsworth Publishing Co., 2nd ed., 1990) 339–341.

11 *Pittsburgh Post-Gazette*, August 15, 2002, magazine section, 1.

12 Andrew F. Inglis, *Behind the Tube: A History of Broadcast Technology and Business* (New York: Focal Press, 1990), 19–20.

13 J. M. Fenster, "How Bing Crosby Brought You Audiotape," *Invention and Technology*, Fall 1994: 58.

14 "John (Jack) T. Mullin (1913–1999) Recalls the American Development of the Tape Recorder," http://community.mcckc.edu/crosby/mullin.htm.

15 *The Wall Street Journal* September 19, 1989, B1.

16 Timothy J. Mellonig, "DCC and MD," in Grant, August E., and Kenton T. Wilkinson, eds., *Communication Technology Update, 1993–1994* (Austin: Technology Futures, Inc., 1993) 191–196.

17 For an interesting discussion of this point, see Gary Gumpert, *Talking Tombstones and Other Tales of the Media Age* (New York: Oxford University Press, 1987) 91.

18 Hosokawa, Shuhei (1984) "The Walkman Effect," *Popular Music* 4: 165–180.

19 Steven Levy, *The Perfect Thing* (New York: Simon & Schuster, 2006) 34.

20 Cited by Steven Levy.

21 Richard S. Hollander, *Video Democracy* (Mt. Airy, MD: Lomond Publications, 1985) 132.

22 Levy, 207.

23 According to the Recording Industry Association of America, reported by Adrian Covert, "A Decade of iTunes Singles Killed the Music Industry," as reported on: http://money.cnn.com/2013/04/25/technology/itunes-music-decline/index.html.

8 Photography: Personal and So Much More

Not many centuries ago some of our ancestors believed they lived on a flat Earth patrolled at its edges by dragons and gryphons. If they wanted to know about the world, they could see graphic representations in a church where stained glass windows told Biblical stories in pictures. Some paintings told religious or mythic tales. Then came photography. By the mid-19th century ordinary people could see with their own eyes who or what actually lived beyond the horizon. Photography made the world less strange and more interesting.

Photography was invented before the telephone and the phonograph. Each impressed itself upon us through one of our five senses. Each has had effects beyond calculating. Yet, more than education or entertainment or political calls to action, the greatest effects of photography are personal. Our individual actions attest to the emotional impact of photographs. We put snapshots on our walls and furniture and display them on our mobile devices. They preserve the memories of what matters to us, capturing time and affirming our personal past. Fleeing a burning house, we may leave everything but a photo album that tells the family story. Our wallets hold the thumb-worn images of loved ones. Our computers may hold them by the hundreds. We treasure photographs of distant relatives we never met and search their faces for connections. We take "selfies."

Significant occasions in life seem to need a camera to record them. A wedding is incomplete without photographs; a memorial service means more with old photographs on display. Today, by the push of a few buttons of her camera phone, a young mother takes pictures of her children and transmits them instantly to her soldier husband on the other side of the world.

▶ MANY EFFECTS

Yet we know that photography has affected our lives in so many other ways. The Holocaust photos told the world "never again." During the 1980s photos of the eyes of starving African children with flies hovering at their edges launched cargo planes filled with medicines, blankets, food, and doctors. The pained eyes of brutalized women in Somalia, Rwanda, Bosnia, Congo, and Darfur have shaken the world. Degrading photos of Abu Ghraib prisoners have outraged a nation that prided itself as being above such acts.

The noted photographer Gordon Parks said such pictures change those who see them: "One should not grow tired of witnessing these things—corpses stacked, awaiting the fire of a Holocaust oven; two young black lynch victims, dead before a cheerful white mob; a Viet Cong guerrilla, his eyes tightly shut, grimacing as a policeman fires a bullet into his head—for that is the photographer's charge to us, that we never forget . . . The cameras keep watch as mankind goes on filling the universe with its behavior, and they change us."[1]

There is much, much more. The eyes of baby harp seals just before the fur hunter's club crashed down led in 2010 to a ban by the European Union on seal pelts and other products of the slaughter, just one of many examples of how photographs of animals being killed or abused have generated anger, humiliation, and change.

Photography has served every branch of science from electron microscope photos of the invisible world around and within us to the Mars pictures taken by the Spirit, Opportunity, and Curiosity rovers and the Hubble Telescope's probes for the origin of the universe. What is there that has not been captured through a lens? Photography today is a tool of every occupation, every kind of business, every hobby. As a tool of medicine, photography has helped to improve our health. As a tool of journalists, photography has generated both pride and feelings of despair at human behavior.

Documentary and travel photography have enriched our culture and our awareness of other cultures. Through pictures posted on Internet sites such as YouTube and Facebook, the digital age has enhanced our awareness of ourselves and the people around us. Photography is, in short, an essential part of our lives.

▶ ANCIENT ROOTS

Still photography is less than two centuries old and motion photography a little more than a century old, but the technology has ancient roots. Imagine a sunny street in an old city, a house with a dark room and a tiny hole in the wall facing the street. If you sit inside the room and look at the wall opposite the hole, you might see an upside down image of people walking by. Because the world is full of dark rooms with holes in the walls, this phenomenon has been known for centuries. Aristotle mentioned it in the fourth century BCE. The Arab scholar Alhazen described it at some length in the 11th century. Later, so did Leonardo da Vinci.

A 16th-century engraving demonstrating a camera obscura.

During the 16th century in Italy a room called a *camera obscura* that reflected images aided drafting and painting. The term comes from the Latin "*camera*" ("room") and "*obscura*" ("dark"). To sharpen the image, artists placed a lens over the pinhole. To preserve the image, they traced it onto a sheet of paper. By the 17th century portable rooms were built, usually a kind of tent. When the users realized that they did not actually have to stand inside the room to capture their image, the *camera obscura* shrank to a box carried under the arm, a herald of our own cameras.[2]

Each had a peephole, a lens, and sometimes a mirror, plus a pane of glass on which a thin sheet of paper could rest for tracing an image. An even smaller portable device, the *camera lucida*, invented in 1807, consisted of a glass prism suspended by a brass rod over a piece of paper. Looking through the prism, the artist traced an image. No other way existed to save an exact image, but photography was only a few years off.

Chemical discoveries in the previous century eventually helped to pave the way. For thousands of years it has been known that colors change outdoors, such as colored cloth that fades in the sunshine. It was also known that certain salts of silver darken in the open air, although it was not known if this was due to the air itself or the heat of the sun. In 1727 German scientist Johann Schulze observed that a bottle filled with a silver compound turned violet black on the side that was accidentally exposed to sunshine. Experiments confirmed that *light* was responsible.

About 1790 Thomas Wedgewood, of the family famed for fine china, produced photographic contact prints by placing a tree leaf against chemically treated paper that he exposed to light. In order to show his photographs to visitors, he had to display them for moments by dim candlelight before they blackened.

▶ NIÉPCE AND DAGUERRE

In 1827, precisely one century after Schulze's publication of his discovery and following a decade of experimentation, French inventor Joseph Nicéphore Niépce used a *camera obscura* to produce what until recently was considered the world's first true photograph, an image of the courtyard outside his window. In 2002, the French National Library paid about U.S.$500,000 for a photograph believed to have been taken a year earlier than Niépce's courtyard view, a photo of a Dutch engraving showing a man leading a horse. The photographer is unknown.

Niépce became partners with Louis Daguerre, a painter and theatrical producer, who was also trying to capture a camera image. After Niépce's death in 1833, Daguerre improved the process. In 1837 he produced a photograph of surprising quality on a copper plate coated with silver and exposed to iodine fumes. Daguerre named his result after himself, a daguerreotype. The exposed plate was the final picture; there was no negative.

In 1839 Daguerre delivered a significant paper to France's Academy of Sciences describing his process. It remains a mystery why a century elapsed between Schulze's discovery and the breakthrough experiments of Niépce and Daguerre.[3]

While Daguerre was experimenting in France, amateur English scientist William Fox Talbot, frustrated by the difficulties of drawing with the *camera lucida*, achieved some success in taking contact photographs by laying such objects as a leaf, a feather, and a piece of lace directly on sheets of translucent paper that had been treated with silver chloride. This method created a negative image, the dark and light areas reversed. The translucent paper allowed Fox Talbot to make any number of contact positives, something that Daguerre could not do.

The problem of the darkening image was solved in 1839 with sodium thiosulfate (still used today as a photo fixative, commonly called "hypo") followed by washing with water. Its discoverer, Sir John Herschel, an English scientist and a friend of Fox Talbot, also suggested the terms "photography" to replace Fox Talbot's phrase "photogenic drawing," and "positive" and "negative" to replace the terms "reversed copy" and "re-reversed copy."

Fox Talbot was soon taking pictures of buildings, rooftops, and chimneys. His choice of subject was dictated by their immobility and the need for a great deal of light. Only after years of chemical and optical improvements in photography was Fox Talbot able to take pictures of people, whom he posed stiffly with instructions not to move during the long exposure time his pictures required.

Both Daguerre, the French artist, and Fox Talbot, the wealthy English botanist, had been working independently and unaware of each other, yet they were producing similar pictures with similar chemicals and equipment. While Daguerre's results were far superior, Fox Talbot could make multiple copies of images.

▶ HOBBY AND BUSINESS

Photography as a hobby for the well-to-do spread across Europe and into North America as the technology improved. The daguerreotype process received an enthusiastic welcome in the United States even though the nation was entering an economic depression just as photography was being introduced in Paris in 1839 by Daguerre's paper and lecture to the Academy of Sciences.

Smaller cameras reduced the size of photographic plates, and reduced the time that a subject would have to sit without moving. With the aid of a portrait lens the time needed to pose dropped to a manageable 15 to 30 seconds. One reason subjects in early photos look grim is that it was hard to freeze a smile for so long, resulting in the stiff expressions on the faces staring at us in old photographs. Yet the subjects eagerly posed, sometimes aided by iron supporting stands that stiffened the spine and held the head in place. A photograph of Fox Talbot's half-sister playing (or leaning on) the harp is dated about 1842.[4]

Daguerreotypists took photos not only outdoors in the sunlight but also in the new portrait studios. Their brisk trade took business away from portrait painters such as the artist Samuel Morse, who was one of the earliest American experimenters in daguerreotype photography before he became famous for a different means of communication.

By the 1850s in the United States the cost of a photograph had dropped enough to make them available to most Americans. Miniature portrait paintings were available only to the wealthy, but miniature photographs were affordable to middle-class families.

Family pictures became popular, especially pictures of children, partly because of their high mortality rate. Many children died in infancy or while barely toddlers. Epidemics were common. Photographers in the mid-19th century advertised their readiness to take pictures of the dead in their coffins or for a child in a mother's lap. They appear to be sleeping. One advertising line for postmortem photographs was based on an old saying: "Secure the shadow 'ere the substance fade." A photograph of the deceased would also be mounted in a headstone. Such images were called "*memento mori*" (reminder of mortality).

▶ WET-PLATE PHOTOGRAPHY

The two known methods of taking photographs had severe limitations. *Daguerreotypes* were one-of-a-kind positives, usually on copper plates. They were fragile and had to be kept under glass. They were expensive, hard to copy, and required a number of chemicals, including the dangerous mercury.

The term "mad as a hatter," familiar to readers of *Alice in Wonderland*, could have been matched with "mad as a photographer," because mercury fumes used by both hat makers and photographers affect the brain. The daguerreotype produced a sharper image and was better suited to portraiture than the *calotype*, which was Fox Talbot's improvement on his original grainy and blotchy paper prints. Unfortunately, the calotype prints faded in the light over time. Daguerreotypes, which produced positive prints, could be used as the source for engraving.

In 1851, Frederick Archer introduced wet-plate photography. Within a decade, daguerreotype and calotype methods were obsolete. Wet-plate provided greater sensitivity and a shorter exposure time. It made multiple prints possible from one glass plate, although the process was complicated and untidy. Because photographs had to be developed immediately or the emulsion would dry, chemicals were applied in fairly rapid succession in darkness.

Using the wet-plate method, a photographer on the road brought along a darkroom. For a negative, a glass plate was coated with collodion, a clear, thick, sticky liquid that was also used as a surgical dressing. A layer of light-sensitive silver iodide was applied before the plate was inserted into the camera. After exposure, the still wet glass plate was developed, fixed, and washed on the spot before the negatives could be printed on paper. Photographers needed wagons to haul around hundreds of pounds of bottled chemicals, plus the glass plates, dishes, measures, funnels, and a water pail, to say nothing of the heavy camera, lenses, and tripod.[5]

One version of wet-plate photography was the *ambrotype*, offered by photo studios. Ambrotypes lacked the brilliance of daguerreotypes but they were cheap, easy to produce and, best of all, would be prepared while you wait. *Tintypes*, printed on iron sheets instead of paper, were sturdy enough to be mailed or carried in a shirt pocket, yet thin enough to cut with scissors to fit a brooch or locket. During the Civil War, soldiers mailed them to the families they left behind and received tintypes in return of mothers, brothers, sisters, wives, children. (Tintypes were shown in the film *Cold Mountain*.) Besides the familiar stiff portraits, photographers also took pictures of groups in a variety of activities and settings. Many still survive today.

▶ CAPTURING THE WORLD

The Western public had read and talked of the pyramids or of how different Asian cultures must appear in their exotic clothing. Now, realizing that they had in their hands a new way to record life, travelers using the new wet-plate system could hardly wait to haul their heavy cameras and darkroom equipment to distant corners of the world. When they returned home their photographs were projected on a screen or wall as lantern-slide shows, a popular form of entertainment.

In 1854, an album of photographs of ancient Egyptian monuments was published. Actual prints of photos were sewn into books. For the first time people could not only see but even own such images. However, the *printing* of photos on regular book pages along with text would have to wait until the art of *photoengraving* advanced sufficiently toward the end of the 19th century. After that, newspapers and magazines blossomed with photographs.

Artist Roger Fenton traveled in 1855 with fellow Englishman James Robertson and a darkroom in a covered wagon to the Crimean War. What Fenton saw appalled him, but he took no pictures of the horrors of war. In part because he had been commissioned to shoot only portraits of officers and scenes of the Crimea, and because he was suffering from cholera and several broken ribs as a result of an accident, Fenton spent little film on the misery of war. His task was made more difficult because collodion was a tricky chemical in the Crimea's summer heat.

Felice Beato, an Italian, and Robertson in 1858 recorded the aftermath of an uprising against the British in India. For the first time in history people safe at home saw a little of what went on in a war. Two years later Beato went to China to take pictures of the Opium Wars, then, with new partner Charles Wigman, on to fascinating Japan, newly opened to the outside world. Yet travel photographers sometimes encountered fear by those they photographed that taking a photo entrapped someone's spirit that would be left behind in the journey to the next life.

▶ CIVIL WAR PHOTOS AND MORE

A well-known New York portrait photographer, Mathew Brady, hired other photographers to join him to record the scars of Civil War battle. Several hundred photographers went to the site of battles, traveling in clattering wagons filled with the chemicals and equipment needed for wet-plate pictures. They took more than 7,000 pictures of battlefields, encampments, soldiers living and dead, officers and men, weapons and equipment. At newspaper and magazine offices, lithographers traced the photographs onto wooden blocks or copper plates for the printing presses. War coverage also included large maps for the first time, made possible by technology that eliminated the need for column rules.

The Civil War photographers revealed war stripped of glory—a brutal, wearying misery. Brady himself got so close to the action that he was nearly captured at the First Battle of Bull Run in 1861. When Brady displayed photos at a New York gallery of the dead of Antietam, the *New York Times* commented: "If he has not brought bodies and laid them in our dooryards and among our streets, he has done something very like it."[6]

Photography as an aid to science and medicine began. Studying pictures of how people walk, a physician designed artificial legs for maimed soldiers.

After the war, photographers headed West to continue what, in a few years, had evolved into a tradition of visual documentary. Piling 300 to

Dead Confederate artillerymen at the Battle of Antietam, as photographed by Mathew Brady and Alexander Gardner. Such images revealed to the public for the first time the horrors of war.

400 pounds of wet-plate equipment and chemicals on the backs of mules, they left to posterity a permanent record of the Native Americans, of great vistas without a trace of human habitation, of the coming of the railroads, of the miners, the settlers, the cowboys. William Henry Jackson's photographs helped in the political effort to establish Yellowstone as the first national park. This may have been the first time in the United States that photography influenced political change. It would not be the last.

Photography already had some influence in England. Photographers traveling to distant countries captured images of ordinary life to give visual support to what later would be called *ethnography*. The English traveler John Thomson recorded the life of the people he encountered in Asia. On returning to London he published a four-volume illustrated anthropological study. While in London he continued his documentation by photographing the daily life of the London poor, publishing the results along with written text in 1877 as *Victorian London Street Life*. In doing so, Thomson opened a new door for photography: social documentary. To a comfortable Londoner, scenes of poverty in far-off China were a quaint curiosity. Displaying poverty at your doorstep was something else again, especially if you were in a position to do something about it. Thomson usually photographed reasonably pleasant views in working-class neighborhoods, but not always. One subject for criticism was the failure to deal with annual floods that made life so miserable for those who lived along the Thames River.[7] Eventually an embankment was built to prevent the Thames from periodically spilling over into the slums of London.

▶ SOCIAL DOCUMENTARY

Journalists recognized photography as a means not only to present information but to stir emotion. Jacob Riis, a Danish immigrant hired as a New York City police reporter, was determined to reveal the humanity of the poor that the better-off frequently ignored. One of the first journalists to recognize that photographs could help to bring about social change, Riis used both words and pictures to expose conditions in the New York slums, starting in 1888. He went about his personal mission even when he panicked a roomful of people sleeping or actually set fire to himself and to a house by using flash powder, a recent invention that for the first time enabled photography in darkness. (The flashbulb would not be invented until 1925.) Riis's books, *How the Other Half Lives* and *Children of the Poor*, became an important part of muckraking, dredging up awful conditions for the public gaze.[8]

Sociologist Lewis Hine recorded the miserable lives of many immigrants who were pouring out of Europe onto Ellis Island. From there they often went to fetid homes and sweatshops where they eked out a threadbare existence. Hine followed with camera and notebook. In 1908 the National Child Labor Committee hired Hine as an investigator. He drew public attention to the plight of child workers. For the generations that followed, Hine built a searing record of documentary photography. "I wanted to show the things that had to be corrected," he said.[9] He focused especially on children sent to work in food processing plants, factories, and mines. He found them at every turn, but had to disguise his picture-taking and fact-gathering missions to avoid beatings, or worse. He sometimes pretended to be a fire inspector to avoid detection.

Hine showed his photos in public presentations as he carried his message about the need for child labor laws. He considered himself a social photographer. "Perhaps you are weary of child labor pictures," Hine wrote. "Well, so are the rest of us, but we propose to make you and the whole country so sick and tired of the whole business that when the time for action comes, child labor pictures will be records of the past."[10] Publication of his photos in magazines, books, slide shows, and traveling exhibits stirred efforts against heavy opposition to pass child labor laws that took children out of the mines and factories and into schools.[11]

During the Depression of the 1930s, the Resettlement Administration (RA) was created as part of the New Deal to help small farmers who were driven to bankruptcy because of years of drought in the central and southern states. Crop failures were all too common. Topsoil disappeared down rivers. To help argue its case, the RA turned to social documentary photography. Both still and motion pictures were used to show how bad the rural economy was and how government aid could make a difference. Dorothea Lange, Walker Evans, Carl Mydans, Horace Bristol, and Ben Shahn were among those whose photographs have endured through the decades.

From the wellspring of feeling for the downtrodden and anger at social injustice sprang the social documentary motion picture. This was especially

Lewis Hine in 1911 photographed Manuel, age 5, a shrimp picker at the Mississippi shore, standing in front of a mountain of oyster shells picked by children.

so in Great Britain and the United States. The tradition continues today and has spread internationally in both still and motion pictures. We are now accustomed to seeing images of misery on the streets of Syria, in the desert of Darfur in the Sudan, and in other pain-racked corners of the world.

▶ PHOTOENGRAVING

Documentary photographs found their way into, among other places, photo magazines. The most outstanding, *Life*, was first published in 1936. But the picture press itself had started earlier. In fact, it is just about as old as photography. The weekly *Illustrated London News* was first published in 1842 with engravings usually carved from daguerreotype photographs or artists' sketches into wooden blocks or onto copper plates.

At first, engravers laid tissue paper over a photograph to trace the image, which they transferred to a wooden block. Just before the Civil War, the engravers learned how to coat the surface of a wood block with light-sensitive silver nitrate. Placed in a camera pointed at a photograph, the wood block captured an image good enough to guide the engraver's knife.

Actual publication of photographs would not be possible without a technology that allowed an ordinary photograph to be printed on the same page as type. Until then, readers could find woodcuts next to letterpress type. That began in 1842 with *The Illustrated London News*. Its success was followed by competitors in England, France, and Germany. The main illustrated American magazines, starting just before the Civil War, were *Leslie's Weekly* and *Harper's Weekly*.

The first printed newspaper photograph was of New York's Steinway Hall in 1873, but the first fully captured image was of a New York slum, "A Scene in Shanty-Town." It appeared in the *New York Daily Graphic* in 1880. *Photoengraving* started in England. Results were poor until 1881, when Frederick Ives at Cornell University created a *halftone* process that broke a photograph into tiny dots that could pick up ink, giving the appearance of a continuous tone from light to dark. The *halftone* set pictures next to words, leading to one of the great advances in the history of mediated communication: *photojournalism*.

Although they could be seen in the pages of weekly journals and magazines, photographs would not become common in newspapers until the quality of newsprint—the paper itself   improved toward the end of the 19th century.

▶ MORE TECHNICAL IMPROVEMENTS

Based on 19th-century inventions, *offset lithography* became the basis of most photo publication in the 20th century. In the 21st century, the process of putting photos in newspapers has become entirely digital as an image moves from the photographer's camera to a page plate containing photographs and printed matter that will be mounted on a press.

From the beginning, photographers felt frustrated by the time it took to expose a picture. Because the early cameras lacked shutters, the photographer simply took the lens cap off for several seconds to expose the plate. As film improved, inventors formulated ideas for exposing the film for shorter and shorter time periods. Demand for stop-action pictures pushed the inventors of optical and mechanical equipment and photochemistry to bring new products to the marketplace. By the end of the 19th century, focal plane shutters, located between the lens and the film, could limit exposures to 1/1000th of a second.

The wet-plate process gave way to a gelatin silver bromide dry-plate process that provided even greater sensitivity and shorter exposure. It also freed the photographer from carrying a darkroom wherever he went. Yet as long as glass plates served as the recording medium base, cameras would remain bulky. Glass plates, limited by weight and fragility, required special chemicals and special handling.

These difficulties led to a search for a substitute material, something lightweight but flexible enough to be rolled around a spool, yet tough, transparent and impervious to photographic chemicals. Inventors turned to nitrocellulose, the source of collodion, an important chemical in glass plate photography. Simply put, they threw away the glass and kept a version of the sticky stuff that stuck to the glass. At first, flexible film on a roll holder was fitted to the back of a folding-bellows camera. Later, cameras small enough to hold in the hand plus fast shutters removed the need of a tripod.

During the 19th century it was common to color photo prints with paint. Retouching by hand was a feature of studio work. Delicate daguerreotypes demanded special care by colorists. By the turn of the 20th century, color film and color filters had become the basis of attractive color photographs.

Photography also became art. Alfred Stieglitz led a movement devoted to the idea of photographic art as a means of personal expression. Stieglitz and Edward Steichen built reputations rivaling painters who used brush and palette. Henri Cartier-Bresson, Ansel Adams, and Edward Weston followed them. Stieglitz pioneered the one-man show for photographers and founded *Camera Work*, a magazine for fine photographic art.

▶ TAKING YOUR OWN PICTURES

Having your picture taken is not nearly as desirable for most people as having your own camera. Changing technology and lower costs have enabled people all over the world to own cameras and participate in the making and acquiring of photographs of better and better quality.

A self-taught inventor in upstate New York, George Eastman was instrumental in making photography simpler and more affordable. Determined to make the camera "as convenient as the pencil," Eastman in 1888 introduced the Kodak, with roll film, fixed focus, fixed aperture and one speed. It reduced the somewhat complex process of taking a picture to the three steps of pulling a cord, turning a key, and pressing a button. The first Kodak was a wooden box encased in leather; it sold for U.S.$25.

Once they snapped their photos, owners returned the camera to the company, where the film was unloaded, processed by transferring negatives to glass plates for printing, and returned to the owner with paper prints and a fresh roll installed. Eastman's slogan was, "You Press the Button, We Do the Rest." His U.S.$10 charge for this service wasn't cheap, but if you could afford the hobby of photography it was certainly convenient.

By the 20th century some 50 different camera models were manufactured. Almost overnight, it seemed that everyone who could pay for a camera wanted to take pictures. The photographer did not need to understand chemistry when, for the first time, if you could press a button you could take a picture. As prices came down, millions of people carried cameras to outings and events. Camera clubs sprouted everywhere. Eastman said his cameras brought photography "within the reach of every human being who desires to preserve a record of what he sees."

When Eastman's Brownie camera in 1900 sold for U.S.$1 with a six-exposure roll of film that cost 15 cents, photography was truly available for "the man in the street." Eastman had designed the Brownie for children, but adults used it, too. Another Eastman slogan was, "Plant the Brownie acorn and the Kodak oak will grow." He also sold a developing and printing kit for 75 cents. Pictures that could be taken so easily came to be known by the same term as that used for firing a gun at a fast moving target: a snapshot.

▶ POSTWAR YEARS

The years following the end of World War II saw Americans flush with cash, soldiers returning to civilian life, ready to buy homes, cars, television sets, kitchen appliances. Into this happy situation came new models of the 35mm camera from Germany and Japan. The 35mm camera was just the thing to take along on that long delayed vacation. Some models were single-lens reflex. Some had rangefinders. The German Leica and Rolleiflex returned to the American marketplace along with Japanese newcomers Nikon, Canon, Minolta, Ricoh, and Pentax.

In 1947, Edwin Land's Polaroid camera process allowed film development and printing inside the camera. The back of the camera carried separate negative and positive film rolls. The act of tugging the film out of the camera pulled it between two rollers that broke small pods of developing fluid, spreading them evenly across the film surface. One minute later the positive print was ready to peel away. This "instant print" process was available in color by 1963. It combined the negative and positive materials in a single unit, thanks to fourteen separate coatings.

Obtaining quality pictures required training, practice, and skill. But help for everyone came from Japan with the point-and-shoot, automatic everything camera with coated lenses and synchronized internal flash. The focus adjusted instantly to whatever stood in front of the lens. Like so many inventions, the camera itself grew more complicated in order to make its operation simpler. French sociologist Jacques Ellul offered the same point about computers: they become more complex as they grow easier to use.[12] Cameras now are crammed with micro-circuitry and intricate mechanical and optical parts, yet the instrument responds to the press of a button by a child. Eastman's old advertising slogan, "You press the button, we do the rest," could hardly be truer for the automated single-lens reflex camera controlled by computer chips and infrared sensors.

The filmless camera arrived from Japan in 1981 with Sony's Mavica, but only as a prototype. It did not go into full production because of its poor images. Five years later another Japanese firm, Canon, marketed a better camera. The SVC (still video camera) popular in the late 1980s recorded images onto a small magnetic disk. Without chemical processing and after transmission over ordinary telephone lines or by satellite, stills were immediately available for viewing on television screens around the world. One day they would be posted on websites.

One of the social effects of the digital revolution has been to enable average people to do what only professionals using expensive equipment were able to do in the past.[13] Great numbers of people—tens of millions—throughout the world express themselves through high-quality photographs. Facebook, YouTube, Instagram, and Flickr display images that others can click on, needing no particular skill. Call it "crowdsourcing." If you can be energized for a political cause by looking at videos, YouTube will provide them by the hundreds. As *Time* put it, "It's not just a new medium; it's several in one . . . It's a Surveillance System . . . a spotlight . . . a microscope . . . a soapbox . . . . This is just one sign of how much YouTube—and similar video-sharing sites—has changed the flow of information."[14]

▶ PICTURES THAT LIE

Truth and photography have been separated almost from the start. Manipulation dates back at least to the early 1860s, when the head of Abraham Lincoln was placed atop the body of Senator John C. Calhoun, the result placed on the original U.S.$5 bill.[15]

Photographs became an instrument of propaganda by the French government against the uprising of the Paris Commune in 1871 in opposition to the Franco-Prussian War. After soldiers killed an estimated 40,000 of the alleged Communards who supported the rebellion, photographers were summoned to take pictures of the dead in the streets and the revolutionaries who were executed. One photographer did not stop there. He produced fakes to display what seemed to be atrocities committed by the Communards.

During the 1920s, a few newspaper editors combined pictures into "composographs," a combining of photographs, which brought images of people from different photographs together in close proximity. Publishers justified using them because they sold newspapers. Around the time of World War I, five photographs of the "Cottingley Fairies" led Sir Arthur Conan Doyle, the author of the Sherlock Holmes stories and a believer in spiritualism, to publicly assert that the photographs were real.

Such distortions also had political value. Enough voters were deceived during the McCarthy "Red Scare" era of the 1950s to defeat liberal Senator Millard Tydings in his bid for re-election after he was shown standing beside Communist leader Earl Browder, an event that never happened. During the 2004 election campaign a fake photograph circulated on the Internet showing John Kerry on a podium with Jane Fonda in a demonstration against the Vietnam War. The two never shared a podium, but the toxic effect of this digital imagery may have affected a presidential election. A character in the film *Flags of Our Fathers*, recalling U.S. propaganda efforts during World War II, remarked, "A picture can win or lose a war."[16]

For decades newspapers routinely used darkroom techniques to alter photographs. After 1989, photos could be digitally manipulated on a home computer. Now the tampering could be almost impossible to detect. Digital imaging converted images into dots—pixels—that could be moved or removed, but retouching can still lead to public embarrassment. Computer software for digital retouching shifted the pyramids at Giza for a *National Geographic* cover in 1982. That improved the framing, but chipped away at the magazine's reputation for authenticity. A *Newsweek* cover in 2005 placed Martha Stewart's head on a slimmer body to show that she had lost weight upon being released from prison.[17] Magazines for years have airbrushed models and celebrities to make them appear slimmer, a practice that reportedly has many women and teenage girls in distress because their own bodies cannot match these almost impossible images.

To enhance old photographs that had seen better days, customers went to the shops of experts who cleaned up the damaged areas. Actually, it is no longer necessary to turn to the experts for much of this. With off-the-shelf software like Photoshop and Inpaint, images can be altered or replaced by whatever color and pattern is in the background. Another feature allows the combining of images from more than one photograph into a seamless whole. Changes have included taking unidentified people out of a photograph, removing a divorced spouse from a family scene, adding missing relatives to a family reunion, bringing grandmother, mother, and daughter together for a three-generation portrait, closing gaps in a photograph of relatives to make the scene cozier, erasing wrinkles and warts, and eliminating braces from teeth before the orthodontist does. Several dozen applications now are sold for displaying, altering, or adding text and ornamentation to photographs on mobile devices. [18]

▶ CARTOONS

Photography is not the only way to communicate messages with images. Sketches that originated with political cartoons and the sharp drawings of the 18th-century English artist William Hogarth gave birth to a worldwide phenomenon of comic books, newspaper comic strips, magazine cartoons, Internet drawings and, of course, the ever popular political cartoons.

In 1896, a few years after photographs started to appear in newspapers, the technology supporting color in newspapers improved enough for William Randolph Hearst to bring out a comic strip supplement in the *New York American*. Yellow ink was added to an outlandish skirt worn by a little boy in one strip, Hogan's Alley. Renamed The Yellow Kid, it was a hit with readers and opened the way for a major industry with dozens upon dozens of comic strips.

Some comics were intended to be comical. Others were intended to be serious, but in the United States the term "comics" has stuck to them all. Italians call them "*fumetti*," meaning "smoke." In Portuguese they are "*história em quadradinhos*" (a story in little squares). The French prefer the no-nonsense "*bande dessiné*" (drawn strip). Whatever they are called, they are a staple of the modern newspaper, frequently the first place a reader turns. "*Manga*" is the Japanese word for "comics." Its style has spread worldwide both to children and adults, a billion dollar industry.

For many newspaper readers, the comic strips are the one part of the newspaper they would never do without. Reading Dilbert or Doonesbury is as much a part of their morning routine as a cup of coffee. The effects on society of single cartoon panels, comic strips, and comic books have been debated, but little doubt remains that cartoons stir something in many readers. Psychologist Fredric Wertham's accusatory book *Seduction of the Innocent* (1954) argued that comic books corrupted youngsters with pornographic images and excessive violence. Untold numbers of adults have complained that comics rot the brains of youngsters. The youngsters themselves just keep on scanning these durable media.

Some comics have a stronger appeal to adults than to children. Art Spiegelman's *Maus* won a Pulitzer Prize in 1992 as it introduced an increasingly popular genre with adults—the graphic novel—combining text and drawings in stories that are more complex and frequently darker than traditional comic book tales. *V for Vendetta* and *Sin City* became films not only drawn from graphic novels, but produced to look like them. Purists may scoff at the notion that what appears in comic books can be considered art, but when a museum hangs a Roy Lichtenstein painting of a single comic book panel, admiring visitors gather.

▶ SUMMARY

Susan Sontag, writer and filmmaker, said "photography takes the whole world as its subject, cannibalizes all art forms, and converts them into images."[19]

It is not uncommon in places where uncomfortable events are happening to see a policeman, a soldier, or a militiaman walk up to a camera with his hand out to block the lens. Damning words may be forgotten, but damning pictures sear our memory. As noted, they have led to change.

As a result, like our reaction to all media of communication and more than most media, we have adapted to photography. Our reaction may be as minor as running our fingers through our hair before a snapshot is taken or as significant as passing child labor legislation to end the shame that Lewis Hine's photographs laid before the nation's eyes, pulling children out of cotton mills and coal mines and sending them to school, giving them a chance at life. He said, "If I could tell the story in words, I wouldn't need to lug around a camera."[20]

▶ TIMELINE

1038   Arab scholar Alhazen describes a room-size *camera obscura*.

1727   Johann Schulze sees silver nitrate darken, begins science of photochemistry.

1802   Thomas Wedgewood produces silhouettes with silver nitrate, but they darken.

1816   Joseph Nicéphore Niépce captures a negative image on paper, but it darkens.

1825   Copy of a Dutch print. It is now thought to be the first true photograph.

1827   Using a *camera obscura*, Niépce produces a photograph on a pewter plate.

1835   In England, W. H. Fox Talbot produces his first photographs, the first negatives.

1837   In France, Louis Daguerre creates daguerreotype photographs.

1839   John Herschel's hypo fixative stops darkening of photographs.

    Daguerre's paper to the French Academy of Sciences begins a photography craze.

1849   Photographs of Egyptian pyramids begin travel photography.

    Twin-lens camera can take pictures for stereoscopic viewing.

1851   Frederick Scott Archer invents wet-plate photography.

1861   Mathew Brady and others begin to photograph the American Civil War.

1880   A halftone photograph, "Shantytown," appears in a newspaper.

1881   The first photographic roll film is available.

1888   The inexpensive "Kodak" box camera. The "snapshot" is born.

1896   X-ray photography appears.

1900   George Eastman's U.S.$1 Brownie puts photography within almost everyone's reach.

1902   Alfred Stieglitz publishes *Camera Work* to promote photography as art.

1937   An American, Chester Carlson, invents the photocopier, Xerography process.

1947   Dennis Gabor, Hungarian engineer in England, invents holography.

    Edwin Land's one-minute Polaroid method prints pictures in the camera.

1978   From Japan, an automatic focusing, point-and-shoot camera goes on sale.

1982   Japanese filmless cameras store pictures electronically.

1991   An x-ray photograph is taken of the brain recalling a word.

2004   2D and 3D photos taken by Rover vehicles are beamed back from Mars.

2007   Camera phones are everywhere.

2013   "Selfies" are posted by the millions on websites such as Snapchat.

▶ NOTES

1 *100 Photographs That Changed the World* (New York: Life Books, 2003) 7.

2 For a fuller description read Richard G. Tansey and Horst de la Croix, *Art Through the Ages* (New York: Harcourt Brace Jovanovich, 1986).

3 Geoffrey Batchen, *Each Wild Idea* (Cambridge, MA: MIT Press, 2001) 4.

4 The photograph is hosted, among other places, at Wikimedia Commons: http://en.wikipedia.org/wiki/File:Talbot_Harfe.jpg.

5 Daniel J. Boorstin, *The Americans: The Democratic Experience* (New York: Random House, 1973) 398.

6 *New York Times*, October 20, 1862. An online version of the original article can be found at http://www.nytimes.com/1862/10/20/news/brady-s-photographs-pictures-of-the-dead-at-antietam.html?smid=pl-share.

7 An earlier photographer, Richard Beard, had taken daguerreotypes in London streets that were used for illustrations in another sociological study of the travails of the London poor. Henry Mayhew, *London Labour and the London Poor* (1851) 62.

8 *How the Other Half Lives: Studies among the Tenements of New York* (New York: Charles Scribner's Sons, 1980); *The Children of the Poor* (New York: Charles Scribner's Sons, 1892).

9 See http://www.photoquotations.com/a/322/Lewis+Hine, dated 1909.

10 "Lewis Hine," entry at http://www.spartacus.schoolnet.co.uk/IRhine.htm.

11 Richard Hofstadter, *The Progressive Movement, 1900–1915* (New York: Simon & Schuster, 1963).

12 Jacques Ellul, *The Technological Bluff* (Grand Rapids, MI: Wm. B. Eerdmans Publishing Co., 1990) 182.

13 It is also a cheaper way to acquire good photos and videos than hiring staff photographers. See Jeff Howe, "The Rise of Crowdsourcing," *Wired*, June 2006: 177–183.

14 *Time*, December 25, 2006: 63–64.

15 Hany Farid, "Photography Changes What We Are Willing to Believe," *Click*, http://click.si.edu/Story.aspx?story=178.

16 Giving other examples, Arthur Goldsmith wrote, "With the new technology we can enhance colors or change them, eliminate details, add or delete figures, alter the composition and lighting effects, combine any number of images, and literally move mountains, or at least the Eiffel Tower, as one magazine did to improve a cover design. *TV Guide* didn't even stop at decapitation—it placed Oprah Winfrey's head on Ann-Margret's body." Arthur Goldsmith, "Reinventing the Image," *Popular Photography*, March 1990: 49.

17 *Newsweek* in its issue of March 7, 2005 not only placed Martha Stewart's head on a model's body, but in the accompanying article freely admitted doing so and saw nothing wrong with such a "photo illustration."

18 A listing of "The 30 Best Photo Apps" was available at http://www.creativebloq. com/design-tools/best-photo-apps-513764.

19 Speech delivered at Wellesley College, April 21, 1975. Reprinted as "Photography Within the Humanities," in Liz Wells, ed., *The Photography Reader* (New York: Routledge, 2003) 60.

20 Steve Meltzer, "Celebrating Social Documentary Photographer Lewis Hine," *Imaging Resource*, November 1, 2013, http://www.imaging-resource.com/ news/2013/11/01/appreciating-master-social-documentary-photographer-lewis-hine.

9 Silent Film: The Audience Waits

Commercial entertainment during the last quarter of the 19th century and into the 20th century included opera and symphony concert halls for the well-to-do, plus city park band shells, baseball parks, amusement parks, vaudeville halls, and dance halls for the less well-off. Thomas Edison offered phonograph parlors as respectable family entertainment. Despite the scratchiness of the songs and the marching band music, phonographs were welcomed with enthusiasm at fair midways, hotel lobbies, train stations, and summer resorts, wherever people gathered.[1] Americans did not have as much entertainment as they enjoy today, but those who lived in urban areas went out far more often than their European cousins.[2]

The motion picture brought something new into the world, the prospect of all-day entertainment. Starting with vaudeville theaters and expanding significantly with the nickelodeons that sprang up in street front rooms during the first decade of the 20th century, commercial entertainment was available from morning until late into the night every day. The audience was predominantly white collar, but not wealthy.[3] Obviously a large segment of the working class would be toiling at their jobs, but there must have been enough others with the free time and the coins to keep the entertainment doors open.[4] When the working classes had free time and some coins they could spare, they too went to the pictures.

▶ HOMEMADE VIDEOS

The first moving pictures were brief slices of real life. So are the newest, as homemade videos on YouTube go viral to the world. If something is strange or funny or if you are upset enough about an injustice, you can do more than blog about it. Film it and upload your video. The digital revolution makes it easy and cheap. If you can make a persuasive documentary, Netflix and Sundance are open to you. Camcorders and phone cameras are everywhere, more common than George Eastman's Brownie once was. And you can watch a movie on a smartphone.

Like so much of mediated communication, videotape and its successor digital technologies have been egalitarian, empowering ordinary users. The beating of Rodney King, an African American, by four police officers in 1991, taped by an amateur from an apartment window, reverberated nationwide and has affected the way police behave during arrests. It played again and again on television, fueling the African American, anger behind the Los Angeles riots. Now think of all the camera phones that are being pointed at police during recent demonstrations in country after country, and their images going viral. Or think of the video coming out of Syria and Gaza of cities in ruins and the dead and dying adults and children.

Production and distribution of moving images are decentralized as never before. People of a great variety of beliefs and agendas use the powerful medium of movies to try to persuade us. And, of course, the established motion picture industry continues to exert its influence on everything from political and social views to haircuts.

▶ MORE THAN A DIVERSION

It would be easier to find someone who has never read a newspaper, a magazine, or a book than to find an adult who has never seen a movie.[5] From our childhood, movies have been part of our lives. To watch a movie with enough understanding to have an emotional response, literacy is not necessary. Steven Spielberg called films "the most powerful weapon in the world."[6] For most of us, a world deprived of film would be grayer, less pleasant. Watching movies has also substituted for other activities and for direct contact with other people. The movies have encouraged us to sit back and let the people who make movies entertain us. We have less need to entertain ourselves.

The movies are more than occasional diversions. Beyond the plots, the action, the actors, and the computer graphics, both fiction and non-fiction movies carry messages. And the messages get through despite cultural differences.[7] Only some messages are intentional, but films that do not set out to send a message still do so in subtle ways: the condition of the streets and buildings, the cars, the food, what the participants wear and their attitudes, the behavior of police and politicians can tell an audience that this is how things are in other places. If life is different where you live, maybe you will want changes where you live, or maybe you will decide to move somewhere else. Sukarno, the first prime minister of Indonesia, reportedly once said that Hollywood, in effect, preached revolution because it showed a society in which ordinary people had houses with several rooms and possessed automobiles.[8]

Movies have knocked down barriers among races, religions, and nationalities. Movies can help to turn our focus from local and parochial matters to broader perspectives. Sometimes they firm flabby sympathies into the sinews of active commitment. And they have also encouraged ridicule. Even when no hostility was intended, the movies, especially in their early years, got cheap laughs out of stereotypes. Historian David Nasaw recalled, "Most of the early comedies borrowed their characters, if not their plots, from vaudeville skits. As in vaudeville, ethnic and racial parodies were prevalent, with dim-witted Irish servants blowing themselves up trying to light the stove or taking off their clothes when asked to serve the salad without dressing, unscrupulous Jewish merchants in full beards and long black coats cheating their customers, and blacks behaving like children—cakewalking, grinning, shooting craps, stealing chickens, and eating watermelon."[9]

Considering the diversity of those who contribute their skills and considering where in the world the product goes, the motion picture industry is among the most international of enterprises. All leading nations of the world and many of the smaller nations have their own film industries, a point of pride like a national airline. Some have had notable histories, such as the film industries of Russia, Britain, France, Germany, and Japan.

▶ THE ROOTS

Motion picture technology has three roots that go back for centuries. The *chemistry* of film has its roots in still photography. The other two roots are *projection*, which had its origin in the magic lantern, and *stills-in-motion*, which began as toys that depended on *persistence of vision*. Because it takes the eye and the brain a fraction of a second to lose an image, a series of still pictures presented in quick succession will appear as a single moving image. An examination of the flickering images of the persistence-of-vision devices built throughout the 19th century may lead to the conclusion that the invention of the motion picture was inevitable.

From the Thaumatrope, invented in the early 19th century, to devices with complex names such as the Phenakistoscope, the Praxinoscope, the Zoetrope, and the Zoopraxiscope, inventors strove to fool the eye. The Thaumatrope is a disk attached to a string. On each side of the disk is a different image, such as a cage and a canary. Spinning the disk gives the illusion of the canary inside the cage. The inventor was possibly influenced by a scientific paper on persistence of vision by the remarkable physician Peter Roget, creator of Roget's *Thesaurus* of English synonyms and the inventor of the logarithmic slide rule.

Railroad baron Leland Stanford, ex-governor of California and founder of Stanford University, wanted to settle a bet on whether a trotting horse lifted all four hooves off the ground at the same time. In 1878 he hired professional photographer Eadweard Muybridge, who, after several trials, set a row of 24 cameras along a racetrack. Strings that stretched across the track tripped the camera shutters as the horse trotted by. That resulted in a series of stills. Flipped in rapid succession, they displayed the horse in motion. (Stanford won his bet; all four feet lifted off the ground.)

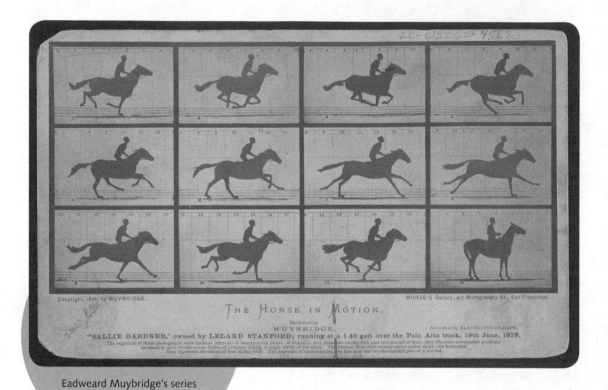

Eadweard Muybridge's series "The Horse in Motion," 1878.

Muybridge continued his experiments by photographing the movements of a variety of animals. Exhibiting his work in Paris, he met physician Etienne Jules Marey, who was doing research into such animal locomotion as the flapping of a bird's wings. That meeting led Marey to take an inventive step forward. Adapting a "photographic revolver" designed by astronomer Pierre Janssen to record the transit of Venus across the sun, Marey built a single camera that rapidly shot a series of images on a single plate. It did not require strings, which would have interfered with the fluttering wings. Inventors in several countries solved other mechanical difficulties. Among them were William Friese-Greene in England and the brothers Louis and Auguste Lumière in France.

▶ EDISON AND THE LUMIÈRE BROTHERS

Thomas Edison, who originally thought of motion pictures to accompany the sound in his phonograph parlors, assigned assistant W. K. L. Dickson to build a motion picture system, based on the French photographic revolver. Working in Edison's New Jersey laboratory with strips of celluloid film manufactured by George Eastman for his Kodak, Dickson in 1889 invented the Kineto-graph camera and the motor-driven "peep show," running 50 feet of film in 30 seconds. Sprockets guided the film's perforated edges past the lens with a controlled, intermittent movement like the ticking second-hand of a watch.

To produce something to display, Dickson erected a studio building that could be turned to take advantage of sunlight. Workers referred to the studio building as the "Black Maria," because with its tarpaper covering it vaguely bore the shape of a police wagon with that nickname. Trained animal acts, circus entertainers, and the like performed there.

In 1894, Kinetoscopes for viewing the films went into parlors modeled after Edison's successful phonograph parlors, with the difference that admission was not free; customers paid one quarter for tickets allowing them to peep into five machines. Start the electric motor, gaze into the peephole, and there was magic! The viewer stared into a box to see the frames of film flicker by. The inventive Dickson later built the Mutoscope peephole machine, with a series of cards that were flipped by a handle; Dickson made the Mutoscope different enough from his early Kinetoscope to get around Edison's patent. (Mutoscopes can still occasionally be found in old-fashioned penny arcades.)

Yet it was not *projection*, which appeared first in France. The Lumière brothers, Louis and Auguste, owners of a photo products manufacturing business, set about to improve a Kinetoscope they saw on display in Paris. This they did with their Cinematographe, a combined camera, film printer, and projector. Substituting a hand crank for Edison's electric motor, the Lumières reduced the machine's weight so that it could be carried to any location. Edison's bulky, fixed Kinetograph required performers to appear before it in the studio. Where Edison's films gave the view of a stage, Lumière films were like looking through a window. In addition, the Lumières projected their films onto a screen where a number of viewers saw them at the same time. Only one viewer at a time peered into the Kinetoscope.

The Lumières' first film, of workers leaving their factory, was shot in March 1895, and was shown at a special exhibit for photographers. On December 28, 1895, in the basement of a Paris café, they showed the first motion pictures projected to a paying audience. For 1 franc apiece the audience saw a 20 minute program consisting of ten films, accompanied by a piano, commentary by the Lumières' father and their own gasps of amazement.[10] In no time at all, long lines formed outside the café to see the show. The movies were born.[11]

Two months later, projected films were shown in London. Two months after that, New York. Soon after, Bombay, Rio de Janeiro, Johannesburg, Melbourne, Mexico City, Osaka. Audiences were soon drawn not only from the wealthy and the middle class, but from the working class who previously had no opportunity to dress up for a night at the theater, the concert hall, or the music hall. The wealthy had the opera, the symphony, and private amusements to occupy their leisure and had little use for social mixing. The middle class enjoyed music hall vaudeville. A strong sense of "middle-class morality" based on Victorian scruples kept many Americans out of any theaters.

▶ THE NICKELODEON

The businessmen who ventured into the new motion picture industry at first saw films as part of vaudeville shows. Unimagined by Thomas Edison and the other early filmmakers, a huge mass entertainment market was waiting. The novelty did not wear off. The movies would change mass culture. One way or another, budding entrepreneurs acquired projectors, buying them or building their own. In the cities they converted stores, restaurants and dance halls to look like vaudeville houses, or they cordoned off a section of a parlor or penny arcade and placed wooden chairs in front of a screen, even if it was no more than a white wall or a bed sheet. At county fairs a tent wall would do. Lecturers who illustrated their talks with slides adopted the new medium when they recognized how moving pictures would improve their presentations.

A decade after the first paying audience gathered in the basement of a Paris café to see pictures that moved, a series of short films were shown in new venues. Not everyone saw the same films. People in small towns might see uplifting or educational films in traveling shows or in church-sponsored venues. The urban working classes saw slapstick comedies and dramas in storefront nickelodeons—a nickel (5 cents) admission—started in Pittsburgh in 1904. The first day 450 people ventured in. The second day, more than 1,500.[12] The crowds kept coming. Storefront rooms, folding chairs, a white sheet or canvas for a screen, and a rented or purchased projector cost relatively little to start a business that rained nickels and dimes. In the big cities several nickelodeons might share the same block, and patrons walked from one to the other. Audiences ignored the grime and the foul air to stare at the screen and perhaps dream of a connection with the attractive actors looming over them. In some theaters the attendants squirted the air with a solution to mask the foulness, which did nothing about the pestilential germs that worried city inspectors.

Audiences adapted their personal standards to the new medium, for here was something entirely different and surprisingly desirable: sitting in the dark among strangers to share the laughter and tears and thrills of an unfolding story that was easy to understand. Reading a magazine or book was mediated communication, but it was a solitary pursuit. Attending a lecture, a circus, or a concert was a direct experience, not mediated and these events took place in lighted halls or outdoors. The poorer working class was unlikely to afford the price of admission to vaudeville shows, which were a succession of actors, singers, dancers, jugglers, and trained dogs. However, a few entrepreneurs foresaw that customers who so eagerly parted with their hard-earned coins to look moving pictures in a box at one of Thomas Edison's Kinetoscopes would, even more willingly, spend those coins if the pictures were projected against a screen, and this might attract even the poor including the millions of immigrants pouring onto America's shores.

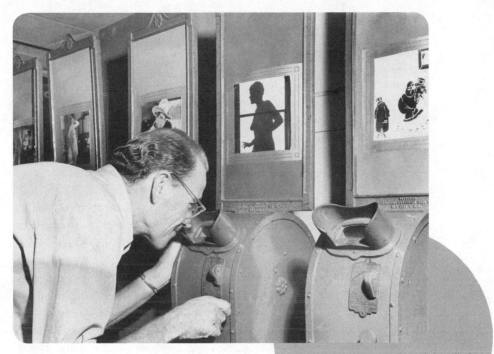

Kinetoscopes and crank-handled Mutoscopes may still be found in old-fashioned penny arcades. Drop in a coin and enjoy.

The films were silent, but the nickelodeons were boisterous and noisy when families gathered for a brief escape from their limited lives, for the audience kept up a cheerful racket. Slides carried the message, "Please Do Not Stamp. The Floor May Cave In." That seemed to young patrons like an invitation to stamp.

The entrepreneurs themselves arose from the masses of the poor. Some of the more successful were immigrants, often Jews born into the poverty and the anti-Semitism of Russia and Eastern Europe, not fully comfortable with the English language or the dominant Protestant culture of their new country.[13] Yet they were totally at home with the Protestant work ethic that has infused the lives of so many immigrants: work hard and success will follow. They had an instinctive sense of the simple narratives that would appeal to the poor, working-class families who crowded into nickelodeons. Marcus Loew, who started as a furrier, would one day see his name identifying a large national chain of cinemas. Louis B. Mayer started out as a scrap dealer who switched over to nickelodeons. Samuel Goldwyn and Mayer started MGM. William Fox gave his name to 20th Century Fox; his name now identifies the Fox media empire. Adolph Zukor began Paramount. Out of a clothing store in Oshkosh, Wisconsin, Carl Laemmle came to run Universal. The four Warner brothers began in Manhattan by borrowing chairs from a nearby funeral parlor; when the chairs were needed for a funeral, movie patrons stood.

Albert E. Smith and a partner bought a projector and a supply of movies from Edison, who sold projectors but refused to sell cameras in an effort to control movie production. It dawned on Smith that he could make more money producing films and that a camera was a kind of backwards projector. Converting one into the other, he and two partners created the Vitagraph Company in 1899 and went into competition with the powerful Biograph Company, which had begun four years earlier as the nation's first motion picture production company.

▶ COURT BATTLES

Battles over patent infringements were fought in the courts as a trust of bankers and businessmen sought to acquire enough patents to monopolize the motion picture industry despite anti-trust laws. Established companies fought the newcomers fiercely. The trust, the Motion Picture Patents Company, charged cinema owners fees for a projector, a projectionist, and films. Cinemas could not show unauthorized "outlaw" movies. Eastman at first sold raw film stock only to members of the trust. The trust did not care that their heavy-handed methods choked efforts to produce more imaginative pictures, especially the fictional stories that audiences by this time wanted to see. Business was business. The legal warfare lasted for seven years until a federal court outlawed the trust.

D. W. Griffith and actors from the Biograph Company, including Lillian Gish, Mary Pickford, and Lionel Barrymore, went to southern California in 1910, moving as far away from the heart of film making in the New York–New Jersey area as they could manage.[14] In Los Angeles they could escape the subpoenas and the heavy hand of the trust's Pinkerton detectives and at the same time find cheap labor and adequate sunshine for their filming. Nearby ocean, mountains, lakes, desert, woodlands, pasture, Spanish architecture, and town settings including streets with trolley cars offered a variety of outdoor locations.

In a friendly southern California village called Hollywood, the relocated filmmakers knocked outdoor stages together and began cranking their cameras. Soon, the motion picture companies started by Laemmle, Jesse Lasky, and a few others joined them. They rented barns and hammered stages together. The first movie studio occupied a converted saloon. In the United States, New York would remain the distribution center for films, but Hollywood would become the production center. These breakaway moviemakers would become the Hollywood studio establishment. One day the studios themselves would battle television and independent moviemakers just as hard as the trust once battled them.

▶ THE AUDIENCES

Working-class families could sit with friends and neighbors to watch a string of silent films, while snacks were sold up and down the aisles by children of the owners of the nickelodeons and the gaudy movie palaces that followed. Some movie palaces boasted orchestras, organs, or sound effects machines like the Noiseograph, the Dramagraph, and the Soundograph, whose keyboards imitated crashing glass and galloping horses. Professional actors working in the movie houses interpreted the dialogue behind the screen.

Lloyd Morris, popular historian of the early 20th century, described the urban audiences:

> In the slums of the great Eastern and Middle Western cities there were herded vast immigrant populations. Largely unfamiliar with the English language, they could not read the newspapers, magazines, or books. But the living pictures communicated their meanings directly and eloquently. To enjoy them, no command of a new language was essential. They made illiteracy and ignorance of American customs seem less shameful; they broke down a painful sense of isolation and ostracism. At the movies, dwellers in tenements, workers in sweatshops, could escape the drabness of their environment for a little while at a price within their means.
>
> The nickels rattled down like hailstones as workingmen and their families crowded into the lobbies, overflowed in long patient lines on the street. Inside, the program lasted from twenty minutes to an hour: a brief melodrama or chase; a comedy; a news picture or travel picture; a glimpse of dancers or acrobats . . . Youngsters carrying trays piled with peanuts, candy, popcorn and soda pop rushed up and down the aisles, crying their wares. Presently the machine resumed its sputtering, and the screen came alive again. There was a ripple of applause, a fluttering sigh of contentment. Then silence, broken by the crackling of peanut shells and popcorn, the whimpering of a frightened child. In the fetid darkness, tired men and women forgot the hardships of poverty. For this was happiness. This was the Promised Land.[15]

Morris also said, "In the penny arcades, moving pictures took a deep root, both as an agency for information and as a cheap form of entertainment for the masses. In the small rural communities to which they were taken by traveling showmen, they met equally responsive audiences. A broad popular foundation was being laid for a major industry, as well as a social instrument of incalculable power."[16]

Even if the immigrant unfamiliar with English or the illiterate farmhand could not read the inter-titles, and if an accompanying friend could not whisper the words on screen, the unfolding story could still be enjoyed.

Attracted by their gaudy lights, phonograph music piped outside, and shouting barkers, the public poured in by the hundreds of thousands daily. To keep up with demand for new movies, exhibitors changed the bill daily or even twice a day. Customers packed in from morning to night, one show after another, seven days a week. They streamed out of one nickelodeon into another, beguiled by the barkers, the flashing lights and the colorful posters outside until endurance and pockets were drained.

The nickelodeons, the storefronts, the backs of the arcades, and the circus tents were joined as movie venues by cinemas built specifically for watching films. The architecture became gaudier and grander with the construction of movie "palaces" in the downtown sections of large cities. These new motion picture palaces featured orchestra pits, pipe organs, and plaster Byzantine architecture. Some advertised "Air Conditioning" in marquee letters as big as the names of the stars. The palaces were designed to attract those middle-class patrons who wanted to see motion pictures but did not want to sit in dingy, crowded nickelodeons. The largest movie palaces could seat several thousand patrons, with uniformed ushers to guide them down the aisles.

The appeal of the movies expanded to middle-class Americans in the early years of the new century. An unexpected mingling of social classes followed into other commercial amusements in the American melting pot.[17] But this was likely to be a whites-only audience. At many nickelodeons, African Americans were barred. When the nickelodeons were replaced by large, permanent cinemas, African Americans were often directed by ushers to the balcony or along the sides.

David Nasaw wrote, "Going to the movies had become the hallmark of a new American civilization. In myth, and to a slightly less extent in reality, the picture palace represented the partial fulfillment of the American dream of an interethnic, cross-class, genderless, luxury-laden urban democracy. While that democracy was founded on the segregation of African Americans, it was nonetheless a remarkable achievement."[18]

For women, who had limited options for entertainment, the nickelodeon and the movie palace were safe, affordable, interesting. Historian Miriam Hansen wrote:

> More than any other entertainment form, the cinema opened up a space—a social space as well as a perceptual experiential horizon—in women's lives . . . Married women would drop into a movie theater on their way home from a shopping trip, a pleasure indulged in just as much by women of the more affluent classes. Schoolgirls filled the theaters during much of the afternoon, before returning to the folds of familial discipline. And young working women would find in the cinema an hour of diversion after work, as well as an opportunity to meet men.[19]

Simon Patten, an economist studying consumption practices, added:

> Opposite the barren school yard was the arcaded entrance to the nickelodeon, finished in white stucco, with the ticket seller enthroned in a chariot drawn by an elephant trimmed with red, white and blue lights . . . Here were groups of working girls—now happy "summer girls"—because they had left the grime, ugliness, and dejection of their factories behind them, and were freshened and revived by doing what they liked to do.[20]

In close-ups the matinee idol actors and actresses loomed over the audiences who idolized them and sometimes managed to learn more about them than their own family members. Writing about the enchanting Greta Garbo, media theorist Roland Barthes observed, "Garbo still belongs to that moment in cinema when capturing the human face still plunged audiences into the deepest ecstasy, when one literally lost oneself in a human image."[21]

The entertainment bill of fare changed, too. Instead of a series of one- or two-reelers, the cinemas showed the longer feature films the public had already come to love. Film exchanges, instead of *selling* films to exhibitors, *rented* them. In time, as the industry matured, distribution centers and chain owners would dominate the mom-and-pop beginnings of film exhibition. Movie theater chains with hundreds of outlets either contracted with studios or had the same corporate ownership, guaranteeing both a steady supply of product and dependable distribution. Warner Bros. films opened in a Warner Bros. theater, Paramount films at a Paramount, MGM films at a Loew's theater.

▶ PEOPLE WANT FICTION

The sight of ocean waves coming toward the camera elicited squeals from the early patrons, who half-expected to be soaked. The earliest Lumière and Edison films were scenes from real life: people in a park, workers leaving a factory, a man playing a fiddle, a baby being fed, a parade. In time, audiences tired of such banal fare.

For audiences that loved stories, French magician George Méliès produced the first openly fictional films. Even today, audiences enjoy his *A Trip to the Moon* (1902), which is shown as a whimsical introduction to the history of space flight. Méliès was among the first to stretch the film from less than 1 minute to an entire reel of 10 to 15 minutes.

Méliès's humorous moon fantasy was innocent, unlike a number of serious efforts that were patently fraudulent. Perhaps the actualities were intended to deceive a naïve public, but many in the audience realized they were not seeing reality. After tub-thumping newspaper publishers promoted American entry into the Spanish–American War, the first film photographers added to the media-created jingoism with phony film. Imagined Spanish atrocities in Cuba were filmed in New Jersey. The famous charge up San Juan Hill went up another hill considerably later. South Africa's Boer War was filmed on a golf course. Mount Vesuvius actually erupted somewhere else. A safari into the heart of Africa featured two elderly zoo lions who politely allowed themselves to be shot on camera.

Motion pictures might have ended as just another novelty. What made the difference was *fiction*. Director–photographer Edwin Porter tried to tell stories when in 1903 he made both *Life of an American Fireman* and *The Great Train Robbery*, the first memorable story film and the first to utilize film editing to establish relationships. In eight minutes, bandits hold up a mail train, a posse is formed to chase after the bandits, a shoot-out follows, and the bandits are wiped out. For the first time, too, the camera moved with the action, indoors and out. Excited audiences lined up to get in.

A distinct preference emerged for the scripted fiction narrative film. Realistic films led to newsreels and documentaries, but the movie-going public by their ticket purchases made their choice clear. They had enough troubles

THE BIRTH OF A NATION

The popular melodrama easily made the transition from stage to screen. The melodrama evolved into the romantic drama with *The Birth of a Nation* (1915), a feature film nearly three hours long. Director D. W. Griffith's manipulation of long, medium and close-up shots, pacing, crosscutting and optical effects, plus his choice of locations and his attention to actors' movements, set new standards for the motion picture. He insisted on close-ups of actors despite protests from studio executives that audiences wanted to see the actors from head to toe and would not accept "half an actor."

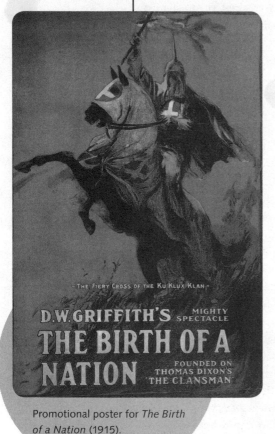

Promotional poster for *The Birth of a Nation* (1915).

Starting with *The Birth of a Nation*, movies would create a visual language that the public understood, a language to which it responded. Although a silent film, *The Birth of a Nation* had the accompaniment of live music, anything from a 70-piece symphony orchestra to a single pianist playing a musical score specifically written for the film. After seeing it, President Woodrow Wilson is said to have remarked, "It is like writing history with lightning."[22]

Griffith has been lauded as the single most important individual in the development of the motion picture as an art form, but *The Birth of a Nation* was also a racially biased movie that fostered lingering stereotypes of African Americans as vicious and inferior sub-humans. The Ku Klux Klan was portrayed as noble, galloping up on horses to save the heroine. Griffith was a Southerner, the son of a Confederate veteran, raised amid the post-Civil War resentments of a conquered people. He had not finished high school.

For all its artistry, *The Birth of a Nation* evoked protest marches. The NAACP tried unsuccessfully to have the film banned or at least to have certain scenes removed. Griffith tried to make amends with an even more ambitious film that ran for three and a half hours, *Intolerance*, which identified bigotry during the Babylonian, Judean, Renaissance, and contemporary American periods. It has been called a masterpiece of the silent screen, but it failed at the box office.

at home. Reality in the form of actuality film was not why they entered the darkened theater. The documentary would come to be respected more than enjoyed. Moviemakers knew that, like everything else for sale, money—in the form of box office receipts—would identify the type of movies that they should produce. Hollywood production was measured by that yardstick, not critical judgment or classical theatrical artistry. Little wonder that Hollywood became "the dream factory." In time the public would also express its preference for sound and color. These added even more escapist pleasure to an evening of going out to the movies.

Realism was exaggerated to absurdity by fast-motion film, ridiculous props, split-second timing, and incongruous film cutting. When the screen comic hero's automobile missed the oncoming locomotive by inches, the audience suspended belief and laughed. Director Mack Sennett's pie-in-the-face slapstick competed with silent film actors who took the comic art to yet greater heights. Harold Lloyd, Buster Keaton, and, above the rest, Charlie Chaplin blended slapstick with pathos. His meld of mirth, romance, and sadness created one of the classic characters of any age or culture, the little tramp, in such films as *The Kid*, *The Gold Rush*, and *City Lights*.

Fred Ott's Sneeze (1893), an early Edison film for the Kinetoscopes, began a long tradition of film comedy. Under the guiding hand of Mack Sennett, slapstick grew from its limited roots in burlesque to an art form. The Keystone Kops' nonsensical appearance and incompetence invited people to laugh at a social institution that was anything but funny. For immigrants from repressive police states, regarding the policeman as a figure of ridicule must have been a strange and liberating experience. In the slapstick comedies, danger was constant and hairbreadth escapes were common, but no one died and a pie in the face hurt no one.

▶ THE STARS

People willingly plunked down their cash for visual comedy and stories, especially when they featured actors whom they had learned to adore. The first screen actors were people who appeared in front of the camera only because they were not busy working behind it. Wives, friends, and visitors took a turn.

When trained stage actors rode the trains west heading to the new movie studios to look for work, they were given acting jobs but not the publicity they expected. Studio owners were afraid this would lead to demands for better pay. This situation changed after theater owners reported to producers that audiences looked forward to seeing familiar faces. Word raced through every town that the actor or actress who had appeared in such-and-such a role could be seen again at the Bijou in a new motion picture. That resulted in ticket sales and the start of the movie star system. In 1914, Charlie Chaplin was being paid U.S.$125 a week. By 1915 he was getting $10,000 a week plus $150,000 for signing the contract. Mary Pickford was paid $10,000 a week plus half the profits of her pictures.[23]

Although actors in the early films were not identified, it was soon apparent that the public was developing an affinity for certain featured players and a curiosity about the actors' lives. An early survey of audience preferences for film plots received instead questions about the actors

A poster for D. W. Griffith's *Intolerance* (1916), which explored bigotry throughout the ages.

and actresses. What was he like? Was she married? The fiction film itself was only a few years old when *Photoplay* was published in 1911 to discuss film plots and characters, the first movie fan magazine. As the familiar faces loomed over them in close-ups on the big screen, patrons could feel a closer identity with the stars than with people they had known most of their lives. The mediated pleasure sprouting from this connection has continued to displace flesh-and-blood connections from generation to generation. It has spawned its own world of press agents, fan magazines, Hollywood reporters intent on the smallest private details, paparazzi, bodyguards, and millions of viewers watching the Academy Awards and other events honoring these luminaries.

The star system was one of several ways in which the public determined the direction that movies would take. The love affair between movie fans and the objects of their desire in close-up on the silver screen deepened with the passing decades as the movie studios and actors themselves turned out to be expert at churning out publicity. The movie stars then and now are far better known than the political figures we elect. One of the compliments we pay to a politician is that he or she has "star quality." The star system reached its zenith when the big studios peaked in the 1930s, 1940s and 1950s. Politicians counted themselves fortunate when a movie star agreed to a joint appearance at a rally. Song-and-dance man George Murphy was elected to the United States Senate in 1964. So was actor Fred Thompson in 1994. Arnold Schwarzenegger was twice elected governor of California, starting in 1993. Ronald Reagan was not only elected governor of California but was twice elected president (1980, 1984), and is an iconic figure in American history. Today George Clooney and Angelina Jolie are among many actors who use their celebrity to make positive changes throughout the world.

▶ CENSORSHIP

The impact of movies upon society is too great to be evaluated only on their artistic quality, no matter what the critics may say. Politics matter. No cultural force of such power settles in without opposition, and censorship has consistently been film's companion. From the start, censorship dogged Hollywood's influence.

Nickelodeons troubled those who thought the movies were presenting revolutionary ideas. Starting in the early years of the 20th century, calls came for regulating, censoring, or suppressing films. In 1909, the National Board of Review of Motion Pictures was created, independent of Hollywood. During that year the New York Society for the Prevention of Cruelty to Children stated in its annual report, "God alone knows how many [girls] are leading dissolute lives begun at the 'moving pictures.'" According to film historians Kristin Thompson and David Bordwell, "The quick spread of nickelodeons led to social pressures aimed at reforming the cinema. Many religious groups and social workers considered the nickel theatres sinister places where young people could be led astray. The movies were seen as a training ground for prostitution and robbery."[24]

The Supreme Court in 1915 ruled unanimously in the Mutual Film Corporation decision that free speech protection did not extend to motion pictures. Catholic bishops and evangelical Protestant ministers led the effort to limit the amount of sin that movies could display. Daniel Lord, a Jesuit professor, took the lead in writing the Motion Picture Production Code. Efforts to censor movies marched alongside the years devoted to enact and enforce Prohibition, another effort to legislate morality. Middle-class reformers who attacked working-class drinking also went after the nickelodeon.[25] Before Prohibition, they were cheered by saloon owners who saw business dwindling when potential customers for nickel beer were drawn away to the nickelodeon up the street.

What followed were desperate efforts at self-regulation by the movie industry to stave off even greater censorship. Hollywood in 1922 created the Hays Office, named for its first president, Will Hays, to protect audiences from indecency and violence. The demand for censoring extended to include such liberal political topics as disputes between labor and management, labor strikes, police brutality, and government–business corruption. A socialist undercurrent opposing big business practices was occasionally reflected in the movies, and was particularly popular with immigrant audiences. Upton Sinclair's exposé of the meat packing industry was made into a film in 1914, featuring Sinclair himself. States and even cities established their own censorship boards. Screen violence never got the concern that immorality received.

▶ TIMELINE

1646   In Germany, Athanasius Kircher invents a magic lantern to throw images.

1791   In London, the opening of the first Panorama.

1825   Thaumatrope, a disk with image on each side, demonstrates persistence of vision.

1878   Eadweard Muybridge photographs a trotting horse, forerunner of movies.

1882   Etienne Jules Marey designs a rifle-like camera that shoots 12 photos per second.

1889   Thomas Edison and W. K. L. Dickson construct the Kinetograph camera and peep-show Kinetoscope.

1890   From England, the kinematograph, a combination camera and projector.

1894   A Kinetoscope parlor opens in New York City, 25 cents to see five short films.

1895   France's Lumière brothers' portable movie camera can also print and project films.

In a Paris cellar, a paying audience sees Lumière's motion pictures projected.

1896   Edison's Vitascope, designed by Thomas Armat, brings film projection to the United States.

1900   Much of Europe and Japan begin to make movies.

1902   Film exchange lets exhibitors rent movies instead of buying them.

1903   *The Great Train Robbery* introduces editing, creates demand for fiction movies.

1905   Pittsburgh's Nickelodeon cinema creates template of showing movies for the masses.

1907   Chicago's Police Department gets authority to ban movies in the city.

1909   *New York Times* publishes a movie review.

The first movie star, Florence Lawrence.

1910   D. W. Griffith sets up shop in California at a place called Hollywood.

Edison's Kinetophone is an attempt at sound film. Lasts one year.

1911   Credits appear at the start of a movie.

1912   Movie cameras abandon cranks for motors that smooth motion.

Photoplay, a magazine for movie fans.

1913   *Gertie the Dinosaur*, an animated cartoon, requires 10,000 drawings.

From Hollywood, a feature-length film, Cecil B. DeMille's *The Squaw Man*.

1914   Grand cinema "palaces" start to replace nickelodeons.

1915   Hollywood begins star system. Charlie Chaplin goes from U.S.$125 to $10,000 weekly.

The Birth of a Nation is praised for its film art. Its racism leads to riots.

1919   Griffith, Chaplin, Fairbanks, Pickford create United Artists.

1922   Robert Flaherty's *Nanook of the North* is the first feature film documentary.

1925   *Battleship Potemkin* from Soviet Union elevates film montage to new heights.

An in-flight movie is shown in a plane flying over England.

▶ **NOTES**

1 David Nasaw, *Going Out: The Rise and Fall of Public Amusement* (New York: Basic Books, 1993) 123.

2 For more on leisure time, see Nasaw, 2–9.

3 Nasaw, 31, 127–134.

4 Nasaw, 23.

5 More than a half-century ago, Leo Rosten wrote, "The American press is read only where English is read; the American radio is heard only where English is comprehended; but the American movie is an international carrier which triumphs over differences in age or language, nationality or custom. Even the Sumatran native who cannot spell is able to grasp the meaning of pictures which move, and he can love, hate or identify himself with those who appear in them." Leo Rosten, *Hollywood, the Movie Colony and the Movie Makers* (New York: Harcourt Brace & Co., 1941) 7–12.

6 Speech at the American Museum of the Moving Image, February 24, 1994.

7 For an early take on this, see Rosten.

8 Ian C. Jarvie, *Hollywood's Overseas Campaign: The North Atlantic Movie Trade, 1920–1950* (Cambridge, UK: Cambridge University Press, 1992) 299.

9 Nasaw, 167.

10 Harry M. Geldud, *The Birth of the Talkies: From Edison to Jolson* (Bloomington: Indiana University Press, 1975) 28.

11 One excited Parisian newspaper exulted: "With this new invention, death will no longer be absolute, final. The people we have seen on the screen will be with us, moving and alive after their deaths." David Shipman, *The Story of Cinema* (Englewood Cliffs: Prentice-Hall, 1982) 18.

12 For more information, see "This Day in History, June 19, 1905": http://www.history.com/this-day-in-history/first-nickelodeon-opens.

13 For a detailed set of biographies, see Neal Gabler, *An Empire of Their Own: How the Jews Invented Hollywood* (New York: Anchor Books, 1989).

14 See http://www.u-s-history.com/pages/h3871.html for a brief history of early Hollywood.

15 Lloyd R. Morris, *Not So Long Ago* (New York: Random House, 1949), 34–35.

16 Morris, 29.

17 Nasaw, 152–153.

18 Nasaw, 240.

19 Miriam Hansen, *Babel and Babylon: Spectatorship in American Silent Film* (Cambridge, MA: Harvard University Press, 1991) 117.

20 Simon Patten, *Product and Climax* (New York: B. W. Huebsch, 1909) 18–19.

21 Roland Barthes, "The Face of Garbo," in Susan Sontag, ed., *A Barthes Reader* (New York: Hill and Wang, 1982) 82.

22 Daniel J. Boorstin, *The Image, or What Happened to the American Dream* (New York: Atheneum, 1961) 127–128.

23 "Mary Pickford," entry on the National Women's History Museum site, https://www.nwhm.org/education-resources/biography/biographies/mary-pickford/.

24 Kristin Thompson and David Bordwell, *Film History: An Introduction*, 3rd ed. (New York: McGraw-Hill, 2010) 29.

25 Hansen, 63.

10

A Movie Century: Moving Us

From our childhood, movies have been part of our lives. To watch a movie with enough understanding to have an emotional response, literacy is not necessary. For most of us, a world deprived of film would be grayer, less pleasant. Watching movies has also substituted for other activities and for direct contact with other people. The movies have encouraged us to sit back and let the people who make movies entertain us. We have less need to entertain ourselves. Anyone who thinks that movies have done surprising us should visit the 4D film showing at the Newseum in Washington, DC, where seats move and vibrate in sync with the film.[1] The audience gasped, giggled and yelped, "exactly the reaction we want, said film creator Joe Cortina.[2]

▶ SOUND

Efforts to produce sound to go with film began with the invention of movies. In 1895 Edison invented the Kinetophone, a cylinder phonograph for his Kineto-scope viewers. Later, phonograph records were synchronized mechanically to the projectors. This system worked passably well when the film and the record were new. Unfortunately, the record started to wear out after about 20 plays. After a projectionist spliced a few film breaks, removing a few frames here and there, the soundtrack was totally out of sync with the picture.

Sound heightened the entertainment and informational value of films. But starting with *The Jazz Singer* in 1927, the "talkies" did much more.[3] They gave the movies a cultural value akin to books and plays. The sound motion picture in the United States, along with the radio, helped to standardize American speech. By bringing forth a shared cultural experience, the movies and the radio tightened the bonds that held a large and diverse country together. Like the telegraph and the telephone before them and the televi-sion to follow, the talkies helped to unite the United States.

But sound films presented the problem of dialogue in an unfamiliar language, for international audiences were a source of revenue for Hollywood, and American audiences were a source of revenue for films made in France, Germany, and Russia. Film historians Kristin Thompson and David Bordwell recalled, "Sound filming created a problem for all producing countries: the language barrier threatened to limit export possibilities. Silent film could be translated through the simple substitution of intertitles, but talkies were another matter."[4] Dubbing did not work well because lip movements could not be synchronized. Paramount was among the companies that shot films in more than one language, with different teams of actors trading places for each scene. Laurel and Hardy had voice coaches so they could speak their lines in Spanish, Italian, French, and German.[5] Improved dubbing and the use of subtitles were put in place in the early 1930s and have remained ever since.[6]

In Japan, a unique occupation arose from the Japanese oral tradition. A *benshi*, a kind of storyteller, narrated the films, altering his voice to speak for each of the characters. More popular than movie stars, *benshi* could order directors to alter scenes so they could extend their own performances. When sound films finally arrived in Japan, the *benshi* were able to delay their widespread distribution for several years.[7]

In Hollywood, interest in sound films was propelled by Warner Bros., which was desperate and nearly bankrupt. In 1926, using Vitaphone, a system that paired a phonograph with a projector, Warner Bros. presented some sound shorts and a silent film, *Don Juan*, to which the studio added a music score plus the clash of swords during a duel, but made no effort to lip-sync words. A year later the troubled studio tried again with a silent feature film that had musical accompaniment and four singing or talking sequences. *The Jazz Singer* (1927) starred Al Jolson, who belted out "Mammy" and, in the second reel, uttered those prophetic words, "Wait a minute! Wait a minute, I tell ya! You ain't heard nothin' yet."

Most Hollywood executives wanted to leave well enough alone and stay with silent film.[8] They saw no reason to pay for sound-proofing studios or noisy cameras or figuring ways to position microphones so they would not show up on camera. Efforts to hide mikes can be seen in films of the early 1930s when actors huddled over a prop, like a vase of flowers, to deliver their lines. Some of the best-known actors had thick foreign accents or squeaky voices in sharp contrast to their all-American, matinee idol looks. Changes were inevitable.

Most stars, notably Chaplin, also preferred the silent screen with the dialogue printed on cards that appeared after the words were spoken. Ticket purchases forced the switch to sound. The public again determined the direction that films would take. Lines at the box offices swept aside the argument that talkies were for lowbrows while the more sensitive, intelligent audiences wanted silent films. Hollywood executives should have known better because talkies followed right behind broadcasting, which was spreading as fast as people could afford to buy radio sets. Ticket sales rose sharply for the talkies that soon poured out of the Hollywood studios. Two years after *The Jazz Singer*, the Academy Award for best picture went to *The Broadway Melody* (1929), a splashy musical and the first of a series.

COLOR FILM

The first patent for a color process was issued in 1897, shortly after movies began. At first, a few films were hand painted frame by frame, clearly an impractical solution. In another process, scenes were tinted; segments of black-and-white film were simply dipped into dye so that scenes showing a lot of sky might be blue while scenes of a burning building might be tinted red. These attempts were meant to heighten the mood of the film rather than to add realism. Several optical color processes used colored filters or dyes with less than spectacular results. Only Technicolor, invented by Herbert Kalmus, was successful, emerging in 1922 as a two-tone process. A much better three-tone process followed. This complicated method involved not only printing images on film containing layers of emulsion, but shooting with camera lenses that split the light beam, sending the split images through different colored filters.

Clark Gable and Vivien Leigh in *Gone with the Wind* (1939). Audiences loved the Technicolor spectacle.

Most of the Hollywood establishment did not seem to care about color one way or the other. The public did care and, as usual, prevailed. Long lines for *Gone with the Wind* in 1939 should have convinced any doubters that the public loved romantic stories in lush Technicolor. During the 1980s, when old black-and-white films were colorized for television, the establishment did come out firmly, this time against adding color, arguing that computer generated colors ruined the directors' original visions.

▶ THE STUDIOS

The major studios that dominated Hollywood during its Golden Age, starting about 1930, developed genres and kept stars identified with a particular genre under contract. For MGM, it was the musical and the light comedy. 20th Century Fox specialized in musicals and biographies. Columbia became known for romantic comedies and for the populist films of director Frank Capra. Paramount had European sophistication. Warner Bros. had cowboys, gangsters, and swashbucklers. Republic had westerns and cliff-hanger serials. Universal did well with horror films.[9]

The musicals made from the 1930s onward were Hollywood at its brightest. If audiences loved fantasies mixed with music and glitter, the "dream factories" were only too happy to turn them out on the production lines. That the plots were absurd and always predictable only added to their charm. The audiences wanted to escape into a singing, dancing, Technicolor fantasy. The studios gave them what they wanted.

Westerns could be turned out cheaply and quickly, with familiar plots, pedestrian dialogue, heroes in white hats, villains in black hats, and Indians who said little more than "How!" and were shot off their horses on cue, perpetuating the stereotype. The films of Hopalong Cassidy (actor William Boyd), Gene Autry, and Buck Jones could usually be found in double and even triple features at the neighborhood movie house. Generations of small boys, dreaming of growing up to be cowboys, attacked little brothers assigned to be the Indians.

▶ DEPRESSION AND WAR YEARS

During the Depression years of the 1930s viewers sought lighthearted or escapist fare. In 1940 the average American—adult and child—bought nearly 20 movie tickets a year.[10] The quarter that paid for an average cinema admission could have bought a pound of beef, a gallon and a half of gasoline, or enough postage stamps to mail eight letters, with a penny left over for a postcard. To entice audiences during the Depression and the World War II years, cinemas encouraged attendance by such giveaways as sets of dishes, one dish per week. Attend often enough and the moviegoers could acquire a complete set. A typical family went to a neighborhood movie theater once a week. It was the place for young couples to go on a date. For those who could afford it, a downtown picture palace offered an upmarket alternative.

The neighborhood movie houses were less grand than the downtown plaster palaces, but were cheaper. A typical bill of fare at a neighborhood cinema consisted of two second-run movies, previews of coming attractions, a Walt Disney or Warner Bros. cartoon, and a newsreel. Another favorite of movie audiences were the *March of Time* documentary newsreels on a single subject, usually one of political interest. Because of technical limitations, newsreel presentations of major disasters like earthquakes might be three weeks old by the time they reached cinemas. Dog shows, fashion shows, and ball games in New York and the arrivals in New York of well-known personalities were fresher and easier to cover because New York City had film developing labs and distribution hubs.

Evening admission cost about 30 cents in 1943 at a neighborhood, second-run movie theater. Downtown prices might run 50 cents. A daily newspaper cost about 3 cents; a floor model Silvertone radio, $60; a Victrola phonograph, $110. A three-year-old two-door Chevrolet was advertised for $375. Prices depended on where you lived and the brand you chose, but approximately: a dozen eggs, 52 cents; 2 pounds of coffee, 41 cents; apples, 10 cents a pound; ground beef, 25 cents a pound; a bar of soap, 14 cents; a toothbrush, 29 cents.[11] A pack of Camels cost 14 cents, and a 12 ounce bottle of Pepsi, 5 cents, advertised by one of those radio jingles that listeners could not get out of their heads: "Pepsi Cola hits the spot, 12 full ounces, that's a lot. Twice as much for a nickel, too. Pepsi Cola is the drink for you."

▶ MOVIES WITH MESSAGES

Few moviegoers wanted to see sad or serious films, so the Hollywood studios shied away from making them. Although a few films such as *The Grapes of Wrath* and *Mission to Moscow* were produced in the early 1940s, the studios avoided message films that could provoke trouble. Producer Samuel Goldwyn is supposed to have said, "If you've got a message, send it by Western Union."

The preference for escapist fare changed sharply with American entry into World War II. Besides patriotic, war-themed films, Hollywood turned out films of home-front patriotism, documentaries like the *March of Time* series, weekly newsreels and a variety of training films. All the countries on both sides of the conflict, especially Nazi Germany, recognized the power of motion pictures in their own productions.

After the war a few Hollywood producers summoned up their courage to tackle such social issues as racism and anti-Semitism with *Home of the Brave* (1949), *Pinky* (1949) and *Gentleman's Agreement* (1947). *The Lost Weekend* (1945) dealt with alcoholism, *Brute Force* (1947) with prison brutality, *The Snake Pit* (1948) with horrid conditions in mental asylums, *The Man with the Golden Arm* (1955) with drug addiction, and *Blackboard Jungle* (1955) with juvenile delinquency.

The Cold War that closely followed World War II brought with it the "Red Scare." A deep political division tore Hollywood apart. Actors, writers, and directors suspected of Communist leanings were blacklisted and denied work. They could not be nominated for Oscars. Following hearings by the House of Representatives Committee on Un-American Activities, a few went to prison. The Red Scare blacklisted more than 300 artists, including Charlie Chaplin and Orson Welles, and divided the industry. Frightened studios put a temporary end to films that advocated social change. Escapism was more popular and less worrisome.

It took years, but over time this pain dissipated, though its scars persisted. Social problems reappeared in movies, which became increasingly frank as they attracted the interest of Main Street as well as the critics. Hostile race relations, homosexuality, police brutality, and political corruption became film topics. The best picture Oscar for *Midnight Cowboy* (1969) confronted the subject of homosexuality. Spike Lee won critical applause and lines at the box office with *Do the Right Thing* (1988), which examined the raw reality of black–white race relations. The theme was further explored in the controversial *Malcolm X* (1992). The nomination of *Brokeback Mountain* (2005) for an Oscar reinforced Hollywood's willingness to consider homosexuality

Midnight Cowboy (1969), the only X-rated film to win an Oscar.

as a film theme. There were many other socially relevant films. Movies continue to reflect public opinion, yet today's reflections are more honest than they used to be and less fearful of retribution. Today few controversial social issues lie beyond the boundaries of what mainstream moviemakers will examine.

▶ INTERNATIONAL TRADITIONS

While American motion picture production was shifting to Hollywood at the dawn of the last century, other nations constructed their own film industries. Germany and Denmark each claimed to have built the first motion picture studio. All large nations and many small nations developed their own movie industries even if a limited national language base held only a small promise of any financial success. Having a movie studio was a point of pride. Like a national airline, a film industry seemed essential to national prestige.

World War I gave a boost to Hollywood because almost all the European studios shut down. Among the wartime shortages suffered by the European nations was cellulose, the film base, for it was needed to make explosives. Lacking their own movies, Europeans began to import American product. After the war, their national production resumed, but European audiences had developed a taste for American films, especially westerns. What followed in subsequent decades has been a melding of influences, ideas, and talents into what has truly become an international industry.

France, the early leader, fell behind in building a strong film industry after World War I, but led experiments into unusual forms of expression, notably the avant-garde movement in film as well as in poetry, painting, and music, which looked at the world in new, symbolic ways. Expressions of art that had a shock value were prized, "decadent" or not. After World War II a new tradition swept the revived French motion picture industry. "New Wave" films rebelled against accepted moral standards and normal codes of behavior. With it grew the *auteur* tradition, which evaluated movies as the product of a single mind, that of the director, rather than as a collaboration of the talents of writers, actors, and dozens of others. Orson Welles's *Citizen Kane* and the films of Alfred Hitchcock typify the auteur tradition, which continues to influence movie making around the world.

In Russia after the Bolshevik revolution of 1917, the emerging Soviet film industry and the world's first film school fostered Marxist–Leninist ideology. Recognizing the political power of mass communication, Lenin said, "The cinema for us is the most important of the arts." To build support, "agitprop" (agitation and propaganda) trains fanned out across the countryside to promote Communist ideals for an illiterate proletariat. Meanwhile, radio sent the message across the vast reaches of the new Soviet Union. In rural areas where few radios existed, loudspeakers went up on poles in village squares. The Soviet film industry was led by such brilliant directors as Sergei Eisenstein, whose theory of montage—the relationship of one scene to another—influenced later filmmakers. His *Battleship Potemkin* (1925) has been called the most important film ever made because it showed the broad possibilities of film editing based on rhythm and the connecting of visual images.

In Germany a sturdy film industry grew in the 15 years following World War I, with films that explored more psychological themes than the light-weight American product. German filmmakers reached for darker visions of the soul, reflecting the despair of a once proud nation bitter and defeated, plagued by astronomical inflation, when a barrel of money bought one loaf of bread. It was said that Germany's low point as a nation was the high point of its silent film. Here the techniques of the moving camera expanded. When the Nazis took power in Germany during the 1930s, directors, actors, and technicians fled to Hollywood. The Nazi takeover transformed German cinema into a propaganda arm of the state. In *Triumph of the Will* (1934) and *Olympia* (1938), Nazi Germany's most brilliant director, Leni Riefenstahl, demonstrated the sheer political power of film even in a hateful cause. After World War II a revived German film industry emphasized strong and unusual dramatic themes.

In Britain a social documentary tradition grew during the Depression and World War II that identified national problems and suggested governmental solutions. One of Britain's leading filmmakers, John Grierson, called it "the drama of the doorstep." The British were also able to enjoy a good laugh at themselves. A string of postwar British films such as *Passport to Pimlico* (1949) and *Whisky Galore* (1949) (released as *Tight Little Island* in the United States) tapped a vein of gentle self-mocking humor. They drew appreciative audiences in the United States and the British Commonwealth. Monty Python's humor evolved from earlier examples of dry British wit.

Italy after World War II originated a school of neorealism, the opposite of Hollywood glitter. Films such as *Open City* (1945), *Shoeshine* (1946) and *The Bicycle Thief* (1948) had the gritty feel and look of the documentary as they chronicled the bleak lives of the urban poor.

Japan's film industry after World War II sparkled because of its great directors. Akira Kurosawa, the director best known to Western audiences, made *Rashomon* (1950), a costume drama set in Japan's long feudal era. This classic film is occasionally mentioned in ordinary conversation to argue that people who share the same experience have different memories and recollections of the event. Critics list *Rashomon* among the great films of all time.

More recently, India and China have also developed notable film industries. India's Bollywood produces more films than Hollywood and, in the *masala* films that mix genre, fills them with melodrama, music, and dance. From China in recent years have come award-winning dramas and fantasy films that have captivated audiences with their ethereal action. Iran is among smaller nations that have recognized the influence and goodwill that can follow the distribution of strong film stories of ordinary people dealing with ordinary problems.

In sum, film is an international industry that reveals a shared humanity that all mankind can recognize, existing beyond cultures, languages, and frontiers.

▶ ANIMATION

In the early years of the motion picture, a few moviemakers, in a throwback to 19th-century pre-motion picture devices, drew a series of pictures, each a little different from the last. The first animated cartoon short may have been *Gertie the Dinosaur* (1914), using 10,000 drawings. But audience enthusiasm really began with Walt Disney's *Steamboat Willie* (1928), one of the first animated cartoons with synchronized audio. The first color cartoon reached cinemas in 1932.

During the Depression, audiences expected that a night out at the movies would include a color cartoon. Mickey Mouse was more famous around the world than any actor. Tom and Jerry from MGM and Bugs Bunny from Warner Bros. offered him competition.

The popularity of the shorts led Disney to risk a feature-length animated film based on a well-known fairy tale. *Snow White and the Seven Dwarfs* (1937) combined the story with song. The public, old and young, was enchanted. A long string of feature-length animated films followed, notably *Fantasia* (1940), which introduced stereophonic music to the public, and *Beauty and the Beast* (1991), which earned an Academy Award nomination as the best picture of the year. The cost of frame-by-frame cel animation prompted shortcuts, starting in the 1960s by the Hollywood company Hanna-Barbera and in the 1970s by Japanese animators, at the expense of quality.

During the 1990s, computer-based animation restored and lifted animation standards. In the decade of the 2000s, advanced digital animation from

Pixar, Dreamworks, and other studios pulled in audiences with stories and dialogue that allowed both adults and children to enjoy films like *Shrek* and *Ratatouille* at different levels of understanding.

In 2001, a computer-generated feature film, *Final Fantasy*, tried to make its characters look and move like real people. From England, ignoring computers, the *Wallace and Gromit* films, patiently animated with clay figures, built a loyal fan base.

Computers enhanced movies in still other ways. In live action movies, morphing or shape shifting, starting with *Terminator 2* (1991), could smoothly change one character into another before our eyes. *Jurassic Park* shocked us with hungry dinosaurs (1993). *Titanic* (1997) brought us a realistic ship crashing into an iceberg and sinking. *Troy* (2004) was one of several historical epics that used computers to transform a relatively small number of extras into vast armies. And, of course, the computer has revolutionized feature-length animated films.

Media theorist Lev Manovich speaks of CGI (computer-generated images) as "creating fake realities," and finds examples in television as well as films, such as the meteorologist in front of a map, the newscaster in front of video footage, and the singer in front of animation. In movies, "Digital compositing does represent a qualitatively new step in the history of visual simulation because it allows the creation of *moving* images of nonexistent worlds."[12]

▶ NEWSREELS

The history of motion pictures began at the end of the 19th century with scenes from real life, both true and faked. Fiction films soon dominated the public's interest, but reality did not disappear from the screen. Broadly, it took two forms, the newsreel and the documentary.

Cinemas during the first half of the 20th century showed newsreels shot by independent companies and studios: Pathé, Fox, Movietone, Paramount, Universal, MGM, Telenews, and Gaumont, plus the newsreel-like *March of Time*. Because governments were quick to recognize their propaganda value, a number of countries had their own government-sanctioned newsreels, such as Nazi Germany's Deutsche Wochenschau and Japan's Yomiuri. Networks of film photographers and processing laboratories churned out thousands of feet of film each week, despite technical limitations.

The heavy 35mm film equipment that studios used for features slowed photographers in reaching a news scene and getting the film to a processing lab, with further delays in sending prints to thousands of cinemas. Hand-held 16mm silent cameras shot many stories, with narration and music added in postproduction, but this process was also slow.

As noted, a typical cinema newsreel began with a hard news story a week or two old, followed by several light features whose timeliness barely mattered. Because New York City was a major processing and distributing point, socialites leaving aboard an ocean liner or a New York dog show were newsreel staples. Newsreels often deserved the reputation of being frivolous, even if audiences enjoyed them or did not seem to mind when they were pointless.

When commercial television began in the late 1940s and early 1950s, two kinds of news were available: newsreels and non-visual newscasts transferred from radio. In time, the two melded into the timely and visual newscasts we see today.

DOCUMENTARY

The word "documentary" takes in a great deal of territory, from Michael Moore's filmed political tracts to nature movies. "Documentary" should not be equated with "truth," but may be defined as the creative interpretation of reality, with variations in the degree of creativity.

The first well-known documentary was Robert Flaherty's *Nanook of the North* (1922), a look at the life of an Inuit hunter, his family, and his village. In truth, Flaherty portrayed the more primitive life that Nanook's grandfather had lived.

Today, documentary film festivals are held in cities around the world. Raindance, located in London, offers training courses in directing, producing, writing, and technology. The Academy Awards has Oscars for both documentary short films and feature-length.

▶ CENSORSHIP CONTINUES

Censorship that began in 1909 during the era of silent films with the National Board of Review of Motion Pictures continued as Hollywood entered the era of sound movies. A code of acceptable behavior was adopted in 1934 and a Production Code Administration enforced it. Guidelines have been softened over the years as moviemakers challenged the limits. Church leaders argued that Hollywood's self-censorship code was too weak. Their attack went on for decades. Self-appointed critics soon expanded the focus on sex and violence to include political topics.

Foreign films and television influenced an easing of restrictions in the United States. Some films were banned in certain countries for a variety of reasons related to politics, extreme violence, or child pornography. However, generally more open in regard to sex content, European nations could be stricter about political ideas, but even in the Soviet Union American slapstick comedies were far more likely to attract audiences than political films. *All Quiet on the Western Front* (1930), denounced for its pacifism, was banned by a number of European governments.

A number of American states and cities set up their own censorship boards, but the standards varied from one board to another, creating a difficult situation for a national industry. The Kansas board, for example, banned scenes of smoking or drinking, limited kissing scenes to a few seconds, and even cut a scene showing diaper changing. A series of United States Supreme Court decisions from the late 1940s to the 1970s overturned state obscenity laws and resulted in more leeway for moviemakers. The seats continued to be filled from matinees through evenings.

Films that failed to meet strict standards were blacklisted and boycotted. As an example of how standards have changed, the 1953 romantic comedy *The Moon Is Blue*, was picketed and denied a Production Code seal of approval because the words "virgin," "seduce," "pregnant," and "mistress" were uttered. Kansas, Maryland, and Ohio banned the film, and the Kansas Supreme Court upheld the ban. The U.S. Supreme Court reversed it. The court decision and the box office success of the film weakened the influence of the Production Code. Years later, a *M*A*S*H* episode had the characters learning about the controversy and trying to get a copy of *The Moon is Blue* shipped to them in Korea.

Pressed from all sides, the motion picture industry in the United States decided on new national standards based on age. In 1968, modeled on a British system, a self-censorship code was adopted that we know by the G, PG, PG-13, R, and NC-17 (formerly X) designations.

▶ POSTWAR AND TELEVISION YEARS

After World War II, even before television took hold, movie attendance declined. From 1946 to 1951, weekly movie going dropped nearly 40 percent. Film historian David Thomson wondered why:

> What was happening? It is still an area for speculation: reunited lovers sat in the dark for a few years, then they were pregnant and the owners of new homes and families. Such people have never been steadfast moviegoers: their show is at home; they are tired, and a whole menu of practical realties has usurped the role of fantasy in their lives. Some of them had been educated, matured, or saddened by the experiences of war and travel . . . Perhaps the deepest lesson (though few people perceived it at the time) was that the old unity of the audience no longer existed. There were many who still wanted fun, fantasy, happy endings, and a couple of hours of escape. But the atom bomb's shock waves passed through us, along with the truth about concentration camps and the witchcraft called the Red Menace. Was war really over? . . . Suppose the movies were no longer quite a mass medium. There was some unease over the old models of fantasy and escapism. There was a yearning for new approaches.[13]

McLuhan and Powers observed, "For example, during the studio years (1931–1945) the Hollywood film studios were keyed to a mass audience. Everybody went to the movies, including the educated, and film scripts contained, accordingly, a commensurate amount of literacy (e.g., *Gone with the Wind*, 1939). But as soon as television appeared to further develop the characteristics of a mass medium, movies became specialized according to audience level. The 'art film' suddenly appeared; Disney geared films to the pre-teens, etc."[14]

The Supreme Court, in a 1948 anti-trust decision, *U.S. v. Paramount*, ordered the studios to divest themselves of ownership of theater chains. It took Hollywood several years to recover from the triple blows of divestiture, an influx of foreign films from postwar European film studios, and competition from the newly emerging television industry. Box office receipts plummeted.

With fear and hostility, Hollywood at first tried to ignore television as just a fad, denying the new medium access to its actors, directors, scripts, studio back lots, and film libraries. Little by little, television chipped away at each of these barriers. None stand today. With their heavy overhead and expensive talent on contract, the big studios were losing millions of dollars. To protect themselves they cut their staffs, ended contracts with their stars and other high priced talent, and began renting out their studio facilities to television production companies.

Resultant weakening of the Hollywood studios allowed independent producers to step in to make smaller films, take artistic chances with new approaches to subject matter, and distribute their films to theaters no longer in the tight grip of the major studios. Some independent films tested the limits that censors would allow. A fresh breeze was blowing through studios whose practices had become stiff and stale. Efforts to compete by expanding the screen with new projection systems such as 3-D, Cinerama and Cinema-Scope had mixed success, but greater use by the studios of color and stereo, especially in musicals, showed favorably in comparison with the monaural, black-and-white of the television screen. The 1950s also saw movie stars break away to make independent deals instead of being tied to studio contracts, starting with James Stewart in 1952. The era of the big studios was coming to an end, but audiences still wanted movies.

▶ THE DRIVE-INS

During the 1950s and 1960s, movie theaters closed as Americans stayed home to watch television, but one kind of cinema did well. People were moving to the suburbs and, in an era of gardening, boating, and barbecuing, the drive-in theater, where the movie stars competed with the real stars, was an easy fit. It reflected the return of automobile production as well as the suburban population shift. More families had automobiles, gas was cheap and so was an evening at the drive-in, with free admission for kids and no problem about bringing your own sandwiches, even a whole dinner.

A salesman, Richard Hollingshead, opened the first drive-in near Camden, New Jersey, in 1933, during the depths of the Depression. By 1958 nearly one cinema in every three was a drive-in, nearly 5,000 across the nation, even though the weather forced closure for months in the northern states.[15]

To go to a drive-in you didn't have to pay for parking or a baby sitter, no small consideration in the baby-boom postwar years. The drive-in's fast-food island did a brisk business. Some drive-ins provided playgrounds, laundromats, picnic spots, and even miniature golf courses. All provided a hangout for teens away from their parents, a favorite place to "neck." The double feature was usual, the triple feature not unknown. No cheaply made "B" picture was so bad that it could not be found at some drive-in. (B movies usually ran for less than 70 minutes and depended on action, such as westerns or horror films.) In your car with the windows shut to enjoy the sound coming from a speaker hanging from a side window, you could be as relaxed and talkative as you wanted. It was not unlike an evening with the television of the day, except that the screen was bigger and the movies were in color and more fun than what TV showed on the few available channels. The image was certainly a lot clearer than on a round, gray television tube.

An evening at the drive-in was family time, an evening with friends or a date and no strangers to shush you if you talked. It was not unlike an evening with the television. The drive-in theatre was a harbinger of improved television and later of video rentals. It fitted marketing consultant Faith Popcorn's word "cocoon," which means insulating oneself or hiding from the normal social environment, that may be perceived as distracting, unfriendly, dangerous, or otherwise unwelcome.[16] Technology has made cocooning easier than ever before. The telephone and the Internet are inventions that invite a kind of socialized cocooning, when one can live in physical isolation while maintaining contact with others.

Drive-ins packed them in during the post-World War II years.

Rising real estate values along with the improving quality of television eventually shut down the "ozoner" (so-called because of the car exhaust odor). The adoption of Daylight Savings Time in the 1970s also hurt drive-ins because it pushed movie starting times too close to bedtime.[17] Teenagers found their escape from the family instead at the new shopping center's air-conditioned multiplex. The rest of the family would do their eating, talking, and baby minding in front of the tube, maybe now with a tape, DVD, or download. As the centers of mediated entertainment shifted and fractured into private homes, downtowns in many cities looked forlorn in the evening. The crowds had gone. In the common phrase, "they rolled up the sidewalks."

Movie theaters also evolved. Despite fears about the new medium, television certainly did not kill the motion picture. Nor did it kill the motion picture theater. Economic realities did force changes. Gone are most of the ornate downtown picture palaces, the mom-and-pop single neighborhood theaters and the suburban drive-ins. Instead of downtown palaces and neighborhood cinemas each with a single offering, cinemas were built into suburban shopping malls, where they share parking spaces with supermarkets. Facing economic pressures on all sides, cinemas today derive most of their income from the snack bar. Multiplexes started in 1963 in Kansas City with two cinemas side by side. The landscape would in time be dotted by mega-multiplexes with 15 to 20 screens sharing a lobby redolent of popcorn in an effort to make going out to the movies an event more enjoyable than just watching the same movie at home.

The cinema has become a fixture at the mall. For couples, it is the place to go on a date. For youths, it is a place to meet friends, to hang out, to escape the family for an evening. For kids, it is a Saturday afternoon treat. Nothing was spectacular about them, but they provided what a downtown palace lacked: easy access from homes, plenty of free parking, association based on taste, and, above all, choice.

The drive-in has not totally disappeared. In fact, it has seen a slight resurgence with some new drive-ins using DVD players, digital projectors, iPods and FM transmitters to show films on large outdoor screens.[18] Some cities have begun to hold outdoor rooftop showings allowing families in summertime to enjoy movies under the stars and catching up to what many people in tropical countries have been doing for decades.

▶ RENTING OR OWNING

The neighborhood video store once impressed us with its wide variety of movie tapes. Like so much else in the rapidly changing world of media, the store is gone. Today Netflix does the same with DVDs by mail and download. In addition to the new releases, far more choices are available than are found in all the theaters in town. Hulu is among providers of an online download service.

Centuries ago a book was a precious possession that only the rich could own. Now anyone can own a book and it is just as easy to own a movie. It is by no means unusual for a home library to contain more movies than books. Home entertainment is often scheduled around a DVD that was ordered online or picked up on a shopping trip. The reasons are obvious: choice, convenience, and control.

Business-man Andre Blay made a deal in 1977 to buy cassette production rights to fifty 20th Century Fox movies, but Blay discovered that few customers wanted to buy his tapes, although everyone wanted to rent them at a lower price. Video rental shops soon sprouted like corner groceries. In fact, sometimes the corner grocery itself devoted a shelf to videotapes, making it simple to stop by after work to pick up the fixings for the evening's dinner and entertainment, maybe to be consumed together.

In time, these video shops would be joined by video supermarkets that displayed tens of thousands of titles stored on both videotape and DVD discs in sections labeled *new releases, comedy, adventure, horror, science fiction, romance, children, family, inspirational, exercise, travel, concert, foreign, classics, documentary*, and, in a separate room, *adults only*. Music videos and games got their own sections as did "how-to's" on everything from losing weight to cooking. Candy bars, ice cream, and bags of popcorn for microwaving at home mimicked the cinema. Immigrants from non-English countries kept a shelf of tapes or DVD films in their native language.

▶ WATCHING MOVIES AT HOME

The public left indoor movie theaters for drive-ins partly for the convenience and cheaper cost. Later they left theaters and drive-ins to sit in front of television screens to watch sitcoms and movies, again partly because of convenience and cost. Today we can watch what we download or what arrives in the mail at home without any worry about what friends will say or neighbors will think. There is no need to drive anywhere, dress up or get dressed at all, be quiet, or even sit up. A couch potato can phone a friend, leaf through a magazine, eat a seven-course dinner, stop the DVD to go to the kitchen, the bathroom or the baby's crib, watch a scene over, or set the machine to record a TV program. The satisfied viewer won't miss a syllable. Did Cecil B. DeMille have it any better than this? We time-shift programs, so prime time is any time. Fast-forwarding through taped commercials gave advertising agencies heartburn before TiVo did.

As a result of the appeal of this easygoing lifestyle, we as a society are less social. Like all mediated communication, motion pictures substitute for direct contact with other people. Less reading of books, a drop-off in church attendance, and fewer visits to lectures, concerts, friends and family have also marked our pattern of life. Instead, a routine has developed of staying home to watch instead of going out to dances, sports events, club meetings, or bowling alleys, activities that television and stored media have to some extent displaced.[19]

Robert Putnam, author of *Bowling Alone,* observed, "For the first two-thirds of the 20th century a powerful tide bore Americans into ever deeper engagement in the life of their communities, but a few decades ago—silently, without warning—that tide reversed and we were overtaken by a treacherous rip current. Without at first noticing, we have been pulled apart from one another and from our communities over the last third of the century."[20]

Watching a film with someone provides a limited degree of human contact. When adult friends or relatives drop by for an evening, it does not promise an evening of conversation as it once did, but perhaps a little conversation and a lot of movie or sports watching. When a child's friends visit, look for a video game accompanied by a minimum of conversation.

There is one other thing that home viewing is not. It is not an *event*. Going out and being surrounded in a darkened theater by strangers who are sharing the moment is more so. Seeing the action on a big screen and hearing the sound all around adds to an eventful sense of escapism.[21] Although that sense, along with the heavily advertised first run movies, can pull patrons to the box office line, it is not enough on a blustery evening to coax large numbers of people out of their homes. We "go" to the movies in other ways, using new hardware for the software we love to watch.

▶ WE "GO" TO THE MOVIES

As we know, movie viewing did not stay in the cinemas, but has expanded onto home screens, computer screens, even handheld smartphones. Across the world there are more movie screens than ever. Some screens have widened to IMAX size and films can be delivered over satellite or broadband connections instead of 35mm reels. 3D has made a comeback and some movie theaters worldwide are adding "event cinema" of special showings such as "Cirque du Soleil 3D." The industry has never forgotten public demand and, in fact, has shown the public how much more they could demand.

It is a mistake to think of motion pictures as an industry that begins with production and ends in a movie theater. Considered that way, the old medium certainly suffered with the advance of the new medium of television, just as the television industry later suffered with the popularity of newer media. Videotape suffered in turn with the arrival of DVD, which at this writing has waned in competition with downloading from the Internet. Seen purely from the production standpoint, however, the motion picture medium has expanded. Around the world more movies are being made on a variety of media than ever before and they are distributed through an increasing number of outlets to an increasing number of viewers.

We may travel no further than our comfortable living room sofa, fortifying ourselves with a microwaved frozen dinner or a bowlful of freshly microwaved popcorn as we tune in or pop in a promising movie. Replacing physical film or tape with digital files, the delivery media are different, yet movies are still movies.

In the changing software distribution pattern, a feature film usually starts life in first-run mall theaters in the United States and large cities in other countries. The more popular films next go to cheaper second-run discount theaters, others straight to DVD. While the public still remembers the ads and reviews, films reach cable pay-per-view, the remaining video shops for sales and rental, the red envelopes of Netflix in the mailbox and the Red Box at the supermarket, plus streaming or downloading for computers. In addition, there is HBO, Cinemax, other premium cable channels, and any channels willing to pay a fee for early release line up. Next, network television. Several years after they are first issued, the films are syndicated to stations and free cable channel "superstations." Along the way are strands of an extensive network of foreign distribution and such specialty outlets as airlines. Meanwhile, HBO is among several cable channels that distribute their own films, sometimes in series that win awards for quality.

HOME MOVIES

"Home movies" have been around at least since 1923, when the Cine-Kodak film camera and the Kodascope projector went on sale. They, too, form part of the story of motion pictures. Today, in homes far from Hollywood, more movies are being made than ever before as a result of the availability of inexpensive, easy-to-use desktop video hardware and software.

After the video camera-recorder—camcorder—was introduced in 1982, millions were sold each year, the digital camcorder gradually supplanting the analog version, followed by tapeless cameras. That more people than ever before are shooting video clips or even producing entire movies is due in part to digital technology. Making a film that looks relatively professional has become affordable for many people. It was not possible during the golden age of the studios.

The phrase *desktop video* has found its way into the language next to *desktop publishing*. For U.S.$31,000, two young men made *The Blair Witch Project* and promoted it at almost no cost online (see page 286). Desktop video films can't match the Hollywood product, but they are gaining in popularity and sophistication.[22]

▶ WE ARE DIFFERENT

Film historians Kristin Thompson and David Bordwell offer this perspective:

Around the world, at any instant, millions of people are watching movies. They watch mainstream entertainment, serious "art films," documentaries, cartoons, experimental films, educational shorts. They sit in air-conditioned theaters, in village squares, in art museums, in college classrooms, in their homes before a computer monitor. The world's movie theaters sell 8 billion tickets each year. With the availability of films on video—whether broadcast, fed from cable or satellites or the Internet, or played back from DVD or on cellphones—the audience has multiplied far beyond that . . . The way we dress and cut our hair, the way we talk and act, the things we believe or doubt—all these aspects of our lives are shaped by films.[23]

The term "film" itself is an anachronism both as a noun and as a verb. Filming was done on a photographic film base, then on videotape, and then by discs and other digital memory units but it has left its language behind. "Filmmakers" still "film," no matter what they record on. And despite all the changes, movies are still movies. They are different because of all of us. We are different because of them.

▶ TIMELINE

1927   Al Jolson's *The Jazz Singer* popularizes movie sound.

The Academy of Motion Picture Arts and Sciences is founded.

1929   24 frames/second established as the sound motion picture camera standard.

1930   Hollywood sets up the Hays office to create a new code of decency.

1931   American cinemas routinely show double features.

1933   Camden, New Jersey, sees the drive-in movie theater.

1935   Three-element Technicolor system in *Becky Sharp* sets new standard.

1937   A full-length animated film, Disney's *Snow White and the Seven Dwarfs*.

1939   Blockbusters draw audiences: *The Wizard of Oz*, *Gone with the Wind*, *Stagecoach*.

1945   *Open City* from Italy introduces a gritty "Neo-realism" style.

1946   In France, the Cannes Film Festival.

1947   During the "Red Scare," the "Hollywood Ten" are blacklisted for contempt of Congress.

1948   Supreme Court forces studios to divest themselves of movie theaters.

1952   3D movies make audiences duck.

The Supreme Court gives movies First Amendment free speech protection.

1953   CinemaScope.

1955   Movie studios open their vaults for television rentals, sales.

1956   Foreign language films get an Oscar category. This year: Italy's *La Strada*.

1959   From France, "New Wave" cinema. *Breathless* uses hand-held camera, jump cuts.

1961   In-flight movies shown on regular commercial runs.

1963   In Kansas City, the first multiplex opens: two cinemas side by side.

1968   Hollywood adopts an age-based rating system; at first: G, M, R, X.

1969   X-rated movie, *Midnight Cowboy*, wins Best Picture Oscar.

1973   Marlon Brando refuses Best Actor Oscar as a political protest.

1984   Supreme Court: videotaping is not a violation of copyright.

1990   NC-17 (no children under 17) replaces X-rating.

1993   IMAX 3D digital sound system goes into a New York cinema.

       Lost in Yonkers converted into digital bits, uses computer editing process.

1997   *Titanic* sails into big-budget waters, costs about U.S.$300 million. Grosses twice that.

1999   Two young men make *Blair Witch Project* for U.S.$31,000. Grosses $125 million.

2001   From *Harry Potter* to *Crouching Tiger, Hidden Dragon*, CGI special effects rock audiences.

2002   Desktop video: making movies becomes more affordable.

       DVD burners download movies; film piracy becomes an international problem.

2010   A woman, Kathryn Bigelow, wins the Oscar for best director (*The Hurt Locker*).

       Sci-fi hit *Avatar* revives interest in 3D.

▶ NOTES

1 http://www.newseum.org/news/2007/12/visitors-shake-rattle-roll-through-4-d-film.html

2 ibid.

3 Silent films were still made in early 1930s, such as Charlie Chaplin's *City Lights*, before Hollywood totally yielded to the demand for talkies.

4 Kristin Thompson and David Bordwell, *Film History: An Introduction*, 3rd ed. (New York: McGraw-Hill, 2010) 193–194.

5 To see and hear a Spanish version, go to http://www.youtube.com/watch?v=_U5Z3AS1DDQ.

6 Thompson and Bordwell, 194.

7   For more information about this fascinating occupation, check out the Harvard Film Archive: http://hcl.harvard.edu/hfa/films/2012octdec/benshi.html. See also Thompson and Bordwell, 171, 192–193. Raymond Fielding has argued that silent films were seldom truly silent. "The systematic use of. . . live performers during motion picture presentations began at least as early as 1897 . . . and during the first decade of the century a number of professional actors companies were founded to provide such services to theaters on a regular basis . . . In fact, then, the 'silent film' is a myth. It never existed. Furthermore, the term was rarely used prior to 1926—only afterwards." Raymond Fielding, "The Technological Antecedents of the Coming of Sound: An Introduction," in E. W. Cameron ed., *Sound and the Cinema* (New York: Redgrave Publishing Co., 1980) 5.

8   Ellis, Jack C., *A History of Film*, 2nd ed. (Englewood Cliffs: Prentice-Hall, 1985) 152.

9   The index at http://www.filmsite.org/index.html leads to articles on a broad variety of film genres that studios specialized in and promoted. For instance, Universal, which bills itself as "the movie studio that invented the horror film genre," offers live shows in Hollywood, Orlando, and Singapore.

10 Box office data from 1929 to the present can be found at http://www.waynesthisandthat.com/moviedata.html.

11 Many of these prices were listed in the *Morris County Daily Record*, December 1–15, 1941, at the time of the bombing of Pearl Harbor and United States entry into World War II. Online at http://www.gti.net/mocolib1//prices/1943.html#thanksgiving.

12 Lev Manovich, *The Language of New Media* (Cambridge, MA: MIT Press, 2001) 150, 153.

13 David Thomson, *The Big Screen: The Story of the Movies* (New York: Farrar, Straus and Giroux, 2012) 249–251.

14 Marshall McLuhan and Bruce R. Powers, *The Global Village: Transformations in World Life and Media in the 21st Century* (New York: Oxford University Press) 1989.

15 For more history, see Robin T. Reid, "The History of the Drive-In Movie Theater," at http://www.smithsonianmag.com/arts-culture/the-history-of-the-drive-in-movie-theater-51331221/?page=1. Also, Elizabeth McKeon, and Linda Everett, *Cinema Under the Stars: America's Love Affair With the Drive-In Movie Theater* (Nashville: Cumberland House, 1998).

16 Faith Popcorn, *The Popcorn Report: The Future of Your Company, Your World, Your Life* (New York: Doubleday, 1991).

17 "This Day in History: June 6, 1933," http://www.history.com/this-day-in-history/first-drive-in-movie-theater-opens.

18 *Time*, August 14, 2006: 75.

19 For an extensive discussion, see Robert Putnam, *Bowling Alone: The Collapse and Revival of American Community* (New York: Simon & Schuster, 2000). It should

be noted that the decades following World War II saw an upsurge in social club and community activity. It was the heyday of Lions, Elks, Moose, Rotarians, Shriners, and veterans' organizations.

20 Putnam, 27.

21 David Denby wrote, "[E]ven people who like going to movies alone don't necessarily go to be alone. In a marvelous paradox, the people around us both relieve us of isolation and drive us deeper into our own responses." David Denby, "Big Pictures," *The New Yorker*, January 8, 2007: 56, 62.

22 An interesting examination of this point can be found in the *New York Times*, December 10, 2006, Sec. 230.

23 Thompson and Bordwell, xiv.

11

Radio: Helping Us through the Rough Years

Transmitter earlier

Radio was never just one thing, one isolated invention. It did not have just one effect on us. People involved with radio at its beginning did not consider broadcasting. They were not concerned with connecting with the public; in fact, they did not want intruders tuning in. They thought instead of what the telegraph could not do. Radio was invented as *wireless telegraphy*, a point-to-point service. As *wireless* Morse code communication, radio extended the telegraph where wires could not run. Its main business was to exchange Morse code messages between ships at sea and shore stations.

With the invention of the vacuum tube, radio began to move into the era of *wireless telephony*, replacing the dots and dashes with voices, but still a point-to-point service that extended the range of the telephone. When its potential as a point-to-multiple-point service was recognized, when technology opened a path, and when advertising provided an economic underpinning, radio found a new social use. As *broadcasting*, radio gave uniformity to a diverse population, contact to the lonely, and comfort to scattered listeners. And as it did so, it created a landscape that depended on unseen others for information and entertainment. Out of radio broadcasting has come television broadcasting, and out of television broadcasting has come cable television, a non-broadcast service. Ironically, out of broadcasting, with its effort to reach the broadest possible nationwide radio audience, has come *narrowcasting*, aiming to reach a closely defined audience.

Here is *broadcasting*, a word that previously had been used only to describe what a farmer did when he sowed his field with seed. The U.S. Navy appropriated the word during World War I to describe messages sent to a number of ships at once. The wireless industry derived its word from this. Based on the idea that rays of electromagnetic waves radiated from a transmitter, the word *radio* itself came into general use in the United States only after the vacuum tube sent voices into the air. The term much used in Britain was *wireless*.

Radio broadcasting changed the way in which people chose to be amused and informed at home. Some people alive today grew up in homes where reading aloud was a common activity in the evening. Radio added a new dimension to family entertainment as listeners gathered. Reading aloud in a family setting requires active participation, but radio listeners passively came together around a machine instead of a parent.

As they read, parents look at their children for their silent responses or questions. Even sitting passively in a theater or concert hall requires dressing up or at least dressing before venturing out to share the event with others in an auditorium, making such a trip a social experience. Listening to the radio requires none of this. The listener can sit quietly at home and let the newscasters, DJs, and music do all the work. Once agreement about a program choice is reached, listening is passive. The speakers and musicians do not need your nods of encouragement.

▶ SCIENTIFIC ROOTS

During the 19th century, scientists puzzled over the nature of electricity and what it might be capable of doing, sharing their discoveries in papers and lectures. Michael Faraday in England and Joseph Henry in the United States published papers on electromagnetism.[1] Scottish physicist James Clerk Maxwell added to what was known with his theory of the existence of invisible waves.[2] It was widely believed that light waves and electromagnetic waves could not simply travel through "nothing." Scientists imagined a substance like a thin, colorless, odorless jelly in the air that they named "ether" (not to be confused with the gas used as an anesthetic). That theory has long since vanished, but the word stuck around to refer to radio transmission.[3]

Heinrich Hertz, a German physicist, supported Maxwell's theory by experiments that sent electrical current through the air. French scientist Édouard Branly put iron filings in a glass tube. When he sent an electric current through the air, the filings packed together—or *cohered*—around metal rods at the ends of the tube. This action in his coherer completed a circuit so that electricity passed through the tube. English physicist Oliver Lodge went a step further by tuning the transmitter and the receiver of the current to the same frequency. He wanted to send a Morse code message through the air, but his coherer could do no more than identify brief bursts of electric energy.[4] In Moscow, Alexander Popov in 1895 demonstrated to fellow scientists a practical application of radio waves, but he did not seek a patent.

▶ MARCONI

These researchers were scientists, not businessmen, but entrepreneurs perceived that a practical commercial and military potential existed for the new technology. Guglielmo Marconi, the teenage son of a well-to-do Italian landowner, fascinated by reports of the research, began his own experiments at home in the hope of creating a business with wireless telegraphy. He received some guidance from a physics professor, Auguste Righi, who was a neighbor.[5] In 1894, young Marconi sent a current through a coherer to sound a buzzer 10 yards away. Soon he was able to send Morse code dots and dashes for miles across the hills around his home. Marconi's mother, Anne Jameson Marconi, a member of an Irish family famed for its whiskey, foresaw the possibilities for ships at sea to signal and to receive messages from coastal stations. According to Marconi family lore, a shortsighted official in the Italian Ministry of Posts and Telegraphs turned the invention down as having no value.

Anne Marconi and her son took his wireless equipment to England, the nation with the world's greatest navy. Anne's well-connected relatives arranged meetings with telegraph officials of the British Post Office, including William Preece, who once dismissed Alexander Graham Bell's telephone invention because England had plenty of messenger boys. This time the reaction was different. Successful demonstrations of Marconi's wireless led to financial offers to take over the invention as well as to claims that others had already sent such signals. Marconi held firm. His family arranged to sell equipment to the British army and navy and to train the wireless operators, but they would retain control. They also provided equipment for commercial shipping companies, along with operators on ships and at shore stations. With this, wireless communication emerged from the laboratory and strode into the world of commerce.

Extending the signal's reach in 1901, Marconi transmitted the three dots of the Morse Code letter "S" faintly across the Atlantic from Cornwall to Newfoundland. He formed an American subsidiary, the Marconi Wireless Telegraph Company of America that would eventually become RCA, the Radio Corporation of America.

Competition and new inventions came from several quarters. Marconi's transmission was not too complex to imitate. His efforts to monopolize the wireless business by refusing communication with non-Marconi operators except in emergencies raised a storm of protest. The German government was furious. Its navy was operating its own system, originally based on Marconi's experiments. A rising militant nationalism among the great powers of Europe that led to World War I hardly softened mutual suspicions. A 1906 Berlin conference resulted in the world's first international radio agreement, mandating that international coastal stations must handle all messages, and that the letters "SOS" should be used for distress. Marconi operators generally ignored the decision and continued to use "CQD" ("seek you, distress").

Guglielmo Marconi, 1926.

Other scientists and inventors also saw the business possibilities. They included Oliver Lodge in England and Reginald Fessenden, Lee de Forest, John Stone, and E. Howard Armstrong in the United States. The quarrels over discoveries and patents that resulted among them would end years later in lengthy court battles fought by corporations.

Commercial shipping added wireless equipment, nudged by new laws. In 1909 off the coast of Nantucket the merchant ship *Republic* collided in the fog with the Italian liner *Florida* packed with Italian immigrants. The repeated distress call "CQD" led to the rescue of all aboard both vessels. The next year Congress required most passenger ships to carry wireless equipment but did not require operators to be on duty around the clock, an oversight it regretted two years later after the *Titanic* hit an iceberg and went down with 1,522 passengers and crew on its maiden voyage. The *Titanic* was on a well-traveled sea lane. The *Californian* reportedly was only 19 miles away, but its wireless operator had gone to bed. The ship sailed on, though ships further away responded. Bad as it was, the death toll would have been higher had wireless communication not existed. Like travel by ship, air travel would also find safety in the reach of radio communication. Radio made all travel safer.

Congress followed with the Radio Act of 1912, requiring that a federal license was needed for transmission. Unlike the right of publishing guaranteed by the First Amendment, broadcasting would be a privilege the government could grant or take away. Getting a license was as simple at first as sending a postcard to the Department of Commerce. At the time, no sense emerged of the chaos that would arrive a decade later with the arrival of

RADIO GOES TO WAR

Radio first went into combat in the Russo–Japanese war of 1904. Both the Russian and Japanese fleets had installed the signaling devices, but the Russian admiral chose wireless silence in hopes of eluding the waiting Japanese fleet. Meanwhile, warned by shore radio at lookout points of the impending arrival of the Russian "great white fleet" into Asian waters, the Japanese navy set a trap that sank most of the imperial Russian ships at the battle of Tsushima Strait. The Japanese fleet suffered almost no losses, achieving the most one-sided naval victory in history. Russia sued for peace. Now radio had played a small but vital part in affecting the course of history.

News of the Japanese victory in the Russo–Japanese War was hailed all across Asia and Africa. At last, a non-European country had defeated a European imperialist. Japan was firmly entrenched on the Asian mainland, remaining there and expanding its territory until its turn of fortunes in World War II.

Radio's military possibilities took to the skies in 1911 with the first air-to-ground transmission; World War I airplanes served as artillery spotters using Morse code.

commercial broadcasting. If one purpose of the Radio Act of 1912 was to limit the number of amateur broadcasters, it failed. Most licenses went to hobbyists who used spark transmitters to send Morse code. By 1917 there were 13,581 of them, plus uncounted thousands of other hobbyists who broadcast without a license. Alone among the large industrialized nations, the United States would allow all three forms of mediated point-to-point communication—telegraph, telephone, radio—to remain predominantly in private hands.

▶ OTHER INVENTORS

At the start of World War I, radio mostly meant wireless dots and dashes for military and commercial purposes. The main business of radio was the manufacturing of wireless equipment for ships, shore stations, and military communication. The other part of the business was the sale or lease of communication services to the shipping industry and the government. That would change because inventors who were improving telephone service wanted to apply the results to radio. John Ambrose Fleming built a two-element vacuum tube, or "diode." It sent electrons flowing from a wire filament to a plate. The Fleming "valve" was the first vacuum tube. It would be used in radio receivers and radar for decades. It was the start of electronics.

In 1906, while tinkering, American inventor Lee de Forest added a third element between the filament and the plate, a piece of wire bent into a zig-zag grid. His "audion" tube regulated and amplified the incoming flow of electrons. Now the wireless telegraph could carry a voice. De Forest was not sure what he had accomplished, but a more competent inventor, E. Howard Armstrong, figured out how to use the audion tube as an oscillator that *transmitted* radio waves as well as receiving them.

Reginald Fessenden, a Canadian who had once worked in the Edison laboratory, and Swedish immigrant E. F. W. Alexanderson, a General Electric engineer, designed a high frequency alternator that could send a radio signal thousands of miles. Fessenden was the first inventor to send a human voice by wireless. He did so on Christmas Eve, 1906, from his laboratory at Brant Rock, Massachusetts, to an audience of some amazed Marconi operators on duty at their posts on ships and at coastal stations listening for dots and dashes. He also reached some New England fishermen, a few naval officers, and some reporters whom Fessenden had notified a few days earlier. He read from the Bible, sang, played the violin, broadcast phonograph music, and gave a short speech.[6]

Two years later de Forest went to the top of the Eiffel Tower in Paris to broadcast opera music that could be faintly heard 550 miles away. De Forest saw the possibility of bringing music and voices into people's homes on a schedule, telling a *New York Times* reporter, "I look forward to the day when opera may be brought into every home. Someday the news and even advertising will be sent out over the wireless telephone."[7] By 1909, Charles "Doc" Herrold, who operated an engineering college in San José, California, broadcast news and music on a regular schedule. In 1915, de Forest manufactured equipment that was tuned to his occasional music and news broadcasts plus the commercials he aired to advertise his equipment. He had stumbled onto the vacuum tube by chance, but his vision of the potential of broadcasting was clear long before broadcasting became a reality. Also in 1915, from a transmitter in Virginia, AT&T sent an audio signal that was picked up in both Paris and Pearl Harbor.

▶ LISTENING BY CATWHISKER

Because a single vacuum tube easily cost a week's wages, listening to distant radio signals might have been out of the range of most purses. However, the "crystal and catwhisker" detector, easy to fashion and cheap, was the poor hobbyist's answer. A quartz crystal or a galena rock, by admitting electricity in only one direction, can detect radio waves if the crystal is touched at a certain spot with a fine wire, dubbed a "catwhisker." This discovery opened radio to thousands of hobbyists. Some became the cadre of the broadcasting industry. They wrapped a copper wire around a round, sturdy Quaker Oats cardboard box, the kind you still find in grocery stores. The catwhisker radio could detect a wireless signal and feed it into earphones, although it could not amplify the signal. The hobbyist's pleasure came from picking up call letters from a distant city. That would change when entertainment programs were created in the 1920s to attract listeners to commercial advertisements.

Eager high school and university students formed radio clubs. In 1909, at the dawn of wireless radio, a group of boys in New York with the average age of 12 formed the Junior Wireless Club, the first amateur radio organization. One year later several thousand amateur stations with high power transformers were filling the air across the nation. Their enthusiasm and stubbornness kept them at it day and night. Trying to transmit on the same frequency, the U.S. Navy was not pleased. The children were hogging the available spectrum for the Navy and commercial users, and would not give way. It would take World War I for the Navy to shut down the radio interference, based on the Radio Act of 1912 that provided government control over wavelengths. At this early date, prior to World War I, several years before broadcast mass communication, the public of all ages were communicating by a broadcast medium.[8] Adding an additional wavelength helped somewhat, but the mutual rancor continued. Preachers and educators who wanted to use the airwaves joined the fray.

At the end of World War I, the business of radio was still largely vested in the manufacture of ship-to-ship and ship-to-shore radiotelegraph (Morse code) and radiotelephone (voice) communication equipment, the transmission of messages, and the manufacture of spark transmitters bought by hobbyists, not the broadcasts themselves. The idea that a vast market existed for radio was hardly credible, but in the years immediately after the war there were hints of its future.

▶ THE START OF BROADCASTING

Hobbyists by the thousands had become radio operators for the U.S. Army and Navy. With the war over, some of these operators wanted to start new stations to broadcast voice and music. Frank Conrad, a Westinghouse Corporation engineer who worked on manufacturing portable equipment for the Signal Corps, was among the visionaries. Setting up a transmitter in the garage of his home in Pittsburgh after returning from the war, he was an amateur who broadcast to other amateurs for the pleasure of doing it. He broadcast music by placing his microphone next to a Victrola, requesting postcards from listeners so that he could determine the range of his signals. So many listeners replied to ask for their favorite songs that Conrad started transmitting the broadcasts according to a schedule, adding sports scores and some singing and instrument playing by his children. A Pittsburgh newspaper printed a feature story about it.[9]

To meet requests for music that Conrad did not possess, the owner of a phonograph record shop agreed to lend him records in return for identifying the store on the air. The records Conrad played increased the sales of those titles. All this interest convinced a local department store to offer assembled wireless sets for sale. That prompted Conrad's employer, Westinghouse, to manufacture radio receivers for voice and music. Conrad's garage broadcasting equipment was brought onto the Westinghouse lot, a transmitter went up, and modern broadcasting began on November 2, 1920, with the call letters KDKA. The date was chosen so that the first broadcast would be of the Harding-Cox presidential election. About 100 people tuned in.[10] Following Conrad's idea, Westinghouse offered a regular program schedule.

AIMEE SEMPLE MCPHERSON

Evangelists set up stations to attract worshippers. During the 1920s, Aimee Semple McPherson grew rich and famous as she built a large, devoted national following. McPherson sensed that the "wireless telephone" in the home carried a degree of intimacy and connection to the lonely. She employed it effectively to bring listeners together to share moments of silent prayer, an oddly brilliant use of the talking medium. McPherson lost her license because she would not stick to her assigned frequency, arguing that she needed to operate on "God's frequency."

▶ TOLL BROADCASTS

Newspapers soon erected transmitters to enhance their reputations and attract new subscribers, but not to make money from the broadcasts themselves.[11] Some department stores installed low-powered broadcast operations in a corner of the store to attract curious shoppers, but they did not advertise their goods. Nothing was advertised. No one spent much money on the radio broadcasts or expected much money back. The quality of the sound was poor; scratchy phonograph records did not help. Even so, spontaneous groups got together to listen in stores, hotel lobbies, or speak-easies, legal saloons being outlawed by Prohibition.

The AT&T radio station in New York, WEAF, opened the floodgates to commercial broadcasting when it rented time to a real estate company to talk about its new apartments on Long Island. For its U.S.$300 investment in a soft-sell sales pitch repeated during one evening and four afternoons, the real estate company sold $127,000 worth of apartments. AT&T, normally in the business of renting its equipment by the minute to telephone callers, managed its station like a public telephone booth, initiating what it called "toll broadcasting." After the introduction of commercials, the purpose of programming was to attract listeners to buy something, radio sets at first, then advertised products.

AT&T considered itself to be the sole proprietor of this idea, but other transmitting stations saw the possibility to make money. It took four more years of almost no "toll broadcasts," many arguments among corporations, and a final agreement between the Telephone Group headed by AT&T and the Radio Group headed by RCA, but broadcasting in the United States now was constructing a strong financial base and a new social use, even if not everyone warmed to the idea.

None of the corporations who had taken over the patents from individual owners had total control of the medium. Bitter court battles lasted for years and sometimes ended with compromises in the form of cross-licensing agreements to use each other's patents. Initially, RCA, General Electric, and Westinghouse, the so-called "radio group," concentrated on the receivers of messages, the audience. They regarded broadcast programs as a service to create public demand for their radio sets. AT&T and Western Electric were known as the "telephone group." Their concern was with the senders of messages, later called "sponsors." Today broadcasting, of course, combines programs *and* commercials.

▶ CAUTIOUS COMMERCIALS

A number of listeners were offended that commercials were broadcast over a radio station that depended on a government license. Secretary of Commerce Herbert Hoover told broadcasters, "I believe that the quickest way to kill broadcasting would be to use it for direct advertising. The reader of the newspaper has an option whether he will read an ad or not, but if a speech by the president is to be used as the meat in a sandwich of two patent medicine advertisements, there will be no radio left."[12]

The advertising industry itself, with a nervous eye on the print media, chimed in with editorial comment in *Printers' Ink*: "Any attempt to make the radio an advertising medium . . . would, we think, prove positively offensive to great numbers of people. The family circle is not a public place, and advertising has no business intruding there unless it is invited."[13] The

National Association of Broadcasters used similar language in its first Radio Code in 1929, but soon changed its mind.

Broadcasting stayed in private hands, but the United States government was not totally divorced from it because radio stations needed licenses to transmit. To avoid giving ammunition to opponents, radio stations were cautious about what they advertised. They worried at first, for example, that toothpaste might be too intimate a product to advertise. But the potential of the new medium was just too great to do nothing. Toothpaste found its way into messages.

As the Jazz Age years went by and were followed by the Depression, instead of the hundreds of thousands who read a magazine, tens of millions would hear radio, and its advertising could not be skipped by flipping a page. Having discovered a goose that would lay golden eggs, the industry continued to worry about what the government might permit on the government-licensed stations. In the 1920s, no merchandise samples could be offered or prices revealed. Description of a container, even its color, was left out at first by broadcasters who were nervous about how Congress might react. Actually, at first there were no commercials. Instead, a program would be named for a product, such as "The Gold Dust Twins" advertising a household cleanser or "The A&P Gypsies" advertising a grocery chain. A decade would pass before prices were mentioned on the air. In time, radio advertising would become so deeply ingrained in American culture that a jingle for a product was as likely to be hummed casually by radio listeners as any hit song. For the illiterate, Ipana toothpaste was identified as the one in the red and yellow tube.[14]

De Forest, who insisted on calling himself the "father of radio," attacked broadcasting for presenting commercial "spots." He called them "stains" and he lamented to the industry, "What have you done with my child?"

▶ NATIONAL CHOICES

Other nations chose a different direction. Governments in most nations controlled all aspects of broadcasting. They would have no commercials for decades. The British Broadcasting Corporation, solidly pro-establishment in its programming policy, followed the principle of presenting what those in charge believed listeners *should hear for their own good,* not the American policy of broadcasting what listeners *wanted* to hear. Funds to support the BBC came from annual user license fees on radio sets. Years later, it would license television sets.

During the mid-1950s, as television replaced radio, the British government finally licensed an independent commercial service, ITV, to operate. Most other industrialized nations preferred a version of the BBC model, often with direct government operation, although Canada and Mexico were among countries that permitted a mix of government-owned and privately owned radio stations.

Totalitarian governments funded radio stations the way they funded all their departments, with annual taxpayer-supported budgets, a sure way to manage broadcasters as government employees and to keep them firmly under the government thumb. Radio programming and the television programs that

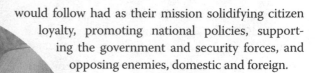

Radio rapidly expanded its audience during the years of the Great Depression.

would follow had as their mission solidifying citizen loyalty, promoting national policies, supporting the government and security forces, and opposing enemies, domestic and foreign.

▶ COMMUNICATION ACTS

The United States after World War I provided only one frequency for all radio transmission, with a second frequency added later for crop and weather reports. Still later a third frequency for music was added, based on the maritime communication model, where sender and receiver exchange brief messages, then go silent. But the broadcast stations were not silent. In fact, the broadcast stations were trying to be heard by boosting their transmission power to outshout each other and were drowning each other out. Government efforts to alleviate the clamor by opening up more frequencies were overwhelmed by new stations coming in to take advantage of commercial possibilities. Shortwave, previously used only by amateurs, was taken over for commercial and government purposes.

Congress preferred not to upset anyone, yet some regulation was clearly needed. Four conferences called by the government in the 1920s had groups at each other's throats. Owners of large stations wanted stronger regulations to control who could broadcast. Small station owners wanted to be under the broadcasting tent. So did hobbyists.

The Federal Radio Act of 1927 created order out of chaos, establishing a permanent commission to grant or deny station licenses, but it had little authority over networks. The commission had no censorship power, but its ability to deny a license renewal gave it a measure of control. Television was scarcely considered. The act was followed by the Communications Act of 1934. Its Federal Communications Commission (the FCC) also took interstate telephone service under its wing. The FCC had the power to regulate both wired and wireless communication on a nationwide and even a worldwide basis. It also had the power to regulate the new medium of television, then still in laboratory development.[15]

Universities involved themselves from the start of broadcasting. Engineering departments established stations. Weather and farm conditions were reported. Union leaders and artists in several fields who saw the cultural promise of the new medium joined professors who liked the broadcasting platform.

However, non-commercial radio fared poorly in the face of strong opposition by the broadcasting industry, which wanted to keep all the frequencies for commercial broadcasters. An effort to create more public radio licenses, the Wagner-Hatfield Amendment, failed in Congress when the 1934 Act was passed, and commercial broadcasters were forced to air public affairs programs. Efforts to get public television licenses fared much better than earlier efforts to get non-commercial radio licenses In 1967, the Corporation for Public Broadcasting was created to organize not only financial support, but also network structure and programming for non-commercial radio and television. The 1934 Act remained in place until it was replaced by the Telecommunications Act of 1996. Among its changes, it included the Internet in its broadcast and spectrum allocation.

Following the concept that the airwaves belong to the public, laws would be based on the government's right to regulate broadcasting and determine who can hold a license. Stations pledged to operate "in the public interest, convenience, or necessity," but neither Congress nor the regulatory agencies ever specified what this means.

By these laws, the government is not permitted to determine what is broadcast, although it can fine stations heavily for broadcasts it considers indecent. The government's power to issue or retrieve the extremely valuable licenses is great but it is almost never enforced. The history of broadcast regulation in the United States has been one of competing influences, intense lobbying, power structures, and the advantage that comes with owning stations that can help or hurt political candidates.[16]

WARDROBE MALFUNCTION

The Federal Communications Commission (FCC) generally stays away from sex and violence in broadcasts. One exception followed the halftime show of Superbowl XXXVIII, in 2004, when a move by Justin Timberlake exposed Janet Jackson's right breast, partially covered by a piece of nipple jewelry, for about a half second. The FCC fined CBS U.S.$550,000 for what was called a "wardrobe malfunction" and "Nipplegate," but a Court of Appeals dismissed the fine in 2012.

"Nipplegate" led to the creation of YouTube, according to its founder, Jawed Karim, and it broke a record for Internet searches.[17]

▶ TECHNOLOGY IMPROVES

The sound of a radio signal was faint until E. Howard Armstrong, around 1912, still a graduate student, did more than convert de Forest's audion tube into an oscillator. He reworked it so sound came booming out of earphones. When radio sets with these redesigned vacuum tubes went on sale, it was the start of the technology necessary to change from a hobby in basements and garages to an instrument of family entertainment fit for the parlor.

It would take more than this, however, to make radio a household appliance. Radio receivers manufactured in the 1920s were large, clunky, temperamental metal boxes with expensive tubes, lots of knobs tricky to adjust for wandering signals, a mess of wires, and a large, smelly battery filled with acid, not unlike the storage battery in an automobile. A radio was hardly a fit thing to put on a good parlor rug or a polished mahogany table.

The batteries and the maze of wires that accompanied them would be replaced a few years later by plugs that went into wall sockets for 110 volt alternating current. A loudspeaker replaced the earphones so that the entire family could listen at the same time. Now the radio set was ready for its new social use as broadcast entertainment. It could come out of the basement or the garage where it was a hobby for Father and the boys listening on earphones. Now Mother and the girls could listen too. Housed inside a wooden cabinet to match the furniture, the radio would take its place in the family parlor beside two other machines in wooden housing that delivered enjoyable sounds, the piano and the phonograph.

Not everyone waited for the AC power that began to replace radio batteries in 1926. During that year, one house in six already had a radio, many equipped with loudspeakers, so that listening took on the pleasure of dinner conversations. Nearly half the population lived in the countryside, far from telephones, daily newspapers, or—at many homes—even electricity. Battery-operated radio became their connection to the world. They may have bought the radio primarily for entertainment, but it also delivered information. A rural public who might have been uninterested and uninformed about the economic and social turmoil in the nation and the world was now learning to care.

Listeners wrote warm letters to radio stations. Magazine articles described the joys of sitting at home alone or with family members to listen to their radios.[18] People *went out* to the movies, but *stayed in* to listen to the radio, as they would later with television. Broadcasting was altering social realities.

HEARING CUBA

During the excitement over the start of broadcasting in the 1920s, an 11-year-old girl, just transplanted from Detroit to a chicken farm outside the city, boasted to a radio singer, "My mother and father heard you sing in Kansas. The first night we got the radio my mother and father sat up till 3 o'clock in the morning. We can hear Cuba with it."[19]

Radios also went into automobiles. In 1930, a battery eliminator that provided DC voltage to power radios from the car engine was a marked improvement. Cars and radios have gone together ever since like ham and eggs.[20]

▶ SURVEYS AND NETWORKS

Audience surveys to determine who was listening came into existence in 1929, started by Archibald Crossley. They increased in size and sophistication as audience growth and network quests for higher advertising rates prodded agencies to insist on better information about who was tuned to what programs. Surveys taken during the Depression years revealed that even low-income homes had at least one radio. The average radio home tuned in more than five hours a day. In fact, low-income families listened to the free entertainment more than middle-income families, just as low-income homes today watch more free television.[21] During the Depression, when Americans cut back on going to the movies or buying subscriptions to newspapers, they spent more time with free radio. Advertisers paid attention.

NBC and CBS by contracting with local stations had built nationwide networks. The United States, a sprawling nation without an authentic national newspaper, now had the means to entertain and inform the entire American public. The tying together of stations, first as temporary "hookups" in a "chain" and later as permanent networks, solved a problem for broadcasters: how to pay for better programs. When stations in different cities broadcast the same program, its cost could be shared. Better programs also drew listeners away from competing stations. National advertisers who ignored individual stations were interested when a network audience could be measured in the millions.

RCA in 1926 assembled stations into two permanent networks, the "Red" (now NBC) and the "Blue" (now ABC). One year later the competitive CBS (Columbia Broadcasting System) network was formed. A fourth national network, the Mutual Broadcasting System, was put together in 1934. In New England, the Midwest and the Far West, regional networks formed. By 1940 more families had radios (82.8 percent)[22] than cars, telephones, electricity, or plumbing. A new means of communication had taken root. People loved it and accommodated their lives to it. Again, they adapted to their media tools.

Radio would replace newspapers as the primary source of news. In addition to the immediacy of a bulletin, radio could offer the familiar voice of a news commentator, a personality attached to an opinion. But unlike newspapers that could operate without the goodwill of politicians, radio stations required licenses. Obscene, indecent, and profane language was barred by the Radio Act of 1927, a limitation not imposed on a press that required no licenses and enjoyed full First Amendment protection. The interconnection of broadcasting that benefitted from political support, and politicians who benefitted from a public presence, has continued.

▶ "GOLDEN AGE"

Radio's golden age, about 1930 to 1950, saw families everywhere gathered in the evening to listen to dramas, comedies, music, quizzes, variety shows, and, of course, commercials. With all this, a culture was being transmitted and absorbed. The broadcast schedule made the radio in the parlor the place for the family to gather. It carried entertainment, information, hope to an American population in need of all three. Comedians became household names.

The dinner hour served up news and commentary. Comedies and drama were broadcast in prime time. Sunday offered church services, opera, and sports. In the midst of the misery of the times, the American public welcomed the free entertainment and did not regard listening to commercials as a cost.

Americans could hardly acquire radios fast enough once broadcasting took hold to bring entertainment at no cash cost into the family home. Rural folks and people living in the South were slower to buy a radio set than urban Northerners, but this was a national phenomenon. In 1930, 40 percent of American households owned radios, a figure than jumped to nearly 96 percent in 1950, despite the arrival of commercial television.[23] Families were buying radio despite the Depression and the fact that radios in broadcasting's early years were not cheap. The average cost of a set in 1930 was U.S.$78, equivalent to about $845 today. That average price dropped to $38 in 1940 and $26 in 1950.[24]

The golden age of radio coincided with the Depression and World War II. Listeners could set aside daily troubles and uncertainties to enjoy the variety of entertainment that radio broadcasting brought into their homes. Weekday morning brought the never-ending drama of soap operas (named because many of the sponsors advertised cleaning products) that delivered overlapping multiple tales and urged listeners to "tune in tomorrow." Afternoons might carry a baseball game. After school children's adventure serials delivered the same tune-in-tomorrow message as soaps. Saturday mornings also brought children's programs such as the award-winning *Let's Pretend* of dramatized fairy tales. In the hour before dinner, five to six o'clock, weekdays, kids presumably had finished playing outside after school and gathered before the family radio to listen to the children's equivalent of soap operas—15 minute episodes like *Little Orphan Annie*, a newspaper comic strip adapted for radio, and *Jack Armstrong, the All-American Boy*.

Soap operas offered escapism to the target audience of housewives. The dramas gave listeners a sense of participation in the lives of people they would never meet who struggled daily with fictional family issues, unrequited love affairs, and moral dilemmas. Listeners responded strongly to stories whose characters were wealthier than they were and lived more interesting lives. The fictional characters became such a part of listeners' lives that when a soap opera character had a baby, fans sent gifts. Letters would be addressed to soap opera characters warning them that other characters were up to no good. Here was still more evidence of the power of mediated communication to transcend physical space and forge distant connections. Soap operas like *Ma Perkins* and *The Romance of Helen Trent* continued for decades. In the 1950s some of the weekday 15 minute radio soaps, such as *The Guiding Light*, became 30 minute television soaps. The real message, from day to day, through plots that never resolved was: stay tuned.[25]

When broadcasting began, the broadcasters programmed what they themselves liked or what their friends suggested. Vaudeville was popular, so some ideas came from there. In time, radio—and the movies—took so much from vaudeville that there was little reason to pay good money for tickets. It has been said that movies killed vaudeville. Radio wielded a knife, too.

Prime time brought comedians who became household names, plus quizzes, dramas, and variety shows. The best-known prime time programs were the weekly comedies based on pretended flaws, such as Jack Benny's stinginess and vanity about his age. Listeners identified the days of the week by the presence of Fred Allen, Red Skelton, Bob Hope, ventriloquist Edgar Bergen, and the duo of Abbott and Costello.

More than any other medium in history up to that time, the radio gave people a sense of sharing with others what the day held for them. If you already owned a radio set—and the price of sets dropped significantly during the Depression years[26]—it delivered all this and more at no cost to you except a minute or two of your time every so often to listen to a commercial, and some of these were just as much fun as the programs. Whether you knew it or not, the commercials were crafted more carefully than any programs.

THE WAR OF THE WORLDS

When the H. G. Wells radio drama *The War of the Worlds* was presented by Orson Welles in the nervous pre-war year of 1938 as a series of news bulletins, many listeners found the broadcast all too believable. Panic sent some Americans and Canadians spilling from their homes to alert their neighbors that the world was being taken over by Martian invaders. According to one set of estimates, some 6 million heard the CBS broadcast; 1.7 million believed it to be true, and 1.2 million were "genuinely frightened." That a twist of the dial could bring in other stations where all was normal was overlooked. It was said that, as a result of the cynicism generated by the hoax, some Americans were skeptical about the Japanese bombing of Pearl Harbor three years later.

Orson Welles, 1937

▶ **NEWS**

As the newspapers themselves were carrying advertising for what the radio programs advertised, free publishing of radio program logs did not sit well at publishers' conferences. During the Depression, radio profits grew while newspaper profits stagnated.

To add insult to this injury, for the 2 or 3 cents it cost to buy a daily newspaper, those radio stations that presented newscasts had access to all the news that a newspaper had labored to assemble. The stations could present the news over the air long before a delivery boy threw a copy of the newspaper onto the front porch. Newspapers struck back weakly. Some newspapers eliminated the free listings of daily radio programs, or they identified a program only as "Music." That did not last long. Irate letters from readers and canceled subscriptions forced newspapers to abandon such tactics. Newspapers continued to list radio programs and then television programs free.

Radio coverage of the 1932 election that swept Franklin Delano Roosevelt into office brought the intense coverage of the kidnapping of Charles and Anne Morrow Lindbergh's baby, for Lindbergh was the American hero who flew solo across the Atlantic. That opened the eyes of newspaper publishers more fully to the competition. This led to the "Press–Radio War" of 1933–1935, when members of the powerful newspaper industry demanded that all newspapers stop including free daily radio logs. They pressured the wire services to deny their feeds to radio stations, except for a restricted feed by the new Press–Radio Bureau that was available only for non-sponsored newscasts. Radio stations rebelled and started their own news gathering units. Newspapers that owned radio stations joined independent radio stations and networks to oppose control. To some extent the "Press–Radio War" was a "Newspaper–Newspaper War."[27]

In a short time, newspapers that tried to limit radio news gave up. As war clouds gathered in Europe, listeners sought more news from both newspapers and radio. Today, wire services are all too happy to sell their feeds, including a special broadcast wire, to radio and television stations.

Radio news reported World War II at home and abroad, delivering more news to more citizens than any other medium.[28] In a nation too large to have a national press because of available technology, radio commentators provided national voices, mixing their commentary with nuggets of the latest news.

If comedies and dramas during the golden age of radio brought people together to share the laughs and shivers, the news explainers pulled them into like-minded groupings. Suppertime was the time for radio commentators to offer a little news and a lot of opinionated analysis. Unlike radio news today but similar to talk radio, the best-known newscasts were delivered by commentators who used a news item of the day as a hook to deliver a partisan monologue, liberal or conservative.

Listeners generally tuned to the commentator whose views made the most sense, meaning the commentator they agreed with. The most popular commentators wielded political clout because their explanations influenced voters. They became household names: Lowell Thomas, Fulton Lewis, Jr., Gabriel Heatter, Raymond Gram Swing, H. V. Kaltenborn, Walter Winchell, and from London during World War II, Edward R. Murrow.

In the early 21st century, radio commentary would be dominated by conservative talk show speakers such as Rush Limbaugh, who frequently referred with pride to his large audience, yet insisted that he himself was not part of media and not a journalist. Limbaugh identified himself as an "antidote" to "the media."

Today, with exceptions such as America's Radio News Network, news on commercial radio has shrunk for the most part to little more than headlines or has disappeared entirely from local stations. However, that is not true of public radio. Both National Public Radio and individual public radio stations feature extended newscasts that include field reports and interviews.

▶ INFLUENCING AMERICAN CULTURE

During the 1930s, in the midst of the economic depression and the international turmoil that preceded World War II, President Franklin D. Roosevelt and his New Deal stirred such vitriolic opposition from the newspaper barons arrayed against him that he took to radio broadcasting with a series of 30 "fireside chats" to reach out directly to American voters to explain in simple language his economic and foreign policies. This was not the local, democratic politics of shaking hands and delivering food baskets on election day; but it was certainly democratic in the sense that FDR was reaching out for support to everyone within earshot. The broadcasts were extraordinarily popular. Every president since Roosevelt has used broadcasting to speak to the nation.

Broadcasting has helped to both push its listeners together and to pull them apart into separate listening groups. The most popular comedies, dramas, and variety programs during the 1930s, 1940s, and 1950s brought listeners of different backgrounds together in a shared experience. If you listened to Jack Benny or Fred Allen last night you could talk about them today at the factory lunch break, at the office water cooler, or on the telephone. Radio broadcasting disseminated national culture and informed its listeners, and it sometimes influenced government leadership.

FDR prepares to broadcast a "fireside chat," 1936.

With all this free, attractive programming, a change in people's lives passed largely unnoticed. Families were spending less time entertaining themselves with such behavior as reading, pursuing hobbies, strolling in the evening, or visiting neighbors. The passive pleasure of sitting in front of the pridefully dusted Philco console or Atwater Kent to hear distant entertainment and information pouring into the parlor had taken hold in the home.

For listeners who lived alone, being alone could seem less difficult. For listeners who disliked silences, here was an alternative that could keep at bay stray thoughts or any thinking at all. As the quality of broadcast programs and technology improved, this shift in behavior strengthened until it had become the norm to sit passively at home in the evening to be entertained. The medium of radio broadcasting has been quite a success.

Radio executives had not set out to alter human behavior or to educate. While evidence aplenty of cultural improvement can be found in American radio programing's long history, that was never the prime purpose of the men who ran the radio industry. Nor did they consider themselves catalysts for bringing Americans together as a nation in order to continue at a deeper level what the telegraph and the telephone had done. They were business-men. What they sold was the attention of audiences to their customers, the advertisers. Programs were never the product. Listeners were never the cus-tomers. Listeners were (and are) product. Programs were (and are) bait.

▶ MELTING POT

The medium of radio was a social leveler and a melting pot. Listeners assem-bled by hearing a common language spoken with a standard national accent. Announcers were chosen for smooth delivery with a non-regional accent, more Oregon than Brooklyn or New Orleans. Millions of immigrants improved their English skills by tuning in. For the millions who could not read English or could not read at all, illiteracy did not matter. Listeners were pulled apart as choices increased. Compared with the few choices available during radio's golden age, broadcasting audiences today are inundated with multiple choices on the AM and FM dials plus those on cable radio.

With announcers chosen for their neutral, non-regional speech pattern, and with strong Southern, New England, and Brooklyn accents used for humor along with exaggerated foreign and ethnic accents, it was apparent for commercial reasons that the best accent was a middle-American way of speaking. The foreign, ethnic, and regional characters were never presented as evil. They were intended to be funny.

However, accents conformed to caricatures and negative public images, notably those of Amos 'n' Andy, whose white actors portrayed the Afri-can American characters as lazy, irresponsible, not very bright schemers.[29] Because of segregated housing and schools, many whites knew of blacks only through these caricatures.

Yet radio also did its part to heat the melting pot of the American immi-grant experience. The Ku Klux Klan, popular in the South and Midwest during the 1920s, did not take hold on American networks. However, in the 1930s, Father Charles Coughlin, an early supporter of the New Deal, turned against Roosevelt and regularly expressed hostility to the British, to Jews, and to issues he branded socialistic or communistic. According to some esti-mates, on any given Sunday one-third of the nation was tuned into "the radio priest." A plea from him could pile 100,000 telegrams on senators' desks.

But as his attacks intensified, stations unplugged from his hookup. Coughlin finally left the airwaves in 1939. He was delivering only slightly veiled Nazi propaganda by the time he was forced off the air under pressure from Roman Catholic Church leaders and the government.

▶ FM

E. Howard Armstrong's invention of FM (frequency modulation) in 1933 held the promise not only of a clearer audio signal than AM (amplitude modulation), but also a bandwidth that could accommodate many new stations. That FM was not diffused until after World War II, more than a dozen years later, was due to the machinations of David Sarnoff, head of RCA and founder of NBC. Sarnoff understood FM's potential all too well but considered it a hindrance to television, which RCA was spending a fortune to develop. Armstrong's frustration over years of legal battles resulted in his suicide in 1954.[30]

After the war, new FM stations did arrive, slowly at first, most of them devoted to music to take advantage of the FM clarity. Also arriving in the postwar years were stereophonic transmission, high fidelity audiotape, LP (long playing) records, and tape cassettes, all promising better sound. America shifted from being a nation of music listeners to a nation of audio appreciators.

Even without FM, the quality of radio sound improved year by year as audio engineers, replacing vacuum tubes with transistors, labored over every part of the sound's path from the microphone in the studio to the speaker in the home radio set. In 1971, AM–FM radios were being installed by car manufacturers. Tuners, turntables, pre-amps, amplifiers, and their connections were improved for the amateur audiophiles who were willing to pay for near-perfect tones.

▶ RADIO SURVIVES TV

Radio in the years following World War II seemed headed for trouble. Television gobbled up radio's best programs, staff, talent, funding, and energy. In the postwar boom years families moved their radio consoles out of their new tract homes to make room for the even larger television consoles with a 7 inch or 12 inch round screen.

Yet, radio did not die. Rather, it was reinvented. Today more radio stations are on the air than ever, and 99 percent of all U.S. homes have at least one radio set.[31] Radio networks bought out independent stations to create radio empires of hundreds of stations. In 2014, Clear Channel Communications owned 850 radio stations.

As television took over evening prime time audiences, radio shifted its attention to drive time, the morning and afternoon work commute. Radios went to the beach and sat unobtrusively on the shelf above the kitchen sink and the factory workbench. Clock radios woke us up and helped put us to sleep, the car radio eased the twice-daily commute, background radio accompanied a meal, and music pouring through Walkman earphones accompanied a jog. Radio broadcasting would be different, but it was far from finished.

One difference between radio during its golden age and today is that we no longer *look at* our radios. When the radio sat in the parlor, the family that gathered around for their favorite programs *watched* the radio that, after all, was talking to them. Today we listen to the radio while we are doing something else. Radio now is an accompaniment to driving, working, or starting the morning. Listeners are too occupied to stare at their radios.

Radio stations today try to reach an interest group niche market, an identifiable segment of the radio market, such as listeners 18 to 35, or an audience who responds to country and western music. Some stations shifted focus to attract ethnic minorities. To the best of the ability of the 14,000 radio stations in the United States, listeners are channeled. The focus is called *narrowcasting*.

Musical tastes are the stations' most effective targeting tool. A playlist stays within an identity like rock 'n' roll, jazz, easy listening, country and western, mariachi, rhythm and blues, classical, big band, hip hop, and so on. Record companies participate because it increases music sales. Combined with all the other choices people now have for mediated communication, less commonality exists at the office water cooler. Instead, those who share our tastes connect electronically from a distance. Emailing and blogging our opinions, we live in a *virtual water cooler world*.

▶ LOOKING AHEAD

The future promises to continue to segment the audience. The first decade of the 21st century brought rapid growth in several types of radio program distribution. Satellite radio services like Sirius and XM carry music with CD-quality sound, plus news and talk, all without commercials. Because the signal arrives from a satellite, it remains constant as a car crosses the nation, unlike local stations with limited range. Spotify streams music free or by subscription to more than 20 million users in much of the world to a variety of mobile devices.[32]

Distance no longer implies static. Nor, as we travel, does it imply listening to the same stations that locals hear. The audio quality of satellite stations may be superior, but we bypass local flavor as we cross the continent. Other changes include AM stereo radio[33] and the conversion of analog radio to non-satellite digital transmission known as HD (hybrid digital) radio with CD-quality sound and without the subscription fees of satellite radio, available through the Internet and on frequencies immediately above or below a station's standard broadcast. Like standard AM and FM radio, HD radio is supported by commercials.

In developing nations where illiteracy rates remain stubbornly high, radio stations are providing low-cost adult education via dramatic programs meant to improve behavior. A radio drama in Papua, New Guinea, for example, had a marine scientist warning a widowed father that dynamite fishing may be initially profitable but his children's future will be better if he practices sustainable fishing. An Ethiopian soap opera brought an increased demand for contraceptives and HIV/AIDS testing.[34]

Thousands of Internet radio stations have come online. Some are off-shoots of large commercial stations, but an Internet station can specialize in, say, Albanian folk music, reaching an international audience of a few dozen if someone is willing to program for them. Established stations also stream news, weather, sports, and traffic reports to the World Wide Web and to iPhones. It all adds up to a huge increase in choices. That, of course, extends both our connections to media sources and to listeners anywhere in the world, and our mediated separation from those living their lives around us.

POINT-TO-POINT RADIO

Aside from broadcasting, radio has continued to serve point-to-point functions. Guardians of the public welfare such as police officers, sheriff's deputies, fire dispatchers, forest service personnel, air controllers, and the Coast Guard all have their own radio frequencies. Radio astronomy has fought for its bandwidth. Citizen's band radio, a continuation of the old pre-broadcasting hobbyists' radio exchanges, at one time counted participants in the millions, most famously the long haul truck drivers who warned each other of the "smokies," the highway patrol officers who lay in wait behind highway billboards. Cellphones have replaced most transmitting rigs, but CB (citizen band) radios, still conveying a sense of what radio was like before broadcasting, refuse to disappear.

▶ TIMELINE

1873   James Clerk Maxwell's electromagnetic theory leads to radio wave discovery.

1887   Heinrich Hertz creates radio waves, discovers photoelectric effect.

1890   In France, Édouard Branly's coherer receives early radio signals.

1895   In Italy, teenager Guglielmo Marconi sends a radio signal more than 1 mile.

1896   Nikola Tesla invents a spark radio transmitter.

       Turned down by Italy, Marconi takes radio gear to England.

1897   In England, the Marconi Company is set up for wireless telegraphy business.

1898   The loudspeaker is invented.

1899   Marconi radio gear signals across the English Channel.

1901   In Newfoundland, Marconi receives a radio signal—the letter "S"—from England.

In Germany, Karl Braun discovers that a crystal can detect radio waves.

1904   E. F. Alexanderson's huge alternator adds distance to radio signals.

1906   International agreement on radio is reached in Berlin.

Lee de Forest's three-element vacuum tube, the audion, puts voices on the air.

Reginald Fessenden's voice surprises wireless operators at sea.

1909   Radio signals bring rescuers after ship collision; 1,700 lives saved.

First broadcast talk; the subject: women's suffrage.

1912   Titanic sinking leads to U.S. government controls on radio transmission.

1915   Radio-telephone carries voice from Virginia to the Eiffel Tower.

1916   Radio tuners.

1920   XWA, Montreal, begins first regularly scheduled North American broadcasts.

Pittsburgh store sells ready-made radio sets.

KDKA begins broadcasting.

1921   Baseball's World Series is reported by radio.

1922   In one year in the United States, from 80 radio broadcasting licenses to 569.

100,000 radios built.

A commercial begins "toll broadcasting."

1924   Radio hook-ups broadcast Democratic, Republican conventions.

1926   Replacing temporary hookups, the United States gets a permanent radio network, NBC.

1928   Home radios use ordinary electric current instead of batteries.

1930   Lowell Thomas begins first regular U.S. network newscast.

A practical, affordable car radio goes on sale.

1933   FDR begins radio Fireside Chats, bypasses hostile newspapers.

1938   Orson Welles's radio drama *The War of the Worlds* panics thousands.

Radio begins real journalism competition with "CBS World News Roundup."

1940   Regular FM radio broadcasting begins in a small way.

1970   FM stations target population segments, introducing "narrowcasting."

1994   Most popular American radio format is country music.

2001   Satellite radio appears; XM begins broadcasting.

13,012 radio stations in the United States.

99 percent of homes have a radio set; average home has six.

2003   Digital AM radio offers FM sound quality.

2005   "Podcast" identifies an online prerecorded radio program.

2007   Podcasts are available on phones.

▶ NOTES

1 In 1886 the Smithsonian Institution posthumously published *Scientific Writings of Joseph Henry* based on research he did from 1826 on. Faraday published two volumes (1839, 1844) of *Experimental Researches in Electricity*.

2 Maxwell published "On Faraday's Lines of Force" in 1855 and "On Physical Lines of Force" in 1861.

3 Gavin Weightman, *Signor Marconi's Magic Box* (London: HarperCollins Publishers, 2003), 56.

4 Stephen N. Raymer, "Fessenden Revisited," *Pavek Museum of Broadcasting Newsletter*, vol. 4, no. 4, 1993: 5.

5 Susan J. Douglas, *Inventing American Broadcasting, 1899–1922* (Baltimore: Johns Hopkins University Press, 1987), 15.

6 Doubt has been cast upon the generally accepted report that the broadcast took place on Christmas Eve. It may have occurred a few days earlier, on December 21, 1906. Similar doubts were not raised about the content of the transmission. See Donna L. Halper and Christopher H. Sterling, "Fessenden's Christmas Eve Broadcast: Reconsidering an Historic Event," *AWA Review*, vol. 19, 2006.

7 Erik Barnouw, *The Sponsor* (New York: Oxford University Press, 1978) 16.

8 "Ham Radio History" at http://w2pa.net/HRH/the-first-regulations/#fn-319-2.

9 For more information, see the biography of Frank Conrad online at http://pabook.libraries.psu.edu/palitmap/bios/Conrad__Frank.html.

10 Ibid.

11 Barnouw, 16.

12 Speech to the Third National Radio Conference, October 1924.

13 *Printers' Ink*, April 27, 1922.

14 For a picture of the tube and more information about the commercials, see the compilation of historical advertisements at http://www.old-time.com/commercials/1930's/Smile.html.

15 For more detail on the changes brought by the Communication Acts of 1934 and 1996, visit Cybertelecom's page at http://www.cybertelecom.org/notes/communications_act.htm.

16 Ithiel de Sola Pool, *Technologies of Freedom* (Cambridge, MA: Harvard University Press, 1983), 122.

17 Julie Hilden, "Jackson 'Nipplegate' Illustrates the Danger of Chilling Free Speech," *CNN.com*, February 20, 2004, http://www.cnn.com/2004/LAW/02/20/findlaw.analysis.hilden.jackson/.

18 George P. Oslin, *The Story of Telecommunications*.(Macon, GA: Mercer University Press, 1992) 283.

19 Elena Razlogova, *The Listener's Voice: Early Radio and the American Public* (Philadelphia: University of Pennsylvania Press, 2011) 40.

20 Douglas, 308.

21 U.S. Labor Department Time Use Survey for 2011, reported in *New York Times*, June 26, 2012, http://economix.blogs.nytimes.com/2012/06/26/the-old-and-uneducated-watch-the-most-tv/?_php=true&_type=blogs&_r=0.

22 U.S. Census Bureau, 1940 census available at http://www.census.gov/1940census/.

23 Steve Craig (2004) "How America Adopted Radio: Demographic Differences in Set Ownership Reported in the 1930–1950 U.S. Censuses," *Journal of Broadcasting & Electronic Media*, vol. 48, no. 2: 179–195, http://dx.doi.org/10.1207/s15506878jobem4802_2.

24 Craig, 186.

25 "If the ultimate goal stops being about capturing an audience's attention once, and becomes more about keeping their attention through repeat viewings, that shift is bound to have an effect on the content." Steven Johnson, *Everything Bad Is Good for You* (New York: Riverhead Books, 2005) 159.

26 Bruce Lenthall, *Radio's America: The Great Depression and the Rise of Modern Mass Culture*.(Chicago: University of Chicago Press, 2007) 56.

27 Robert W. McChesney, "Press-Radio Relations and the Emergence of Network, Commercial Broadcasting in the United States, 1930–1935," *Historical Journal of Film, Radio & Television*, vol. 11, issue 1, 1991: 41.

28 Christopher H. Sterling and John M. Kittross, *Stay Tuned: A Concise History of American Broadcasting*, 2nd ed. (Belmont, CA: Wadsworth Publishing Co., 1990) 239.

29 Robert L. Hilliard and Michael C. Keith, *The Broadcast Century and Beyond: A Biography of American Broadcasting* (Woburn, MA: Focal Press, 2001) 57.

30 See the biography of Armstrong at http://fecha.org/armstrong.htm.

31 According to the FCC's tally as of September 30, 2010, there were 4,784 AM stations, 6,512 commercial FM stations, and 3,251 FM educational stations, a total of 14,547 radio stations. For television: 1,022 UHF commercial TV stations, 370 VHF commercial TV stations, 284 UHF educational TV stations, and 107 VHF educational TV stations, for a total of 1,783 television stations in the United States. This and other data can be found online at http://fjallfoss.fcc.gov/edocs_public/attachmatch/ DOC-302349A1.doc. The National Cable and Telecommunications Association 2008 Industry Overview listed 64,900,000 basic cable customers, or 52.5% of the total homes passed by cable video services. It also listed 35,600,000 high-speed Internet customers. There were 1,212 cable operating companies and 565 national cable networks. This data can be found online at http://i.ncta.com/ncta_com/PDFs/NCTA_Annual_ Report_05.16.08.pdf.

32 Harrison Weber, "Spotify Announces 5M+ Paid Subscribers Globally, 1M Paid in U.S., 20M Total Active Users, 1B Playlists," *The Next Web*, December 6, 2012, http://thenextweb.com/insider/2012/12/06/spotify-announces/.

33 Michael Wusterhausen, "AM Stereo Radio," in Grant, August E. and Kenton T. Wilkinson, eds., *Communication Technology Update, 1993–1994* (Austin: Technology Futures, Inc., 1993) 121.

34 *The Economist*, May 7, 2011: 66.

12 Television: Pictures in Our Parlors

It has been called a fatal attraction, a cultural death wish, blamed for social ills ranging from illiteracy to obesity to childhood hyperactivity to crime. Yet the public adopted the new medium of television with a speed unmatched in history. Even today, with all the competition from other media, television continues to be watched and watched and watched. The average American home is now likely to have more television sets than occupants.[1] Noted French sociologist Jacques Ellul concluded, "Television replaces the missing collective culture that was created by a living group."[2]

Television's influence reaches every facet of life, including judgments about careers, lifestyles, what and how much to buy, ethical standards, relationships, conversations, daily behavior, and how we should spend our free time. Dismissing television viewing as something we can take or let alone ignores its addictive nature, as study after study has shown. This is not just an American phenomenon. Research reported that the Japanese are just as addicted.[3] In every nation, in every culture where television sets are turned on, you will find that stare into the middle distance.

Media theorist Neil Postman wrote, "Television may bring a gradual end to the careers of schoolteachers, since school was an invention of the printing press and must stand or fall on the issue of how much importance the printed word has. For four hundred years, schoolteachers have been part of the knowledge monopoly created by printing, and they are now witnessing the breakup of that monopoly."[4]

Yet the television industry is not immune to the shifting of audiences. New technologies compete with existing means of sending information and entertainment. Television affected cinemas, newspapers, magazines, and radio. Today, video games and the Internet, reached by tablets and mobile phones, are digging into the over-air, direct broadcast satellite, and cable television audiences. Videos of movies and entire seasons of television shows that are available for an evening or two of binge-watching pull audiences away from tuning in to over-the-air channels.

▶ SCIENTIFIC ROOTS

Television, meaning "seeing at a distance," came to mean "seeing by electricity." Its roots go back to 1818, a time of excitement about the properties of electricity, when Sweden's Jöns Berzelius shone light on selenium, a sulfur-like byproduct of copper refining. He noticed variations in how well it conducted electric current. In 1830, England's Michael Faraday sent electricity through a vacuum in a glass bottle. Scotland's Alexander Bain in 1842 sent a current that caused a metal brush to duplicate alphabet letters onto paper. In 1847, the Abbé Caselli, an Italian researcher in France, sent drawings between two cities electrically. In 1873, Irish telegraph operator Joseph May, by varying the amount of light on selenium, sent a signal across the ocean on the Atlantic telegraph cable. American engineer Philip Carey envisioned an array of selenium cells wired to a light bulb in a matching array in a receiver. Other inventors added their efforts during the 19th century, leading in time to wirephotos, facsimile, and the flashing message lights in Times Square.

Sir William Crookes followed Faraday's path in 1875 by shooting electrons from the cathode terminal to the anode terminal of an evacuated tube. Sir J. J. Thomson added to Crookes's work with a magnet that moved the stream of electrons across the tube face. Germany's Karl Ferdinand Braun, in 1897, coated the inner face of a tube with fluorescence so that it glowed when struck by the cathode rays. All these experiments led to the television tube.

What was missing was an image on the face of the tube. In 1884, German student Paul Nipkow introduced this by using two disks with matching patterns of holes that scanned and reproduced a scene fast enough to reach the human eye's persistence of vision. England's John Logie Baird experimented with Nipkow disks into the 1920s and 1930s, but this mechanical system proved to be a dead end, even though Baird managed to send a murky image across the Atlantic Ocean in 1928. The future lay with an electronic system.

▶ SENDING A MOVING IMAGE

Russia's Boris Rosing had a workable system by 1907, partly electronic and partly mechanical, using a cathode ray tube. Others continued electronic experiments. Improbably, one experimenter was an Idaho high school student, Philo Farnsworth, who had read about such investigations in a popular science magazine. In 1927 at the age of 21, Farnsworth filed for the first of many patents for what he called an "image dissector."

Another was Rosing's former assistant, Vladimir Zworykin, an immigrant to the United States, who in 1923 sent a still image from a camera tube that he called an "iconoscope" to the face of a cathode ray display tube that he called a "kinescope." True television is dated from this 1923 demonstration. Zworykin's fellow Russian immigrant, RCA executive David Sarnoff, assembled a team from Westinghouse, General Electric, and RCA under Zworykin to develop electronic television.

In 1925, American inventor Charles Francis Jenkins sent the first transmission of moving objects, windmills, to a receiver 5 miles away. In 1926, a Bell Telephone Labs team under Herbert Ives transmitted a moving picture.

AT&T's Bell Laboratories used a mechanical scanning system to send a black-and-white still photo from Washington to New York in 1927 and color photos in 1929. The quality was poor, an experiment of no apparent commercial use, but everything that anyone did was quickly followed by patent applications. Because no one held all the patents, cross-licensing agreements would be necessary for commercial development, just as radio required them. In 1928, an experimental General Electric station in Schenectady, New York, transmitted programs three times a week, mostly to its own engineers. RCA had its own NBC experimental television station in New York that would become WNBC-TV in 1941. CBS set up WCBS-TV in New York the same year.[5]

As the Depression years leading to World War II went by and the world's attention focused on life-and-death political and economic issues, teams of dogged engineers, scientists, and communication executives in the United States, Britain, Germany, Russia, and Japan pursued the experiments that would lead to television. In England, the British Broadcasting Corporation (BBC) started the world's first regular television service in 1936, testing both mechanical and electronic methods until it became clear that the better system was electronic. Germany began its own electronic television service in Berlin in 1935, broadcasting for an hour and a half three times a week.

The Federal Communications Commission gave CBS and NBC television broadcasting licenses in 1941, but the technology was not ready for commercialization. And World War II loomed. Even the small percentage of people in the New York area who could afford the bulky sets with tiny screens that sold for the price of a new car had almost nothing to see. A prewar home market for television did not exist. Some sets were sold to taverns that bought them for the occasional telecasts of sports events. World War I had blocked the development of commercial radio. Now World War II was blocking commercial television. Electronic research was required for such military needs as radar, sonar, and navigation systems. The government froze television development. Of the ten experimental stations in existence, six fed occasional programs to an estimated 10,000 sets, some of them belonging to station executives and engineers. The DuMont station alone tried to provide service throughout the war.

WHERE TO SHOW IT?

Where to present television was a matter of dispute. The cinema was a likely venue because movies on a celluloid film base already appeared there, and television might be considered another technology for distributing narratives with moving images. Instead, DuMont Laboratories decided to go after the in-home market, and sold its first electronic sets to wealthy individuals starting in 1938 during the depths of the Depression.

Much of the public was introduced to television in 1939 through magazine and newspaper articles, and also at the RCA Pavilion in the New York World's Fair, whose theme was "The World of Tomorrow."

▶ LOOKING TO THE FUTURE

As World War II ground to an end, "Television Past" was only experimental and "Television Present" was dormant. But "Television Future" bustled with energy and promise as people permitted themselves to dream of a postwar future of reunited families and newly married couples moving into single-family homes with one of those new-fangled radios with pictures sitting in their parlor. David Sarnoff's RCA, spending millions to make this happen, actively promoted the dream of television in the home.

By war's end, a huge market for television was ready and waiting, savings in hand because very little had been for sale during war years marked by rationing and self-denial. The public demand was more than matched by manufacturers ready to produce sets, radio broadcasters and newspaper publishers eager for television licenses, and a potential army of workers and entertainers waiting for an industry to come into being.

The postwar years saw the rapid emergence of television as the American populace settled down to build families delayed by the war, created suburbs around their cities, and bought cars to take them to work and shopping at the malls that sprang up. With greater distances to travel and better comforts in their new homes, suburbanites stayed home to watch television. Viewers sat transfixed at their sets as the phrase "couch potato" entered the lexicon, and happy advertisers poured money into the broadcasters' coffers.[6] In 1950, 9 percent of American households owned a television set. Five years later, 63 percent of households did. By 1965, 85 percent did, and by 1975, 97 percent of households owned a set.[7] A Pew Research Center study in 2006 reported that 57 percent of Americans watched a television newscast on a typical day, compared to 40 percent who read a newspaper.[8]

▶ TECHNICAL AGREEMENTS

At first, the pictures were black-and-white, because RCA and CBS could not agree on a color system. As applicants quarreled over who would get the potentially valuable licenses, another battle shaped up over expanding the VHF (very high frequency) spectrum to allow for more television stations, something that RCA resisted, not wanting more competition. With the additional concern that the narrow space between VHF frequencies was causing signal interference, the Federal Communication Commission (FCC) ordered a freeze on new stations that lasted from 1948 to 1952. This was to the advantage of CBS and NBC because most local stations had already affiliated with one or the other, rather than with DuMont or any other group. The technology continued to improve despite the FCC freeze. By 1951, network programs reached from coast to coast. As sales of new television sets soared and pictures became clearer on larger screens, prices of sets plummeted.

By extending the VHF frequency spectrum, (channels 2 to 13) to a new UHF (ultra-high frequency) band, (channels 14 to 69) and later expanding it still further, the FCC dealt with the limited number of channels, assigning local channel licenses in more than 1,200 communities. But many UHF stations failed. Their signals did not transmit as far or with as clean a picture as VHF stations. Early sets were sold without any UHF dials, or lacked click dials. Hunting for signals, inexact tuning, ghost images, and interference reduced audiences. Without audiences, the stations could not attract advertising to pay for network programs, thus further reducing the audiences. But for VHF stations, "A license to broadcast is a license to print money," the Canadian media mogul Lord Thomson said.[9]

The battle over color standards ended in 1953 in favor of RCA. Its proposal for an all-electronic system won out over a partly mechanical system proposed by CBS. Another FCC decision approved a National Television Systems Committee (NTSC) picture made up of 525 lines which were "refreshed" 60 times a second, interlacing the even-numbered lines and the odd-numbered lines that were transmitted alternately. Europeans delayed for a time, then adopted two slightly better systems, the French SECAM and the British–German PAL. Based on colonial, cultural, and trade ties, other nations chose one or another of the three. Because the systems were not compatible, the choice determined what programming these nations received.

HDTV ("high definition television") eventually emerged in the 1990s, offering a sharper and brighter digital image in place of the standard analog pictures. It also offered a cinema screen-like 16 × 9 width-to-height ratio instead of the standard television 4 × 3 ratio, with more than twice the number of scanning lines of NTSC pictures and, therefore, at least twice the sharpness. HDTV offered ten times as much color information as the NTSC system, as well as CD-quality sound.

The possibility that had been raised in the 1930s for cinema distribution of television programs arose again with HDTV—that is, distribution to movie theaters. Most movies still arrived in cinemas as cans of film. A proposal imagined a scrambled HDTV signal sent by satellite at a specific time to cinemas where audiences were waiting. This would not only reduce the cost of distribution but would also allow for films of limited appeal to find their potential audiences. As to the question of abandoning cinemas entirely and simply making all films available as DVDs for home viewing, the answer might well be that going out to a movie is a social event, but sitting at home is not, except for the market of teenagers and young lovers who simply want to get out of the house at any cost. In 2006 another battle over standards saw the Blu-Ray optical disc format win over DVD competitors for recording and playback. Its blue laser technology could store far more information than the red lasers that other DVDs used.

THE REMOTE

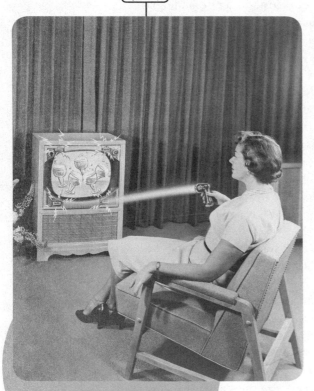

An advertisement for a Zenith remote-controlled TV, 1955.

A less impressive television technology has taken its place as an artifact of modern civilization. Like the telephone answering machine, the remote control is a small, humble gadget attached to a more important device. We use the remote but pay little attention to its influence on our behavior, such as that family members frequently fight over its possession. It confers status on the holder. In more traditional families, the husband and father may regard the remote as his by right. A poll reported in 2013 that more couples (36 percent) fight over control of the remote than over anything else, including money and housework.[10] In 2014, a 17-year-old girl in Kansas City stabbed her stepfather in a quarrel over the remote,[11] and a Yemeni man shot and killed his brother.[12] Again, we adapt to our media tools, although in this case not everyone adapts well.

Remotes predate commercial television. During World War I, Germany used them for motorboats. After World War II, remote-controlled automatic garage door openers helped sell new houses. Requiring a wire connection, Zenith in 1950 introduced "Lazy Bone," the first television remote control; unfortunately, people tripped over the wire. Five years later Zenith came out with the "Flash-matic," a wireless version. Unfortunately, again it failed, this time because the remote depended on photocells. Television sets might change channels by themselves on sunny days.

The following year, Zenith did it better with the "Space Command," a remote control based on ultrasonics. However, their need for extra vacuum tubes raised the price and the size of a television set. The arrival of transistors reduced both. During the early 1980s, the technology changed once again when infrared remote control units replaced ultrasound. They are now included in television set purchases.

▶ PUBLIC BROADCASTING

Not all U.S. broadcasting was for profit. A few educational radio stations had hung on during the early years of commercial television despite poor funding that translated into weak programming. Educators had learned some hard lessons in competing for radio licenses with take-no-prisoners commercial broadcasters.

The educators did much better in securing non-profit television licenses from the FCC, thanks in part to help from major organizations, especially the Ford Foundation. The Public Broadcasting Act of 1967 created the Corporation for Public Broadcasting to establish standards and develop public media. Federal grants also helped, progressing over the decades of the last half-century to a national public television network, originally named National Educational Television in 1952, changed to the Public Broadcasting System (PBS) in 1970. Other public radio networks and distributors also emerged, such as National Public Radio (renamed in 1970 from the National Educational Radio Network), American Public Media (1967), and Public Radio International (1983). As funding arrived, programming improved.

Of the various ways to support the television industry everywhere and pay for programs, commercials won the greatest favor as being the least painful and the least subject to government involvement. Despite some displeasure at the thought of any commercials in public television, American public television has gradually shifted from total rejection of commercials to sponsorship announcements that identified and even promoted a company or product.

Product placement goes back to Jules Verne's novel *Around the World in Eighty Days* (1873), serialized in magazines, when shipping companies lobbied to be mentioned. Today products are displayed in movies and television shows as a source of funding. For example, they regularly appear in James Bond films, such as the bottle of beer Bond holds in *Skyfall* (2012). Products are also displayed in some video games.

▶ INTERNATIONAL CHANGES

While television in the United States continued down the private path begun by the telegraph, most of the rest of the world saw government controls retained in the expansion from radio to television. The BBC's dependence upon annual license fees on television sets to fund public broadcasting was copied by several countries, but all of them had stations that broadcast commercials as well.

Television commercials became the principal means of political campaigning, notably in the United States. Political managers remained convinced of the efficacy of spending hundreds of millions of dollars for commercial time. The money that a candidate raised became one of the surest ways to predict the probability of victory. Totalitarian governments still preferred direct government subsidies to broadcasters because of the direct control it provided, but nevertheless allowed some commercials.

Audiences for the entire television industry declined in the competition with new forms of media, notably the Internet and video games. European government television networks, complacent and overstaffed, suffered far worse than ABC, CBS, and NBC. Wracked by commercial competition that was permitted in the later decades of the 20th century, plus the growth of cable channels, the use of satellites and the expansion of videotape rentals, Italy's RAI, Spain's RTVE, and Germany's ARD and ZDF faced financial ruin.[13] State-run Asian television networks were also hurting as viewer choices increased. In France, Russia, the nations of Eastern Europe, and Mexico among others, state-owned stations were sold to private interests. To keep viewers in the huge and tumultuous Indian market after private channels were allowed to compete in 1991, the government service Doordarshan reduced its educational fare and added more commercial programs. As the 21st century unfolded, the television industry everywhere was undergoing significant change.

▶ PROGRAMS

When radio broadcasting was new in the late 1920s, it was not uncommon, at those times when a popular show such as *Amos 'n' Andy* was on, for neighbors to seek out neighbors who owned a radio set. The first television programs had the same effect. Programs were broadcast to viewers who crowded into the homes of neighbors who owned sets, or who gathered in front of stores that sold sets. Radio store owners put a television in the window and piped the sound outside. In time as the novelty wore off and television became another part of daily life, television sets might remain on to provide background sound. Because many households had one set for each family member and because of the increased variety of choices of programs and videos, watching a television screen alone was common.

Marshall McLuhan observed that a new medium chooses for its content the medium it displaces.[14] Television displaced, among other entertainments, novels and movies, both of which became television content. The radio variety show, born out of stage vaudeville, was reborn to be presented to national audiences as the television variety show. The crowds outside the stores were largest for such popular fare as the variety shows hosted by Milton Berle and Ed Sullivan. Also popular were B-movie westerns owned by their cowboy stars.

Did television hurt the movies? It was not films themselves, but the cinemas that were partially displaced when people began to prefer to view movies in the comforts of home. The success of drive-in theaters should have served as a wake-up call. The inevitable close alliance between the television industry and the motion picture industry was delayed due to the concerns of Hollywood executives who thought that television would erode their profitable business.

Their fears were justified insofar as the Hollywood studios were linked financially to theater chains. The 1948 U.S. Supreme Court decision, *U.S. v. Paramount*, had ordered those links severed. In time a revived, restructured, and thriving motion picture industry came to see television as a valuable distribution channel. The studios had the talent both in front of and behind the camera and the equipment, the sound stages, and the back lots where scenes could be shot. The television networks had the audiences and cash. It was a natural fit. The live dramas that marked television in the 1950s were partially replaced by filmed dramas and comedies that could be filmed, edited, and kept on a shelf until aired and aired again.

QUIZ SHOW SCANDAL

Radio's *$64 Question* became television's *$64,000 Question* and was among the most popular television programs of the 1950s. History professor Charles Van Doren was a favorite contestant for the millions of weekly viewers of the show *Twenty One*. The producers fed him and a few other contestants the correct answers, while instructing the less favored to lose. Contestants were coached to bite their nails and delay their answers to the last moment as they stood in "isolation booths" with the air conditioning off to make them sweat. Another quiz show, *Dotto*, was also revealed to be a fraud.

Quiz show *Twenty One* host Jack Berry (center) with contestants Vivienne Nearine and Charles Van Doren.

When it was discovered that some shows had been rigged to favor certain contestants to whom the audience had taken a liking, congressional inquiries followed. Television quiz show fixing became a federal crime. No one went to jail, but reputations were ruined. Van Doren, the son of a famous family of educators, was fired by Columbia University. The public, at least as the headlines told it, felt betrayed. The embarrassed networks adopted stringent guidelines for future quiz shows and embarked on a period of documentary production. Documentaries did not draw the large audiences beloved of networks but their purity of purpose was laudable.

▶ CULTURAL EFFECTS AND CRITICISM

As an audio-visual representation of a written culture, television programs, like radio programs before them, are positioned to take the best of both oral and written cultures. As an audio-visual medium, television reaches audiences who receive entertainment and information without the effort of reading. Literacy is no problem for viewers, although television calls upon the breadth of written culture with its infinite resources. With programs available to view on TV sets, with computers, mobile phones and iPods, arriving wired, wireless, downloaded, mailed, stored on tape or disc, bought or rented, watched for hours daily, television is—in a word—*us*.

Television has drawn families together but not necessarily to communicate with each other. Often as not the arrival of a guest does not result in the television set being turned off or the sound lowered. The visitor is welcome to share the sofa and the snacks, and join the watching. The sofa is often where meals are eaten. Again, we adapt to media imperatives.

As the home audience stared at their television sets, the television industry stared back with even more intensity. With advertising rates spiking, the advertisers and the ad agencies wanted better information about just who was watching what. What ages, gender, income, and other factors were involved? Demographic data would later be augmented by focus groups and by psychographic data that considered social class, lifestyle, and the personality characteristics of the audience. In time, marketing decisions would do their part in converting television broadcasting into narrowcasting, removing certain groups from some marketing considerations, notably the elderly, who became almost a shadow audience for programs aimed at a younger demographic.

It has been said that viewers do not watch programs; they watch television, pushing buttons until they find something that might not bore them. The term "moderate liking" seems to fit, producing a compromise when several people are watching. If this theory, once prevalent in television network circles, still affects programming decisions, it would lead to bland, copycat programs not likely to offend viewers. In fact, the "LOP" (least objectionable program) theory actually guided programmers and may still influence them.[15]

Because television broadcasting not delivered by cable or satellite has traditionally been free and because most programs require little if any education on the part of viewers, broadcast television has been called a consolation prize for the powerless.[16] In the age of the Internet, broadcast television remains the medium of choice for the poor, the uneducated, children, and the elderly.[17] A couple of generations earlier, a study of radio broadcasting found that our level of income influenced our listening choices.[18]

▶ "A VAST WASTELAND"

In 1961 the chairman of the FCC, Newton Minow, challenged television executives to watch a single day of their own station's programs from start to finish. "I can assure you that you will see a vast wasteland," he said.[19]

So what to do about the vast wasteland? To the industry's standard answer that the unhappy viewer should hit the "off" button comes the complainer's equally standard answer that the family did not buy a television set to turn it off. To the industry's argument that the critics want to impose their personal tastes and morality upon everyone comes the argument that the airwaves belong to the public and the industry is giving back next to nothing in return for the public's gift of valuable licenses. To the industry's argument that television is a business, not an educational institution, comes the reply that, like it or not, television *is* an important educational institution. So go the arguments around and around without resolution. A Sisyphus quality attends both the criticism and the industry response. Those who want change push the rock of reform up the hill, only to be met by resistance and indifference that will lead to new efforts, over and over.

Before TV, people did not go to the movies for hours each day. What neither side in the endless quarrel talks about much is the amount of time spent daily watching television. The set is on about 8.5 hours a day in the average American home.[20] Neither side is campaigning to reduce the substantial amount of discretionary time spent each day staring at phosphor dots. For the industry it is a bread-and-butter issue. For those who complain, a campaign to limit viewing would be hopeless. Television is not something you and I can just take or leave alone. As noted in the Introduction, in one of several studies of families asked to do without TV for a specific length of time, a participant in Minneapolis reflected the sentiment that doing without TV is like "a death in the family."[21]

Ellul was one of the media ecology critics who took a dim view of the hours spent with television: "Again, what use is the video recorder? It enables us to see films as we want and to record television programs that interest us. But do we not spend enough time in front of the television without adding to it, without doubling the brutalizing and dispossession of the self which four hours of daily viewing produce?"[22]

Critics of the commercial-based system had limited followings. Millions of viewers liked television they didn't have to pay for. They even liked looking at a favorite commercial, no matter how often they saw it. Children sometimes enjoyed commercials more than programs.

Edmund Carpenter wrote, "The child is right in not regarding commercials as interruptions. For the only time anyone smiles on TV is in commercials. The rest of life, in news broadcasts and soap operas, is presented as so horrible that the only way to get through life is to buy this product; then you'll smile. Aesop never wrote a clearer fable."[23]

▶ THE SOAPS

Soap operas moved seamlessly from radio to television and from daytime to prime time. Their appeal spread from mostly housewives to the workplace, retirement homes, and campuses. Viewers spend hours each day with "their" soaps. For some, the anticipation of the coming day's episode salvages a dull or difficult life.

According to writer George Wiley in 1961, "The listener's sense of security was enhanced by emphasis placed in the episodes upon such matters of special interest as marriage ties, the problems encountered by career women (a role the listener had avoided), the importance attached to the role of the wife and homemaker, and, in all things, the triumph of good over evil . . . The punctuality and dependability of the daily visits doubtlessly lent a sense of order to many a pointless day."[24]

On September 23, 2011, the day that *All My Children* went off the air after 41 years, some college classes were cancelled so students had the chance to watch the last episode along with everyone else. Something real and important had gone out of their lives. Someone wondered if she watched *All My Children* more than her own children.

PROMOTING TOLERANCE

If the United States is a more tolerant nation than it once was, give some credit to television. Starting with *All in the Family* and its comically racist Archie Bunker, some prime time television programs have tried to be on the cutting edge of social change. However, a not insignificant segment of the audience agreed with his bigoted opinions and considered him one of their own. *All in the Family* producer Norman Lear, a liberal, intended to ridicule prejudice, but it partially backfired. "To critics, the show wasn't the real problem; its audience was."[25]

Social change in media portrayals has been most obvious for African Americans, who were almost invisible at the start of television in the 1940s and 1950s, and were hardly visible in films except in minor or demeaning roles.

In television entertainment, the color bar that kept out most racial minorities, especially African Americans, was broken by the 1970s. The civil rights movements for African Americans and women no doubt would have progressed more slowly without the films, television programs and broadcast coverage of recent decades.[26]

THE V-CHIP

Almost no topic is off limits to television today. Ellul has written about what he calls "determining factors in the eroticizing of society and the growth of violence" in the content of television programs and advertising.[27] Think about the growth of reality shows and the placing of contestants in humiliating or seemingly dangerous situations, or focusing on nasty quarrels between couples until they break apart. Again, the public gets what it wants, however shameful.

As for hour-long police or medical procedurals and the half-hour sitcoms, the social message has changed in two important ways. First, like all mediated entertainment, and most notably movies and popular music, the content has been coarsened by violence and crude behavior. Second, sexual activity that would not have been tolerated at the start of televised entertainment is commonplace.

Congressional committees have held hearings into the role of television in encouraging juvenile delinquency. The Telecommunication Reform Act of 1996 put some changes in place. A "V-Chip" was mandated for each new television set so that parents could block violent and sexually explicit programs. Networks and cable channels accepted an industry rating system that went into effect in 1997. A Comics Code seal of approval on the covers of comic books, in place since congressional hearings in 1954, has mostly disappeared. Marvel comic books added its own rating system in 2001, modified four years later. Video game makers adopted rating standards in 2005. Ratings vary from country to country .

In 2007 the Federal Communications Commission asked Congress for legislation that would allow the FCC to regulate violence on TV, but Congress has not acted. For decades the FCC has fined stations for stepping over the line regarding sexual material or language, but has lacked the muscle to do much about violence. In defending itself against attacks that sex and violence encourage promiscuous and violent behavior among younger viewers, the industry argues that normal viewers are not influenced. This is a position that flies in the face of the billions of dollars, euros, and yen spent on television advertising, which is based on the opposite conviction that what appears on television does indeed influence behavior.

The overall total number of children's programs has increased over the years. In 1975 a Family Viewing Hour, the first hour of prime time, was established, only to be overturned by a court decision. Plans for voluntary compliance gradually dissolved into standard evening fare. However, good children's fare could be found on PBS, notably the award-winning *Sesame Street*, and frequently on cable channels that were striving for a young audience. Actually, *Sesame Street* itself has been accused of affecting children negatively by conditioning them to have a short attention span.[28]

A nationwide study as early as 1960 funded by CBS concluded that television had replaced other means of socialization for everyone except people of high education and income. Of all household items, television was the one non-essential item in the home that nearly everyone regarded as essential.[29] There were reports of changes caused by television viewing in family lifestyles, sleeping habits, children's entertainment, and activity preferences. It was much easier for some children just to tune to *Sesame Street* than to go outside and actually explore.

▶ THE EXPANSION OF NEWS

Radio newscasts and cinema newsreels came together as television news. Television newscasts added a human dimension to the daily reports of events. Network news anchors, particularly Walter Cronkite at CBS and the team of Chet Huntley and David Brinkley at NBC, were welcomed each evening into millions of homes almost like members of the family. One survey voted Cronkite the most trusted man in America.[30]

Connecting stations into networks, adding telephone "tie-lines," and making film technology quicker, television news raised the level of visual reporting, first in black-and-white, then in color. Electronic news gathering (ENG) improved on film. Satellite news gathering (SNG) would bring in visual news reports instantly from all over the world. The digital revolution further improved news reports even from the most distant places.

Walter Cronkite during the first presidential debate between Gerald Ford and Jimmy Carter, 1976.

Television's power to move the nation showed itself in both the rise and the fall of Senator Joseph McCarthy. His unsupported announcements that he had lists of communists in government generated headlines and television coverage and led to the Red Scare that traumatized the nation during the 1950s. It was also on television that Edward R. Murrow's devastating attack on McCarthy and the coverage of the Army–McCarthy hearings in 1954 finally brought McCarthy down.

Presidents learned to give televised news conferences. Campaigns for quadrennial presidential elections shifted their most important events from national party conventions, which mattered less, to presidential debates that were analyzed over and over, and could win or lose an election. The focus in future would be on television. To refuse to participate in a televised presidential debate is now unimaginable. The 1960 televised presidential debates between John Kennedy and Richard Nixon further changed the political landscape of the nation, turning away from locally based ward politics and party loyalties. Kennedy dominated the televised debates, especially the first debate, which showed Nixon, a pale and sweating vice president, facing a tanned and confident young senator. Curiously, radio listeners believed Nixon had won, but those listeners were not enough when the votes were counted. Political campaigns were forever changed.

The reputation of television news rose in its four days of coverage of President Kennedy's assassination and the subsequent events in November 1963. In some nations, street riots might have followed the assassination of a popular leader. In the United States viewers were glued to their television sets. At one point, nine out of ten Americans were watching.[31]

Amid the changes was a growing awareness of television's reach. The Civil Rights movement blossomed in the turbulent decades of the 1950s and 1960s with the popularity of television news. That was no coincidence. Martin Luther King, Jr. and other Civil Rights leaders saw their chance to expose segregationist unfairness and brutality before the nation and force change, so they chose the harsh racial climate of Selma and Birmingham for their demonstrations instead of the gentler reception they would receive in Atlanta. With its coverage of snarling police dogs, high-pressure water hoses, and unarmed demonstrators being beaten by police, television news shone a glaring spotlight on the South's response to the civil rights movement.

As the years went by, with comedy shows about African American families and with African American actors regularly appearing in dramas and variety shows, television moved to the forefront of efforts to improve racial relations.[32]

During the 1960s, network television expanded from 15 to 30 minutes and added color, plus morning shows that included news and weather segments. Local stations scrambled to keep up. Large city stations had news blocks of two hours or more. In addition, morning programs would not be complete without news reports.

Editors were given the authority to break into entertainment programs to report momentous events, and could take over completely, as they did to report the assassination of President Kennedy in 1963 and later, in 2001, the 9/11 attacks. Less overwhelming breaking news was reported by briefer interruptions or as crawls of text along the bottom of the television screen.

In the late 1960s came coverage of the Chicago police mishandling of demonstrators during the Democratic Convention in 1968, Vice President Spiro Agnew's blistering attack on network news in 1969, the 1972 Watergate saga led by the *Washington Post* but widely seen on television, and publication in 1971 by the *New York Times* of the Pentagon Papers revealing U.S. policy regarding Vietnam. Conservatives blamed "the media" again and again, accusing major newspapers and television news of everything from liberal bias to treachery.

Like the Asian proverb that the nail that sticks up gets hammered down, the new visibility of television news had its price. Agnew attacked network news in a speech denouncing network news "liberal bias" by a "small, unelected elite."[33] Tens of thousands of angry letters, phone calls, and telegrams to the networks quickly reinforced the message. Stung by the threats to station licenses, television news started out slowly and nervously in covering the Watergate story. Newspapers did the heavy lifting, but no newspaper could match television's ability to reach a mass audience, to convey the tension and the immediacy of the Senate hearings on impeachment in 1974, and the presidential speeches that showed viewers a tired and troubled Richard Nixon losing his grip on power.

NEWS MAGAZINES

News interview programs were matched in popularity by prime-time news magazine programs like the iconic *60 Minutes* that explore news issues and events in depth, although documentaries were usually left to public television and cable stations. Magazine programs, led by *60 Minutes*, which began in 1968, consisted of extended news reports of about 15 minutes, and were less susceptible to accusations of bias. Through much of the last half of the 20th century, *60 Minutes* was among the most watched programs of any kind on television. Its combination of hard news, exposés, feature news, and interviews resonated strongly with viewers. Its success spawned other magazine shows, such as *20/20*, *Dateline*, and *Primetime*.

From morning network programs like the daily *Today Show* and the weekly *Meet the Press* to evening programs such as *Nightline*, programs dealing with current events were an important part of television schedules, with individual stations matching locally what networks did nationally. Politicians used these programs to garner support for themselves and for their views on controversial issues.

▶ "THE LIVING ROOM WAR"

The Vietnam War was filmed in color, with images reaching television screens only one or two days after battlefield film was shot. It has been called the first "television war" and "the living room war." Daily reports brought the reality of bloodshed, pain, and frustration home and created an intimate contact with warfare never before experienced by a whole nation. The war coverage did much to spark the student demonstrations that ignited the anti-war movement.

Television coverage was from an American perspective, for a Vietnamese perspective was not possible, and was generally sympathetic to the American military experience, but not entirely so. It was those other verbal and visual views that startled and enraged Americans at home. The napalm bombings, the village burnings, the scenes of terrified old people and children, and the body bags of American soldiers being sent home infused the anti-war movement and led to counter-accusations that the media were to blame for not supporting the troops, for adding to American casualties, and even for losing the Vietnam War by encouraging the antiwar rallies. Nor did entertainment programs escape censure. The mildly cynical and very popular series *M*A*S*H*, following the hit movie, did not fool its entire audience into thinking it was really about the Korean War.

Cronkite went to Vietnam in 1968 after the Tet Offensive and, in a special report, concluded:

> To say that we are closer to victory today is to believe, in the face of the evidence, the optimists who have been wrong in the past. To suggest we are on the edge of defeat is to yield to unreasonable pessimism. To say that we are mired in stalemate seems the only realistic, yet unsatisfactory, conclusion. On the off chance that military and political analysts are right, in the next few months we must test the enemy's intentions, in case this is indeed his last big gasp before negotiations. But it is increasingly clear to this reporter that the only rational way out then will be to negotiate, not as victors, but as an honorable people who lived up to their pledge to defend democracy, and did the best they could.[34]

Public reaction was intense. President Lyndon Baines Johnson reportedly said, "If I've lost Cronkite, I've lost Middle America."[35] Whether he said it or not, a few weeks later he announced that he would not seek re-election.

Television reporters and photographers had been free to go where they wanted during the Vietnam War. That casual military attitude would not continue. As a result of lessons learned to its dismay, the Pentagon would handle the media differently in future conflicts. War planning would change in the future to take into account home front reaction to instant battle coverage. During the Gulf War of 1991 and the Iraq War of the 2000s the Pentagon more closely monitored movements of reporters and television photographers. Journalists were "embedded" with designated military units, and that resulted in more sympathetic coverage.

The United States government was not alone in finding itself in the television news crosshairs. Protests shown against the policies of many governments, from Tiananmen Square in 1989 to the 2009 Iranian elections, the 2011 uprisings across the Middle East, and the Syrian civil war bloodbath beginning in 2011, demonstrated television's power to bring world attention to unpopular government actions. Dictatorships may block their own television channels, but when the pictures from inside their nations reached the rest of the world, it was primarily television that distributed them. YouTube has now joined that distribution.

First videotape and later the digital revolution expanded what television news could offer viewers. Videotape and accompanying signaling led to electronic news gathering. The time it took to process film disappeared. Being reusable, videotape did not force photographers to ration the amount of footage they shot, as film did. With the addition of electronic transmission from a photographer's truck to a television station and the bounced signals of satellite news gathering, television reporting and photography expanded so that the Iraq War could be covered live by reporters embedded with front line troops. Television news also adopted computerized non-linear video editing. The result was quicker, more precise, and more complex editing at lower cost.

▶ SPACE RACE

Television was also part of what came to be known as the Space Race that started with the Soviet Union's launch of the first *Sputnik* in 1957. Americans had been living with the comfortable assumption that, as one journalist remarked after visiting Moscow, the Russians couldn't manage to build a ladder that reached from an airplane to the ground.[36] The fear of communist domination of outer space, from which nuclear weapons could be launched, put an American space program into overdrive. Media covered it in depth for its international and domestic, political and economic implications as well as for the gee-whiz visual coverage of Cape Canaveral (known as Cape Kennedy from 1963 to 1973) launches. From the start, the competition between the United States and the Soviet Union was especially tense for American viewers because many of the first American rockets were failures. The Soviet Union had its share of disasters, but it kept those hidden from the public. It did not help when Yuri Gagarin went into orbit in 1961, a year before John Glenn did.

When the *Eagle* landed on the moon on July 20, 1969, one-sixth of the world's population was able to tune in live and to hear Neil Armstrong say, "That's one small step for man, one giant leap for mankind." It was also a giant leap for communication as an estimated 600 million people watched. Marshall McLuhan's image of a "global village" was realized, however briefly.[37]

The concept of the global village is also realized in television programs that enjoy a wide international following. The bikini-filled *Baywatch*[38] that has stirred comment in countries where women's bodies are fully covered and *The Simpsons* cartoons showing a stupid father qualify as global village fare. So does the annual Chinese Lunar New Year program, attracting an estimated 700 million viewers worldwide for the commercial-free, four-hour extravaganza.[39] Yet, for the most part, the enormous number of media choices encourages people to go their separate ways. There are just too many books, magazines, radio and stored music, television programs, and Internet sites for the concept of a village that shares.

▶ CABLE

Let us back up more than a half-century. The story of cable television is as American as a Horatio Alger tale of the poor country boy who found success in the city. Unlike cultural changes that begin in major cities and find their way to rural villages and towns, cable was the country boy who went to the big city. Born in humble circumstances in rural Pennsylvania to help folks living out in the countryside to enjoy something that only city folks had, cable TV eventually migrated to cities, where it challenged a major indus-try—over-the-air broadcasting—and succeeded beyond all expectations in affecting our way of life.

When cable began in 1948 as community antennas, it was just a means to bring television signals to towns too far from a large city station for good reception. The broadcast industry, if it thought about the matter at all, wel-comed community antennas because they added viewers at no cost to the stations. That would change when cable signals began to compete with what the stations were broadcasting. Complaints from broadcasters grew louder when the CATV (community antenna TV) owners added program-ming of their own such as a locally produced variety show and coverage of city hall meetings and local high school sports. That began in 1951 in the town of Pottsville, Pennsylvania, when a CATV owner used a small, personal television camera to pull together a 30-minute variety show with Pottsville residents as entertainers. Neighbors were delighted with its local origination.

With the addition of locally produced content, CATV evolved into cable television. All this was taking place in the midst of the FCC freeze on new television licenses, when only 108 stations were on the air. Some broadcast-ers observing this fast growing business invested in it themselves. In time, media conglomerates would own cable systems as well as television stations as part of their communication empires.

▶ HBO AND TED TURNER

Cable underwent an important change in 1975 with a test in Wilkes-Barre, Pennsylvania, to deliver programming that had been unavailable anywhere until then. It was called Home Box Office, a pay channel that for three years had been feeding videotape recordings of recent movies and some sports coverage to nearby cable systems. More and more cable systems wanted to add the popular channel to their service. So many inquiries came that HBO decided to take the financial risk to sell the service across the nation by bouncing a signal off RCA's domestic communications satellite, SATCOM. To attract a large audience, HBO chose as its first offering a boxing match in the Philippines between Mohammed Ali and Joe Frazier. What Ali dubbed the "thrilla from Manila" in 1975 went to cable systems that had installed a satellite dish 10 meters in diameter. The fight was shown in 380 locations in the United States and broadcast to 68 countries worldwide.[40]

Atlanta UHF station owner Ted Turner decided to provide a similar service via the same SATCOM satellite, but with a different financing method. Instead of charging individual subscribers, Turner offered an extra channel of movies and sports that the cable systems themselves would pay for on the basis of a few cents per subscriber.

Each cable system would be using the same dish it had installed for HBO. The extra channel gave viewers still more choices, so it was attractive to cable systems in their efforts to win customers. Turner's WTCG-TV (later WTBS) became the first "superstation."[41] His ownership of a UHF station on which he showed the ball games of two teams that he owned— baseball's Atlanta Braves and basketball's Atlanta Hawks—not only gave Turner additional programming, but also a national audience that he parlayed into much higher fees for commercials. Chicago's WGN, New York's WOR, and several other new superstations followed. HBO was followed by pay channels Cinemax, Showtime, and The Movie Channel. Several dozen cable channels have since been created on the way to what futurists predicted would become "a 500-channel universe," actually meaning a universe of channels limited only by audience demand.

As the programming choices increased, the technology of cable television itself was given competition by DBS (Direct Broadcast Satellite), also known as DTH (Direct-to-Home). In some communities a non-satellite wireless service that used microwave also competed with cable. DBS suffered in competition with cable until a 1999 law allowed it to retransmit local signals back to the local community. In the first decade of the new century, more than two-thirds of all the households in the United States received a cable or DBS service. Said one cable executive, cable television was like air conditioning, "You don't need it, but once you live with it, you can't live without it."[42]

Among the channels created for cable systems were those specifically devoted to shopping at home and those channels that were given over at night to infomercials (program-length commercials). It gave viewers the opportunity to shop without leaving home. As watching television and shopping were two of the favorite activities of millions of people, "electronic retailing" seemed a sure bet for success. Selling goods this way started displacing the mailed catalogues, just as Sears and Montgomery Ward catalogues had once invaded the business of the small town general store. Communication technology was again forcing change. As the Internet came into being, online shopping was sure to follow.

Still more choice was available to those willing to pay. Known variously as PPV (Pay-per-View), STV (Subscription Television), or pay-TV, it delivered recent first-run movies, plus original entertainment and sports events to homes and hotel rooms. What was happening was little different from what always happens as mediated communication grows. Viewers who are offered the opportunity for making choices will always prefer to have them. The proliferation of radio stations after World War II had brought so many choices that radio stations, for their own survival, opted to focus on a specific market segment such as youth, just as magazines did. With so many choices, it was inevitable that the cable industry would fracture into narrowcasting, with programmers shifting away from trying to reach a general audience. On occasion, television audiences coalesced around a single program or event, such as the coverage of the Olympics or a truly major worldwide news story, but for the most part, viewers went their separate ways to their channels of choice.

▶ CHANGES IN NEWS VIEWING PATTERNS

The arrival of the Internet as a news venue, the growing popularity of blogs for news and opinions, and the 24-hour news cycle of CNN and other cable channels sharply cut into network audiences, just as newscasts had cut into newspapers readership. Both network news audiences and newspaper readership have been skewing toward the elderly, with young people going elsewhere for news, or going nowhere. Credit—or blame—for this includes a significant national shift toward increased choices, especially among the segment most desired by advertisers and networks, the better educated younger viewers who prefer to get their news at the time of their choosing and know how to surf online for the topics that interest them. Impatient, they no longer need to wait.

News organizations of every medium have created their own websites, offering video reports sometimes in greater depth than newscasts and print stories permit, and sometimes before they are presented on the evening newscasts. Like entertainment programs, newscasts can be downloaded for viewing anytime on a variety of devices. So can podcasts that anyone can create.

On most days, Americans tune in and out of television news, radio news, and the Internet news services. When we awake, tuck into dinner, or go to bed, we may check to see if the world has altered. Satisfied that it has not, we go about our lives or use the media for diversion or for learning facts that we can act upon. That is why weather reports occupy so much of local newscasts each day; we can grab an umbrella or stuff a child into a heavier jacket. News is also diversion, which explains much of what else we see on newscasts. Many viewers prefer local newscasts and their reactive response to crimes, accidents, fires, and other nearby events, plus lighthearted features, all delivered by attractive anchors who adjust their expressions to suit the story.[43]

▶ NEW WAYS TO WATCH

The new century has seen popular television programs sold as video-on-demand (VOD) for downloading without commercials. For fans who missed a favorite episode, such a piecemeal purchase—quickly available—was a desirable alternative to waiting for reruns or acquiring a DVD of an entire season. Viewing would happen when it was more convenient for the viewer, and over other media than the TV set, including laptops, tiny iPods and cellphone screens. A program could be watched anywhere that a cellphone could be carried. A couple lying side by side in bed at night, instead of each reading a book, might each separately be watching and hearing a favorite program.

In retrospect, it seems inevitable that the advances of digital storage media would lead to the personal video recorder (PVR) such as TiVo that allows a viewer to pause or rewind live programs and skip over commercials. Even more than videotape, TiVo is convenient. As with any recorder, TiVo or DVR could be paused for a baby's cry, a ringing phone, or a bathroom break.

Because of its widespread adoption, the television industry and the advertising industry have searched for new ways to reach those "eyeballs," such as product placement. Firms that do television viewer research are being compelled by fast-changing communication technology to rethink the basic broadcasting model, which is that viewers are given free entertainment in return for minutes of their time to watch commercials.

The new century also saw the growing popularity of alternatives to the cathode ray tube home television and the rear projection set. The liquid crystal display (LCD) and the plasma tube offer large screens and panels that may be thin and flat enough to hang on a wall. Among the experimental technologies that are likely to bring new choices is optical transmission based on digital light pulses rather than electrical signals. A single hair-thin optical fiber is able to transmit 167 television channels, while a bundle of six strands can feed out more than 1,000 video signals. This broadband opens the possibility of interactive cable television. In 2007, Sony tested a TV screen as thin and flexible as paper.

▶ CHOICES IN THE 21ST CENTURY

The 21st century is seeing popular television programs sold or given away for downloading through websites such as Hulu as video-on-demand and through distribution systems like Netflix, where an entire season of programs can be viewed in sequence and without commercials, a process often called "binge-watching."

In 1938, when it began to attract public notice for its future potential, television drew the attention of a leading American essayist, E. B. White: "I believe television is going to be the test of the modern world and that in this new opportunity to see beyond the range of our vision, we shall discover either a new and unbearable disturbance of the general peace, or a saving radiance in the sky. We shall stand or fall by television, of that I am quite sure."[44]

So, three-quarters of a century after White's prediction, at the end of the television viewing day, is the television set a positive or a negative? Certainly a little of each. Its supporters say it educates and entertains. Its detractors say it corrupts. Everyone can agree on two things. First, television continues to influence our society. Second, it is not going away anytime soon.

▶ TIMELINE

1817   Jöns Berzelius discovers that light changes selenium's electric flow.

1873   Joseph May uses selenium to send a signal through the Atlantic cable.

1875   In England, William Crookes builds a forerunner to the TV cathode ray tube.

1884   In Germany, student Paul Nipkow builds a scanning disc.

1890   In Germany, Karl Ferdinand Braun invents the cathode ray tube.

1907   Boris Rosing builds a working electronic/mechanical system in the lab.

1922   15-year-old Philo Farnsworth designs a television "image dissector."

1923   Vladimir Zworykin patents an electronic camera tube, the iconoscope.

1925   A moving image is telecast in a lab experiment.

1936   BBC starts world's first regular television service, three hours a day.

    In Germany, television cameras transmit the Berlin Olympics.

1939   NBC starts the first regular daily electronic TV broadcasts in the United States.

1940   Peter Goldmark at CBS demonstrates television in color.

1947   *Meet the Press* shifts from radio to TV; will be longest running TV program.

1948   CBS and NBC begin nightly 15-minute television newscasts.

    Before cable there was Community Antenna Television, CATV.

1951   Color television sets go on sale.

1952   FCC ends four-year freeze, sets VHF, opens UHF, reserves education channels.

1953   *TV Guide*; initial press run is 1.5 million copies.

1954   United States is shaken by Murrow documentary on U.S. Senator Joseph McCarthy.

1955   Research shows TV viewing correlates inversely with education, income.

1958   Videotape delivers color.

1960   Kennedy–Nixon debates draw huge numbers of viewers.

1963   John F. Kennedy assassination sends millions to around-the-clock newscasts.

Communications satellite Syncom II goes into geo-synchronous orbit.

1965   Vietnam War becomes first war to be televised: "the living room war."

1975   HBO bounces signal off satellite to reach cable systems.

1980   CNN begins round-the-clock reports from Atlanta to 172 cable systems.

1995   Direct Broadcast Satellites (DBS) beam digital programs to home dishes.

1999   TiVo offers personal television control: storing programs and skipping ads.

2006   Television signals available digitally.

2010   3D television arrives.

▶ NOTES

1 U.S. Census Bureau reports an average in 2010 of 2.58 persons per household, compared to 2.59 persons per household in 2000. The average number of sets per home in 2005, the latest figure released, reported 2.6 sets per household, compared to 2.4 sets in 2000.

2 Jacques Ellul, *The Technological Bluff* (Grand Rapids, MI: Wm. B. Eerdmans Publishing Co., 1990) 261.

3 Motorola's *Mobility Global 2010 Media Engagement Barometer* study reported that American and Japanese viewers spend 21 hours per week watching television and video content, the most of any nations in the world. Don Reisinger, "Study: Americans, Japanese Watch the Most TV," November 17, 2010, http://www.cnet.com/news/study-americans-japanese-watch-the-most-tv/.

4 Neil Postman, *Technopoly: The Surrender of Culture to Technology* (New York: Knopf, 1992) 10. Postman also wrote: "Television is different because it encompasses all forms of discourse. No one goes to a movie to find out about government policy or the latest scientific advances. No one buys a record to find out the baseball scores or the weather or the latest murder. No one turns on radio anymore for soap operas or a presidential address (if a television set is at hand). But everyone goes to television for all these things and more, which is why television

resonates so powerfully throughout the culture." Neil Postman, *Amusing Ourselves to Death* (New York: Viking Penguin, 1985) 92.

5   The New York station began commercial broadcasts in 1941 with the call letters WCBW. It changed to WCBS-TV in 1946.

6   According to one source, the term "couch potato" originated with a friend of comics artist Robert Armstrong, who used it in a series of comic panels: http://en.wikipedia.org/wiki/Sedentary_lifestyle.

7   U.S. Census Bureau, "20th Century Statistics," http://www.census.gov/prod/99pubs/99statab/sec31.pdf, Table #1440.

8   Pew Center for the People and the Press report *Online Papers Modestly Boost Readership: Maturing Internet News Audience Broader than Deep*, released July 30, 2006. Reported on *Frontline*, http://www.pbs.org/wgbh/pages/frontline/newswar/part3/stats.html.

9   William Prochnau, "State of The American Newspaper in Lord Thomson's Realm," October 1998, http://ajrarchive.org/article.asp?id=3285. Thomson may have used the phrase "a permit to print money" referring to a television station he acquired in Scotland.

10   Reported by Charlie White on Mashable, "What Couples Fight about Most: The Remote," January 3, 2013, http://mashable.com/2013/01/03/poll-couples-fight/.

11   See http://www.kansas.com/2014/02/05/3269383/kc-police-stabbing-capped-fight.html.

12   See http://gulfnews.com/news/gulf/yemen/fight-over-tv-remote-control-kills-one-hurts-two-of-a-yemeni-family-1.1318816.

13   *The Economist*, February 13, 1994: 12.

14   Marshall McLuhan, *Understanding Media: The Extensions of Man* (Cambridge, MA: MIT Press, 1994) "This fact, characteristic of all media, means that the 'content' of any medium is always another medium. The content of writing is speech, just as the written word is the content of print, and print is the content of the telegraph."

15   The concept is credited to Paul Klein of NBC, whose obituary in the *New York Times* may be read here: http://www.nytimes.com/1998/07/13/business/paul-l-klein-69-a-developer-of-pay-per-view-tv-channels.html.

16   Todd Gitlin, "Flat and Happy," *Wilson Quarterly*, Autumn, 1993: 48.

17   *TV Viewing and Income* report (2013), available here: http://www.marketplace.org/opics/wealth-poverty/income-upshot/behind-data-tv-viewing-and-income.

18   Bruce Lenthall, *Radio's America: The Great Depression and the Rise of Modern Mass Culture* (Chicago: University of Chicago Press, 2007) 57–58.

19   Speech to the 1961 Convention of the National Association of Broadcasters.

20   According to 2009 statistics generated by TVB, which represents the commercial television industry, men on average spent 4 hours, 54 minutes watching

television daily, women spent 5 hours, 31 minutes, teens spent 3 hours, 26 minutes, and children spent 3 hours, 21 minutes. The television set in the average household was on 8 hours, 21 minutes. This data is available online at http://www.tvb.org/media/ file/TVB_FF_TV_Basics.pdf. They do not include watching DVD rental movies, downloads, or videogames on the television screen.

21 WCCO-TV used that comment as the title of a documentary about the experience: http://tcmedianow.com/video/wcco-tv-dave-moore-report-death-in-the-family-a-report-on-the-effects-of-television-viewing-from-1979/.

22 Ellul, 265.

23 Edmund Carpenter, *Explorations in Communication* (Boston: Beacon Press, 1960) 165.

24 George A. Wiley, "End of an Era: The Daytime Radio Serial," *Journal of Broadcasting*, Spring, 1961: 110.

25 Emily Nussbaum, "The Great Divide," *The New Yorker*, April 7, 2014: 64 68.

26 Christopher H. Sterling and John M. Kittross, *Stay Tuned: A Concise History of American Broadcasting* 2nd ed., (Belmont, CA: Wadsworth Publishing Co., 1990) 582.

27 Ellul, 336.

28 Vern Boerman, "Potholes on Sesame Street," *The Banner*, October 20, 1986, reprinted online at http://www.catapultmagazine.com/saturday-morning/article/potholes-on-sesame.

29 Sterling and Kittross, 418.

30 Survey by Oliver Quayle and Company, 1972.

31 A Nielsen survey estimated that during the funeral on Monday afternoon, 41,553,000 sets were in use, 81% of all homes. *TV Guide*, January 25, 1964.

32 Sterling and Kittross, 582. For one observer's list of "The 25 Best Black Sitcoms of All Time" go to http://www.complex.com/pop-culture/2013/02/best-black-sitcoms/.

33 Delivered by Vice President Spiro Agnew in Des Moines, Iowa, November 13, 1969. Text of speech: http://www.americanrhetoric.com/speeches/spiroagnewtvnews coverage.htm. Video: http://www.youtube.com/watch?v=SQpQyJQm2Mk.

34 The video can be seen at http://www.youtube.com/watch?v=Nn4w-ud-TyE.

35 Go to http://mediamythalert.wordpress.com/2012/05/21/kurtz-invokes-if-ive-lost-cronkite-myth-in-reviewing-new-cronkite-biography/ for a discussion about what LBJ actually said, or didn't say.

36 John Gunther, *Inside Russia Today* (New York: Harper, 1958): "The first physical impression I had of Russia, as we descended from the plane, was the quality of the metal ladder—flimsy, antique, short by half a step, and made of some queer light metal, ornately engraved." Accessible online at http://content.time.com/time/magazine/article/0,9171,864269,00.html.

37 Andrew Chaikin, "For Neil Armstrong, the First Moon Walker, It Was All about Landing the *Eagle*," *Scientific American*, July 17, 2009, http://www.scientific american.com/article/neil-armstrong-apollo-11/.

38 *Baywatch* was produced from 1989 to 2001, but reruns have continued worldwide.

39 Wilfred Chan, "Thought the Super Bowl Was Big? Try China's Lunar New Year TV Gala," February 5, 2014, CNN World, http://www.cnn.com/2014/02/05/world/asia/lunar-new-year-super-bowl/.

40 See BoxRec page, http://boxrec.com/media/index.php/Muhammad_Ali_vs._Joe_Frazier_(3rd_meeting).

41 Matt Stump and Harry Jessell, "Cable: The First Forty Years," *Broadcasting*, November 21, 1988: 42.

42 Lloyd Trufelman, Cable Television Advertising Bureau, http://articles.sun-sentinel.com/1989-07-17/business/8902210320_1_cable-industry-cable-rates-cable-service.

43 For a deeper discussion about news preferences, see Leonard Downie Jr. and Robert G. Kaiser, *The News About the News* (New York: Alfred A. Knopf, 2002) 172.

44 E. B. White, *Harper's Magazine*, October 1938.

13

Computers: Beyond Calculation

A four-year-old child of the early 21st century doing homework or playing a video game has more computer power at her fingertips than all the scientists during World War II.

Pick up a current computer magazine. Its articles and ads will describe devices that have nothing at all to do with what computers were invented to do. They were not invented to process words or do anything with language. They were not invented to communicate. They certainly were not invented to play games or to entertain in any way. Computers were invented solely to calculate, to compute, but that is no longer their principle use. Computers now exercise our people skills more than our math skills.[1]

It can be argued that the "computer revolution" is more significant than the introduction of the printing press in the 15th century, photography in the 19th century, or any other media "revolutions." Media theorist Lev Manovich has contended that the printing press affected only one stage of cultural communication information distribution; photography affected only one type of cultural communication—still images; and, by contrast, computers affect all stages of communication and all types of media, including texts, still and moving images, sound, and spatial constructions.[2]

Yet, agreeing with him or not, beyond the "gee whiz" factor lies the question of the value of the uses made by these technological advances. Noted media critic Jacques Ellul put it this way: "The introduction of computers into schools and homes might make things more efficient but this turns inevitably into irrationality. Why save time if the time thus saved is empty and meaningless?"[3]

▶ ANCIENT ORIGINS

The need for a device to calculate started with counting boards on which pebbles were moved around ("*calculus*" is Latin for "pebble"). The oldest surviving counting board is the Salamis tablet used by Babylonians about 300 BCE. That may have led to the invention of the Roman hand abacus. The more familiar stringed and beaded abacus dates back at least to the Chinese *suan-pan* used since 1200 BCE. Partitioned to match the fingers on one hand, the abacus aided merchants and tax collectors across the ancient world to add, subtract, multiply, and divide. Here and there, even in our current age of cheap, hand-held calculators, the abacus is still in use.[4]

Calculating all day long is tiresome work. The abacus and counting tables of the Middle Ages helped to ease the tedium, but there was an impetus to build a better device. Leonardo da Vinci designed one. During the 17th century, German professor Wilhelm Schickard constructed a "calculating clock," and in France, at age 19, the future philosopher Blaise Pascal built a shoebox-size device to help his father, a tax collector.

In Germany, while still in his twenties, the philosopher Gottfried Leibniz designed a decimal calculator, "for it is unworthy of excellent men to lose hours like slaves."[5] Leibniz also conceived of binary calculation, but found no practical use for it. Efforts in England and Scotland brought forth the slide rule and logarithms. The first widely marketed mechanical calculator, the "Arithmometer," was built in France in 1720.

▶ CHARLES BABBAGE

The foundations for a true computer were laid in the 19th century by a British mathematician. Charles Babbage grew frustrated at reading newspaper accounts of English ships foundering on rocks because published navigation tables had been calculated in error. In 1822 he began to build an "engine" to figure the tables accurately. He imagined that the machine could also help in banking, surveying, mathematics, and the sciences.

Part way through the construction of his "difference engine," and after being appointed as a professor of mathematics at Cambridge, Babbage had a better idea. He imagined an "analytical engine" that could solve any arithmetic problem. It would grind out the answers in a "mill" and place them in a "store." Punch cards would feed the problems into the machine. A new problem required a new set of cards. When a certain point was reached (e.g., at a tally of 200), a different sequence of steps would begin.

Building on these ideas, Babbage invented programming and the computer. Babbage's idea for using cards came from Joseph-Marie Jacquard, owner of a French weaving factory, who used thousands of wooden cards in series with holes punched to guide threads into complex patterns on a loom.

Babbage did not complete his analytical engine, but he explained his ideas to family friend Ada, Lady Lovelace, the daughter of the poet Lord

Byron. She published them in 1843 in a series of *Notes*, writing that the engine would weave algebraic patterns the way the punch card loom weaves flowers and leaves. She saw a use for his machine in composing music and making graphics. It has even been suggested that it was she, not he, who was the brains behind both the difference engine and the analytical engine.[6] Much later, in 1979, the programming language Ada was named to honor her contribution.

Cards were at the heart of a different effort in 1890 when a U.S. Patent Office employee, Herman Hollerith, set out to cross-tabulate census data, such as determining the number of Minnesota bachelor farmers born in Norway. This was data processing. The holes in each card allowed for electrical contacts so that counting-registers for each variable could advance one digit. This would be the basis of future computer binary calculation. Hollerith left the Census Bureau to start a company that would one day become International Business Machines, or IBM.

Charles Babbage, 1791–1871.

▶ FIRST LARGE COMPUTERS

World War II and the postwar years saw considerable advances in both computer theory and construction. A British computing effort joined by Alan Turing, one of the geniuses in the history of computing, cracked Germany's secret Enigma military code and helped to win the war. Turing went beyond Babbage in describing the structure of a general purpose computer in which programs could be stored in its memory.

In the United States, ENIAC, a digital computer, was built at the University of Pennsylvania during World War II. It was completed too late for its objective of calculating the trajectory of artillery shells, but it managed to examine a postwar plan to build the hydrogen bomb.

Ideas from mathematicians Norbert Weiner and John von Neumann charted the path taken by postwar computers. Meanwhile, Bell engineers Claude Shannon and Warren Weaver raised communication theory from a kind of guesswork to science. Universities constructed research computers with acronym names: ENIAC, EDSAC, ILLIAC, JOHNNIAC, SWAC, BINAC, MANIAC. The Air Force's Whirlwind, completed in 1951 at the Massachusetts Institute of Technology (MIT), was also groundbreaking

A technician changes one of ENIAC's 19,000 tubes, early 1940s. US Army Photo.

in using video displays and operating in real time. Each of these advanced our knowledge of what computers could do.

▶ THE K-MODEL

Boolean logic (with symbols for AND, OR, and NOT) and binary arithmetic (base 2, composed of zeros and ones, not the base 10 decimal system) set researchers on the digital path used today. In 1937 Bell Labs engineer George Stibitz had a flash of insight about using Boolean logic and binary arithmetic in an electrical device.

One evening he took home two telephone relays, two flashlight bulbs, a dry cell battery, and some wire that he hooked up to a strip of metal he cut from a tobacco tin. He sat at his kitchen table and wired together what his wife dubbed "the K-Model" ("K" for "kitchen table"). He had created the world's first digital calculator.

The K-Model led to calculators to solve telephone engineering problems. Stibitz realized that a full-size calculator could perform a sequence of calculations under the direction of relay circuits and could store the results. The calculator that was built went through several versions during World War II and solved problems concerning the aiming of anti-aircraft guns. In 1940 Stibitz went further. He hooked a teletype and a calculator into a telephone circuit between New York and New Hampshire to expand the world of telecommunications by allowing numerical data to be transmitted.

Stibitz was unaware of similar research being done in Berlin by another engineer. Before and during World War II, Konrad Zuse built four increasingly sophisticated versions of a computer guided by software instructions, the world's first programmable computers. Daily Allied bombing of Berlin forced Zuse to flee the city. He hid his semi-finished last version in a barn. He also wrote the first high-level programming language. Despite Zuse's ingenious solutions to several problems, his device was never used to help Nazi Germany.

A COMPUTER GOES ON TV

In 1952 the UNIVAC introduced the public to computers when CBS used one to help forecast the presidential election results. Instead of the close results the experts expected, it forecast an Eisenhower landslide (odds of 100 to 1). According to one version of what happened next, CBS executives nervously ordered the results adjusted so that UNIVAC would agree with the political experts. According to another version, someone accidentally dropped a zero resulting in 8 to 7 odds. The final electoral vote was 442 to 89, a landslide for Eisenhower. UNIVAC had been off by less than 1 percent. Newspaper columnists later had fun writing about how unfair CBS had been to the computer.[7]

▶ MICROCHIPS

In 1957 millions of moviegoers heard the word "computer" for the first time when a computer figured in the Spencer Tracy–Katherine Hepburn comedy *Desk Set*. The romantic story centered on a secret effort to computerize the research department of a television network. In 1959 British scientist Charles Percy Snow told an MIT audience, "We happen to be living at a time of a major scientific revolution, probably more important in its consequences than the first Industrial Revolution, a revolution which we shall see in full force in the very near future."[8]

Yet, as long as computers depended on vacuum tubes that could burn out, were unreliable and expensive, they would remain limited devices, a handful scattered around the world in universities, military installations, and a few big government agencies and business firms. Change arrived in 1948 with the invention of the transistor to replace the vacuum tube, also useful for all electronic communication equipment. That led in 1959 to the integrated circuit in a microchip and in 1970 to the microprocessor.

The romantic comedy *Desk Set* (1957) starring Katherine Hepburn and Spencer Tracy featured an "electronic brain" called EMERAC.

The history of the computer has also been, in part, a history of information *storage*, from vacuum tubes and punch cards to terabytes of crystal-based optical memory. The ancient Greeks had learned that if we can store information, we can reflect upon the past in considerable detail and build upon the information. We can share it systematically. But transistors are unsuited to computer memory because when the electricity is turned off a transistor loses its on/off state, its memory. The first solution beyond punch cards was magnetic core memory, a wire mesh strung with tiny ferrite ceramic doughnuts. In 1968 computers got random access memory (RAM) microchips, which can be erased and reused, and the permanent read-only memory (ROM) microchips. Memory today is measured in terabytes, or trillions of bytes.

▶ PERSONAL COMPUTERS

The end of the decade of the 1950s saw the end of hand-built, one-of-a-kind computers. Commercial firms assembled new computers on assembly lines. The first were the large mainframe computers. Then came the mini-computers, and in the 1970s came the microcomputer.

The computer was meant to be a serious tool for scientific, government, and business use. Did anyone imagine that children would use computers? The notion that a computer would ever be a common household device like a washing machine would have been considered ridiculous as recently as 1974, when the Altair 8800, a kit for hobbyists to assemble, started the move to the personal microcomputer. The hobbyists had to write their own binary code and flip a switch on the front panel for each binary digit.

Three years later the already assembled Apple II, Commodore Pet, and TRS-80 opened the floodgates. The Apple II was the first personal computer with color, high-resolution graphics, sound, and a way to control games. The Atari video games went into arcades and the first Osborne portable would soon be at the fingertips of reporters on assignment. When ordinary people realized how a computer could extend life's choices, they could hardly wait to get one. *Time* named the computer as "Machine of the Year" for 1982.[9]

The hand-held personal digital assistant, or PDA, recognized handwriting to a limited extent and acted like a memo pad that connected to a computer. Apple introduced the first of these, the Newton, in 1993. Like most electronic devices, it was soon superseded by more advanced devices. Succeeding the Newton was the smaller, cheaper, easier-to-use, feature-filled Palm Pilot. During the 1990s, PDAs were pulled from briefcases, purses and even pockets, used everywhere from business meetings to supermarkets just as smartphones have been in the 21st century.

Engineers have added more features to hand-held computing devices, including voice recognition software. Other engineers combined features of the PDA and the cellphone into such units as the BlackBerry and the iPhone, which is also a handheld emailer and Web access device, the camera phone, and the smartphone. Owners use them to blog, send instant messages and pay bills at any convenient opportunity, including sitting in a car while waiting for a red light to change. They access the Internet, show movies, allow videophone calls, and do hundreds of other tasks through apps.

▶ WORD PROCESSING

The history of the computer is also the history of input devices like the card readers, tape drives, disk drives, the mouse, the joystick, and the scanner. It is also the story of such output devices as printers, synthesizers, modems, and routers, plus wireless technology like Bluetooth to connect them. Of particular application to communication, the laser printer arrived in the mid-1970s with a price tag of around U.S.$500,000. Today they can be found for less than $100.

In addition, it is the story of software, from the ones and zeros of the era of vacuum tubes to assembly languages, compilers, programming languages, and eventually application programs (apps) available off the shelf to do hundreds of tasks.

Word processing programs gave the computer a communication capability deserving the overused word "revolutionary." The first word processors were standalone machines, faster than typewriters, could edit and move text around, and could store text. However, as single-minded computers that could do nothing else, they were bypassed when word processing software was written for general-purpose computers. Page layout, graphics, photo, and video editing programs have followed to aid communication tasks. Automatic language translation proved more stubborn because languages themselves are so idiosyncratic, but considerable progress has been accomplished even here.[10] And voice recognition software has made strides as anyone who contacts a bank or phone provider knows.

The computer made other forms of communication easier. Most newspapers, magazines, radio and television stations now have computer-based online versions of their output. Computers assist the newspaper publishing process at each step from the reporter's laptop to the delivery trucks.

Computers have transmitted news since 1970, when the Associated Press switched from teletypes. Some large magazine publishers use computers to sort subscribers by targeting advertising to specific groups. Book publishers require authors to submit their work in electronic form. For research, the information age has added electronic archives. LexisNexis is among the better known of more than 4,000 databases available for retrieving information from archived magazines, academic journals, and other sources. Archive.org has archived billions of pages of text and audio that appeared on the Web.

▶ DESKTOP PUBLISHING

Desktop publishing began with word processing, and that began with a wish to duplicate what was typed.[11] Early attempts to do this consisted of attachments to an electric typewriter. The M. Schultz machine of the 1930s used rolls of paper much like player piano rolls to record typing. Form letters could be turned out one after the other with only the address and salutation changed. Paper rolls were succeeded by the paper tape of the Flexowriter sold from the 1930s to the 1960s. It allowed for correcting mistakes and the physical cutting and pasting of text, a precursor to what word processing would do electronically. An IBM Selectric typewriter with a magnetic tape drive began true word processing at a basic level in 1964.

The term "word processing" came from IBM and encompassed writing, editing, printing, and storing text that could be punched on standard 80-column punch cards. In 1969, IBM's MagCards increased what could be stored on a single card from 80 characters to a page of characters. Three years later came video screens for display and tape cassettes for storage. In the early 1970s, floppy disks permitted the storage of one hundred pages of text on each disk.

A Chinese immigrant to the United States, Dr. An Wang, designed his Wang 1200 automatic typewriter with limited editing functions in 1971. Next came word processing software that could run on general-purpose microcomputers. The Electric Pencil program in 1976 was followed by WordStar and WordPerfect. Microsoft Word has dominated the field of word processing for a number of years.

Xerox Corporation researchers conceived of a graphics-based computer that not only could be controlled by a mouse, but also displayed typefaces on a screen and sent the displayed output to a laser printer. This would be the foundation of what would become known as WYSIWYG: "What you see is what you get."

Although Xerox did not take advantage of the ideas flowing from its research division, Steve Jobs of Apple did with the introduction in 1984 of the Macintosh. In addition, the PostScript page description program and the Hewlett-Packard low-cost laser printer brought to the public the reality of "desktop publishing," a term coined in 1985 by Paul Brainerd, developer of PageMaker, which became the leading page layout program.

By themselves, computers and laser printers, the principal equipment in desktop publishing, have not created the first opportunity for people of moderate means to publish. After all, typewriters and mimeograph machines had been around for decades. What computers and printers provide is much more egalitarian, the means to offer an attractive and professional looking product at low cost.

Tens of thousands of people now do what relatively few people could do in the past. They package their writing without having to turn to printing companies for help. Businesses, schools, government offices, clubs, and organizations of every sort turn out innumerable newspapers, newsletters, magazines, and flyers. Restaurants print menus and theaters print programs. Students hand in slick-looking term papers.

Today, for surprisingly small sums of money compared with what was once required, someone working out of a garage can publish a newspaper, magazine, or book. Inexpensive microcomputers and easy-to-learn desktop publishing software today enable output of a quality that once only a skilled printer could produce with bulky machinery. Today a printing-on-demand machine runs a copy of a book off on standard 20 pound office paper, trims it to book size, and binds and covers it with a perfect binding. Companies such as Smashwords let you download an e-book for a dollar or two to any device a reader prefers, skipping printers entirely.

In a historical sense desktop publishing is as old as the start of printing in Europe. Gutenberg and those who followed him a half-millennium ago were printer-publishers. So was Benjamin Franklin. Things changed with the introduction of big and costly machinery two centuries ago as part of the Industrial Revolution. Desktop publishing has, in the sense of personal empowerment, turned the clock back. Going a step further, with the Internet, even the computer printer is no longer needed to publish.

Email and word processing did not bring the "paperless office," a promise that always seems a decade away but never arrives. The world continues to convert forests into sheets of paper. One change is a shift from the practice of first printing, then distributing, which is the way the output of printing presses and mimeograph machines are handled. With email, information is first distributed electronically, then, if the recipient wishes, printed.[12]

▶ DESKTOP VIDEO

Desktop video expands the producer base for motion pictures as well as expanding distribution through film festivals and online venues like YouTube. In professional hands, computers are involved in every stage of major film production, just as they are involved at every step in getting a newspaper or a magazine into a reader's hands.

Technology that supported motion picture production during the decades of the golden age of Hollywood required enormous sums of money. Although this helped to concentrate in just a few hands the ability to make feature films (and still does in the rarefied world of high-budget film making), more recent technology has pushed in the opposite direction—outward to many hands. Production and distribution of motion pictures are broader than ever. While big budget movies are still being turned out, so are shoestring movies of quite good quality. *Desktop video* found its way into the language next to *desktop publishing*.

Computer-based technology brings within reach of the average family non-linear editing processes (providing random access) with such video effects as morphing (seamlessly flowing from one image to another) that only recently were limited to machines costing hundreds of thousands of dollars, if they were available at all. Production facilities to shoot and edit digital motion pictures, and off-the-shelf software for inexpensive digital animation, are used in schools, offices, and businesses that once would not have considered making a movie. In addition to editing software like Final Cut Pro and Premiere, even simpler online editing programs such as Jumpcut and Eyespot string video clips together and add soundtracks, titles, and effects.

The most spectacular use of computers is in CGI (computer-generated imagery), which can create such effects as a Greek fleet of a thousand ships for the invasion of Troy or a race of large blue humanoids. Animated films using computers have improved to the level of Oscar competition. *Toy Story* (1995), created by Pixar Animation Studios and Walt Disney Pictures, was the first feature-length CGI animated film. Computers based on AI (artificial intelligence) have emerged as central characters with feelings, starting with HAL in *2001: A Space Odyssey* (1968). The computers are often villains. *Her* (2013), the story of a computer user and his romantic relationship with an operating system, is an exception.

THE BLAIR WITCH PROJECT

In 1999, two college students in Florida, Dan Myrick and Eduardo Sanchez, made a feature film, *The Blair Witch Project*, purportedly a documentary, for U.S.$31,000, with early marketing done mostly on the Internet. It reportedly brought in about $240 million, although the two young filmmakers sold their interests long before that stratospheric sum was realized.

The Blair Witch Project, admittedly a remarkable example, showed that low-cost video production could produce a motion picture of technically acceptable quality at a price that would have seemed ludicrous just a few years before. In 2003 the technology market research firm IDC estimated that as many as 1 million camera owners have been making movies intended for a wider audience than family and friends. Some filmmakers rented theaters and advertised, and numerous film festivals exist for these hopefuls who dream of finding a willing distributor.

▶ TELECOMMUTING

Peter Leyden, director of the New Politics Institute, observed:

> When transportation meant ships, people built Venice. When it meant trains, they built Chicago. When it meant cars, they built Los Angeles. Cities have always been fundamentally shaped by the dominant transportation of their time. It's one of the givens of urban planning. But today planners are beginning to see that society is on the verge of building a new kind of city in an era driven not by transportation but by *telecommunications*.[13]

For example, a young mother used to drop her two sons off at a daycare facility at 6 a.m., drive about 50 miles to work as an insurance claims adjustor, and then hope to be home again around 5 p.m. With telecommuting, 6 a.m. had her making a "two-second commute" to her basement office and taking a break at about 7:30 a.m. to get the boys off to the school bus. Then it was back to work until about 4:30 p.m., when the bus brought her boys back home. In this and so many other ways for so many people, communication replaces transportation with all its obvious advantages, and some hidden costs.

Not all mediated communication change is positive. The middle management employee who carries his work-supplied cellphone when he is off duty has no certain escape time in his workweek. That week now contains seven days, not five. It's morning, noon and night. In France an agreement was reached in 2014 to put a cap on this practice.[14] On the positive side, many white-collar workers are now able to spend at least part of each week telecommuting. Among the work-at-home occupations are accountants, architects, bankers, bookkeepers, clerical workers, computer operators, programmers, systems analysts, counselors, data entry clerks, engineers, journalists, lawyers, real estate agents, secretaries, brokers, travel agents, and, of course, writers.[15]

A broadcast journalist who must file a story or update one in a hurry can do so from a mini-studio at home. Some doctors even e-visit patients, and medical insurers are covering the activity. Hospitals post medical test results and doctors' notes on websites that their patients can access.

Interactive video for judicial proceedings cuts legal costs. Defense attorneys, prosecutors, witnesses, judges, victims and parole officers have all used the technology. The arraignment in a New Jersey federal court of Theodore J. Kaczynski, the Unabomber, was held in Sacramento, California, in 1997. Estimated cost of transporting Kaczynski would have been U.S.\$30,000. Using "TeleJustice," the court conducted the arraignment on murder charges for about \$45.[16]

Telecommuting holds advantages and disadvantages for both employer and employee. Employers may need less office space, saving on rent, furniture, and utility bills, but at the expense of close connections to their staffs. In many cases the employers have eliminated full-time staff positions, substituting part-time contract workers or consultants, saving not only on healthcare and other costs but changing the employer–employee dynamic in favor of the employer. For the employee who manages to hang onto a job, the time, expense, and frustration of the daily commute are eliminated. Concern about caring for small children may determine whether the employee is even able to hold a job outside the home. The isolation of being apart from other adults during the workday is offset for parents by the benefit of spending time with their children, other family members, and neighbors. In fact, with social media, phone and email, colleagues are not fully isolated from each other. Futurist writer Alvin Toffler used the metaphor of "the electronic cottage" to describe the increasing shift of work from office and factory to the home.[17] "The communication toolshed" would also be an apt metaphor.

Some observers predict that if telecommunications succeed in pulling people out of cities, the exodus will be primarily of the middle- and upper-income groups, those who most easily travel the electronic pathways, leaving the poor and the elderly behind. Such a movement often erodes a city tax base, with potentially dire consequences.[18]

For at-home workers who miss the fellowship of an office but dislike a long commute, the concept of "co-working" has led to chains of offices dedicated to meet their needs and to the renting of desks by businesses that have unused capacity. By 2012 an estimated 760 co-working facilities were operating in the United States.[19]

Telecommuting has also led to outsourcing as white-collar jobs follow factory jobs to low-wage countries, a change of decidedly mixed blessing that mediated communication makes possible. While it has resulted in white-collar layoffs in developed nations, outsourcing has made life better in developing countries for quite a few skilled workers, especially in English-speaking nations such as India and the Philippines. In Bangalore and other Indian cities with a cadre of educated, English-speaking workers, entire industries have sprung up to do computer programming, telemarketing, banking, online product support, plus a variety of different jobs that can be handled through global communications at lower costs.

Mediated communication allows some self-employed workers to settle wherever their dreams take them. The home, filled with communication and computation equipment, may be a van or a boat. A home address may be a website and an email address. As for anyone whose work requires neither a daily commute nor relocating, the choices of where to live are limitless. By adapting their lives to this useful tool, the computer, many people are reaping rewards that were never imagined just a few decades ago.

▶ TIMELINE

1801   Joseph-Marie Jacquard's loom uses punch cards.

1823   Charles Babbage starts building a calculating machine, a "difference engine."

1834   Babbage plans an analytical engine, a computer device.

1843   Byron's daughter, Ada Lovelace, explains concept of computer programming.

1854   George Boole's *An Investigation into the Laws of Thought* logic system.

1873   Lord Kelvin calculates the tides with a machine.

1890   Herman Hollerith use punch cards as data storage for U.S. census.

1928   IBM punch cards.

1931   In Berlin, lone genius Konrad Zuse invents a computer but is ignored.

1936   Alan Turing develops the theory of a general-purpose computer.

1937   George Stibitz invents the "K-Model," an electrical digital calculator.

1939   In Iowa, Atanasoff and Berry build an electronic computer; it is lost during World War II.

1940   Teletypewriter, calculator tied by phone line to demonstrate remote computing.

1943   British machine Colossus cracks Germany's Enigma code.

1946   University of Pennsylvania's ENIAC, the first modern electronic computer.

1948   From Claude Shannon and Warren Weaver of Bell Labs: information theory.

1952   Grace Hopper invents a compiler for a programming language.

Claude Shannon uses an electric mouse and maze to prove computers can learn.

1953   Magnetic core memory is installed in a computer, the Whirlwind.

1956   A transistorized computer and the first hard disk random access drive.

1957   A leap forward in software: FORTRAN.

1958   The microchip is invented. It will enable the computer revolution.

1964   IBM's OS/360 is first mass-produced computer operating system.

1967   The light pen and the floppy disk.

1968   Douglas Englelbart links keyboard, keypad, mouse, windows, and more.

1971   The microprocessor.

1975   Microcomputers are sold in kits to hobbyists.

1981   From Tandy: the laptop.

1982   The computer is *Time*'s "Man of the Year."

1994   Almost one-third of American homes have a computer.

1999   Hand-held BlackBerry can email.

2004   Wi-Fi goes nearly everywhere.

2009   "Cloud computing" moves to central data storage, away from PCs.

2010   The iPad.

2013   More than 100 billion mobile apps are downloaded.

▶ NOTES

1 Will Wright, "Dream Machines," *Wired*, April 2006: 112, http://archive.wired.com/wired/archive/14.04/wright.html.

2 Lev Manovich, *The Language of New Media* (Cambridge, MA: MIT Press, 2001) 19.

3 Jacques Ellul, *The Technological Bluff* (Grand Rapids, MI: Wm. B. Eerdmans Publishing Co., 1990) 108.

4 The abacus is used in villages and cities by clerks and merchants throughout Africa and in much of Asia. The user is sometimes known as an abacist. It is also a valuable counting tool for the blind (http://www.aph.org/tests/abacus.html).

5 James Redlin, "A Brief History of Mechanical Calculators," http://www.xnumber.com/xnumber/mechanical1.htm.

6 Management historians Daniel A. Wren and Arthur G. Bedeian wrote that Lady Lovelace "expressed his ideas better than he could" (*The Evolution of Management Thought*, Chichester: John Wiley and Sons, 2009) 68.

7 Steve Henn. "The Night a Computer Predicted the Next President," *NPR*, October 31, 2012, http://www.npr.org/blogs/alltechconsidered/2012/10/31/163951263/the-night-a-computer-predicted-the-next-president. The story was also the subject of a doctoral dissertation by Ira Chinoy, available at http://drum.lib.umd.edu/bitstream/1903/10504/1/Chinoy_umd_0117E_11395.pdf.

8 Martin Greenberger, ed., *Management and Computers of the Future* (Cambridge, MA: MIT Press, 1962) 8.

9 *Time*, January 3, 1983.

10 For an example of how difficult the process is, read "Why Computers Still Can't Translate Languages Automatically" by Konstantin Kakaes, *Slate*, May 11, 2012, http://www.slate.com/articles/technology/future_tense/2012/05/darpa_s_transtac_bolt_and_other_machine_translation_programs_search_for_meaning_.html.

11 A number of websites review the history of desktop publishing. Two of the better sites are http://www.brighthub.com/multimedia/publishing/articles/1912.aspx and http://www.tsd.state.tx.us/cte/careertech/desktoppublishing/historyDTP.HTM.

12 Abigail Sellen and Richard Harper, *The Myth of the Paperless Office* (Cambridge, MA: MIT Press, 2002) 13.

13 Peter Leyden, "Teleworking Could Turn Our Cities Inside Out," Minneapolis *Star Tribune*, September 5, 1993: 1A, 16A.

14 Scott Sayare, "In France, a Move to Limit Off-the-Clock Work Emails," *New York Times*, April 11, 2014, http://www.nytimes.com/2014/04/12/world/europe/in-france-a-move-to-limit-off-the-clock-work-emails.html?_r=0.

15 Marcia Kelly, "Work-at-Home," *The Futurist*, November/December 1988: 32.

16 John Matthias and James Twedt, "TeleJustice—Videoconferencing for the 21st Century," 1997, http://ctl.ncsc.dni.us/bbsfiles/ctc5_rom/208.htm.

17 Alvin Toffler, *The Third Wave* (New York: William Morrow, 1980) 210–223.

18 See Manuel Castells, *The Information Age: Economy, Society, and Culture* (New York: Oxford University Press, three volumes, 1996–1998).

19 *The Economist*, December 31, 2011–January 6, 2012: 46.

14 The Internet: The World at Our Fingertips

The Internet touches us all. What is happening today is sometimes compared with what Gutenberg began in the 15th century. It can also be compared with ancient Greece, when thoughts on many subjects could be stored in the form of writing for future generations and knowledge could build upon knowledge (e.g., an astronomer sending his observations to another astronomer in a distant place). Writing overcame barriers of time and space. The Internet works in much the same way but for more people and at a much faster pace. The creation of computer networks has produced a change in human communication as its World Wide Web and email reach across the globe almost instantly.

The Internet—and especially its World Wide Web[1]—brings together newspaper, magazine, book, postal service, telephone, radio, and television. Each originally found public acceptance for a reason. When we deplore the decline of the traditional newspaper we are really mourning the technology that once put a fat package of inked paper in our hands at the breakfast table, not the reasons we read the newspaper. That the newspaper-reading public is diminishing represents a shift in technology, not a lack of interest in news itself. This example also applies to all the other media that cannot do their jobs as well as the Internet can. Just as we no longer need to read a newspaper to learn how the local team did or whether to pack an umbrella, we do not need a telephone to call a banker or broker to buy a bond or sell a stock and we no longer need to buy a stamp to pay a bill.

▶ HOW THE INTERNET BEGAN

The Internet began when researchers working at mainframe computers wanted to communicate with each other. What once was a strictly professional connection quickly evolved into friendly chat and interest groups. It was the start of computer-based social networking. Their path led to chat rooms that filled an apparent need for a remote version of social interaction. The path has continued to Facebook and Twitter and goes on from there.

Like the phonograph, the telephone, and the computer, the Internet was conceived for purposes other than its main uses today. Along with so many communication media technologies, the Internet has become more of what its users wanted and less of what its inventors intended. Its inventors could not have contemplated its use for myriad private purposes by the folks who live down the street. They certainly did not envision the Internet as a global means of entertainment.

The Internet began quietly when some science researchers at universities and in industry wanted a better way to contact each other through their mainframe computers that were connected by telephone lines. In 1969, they sought a grant from the Advanced Research Projects Agency of the Department of Defense, which had been organized in 1958 as a government think tank in response to the Soviet launching of Sputnik.

With the grant the scientists set up the ARPANET, the Advanced Research Projects Agency Network. ARPANET was to be a test area for computer networks, a link-up of time-sharing systems. Because of the heavy cost of constructing and operating mainframe computers, sharing made sense. A principal goal of the ARPANET was to share data and programs in the days when data existed on punch cards and programs were not sold at the computer store (because there were no stores), but had to be written by individual researchers for their own projects. Computers then were employed mostly as mathematical tools and calculators, although by the 1960s some non-mathematical research was done, such as language analysis (including one study by the author of this book[2]).

The ARPANET was seen as something more than a *research* tool. It was also a *communication* tool, an important distinction. No one had ever used a computer for ordinary communication the way people made a telephone call or sent a telegram. The ARPANET was not intended to connect computers but rather to connect the researchers who used the computers, another important distinction.

To accomplish that goal, it was necessary to establish protocols—agreed-upon ways of communicating—such as a file transfer protocol (FTP) and a remote login (Telnet). These signals would open up channels to allow data to pass through and then close the channels. J. C. R. Licklider, first head of ARPA's Information Processing Techniques Office, envisioned a network that could spread everywhere, an "intergalactic network," as he put it. The idea caught on. Licklider also moved ARPANET thinking away from a military focus to exchanging information about basic computer research.

▶ WHO SHOULD USE THE NETWORK?

One question that arose early was access. Who should be allowed to use the network? If access were to be limited to certain universities, certain industries, and certain government and military offices, it would not be "intergalactic." To be that, to be so universal that the network's potential benefit could reach all of mankind, access could not be limited, nor could control of the network.

It was decided early that the network would not have a single central command and control point. Each node—each point of connection—would be able to connect with any other node. In the event of an atomic bomb attack, the network would not be brought down by the destruction of a headquarters site. That concept grew out of a 1962 Rand Corporation study, *On Distributed Communications Networks*, by Paul Baran.[3] He called for what amounted to a new kind of public utility. In describing such a utility, Baran created the concept of packet switching and store-and-forward technology that now lie at the heart of email data transmission.

By the end of 1969 ARPANET had connected computer nodes at four universities: UCLA, Stanford, the University of California at Santa Barbara, and the University of Utah. Four years later 40 nodes existed, including a satellite link to Hawaii and low speed links to England and Norway. Ten years later there were 4,000 nodes, and the project was no longer the original ARPANET.

In 1975, as messages flew from node to node, ARPANET was declassified as a research project. Responsibility for it was given to the Defense Communications Agency. That same year the Xerox Corporation started an experimental Internet. The ARPANET was eventually split in two, into a civilian Internet and the military network, MILNET.

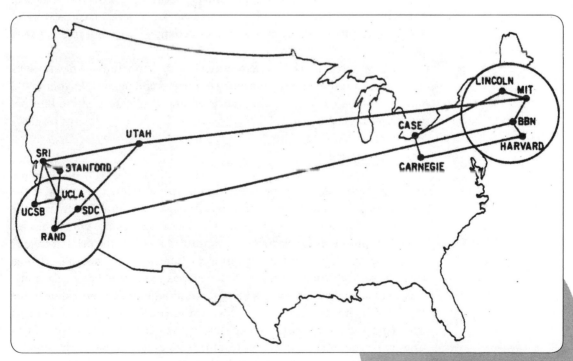

A 1970 map of ARPANET, showing the number of nodes already expanding across the United States.

▶ USENET

Because humans are social animals, the researchers were also using their new pathways to create interest groups. Are there other lovers of home-made beer out there among computer users? How about science fiction fans? How about gardeners? Such personal communication lay outside the formal research-purposed structure of ARPANET, but those using the connected computers enjoyed the extra social benefit. Few complained.

In 1979, two Duke University students, Tom Truscott and Jim Ellis, created a separate online network, a kind of computerized bulletin board that they called Usenet.[4] Anyone could offer news or information articles in the form of files. The network began at two sites: Duke and the University of North Carolina. Other universities soon signed on. The University of California at Berkeley provided a gateway between the mailing lists of ARPANET and the more open Usenet.

Whereas ARPANET tried—not too successfully—to limit its discussions to research issues, any topic was fair game for Usenet bulletin boards: find a few like-minded souls and set up a newsgroup. The question of distasteful postings came up. It was decided that peer pressure via emails should nip offensive postings. Repeat offenders would be removed from the Usenet.

By 1983 Usenet had leaped the Atlantic as European sites connected to the growing network. It wasn't cheap. With the standard 300-baud modems, the transfer of data was slow enough to run up considerable phone charges, especially burdensome for impoverished college students. The arrival of the 1200-baud modem helped somewhat. So did an organized network of *backbones*—main trunk lines—in different countries to connect UNIX user groups.

Eventually Usenet spread across the world. Thousands of newsgroups discussed everything from philosophy to recipes and movies. Anyone could post. Everyone could read. The free, even anarchic nature of the Internet was never more obvious.

▶ THE WEB

In many homes entire sections of a newspaper delivered each day at the front door go straight to the recycle bin. The use of natural resources in the printing and delivery of newspapers and magazines that are unread has led to several proposals for electronic substitutes to replace the printed page.

During the 1970s and 1980s, prior to Internet news and advertising, there were teletext and videotex. Teletext was a one-way broadcast transmission via a television signal's unused scanning lines, or vertical blanking interval (the horizontal bar on a television screen visible when the set isn't tuned perfectly). Videotex, using telephone lines, had an interactive feature. The user requested information from a computer data bank, the precursor of current online news retrieval. Neither service succeeded in meeting an obvious desire for a way that individual users could gather requested information from a database, but they pointed the way to technologies that did.

In 1990, British engineer Tim Berners-Lee wrote the first browser program, a software program that guides a user to read hypertext (non-sequential) files. He called it WorldWideWeb (written as one word). With it he created the first web server and the first website, put online in 1991. It would link directly from any website to any other and also enable the user to edit files with point-and-click ease.[5] The address of the first website was Info.cern.ch, referring to the European Organization for Nuclear Research, where Berners-Lee worked.

At a time when incompatible computers ran on idiosyncratic operating systems, Berners-Lee's browser became a means to scan networks of computers to see what was out there and to summarize their contents. It started as a tool to enable researchers to browse for other research. Later the browser was distinguished from the virtual space filled with websites. The virtual space itself retained the name: the *World Wide Web*. Over the years the World Wide Web—or "the Web"—has become synonymous with the Internet, but, they are two different things. The Internet is a broader designation that includes email, Usenet, and other systems and networks. Each quickly swelled to enormous size. The Web's virtually uncountable number of sites would be of little use if not for browsers to organize and read them, and search engines to locate what the "net citizen" (the "netizen") wants. A browser enables us to retrieve and read the documents at websites.

At first, college students wrote most of the browsers and search engines in their spare time. The name "Archie" for a Web navigator was intended to conjure up "archive," not the comic book character (an association that its designers detested). An improved search engine called "Gopher" took the user from directory to directory. That was followed by a new search engine called "Veronica," named just to tease the "Archie" team. Among other browsers were Erwise, Viola, Lynx, Arena, Amaya, and Midas.

In 1993, college students Marc Andreessen and Eric Bina designed Mosaic, the most efficient browser at the time. To overcome its weaknesses, two years later they wrote Netscape. Unlike Mosaic, it worked almost identically with the Windows, Macintosh, and UNIX platforms. It was modem friendly, enabling the user to act on the quickly available text and hyperlinks while it more slowly downloaded graphics.

In addition, service providers such as AOL and CompuServe came along to improve and extend access. AOL tried to look hip for a young, with-it clientele. The Dow Jones News Retrieval began as a business information service before reaching out to the general public. Prodigy, another online service, hired women to help design and market its product. Its goal was a family-oriented service, but it captured only a small fraction of the market. At this writing the most popular browsers include Explorer, Safari, Firefox, and Chrome.

A variety of search engines followed, including AltaVista, Dogpile, Hotbot, Lycos, and Yahoo plus hundreds more that specialized in specific information areas. The dominant search engine today, Google, almost instantly replies to any topic request by identifying websites that relate to the topic. According to its 2014 statistics of usage, Google in 2013 handled more than 2 trillion requests for information.[6] Google offers several search pages. The best known is for text websites. Others are for images, videos, Google maps, and shopping items. There is also a news search and a finance search that keep up with current events across a broad range of topics. News editions are available for many different countries and in a number of languages.

▶ USING THE INTERNET

The U.S. Department of Defense had originally provided the money to set up the Internet in order to improve communications with the private sector. The National Science Foundation, which ran the Internet backbone, soon realized that the Internet had grown into much more than an accompaniment to research. In 1995 the foundation allowed commercial invasion of a nonprofit online network, and it was the year of the Netscape browser using hypertext and the hyperlinks of the World Wide Web, changing everything again. Netscape allowed almost anyone to find almost anything, learn almost anything, write anything, and buy or sell anything.

It opened a world that was, in William James's phrase of another era, "a blooming, buzzing confusion" that now holds more than 100 million websites with domain names and content. The total number of Web pages is, of course, much larger. It is a world dominated for the most part by ordinary people, not by governments that try with marginal success to control what goes on within their own borders, and not by large corporations.[7]

What do we do with the Internet? A 2014 Pew survey taken at the 25th anniversary of the World Wide Web reported that 53 percent of American users say that it would be "very hard" to give up the Internet, while 46 percent say that about their cell phones and just 35 percent now say that about television. Three of four users think online communication enhances their social relationships, while about one in eight think it worsens them.[8]

Computer usage continues to skew toward the young: 89 percent of 18- to 29-year-olds use a computer compared to 56 percent of adults 65 or older, but there has been a shift of access to the Internet; now 68 percent of adults access the Internet on mobile devices.[9] Internet access is available in virtually every school and library in the United States and in most homes with children. Nevertheless, more and more older adults go online and they are doing more, especially emailing.[10] Women above 55 have been joining Facebook at a fast clip, according to an informal 2009 survey.[11]

Online dating sites have grown in popularity, but have yet to become the way to romance for most Americans. A Pew Research Center study in 2013 reported that 11 percent of men and 9 percent of women have used online dating sites or apps. Younger adults and those with some college education are more likely online daters, with more urban than rural romance seekers.[12]

As for couples, 21 percent of cell owners or Internet users in a committed relationship have felt closer to their spouse or partner because of exchanges they had online or via text message, and 9 percent have resolved an argument with their partner online or by text message that they were having difficulty resolving in person.[13]

Compared with women, men are more likely to use the Internet for weather, political and financial news, sports, and do-it-yourself information. Men are more likely to do job-related research, download software, listen to music, use a webcam, participate in interest groups, or take a class. Women are more likely to email, get maps and directions, and look for medical information, religious information, or support for personal problems. More women said the Internet helped them find people they needed to reach. Women are also more likely than men to value the positive effects of email for improving relationships. And they are more likely to forward jokes and funny stories.[14]

The Web has shaken the traditional merchant–customer relationship. As always, when something is gained, what it replaces is diminished or is lost. The handshake and smile that concluded a sale is gone, exchanged for a global outreach for goods and customers accompanied by an impersonal, standardized acknowledgment. Thousands of websites provide online shopping that is—to paraphrase Marshall McLuhan—knocking down the walls of the store on the corner. Electronic merchandise such as books may be downloaded so the entire buying process never departs from a computer screen.

Thousands of sellers make money on eBay, the electronic sales floor created in Pierre Omidyar's San José, California, living room in 1995. Tens of millions of buyers make purchases. It has all become a significant change to an important part of life.

▶ EMAIL

Of all aspects of the Internet, the most powerful and transformative for many people has been email. The potential to connect distant family and friends is a feature that changes many former non-users of computers into users. Hundreds of millions of people use email daily. Like all communication technologies, the Internet reduces our face-to-face contact with other human beings while expanding our contacts with people beyond our reach. Humorist Dave Barry wryly commented, "I prefer email because it's such an effective way of getting information to somebody without running the risk of becoming involved in human conversation."[15]

Small talk isn't needed for asynchronous email "conversation," nor is suitable clothing. At the same time it takes just a click to receive an article or a joke from anyone anywhere, another click to add it to our personal hoard, and another click to send it on to distant friends wherever in the world they live. Some companies find email too time consuming for their staffs and have declared email-free days. To communicate, those employees actually have to talk to each other. Of course, if looking at someone's face is too intense there is that older communication tool, the telephone. And if even synchronous telephone conversation is too intense, texting adds an intermediate social distance.

Emails seem to have revived letter writing, but without the gracefulness of pen and ink. Sloppy writing is less of a problem.[16] Words are less likely to be weighed if a message disappears at the tap of a finger, and sentences can so easily be changed, added to, eliminated, or moved around. Beyond email we now have Twitter, limited to 140 characters at a time. This has led to new protocols of abbreviation. LMAO says in four letters what otherwise consumes 19 characters (including spaces): laughing my ass off.

▶ HOW EMAIL BEGAN

How did email begin? Around 1965, users who shared a computer could put messages in one another's file directory so they would be seen when the user logged on. The users were at "dumb terminals" that connected to the same mainframe computer.

In 1971, after distant computers began talking to each other over phone lines, Ray Tomlinson, an ARPANET contractor, invented email so that messages could be sent over connected networks. He chose the @ sign as a standard between the name of the sender (or recipient) and the computer location.

Email grew rapidly because it met fundamental communication needs. Within two years three of every four ARPANET messages were email. In a wisp of time the messages expanded from the military and scientific to the commercial and the personal.

This amount of communication might have been prohibitive in countries where telephone calls are expensive, but costs were kept down by the asynchronous practice of delivering a text message quickly to a computer location that a message receiver could access at any time. Protocols and mail programs were developed to set standards for message transfers. Photos, videos, and sound soon joined text messages.

▶ YOUNGER INTERNET USERS

If more of the older users are emailing, a percentage of the young have now moved on from email to cellphone texting, with social networking and blogging at their fingertips. Internet users ages 12 to 32 are the most likely to use the Internet for all kinds of communicating and for such entertainment as downloaded music, online videos, games, and virtual worlds. They are more likely than older users to read other people's blogs and to write their own, happily blogging and tweeting throughout the day.[17] By a large margin, the favorite online activity of the younger generation is game playing.

Computer users in high schools not too many years ago were dismissed as "geeks" and "nerds." No longer true. Something else is going on. "Nerds" created Silicon Valley; today some are billionaires. They have set up communication enterprises like Facebook and YouTube into which everyone is welcome to provide content, an activity that can be traced back to the first letters-to-the-editor column in a newspaper. As eager, unpaid content providers, millions of us are naturally curious to learn if anyone is paying attention. Someone who displays a photo on Flickr or a political opinion in a blog on Tumblr wants to know how many passersby clicked on the poster's personal page to appreciate the effort. Tracking hits can be as obsessive as stopping to look at your reflection each time you pass the hallway mirror. Again, this is an example of mediated communication intersecting with our lives.

With the Internet at hand, if students read fewer books and newspapers than their grandparents did, it does not mean they are learning less. (Whether what they are learning is useful is another matter.) Students now have many more choices in their sources. They do their research via *SparkNotes* and Google, bypassing original texts. Parents who once used *CliffsNotes* for their Shakespeare assignments and grandparents who got their literature from *Reader's Digest* Condensed Books can hardly complain. Once again, choice through mediated communication is transforming education.

▶ DISTANCE EDUCATION

The Internet has augmented traditional bricks-and-mortar education and what once were called "open universities" and "correspondence courses" that depended on the mail to move lessons and teacher evaluations. The non-profit Khan Academy, to cite one prominent website, offers a library of more than 2,000 simple videos, each a lesson in math or another school subject. Combined with traditional in-class teaching, the lessons enable teachers to zero in on topics each student has difficulty understanding. Excellent progress has been reported.

With email, instant messaging, newsgroups, and video teleconferencing, the correspondence course has come a long way from its roots. Distance education allows high schools, trade schools, and colleges to offer study courses to earn credentials from a GED to a PhD. Lectures, assignments, questions, and answers flow at electric speed. Books and journal articles are downloaded. Students do not have to scribble notes as the teacher speaks. With a click, students who want to understand a poem are hyperlinked to a literary review along with an author biography. Study sessions with other students may even be separated by continents, but can be just as intense as late night cram sessions in a dorm. MOOCs (Massive Open Online Courses) give student access not only to readings and videos, but also to professors, teaching assistants, and even other students for interactive online discussion. They are a recent development for distance education.

Decades before the Internet, universities used mediated communication in such areas as agricultural extension services. Those services are even more readily available now. Nursing is another field where keeping up to date is essential, but nurses in distant locations may not be able to spare the time to return to a university for that information. Now they don't have to. To cite another example of how the Internet has changed education, students must leave their classrooms if they join a military service, but not their education. Recognizing that outside education as well as military training can produce a better soldier, the Department of Defense has established a tuition assistance program for personnel on active duty, their spouses and dependents (not to be confused with the GI Bill for former personnel). Online educators help by making allowances for military constraints.

▶ WEB 2.0

Web 2.0, comprising the newest additions to the Web, has in the blink of an eye brought about a second revolution. Web 1.0 consists mostly of pages provided by those with something significant to sell or tell. Web 2.0 is provided by the rest of us for the rest of us. *Time*'s "Person of the Year" ("You") for 2006 celebrated this personal shift.[18] The *Digital Futures Report* said, "While the Internet may be subjected to criticism on a variety of fronts, it is unlikely that going online will ever suffer from the same type of scorn that television has received over the years ('the idiot box', 'the boob tube', 'the vast wasteland')."[19]

Why not? Why does the Internet receive far more respect than television? Look for the answer in the comment by Apple's Steve Jobs about computer users who turn their brains on in active engagement and television viewers who turn their brains off, passively receiving whatever comes out of the tube (see page 317). Also, consider that a few television executives decide the content that millions watch. A few newspaper executives and journalists in any given community control the news output available to people in that community. This is the industrial model of *mass* communication. The Internet, especially the old Usenet and the new Web 2.0, is supposed to travel a different path.[20]

Web 2.0 is packed with communal activity; but remember that these are uses that governments neither originate nor control. Yet Web 2.0 is not anarchy. It can be as businesslike as banking. At prosper.com users who want to borrow or lend money directly from or to one another provide the content. At wetpaint.com, stumbleupon.com, and the like, users share observations about stories, music, movies, ads, or websites they run across. Alone, none of the founders of these sites could possibly supply the enormous amount of content or choices that users happily contribute.

However, increasingly some of the most frequented web addresses are being accused of tailoring responses to each individual in ways that are not always helpful. Concern has arisen that some organizations—Facebook and Google have been mentioned—are filtering out the variety that users might want. Blame may go to the automated gatekeepers—not human editors. User A and User B might make the same request of Google for a list of websites on a certain topic, but might be given different sets of websites. This personalizing and tailoring of information are based on such collected data as what people click on most often and where they live. Netflix, for instance, will suggest movies based on those you have already watched and then clicked that you enjoyed.

▶ SOCIAL NETWORKS

We are social beings who will make use of the available tools of online social media to connect with the near and dear. We can also connect with those living who remain dear, even if no longer near. Distance is no longer the barrier it once was. In fact, there are advantages to distant connections with people we never knew and may never meet. Like strangers on a train we unburden ourselves with little inhibition about what we say.

Media historian Tom Standage observed, "Social forms of media based on sharing, copying, and personal recommendation, which prevailed for centuries, have been dramatically reborn, supercharged by the Internet. By making it quick and easy for anyone to share information with others, modern social media gives ordinary people a collective agenda-setting power that was previously restricted to large publishers and broadcasters, and that is capable of striking fear into those in authority."[21]

We keep surprising ourselves. Few could have imagined that what was initially a means for researchers to communicate with other researchers would lead to a massive, global-wide sharing of personal information. During the first decade of the new millennium a handful of visionary entrepreneurs such as Mark Zuckerberg created the social networks of Facebook, YouTube, Twitter, and the other virtual venues that make up Web 2.0. Yahoo has millions of groups dealing with every imaginable subject. Distinctions between life online and life offline have blurred.

Zuckerberg, *Time*'s Person of the Year for 2010, began a social network at age 19 that by the start of 2014 had connected an astonishing total of 1.3 billion monthly active users worldwide. They access 54 million Facebook pages. Three of four users live outside the United States. Worldwide users now speak to each other on Facebook in 70 languages.[22] The award to Zuckerberg was made "for changing how we live our lives," said *Time* in explanation.

Time added, "Most people think of Facebook as a way to enviously ogle their co-workers' vacation pictures, but what Zuckerberg is doing is fundamentally changing the way the Internet works and, more importantly, the way it feels—which means, as the Internet permeates more and more aspects of our lives and hours of our day, how the world feels."[23] Personal privacy has taken a back seat, a point raised by Facebook's critics. Facebook responded by recommending ways to preserve privacy.[24]

▶ WIKI

As part of sharing information, Web 2.0 collaborates. That creates a sense of a global village. Consider JSTOR, a gateway to journals, books, and primary source material. In 2014 it offered access to hundreds of titles in law and medicine, and thousands of titles in science, mathematics, the arts, history, and humanities.

Or consider Wikipedia, the communal encyclopedia, or the Apache Software Foundation, dedicated to open source programming, or the Linux operating system (or systems), the alternative to proprietary systems.

Not many experts thought Wikipedia would work because they believed that revolutionaries, propagandists, and assorted crazies might strangle it. Instead, it would be hard to find a better example of Web 2.0's by-the-people, for-the-people promise. The vandals are there, but so are Wikipedia's protectors. The result is a quick, usually dependable source that even serious scholars use, although they may feel too shamefaced about it to footnote what they find.

Perhaps we should recall that more than a century ago work began on the great *Oxford English Dictionary*. It, too, depended on the contributions of volunteers.

The village breeds its own vocabulary. "Wiki" refers to any collaborative website. Anyone can edit it. Amazingly, it works. At Wikipedia, millions of writers have contributed articles. A curious and controversial version of Wikipedia is located at wikileaks.org to deposit government documents. Where governments control access to newspapers and broadcast outlets, here is an outlet for whistle blowers. The site relies on volunteers to vet the information. Potential for WikiLeaks abuse is great. A storm of protest followed Julian Assange's release of sensitive U.S. government text files in 2010. An even bigger storm followed Edward Snowden's release of documents in 2013 that revealed widespread email and telephone eavesdropping by the U.S. government, especially on government leaders of friendly nations.

▶ BLOGGING

The Internet offers a wealth of source material on almost every topic, and almost anyone can contribute. With an inexpensive digital camera and an MP3 recorder player, a self-appointed journalist can set up a news website and, at least in theory, attract an international readership to the blogger's daily news and opinions. And, with this equipment, photo interviews can be conducted.

Bloggers have broken significant stories. The writing and questions may lack polish and the video may be out of focus or shaky, but the stories have an air of immediacy. Topics ignored by journalists or dropped after a day or two have been kept alive and pushed to the point that politicians felt forced to respond. Memorably, blogs riveted on a CBS News error regarding President George W. Bush's military service led to the resignation of veteran news anchor Dan Rather.[25]

Websites have been helpful to the public in innumerable ways. They have provided nearly instant information about the effects of a disaster, especially the identities of victims for those who search for relatives. On the Internet there is no waiting for a scheduled newscast or the next printed edition. The sequential structure of broadcast newscasts does not exist. The online reader looks at headlines and chooses stories asynchronously from a menu of online news agencies, newspapers, radio stations, television stations, and news channels all over the world, often at no cost to the reader.

SECOND LIFE

Millions of players from all over the world today are living the vicarious existences of *Second Life*, a virtual world created in 1999. *Second Life* may be as close to heaven as you can get on Earth. It is less a video game than a social network set in a fantasy realm created by the players themselves, a parallel dreamland that by 2009 had registered 16 million players from all over the world. It might be described as an Internet activity without rules or an objective or game play. "Residents" choose an avatar (a substitute for themselves), find a plot of land, build a house, start a business, socialize with other residents, and generally live a "second life," just as the title promises. That avatar life can be a person of a different age, race, gender, or physical attributes. People move about in a life that "might-have-been" if only their lives had worked out differently.

Title screen for Second Life.

Within this fantasy thousands of residents "attend" church; different faiths and denominations are a click away. Real auto manufacturers, including Toyota, Nissan, and Pontiac, opened virtual dealerships to offer virtual cars for sale for "linden dollars" to residents who want to express their tastes but don't need a car for transportation in a world where they can teletransport their avatar from place to place.

Researchers in several dozen schools and educational organizations, including the Harvard Law School, could be found there. A number of them were studying how *Second Life* might be used to advance education. The news agency Reuters had a correspondent there. You could watch full-length feature films on the Sundance Channel inside *Second Life*. Linden Labs, the company that runs *Second Life*, added a *Teen Second Life* world. Quarrels over imaginary real estate have led to real life lawsuits. In Japan, a wife who was unexpectedly divorced logged onto the similar fantasy site *Maple Story* and murdered her husband's avatar. She was arrested and jailed.

What better example can there be of how mediated communication distances its users? Isolating themselves totally from the reality of their lives, players enjoy a fantasy world of their own creation. Their connections are with people far away who have also separated themselves from their own lives. This is *playing house* for grownups.

For readers who prefer news heavily seasoned with opinion, informed or not, even laden with invective, thousands of blogs and special interest websites are just a few clicks away. News websites such as *Salon.com*, *The Drudge Report*, *Vice*, *BuzzFeed*, and *The Huffington Post* bring news laden with opinions to hundreds of thousands of viewers daily.

GAMBLING

Among the many Internet groups are online poker players. Online gamblers provide an interesting example of figuring out a social interaction at a distance. They bet against each other with real money but for the most part never meet. In addition to playing cards, they chat with each other using their own conversational conventions. Traditionally, poker is a game full of both spoken and silent social interaction, but online is limited to the chat function that the online poker site provides. In the online game, very few player "tells" (movements that might identify the quality of the cards in a hand) are involved. In live poker, studying your opponents' physical movements is an enjoyable and potentially profitable form of interaction. Online, up to ten people can be "seated" around a poker table. Typically, their only form of communication is via the "chat window." On one poker site, players design their own persona by specifying visual characteristics such as facial features, haircut, and clothing. At the poker table, they can modify their facial expressions and body positions, and they can even talk to each other in various accents, using "emoticons."

▶ KEEPING TRACK ELSEWHERE

No medium of communication with such power can exist without challenges from those who wish to change it to something that it currently is not. Nations that do not allow journalists to speak freely do not always give bloggers a free pass either, but may not come down as hard as they do on traditional outlets such as newspapers. By the start of 2013, China had about 564 million Internet users, 40 percent of the population, three out of four of them using mobile phones to access the Internet. Astonishingly, more than half of the Chinese using the Internet went to blogs.[26] Even in rural areas, where cellphones have become common and the Internet is a click away, unrest among Chinese peasants has grown.[27] Blogs by young Chinese test the limit of what authorities will allow. Thanks to Chinese character words, bloggers bundle a lot of information into short messages.

With all the new sites coming online, authorities are hard pressed to keep track of content. They attempt to do so indirectly by holding Internet service providers responsible for policing the blogs to make sure pornography and political messages hostile to the government do not appear. The ISPs were given lists of forbidden words. Filtering software either replaced the words with asterisks or blocked the message altogether. Chinese authorities provided a microblogging substitute, *Sina Weibo*, the most popular website in China. Chinese bloggers found creative ways around forbidden words such as using Chinese characters that sound like banned words when spoken aloud. Many popular sites not based in China, including Facebook and Twitter, were blocked.

Meanwhile, Iranian college students used blogs to accuse their government of a fraudulent election. The Turkish government briefly tried to ban Twitter in 2014 (but at the time this was written an agreement may have been reached between the Turkish government and Twitter). In Egypt a court sent one blogger to jail for four years for expressing his opinions. Will the Internet replace newspapers and newscasts? For some people, especially educated people living in dictatorships where news is controlled, it already has. Government censors in some nations may not fully know what is being sent and, even if they did, could scarcely halt the exchange of information across their borders short of seizing all computer modems or tracking down all international phone calls.

▶ PENDING LEGISLATION

As this book went to press, the U.S. House of Representatives was debating the Stop Online Piracy Act aimed mainly at websites based overseas that profit from online content such as movies that they do not pay for. Ranged in support of the bill were the National Association of Broadcasters and content providers led by movie and music providers. Opposition includes the Brookings Institute and such Internet sites as Wikipedia, Facebook, and Google, which fear that the legislation could lead to government censorship of the Internet. While the House considers this bill, the Senate is considering the Protect IP (intellectual property) Act. This would give the government and copyright holders tools to limit access to websites that peddle counterfeit media and media that infringe copyright. Like the Online Piracy Act, issues of press freedom are argued.

▶ CHALLENGES

Politicians have used the Internet as a cheap way to get their messages to voters. So have the extreme fringes. It has not been possible to stop hate; websites link the angry, the suspicious, and even the mentally ill on all manner of issues. At the same time, support groups use newsgroups to deal with problems relating to physical disabilities, eating disorders, drug use, AIDS, cancer, diabetes, and mental illness. It is decidedly less embarrassing to type in: "Hello, my name is Susan, and I'm an alcoholic" than to face others at a meeting.

Internet addiction is a worldwide problem. The South Korean, Vietnamese, and Thai governments tried to limit the hours that teens spend online, such as kicking them off network games after five hours. China went further, treating heavy Internet use as a mental disorder and locking teens up in rehabilitation clinics.[28] In the United States, the equivalents of Alcoholics Anonymous groups for cyber addiction have formed online (despite the irony of the venue). It has been called Internet Addiction (IA), Internet Addiction Disorder (IAD), and Pathological Internet Use (PIU). At least one scientific study published in 2012 found brain changes similar to those found among alcoholics and drug users.[29]

Seductive, the Internet coaxes otherwise busy people to waste productive hours, detoured by websites that catch their attention. Lost hours and lost sleep can lead to dysfunctional behavior that destroys marriages and careers. More than a few users rack up large monthly phone bills. They may be addicted to chat lines, porn sites, or game sites.[30] Internet addictions have joined addiction to other forms of mediated communication, particularly television and telephone use.

According to a study covering 16 nations, online time seems to be taken mainly from television viewing rather than from time with family and friends. A study of heavy Internet usage reported unsuccessful attempts to cut down on time spent online. Addicts experienced anxiety when not online and significant relationship discord. Some respondents admit to pre-existing psychiatric problems such as bipolar disorder, depression, or alcohol abuse.

The Internet has the potential for individuals to challenge governments and even dictatorships to an extent far beyond anything ever known, and that has importance for society. Anything is possible in this information revolution including real, bloody revolutions. Consider Internet use during the Arab Spring revolts and the "Occupy" revolts in the United States. The "Power to the People" independence of the Internet holds both positive and negative elements: positive, for example, in opposition to tyrannical governments; negative in enabling child pornographers and sexual predators, con men, and drug dealers to elude justice. Cyber stalkers target victims, and police either cannot track them down or express disinterest in doing so across international borders. Nor can we forget the hackers who disrupt communication for the sake of gain or malicious pleasure or for no fathomable reason at all.

Adolescents may have bullied each other since the dawn of time, but the present generation can call on media technology to extend the reach of the bullies. Because of the willful and repeated threats and humiliations poured on their prey, bullies have caused unrelieved misery and, in a few cases, suicides.

LONELYGIRL15

Lonelygirl15, a widely watched and believed series on YouTube, was an example of the yearning by people all over the world to have intimate communication with a stranger.[31]

An actress pretended to be a 16-year-old video blogger whose ordinary life grew increasingly bizarre. Online fans flocked in from every direction. One fan began a message board discussion that led other fans to seek details of her life that eventually revealed a hoax.

Lonelygirl15 proved harmless. Others are not. Social network scams have been stubborn.

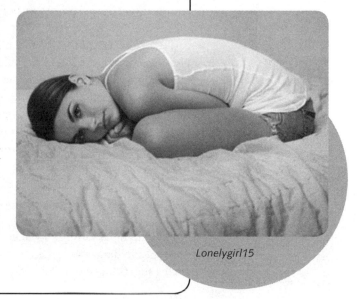

Lonelygirl15

▶ THE DARK SIDE

For some users it doesn't matter that the more public mediated communication that we have, the less privacy. For others, the lack of privacy does indeed matter. Even when we think we are communicating privately, we are not. Digital age author Steven Levy concluded, "We think we're whispering, but we're really broadcasting."[32] And some clever people are listening. From scam to spam, they prowl and phish (attempt to gather personal data with phony email). If email eased communication for millions of people, it also eased the way for the unscrupulous.

Nastiness does not stop there. Malicious hackers spread viruses, worms, Trojan horses, spyware. Motives for writing and spreading destructive programs vary, but none is pleasant. Con artists send email to the gullible, promising fortunes in exchange for bank account information. Pedophiles locate the email addresses of children to whom they send pornographic letters and pictures, or arrange meetings. Sending a youngster a webcam to attach to a computer in the child's room as a "gift" is a favored trick. Stopping pedophiles has not proved easy.

Hate has free reign on the Internet. Many websites have hatred as a particular purpose. Posters welcome the anonymity that the Internet offers. To cite just one example, a call for Muslims to kill all Jews as a preparation for Judgment Day registered 350,000 "likes" on Facebook before the page was taken down.[33]

Like the rain, the Internet is sent on the just and on the unjust.[34]

▶ SUMMARY

The 2014 Pew survey marking the 25th anniversary of the World Wide Web recorded that 76 percent of respondents said the Internet was a good thing for society, and 90 percent said it was a good thing for themselves. As noted earlier, of all communication technologies, like television, cell or landline telephones, or email, the Internet would be the hardest to give up. (Because of the confusion over definitions, it is clear that most respondents meant the Web.) Variations exist based on education, age, income, and ethnicity, but there is still a majority for "very hard or impossible to give up" in every category.[35]

If anyone still wonders what people use the Internet for, the response is obvious: what don't they use it for? As a headline to the Pew study states, the Internet has woven itself into American life. For years access was only through computers. Today it is also reached through mobile devices, and nine of ten adult Americans own a mobile device, although not all can access the Internet. In short, the Internet is readily available in all places at all times day and night, as close as a wallet or a pocket handkerchief.

Who could have imagined that so much information and so much else in such a short time would be today virtually a part of us?

▶ TIMELINE

1945   Vannevar Bush conceives idea of hyperlinks, hypermedia.

1958   Defense Department creates ARPANET, precursor of the Internet.

1960   Joseph Licklider conceives the Internet.

        Americans and Britons simultaneously develop packet switching transmission.

1965   Non-sequential hypertext is created. It will one day build the Internet's links.

1969   UCLA computer sends data to Stanford computer, foreshadowing the Internet.

1971   ARPANET, Internet forerunner, has 22 university, government connections.

        Early version of email.

1973   Xerox sets up a LAN (local area network) called Ethernet.

1979   USENET begins.

1980   Internet users send and receive at 300 baud.

1982   From Carnegie Mellon University professor Scott Fahlman: emoticons :-).

1983   Internet domains get names instead of hard-to-remember numbers.

        TCP/IP becomes standard protocol for Internet connections.

1986   Congress passes Electronic Communications Privacy Act.

1988   "Hacker" and "worm" enter the Internet lexicon. First data crime reported.

1989   Researchers try to index the exploding Internet; they can't keep up.

1990   World Wide Web originates at CERN in Europe. Tim Berners-Lee writes program.

1991   Internet available for commercial uses.

Hypertext Markup Language (HTML) written; helps create the World Wide Web.

The Web gets servers.

1992   Text-based browser opens the World Wide Web for general usage.

1996   Email use surpasses postal mail.

1997   Nearly eight of ten U.S. public schools have Internet access.

Streaming audio and video are available on the Web.

1998   Weblogs, or "blogs" for short, and PayPal are created.

2000   Seven new Web domain names approved, including .info, .pro, .biz.

2001   Internet has thousands of online radio stations.

2002   Google News, an automated service without human editors.

2003   Flash mobs, organized on the Net, start in New York, spread worldwide.

An estimated 5 trillion unwanted messages are sent on the Internet.

2004   Facebook makes friends.

95% of U.S. public libraries offer Internet access.

2008   Internet plays an important part in U.S. presidential election victory.

2009   Applications taken for internationalized domain names.

2010   4G wireless network extends high speed Internet to cellphones.

2012   Wikipedia shuts down for 24 hours, a gesture to oppose anti-Web piracy bills.

▶ NOTES

1 The Internet is a system of networks, a network of networks. The Web is one of these networks, a system of linked pages that are reached through the Internet.

2 My PhD dissertation: "A Computer-Based Analysis of Television News Writing Style for Listening Comprehension," UCLA, 1965.

3 Published in *Communication Systems, IEEE Transactions*, March 1964, vol. 12, no. 1: 1–9.

4 Michael Hauben, "The Social Forces Behind the Development of Usenet," http://www.columbia.edu/~rh120/ch106.x03. Also in *Netizens* (Los Alamitos, CA: IEEE Computer Society Press, 1997) 48.

5 Michael Dertouzos makes the point in his foreword to Tim Berners-Lee, *Weaving the Web* (San Francisco: Harper, 1999) ix.

6 Statistic Brain, "Google Annnual Search Statistics," http://www.statisticbrain.com/google-searches/.

7 See, for example, *Wired*, August 2005: 96.

8 Pew Research Center, "The Web at 25 in the U.S.," http://www.pewinternet.org/files/2014/02/PIP_25th-anniversary-of-the-Web_0227141.pdf.

9 Ibid.

10 Sydney Jones and Susannah Fox, "Generations Online in 2009," *Pew Internet and American Life Project*, January 28, 2009. Information can be found at http://www.pewInternet.org/~/media//Files/Reports/2009/PIP_Generations_2009.pdf

11 Stanford University Professor B. J. Fogg reported that older women join Facebook to "friend" their younger family members, then stay on to connect online with their peers. The Facebook organization, on its Inside Facebook site, reported on April 13, 2009, that 1.5 million women over 55 had joined, a 550% increase in six months. Total membership at the time was 200 million, a larger user base than the population of any country except China, India, the United States, and Indonesia. John D. Sutter, "All in the Facebook Family: Older Generations Join Social Networks," *CNN.com*, April 13, 2009, http://www.cnn. com/2009/TECH/04/13/social.network.older/index.html?iref=t2test_techmon.

12 Drew Desilver, "Digital Dating: Online's Share of the Romance Market," *Pew Research Center*, October 23, 2013, http://www.pewresearch.org/fact-tank/2013/10/23/digital-dating-onlines-share-of-the-romance-market/.

13 Amanda Lenhart and Maeve Duggan, "Couples, the Internet, and Social Media," *Pew Research Internet Project*, February 11, 2014, http://www.pewinternet.org/2014/02/11/couples-the-internet-and-social-media/.

14 Deborah Fallows, "How Women and Men Use the Internet," *Pew Research Internet Project*, December 28, 2005. http://www.pewinternet.org/2005/12/28/how-women-and-men-use-the-internet/

15 Dave Barry, "You've Got Trouble," *New York Times*, May 6, 2007, http://www.nytimes.com/2007/05/06/books/review/Barry.t.html?ex=1335844800&en=33f26214516e2c7d&ei=5124&partner=permalink&exprod=permalink&_r=0.

16 See Hauben, 123.

17 For a take on this point see Steven Johnson, *Everything Bad Is Good for You* (New York: Riverhead Books, 2005) 120.

18 *Time*, December 25, 2006.

19 *The Digital Futures Report, Year Four* (Los Angeles: Annenberg School, USC, 2005) 97.

20 For a discussion of Usenet, see Hauben 1997.

21 Tom Standage, *Writing in the Wall: Social Media, the First 2,000 Years* (New York: Bloomsbury, 2013) 239.

22 These statistics are supplied by Facebook itself. Statistic Brain, "Facebook Statistics," http://www.statisticbrain.com/facebook-statistics/.

23 *Time*, December 15, 2010, cover story.

24 NDTV, "How to Manage Your Facebook Privacy in 5 Easy Steps (with 5 Bonus Tips)," *NDTV Gadgets*, April 21, 2014, http://gadgets.ndtv.com/social-networking/features/how-to-manage-your-facebook-privacy-in-5-easy-steps-with-5-bonus-tips-511506.

25 "Dan Rather Leaves CBS after 44 Years," http://www.pbs.org/newshour/bb/media-jan-june06-rather_06-20/.

26 China Network Information Center, *Statistical Report on Internet Development in China (January 2013)*, http://www1.cnnic.cn/IDR/ReportDownloads/201302/P020130221391269963814.pdf.

27 Kevin Kelly, "The New Socialism," *Wired*, August 2009: 116–121.

28 PBS, "Treating China's Internet Addicts," *PBS NewsHour*, January 20, 2014, http://www.pbs.org/newshour/rundown/treating-chinas-internet-addicts/.

29 Lin et al., "Abnormal White Matter Integrity in Adolescents with Internet Addiction Disorder: A Tract-Based Spatial Statistics Study," *PLOS ONE*, January 11, 2012, http://www.plosone.org/article/info%3Adoi%2F10.1371%2Fjournal.pone.0030253.

30 A number of websites discuss this matter (e.g., http://www.helpguide.org/mental/internet_cybersex_addiction.htm).

31 "The Secret World of Lonelygirl15," *Wired*, December 2006: 236–239.

32 Steven Levy, *Crypto* (New York: Penguin Books, 2001) 1.

33 Niall Ferguson, "The Mash of Civilizations," *Newsweek*, April 18, 2011: 9.

34 The King James Bible (2000) translates Matthew 5:45 as "That you may be the children of your Father who is in heaven: for he makes his sun to rise on the evil and on the good, and sends rain on the just and on the unjust."

35 Susannah Fox and Lee Rainie, "Part 1: How the Internet Has Woven Itself into American Life," *Pew Research Internet Project*, February 27, 2014, http://www.pewinternet.org/2014/02/27/part-1-how-the-internet-has-woven-itself-into-american-life/.

15

Video Games: Leaning Forward

At the start of the film *The Princess Bride*, a boy ill in bed is playing the video game *Hardball III*. His grandfather arrives to read him a story. The grandfather takes for granted the superiority of a fairy tale in a book over an interactive game, with the grandfather, not the child, doing the reading. The audience is expected to agree that the imagination stirred by listening to a story is superior to what a game stirs. Or at least in this instance, passive listening is more fun.

It isn't. And the public knows it and says so with its money. The 2011 release of *Call of Duty: Modern Warfare 3* sold 6.5 million copies in its first 24 hours of sales and grossed U.S.$400 million.[1] In 2013 *Grand Theft Auto V* sold more than 11 million copies in its first 24 hours and passed $1 billion gross in three days.[2] A few weeks later *Call of Duty: Ghosts*, the tenth version of this series, was released and passed $1 billion in a single day.[3] No motion picture release has come close to matching those numbers. Video games and their equipment grossed $56 billion globally in 2010, more than radio, recorded music, or magazine revenues.[4] Today it is not academic research or business that drives microcomputer development to be bigger and faster. It is games.

From their early days, video games sold computers. (*note that for simplicity, all electronic games are identified here as "video games," no matter what platform they use.*) Until they heard about games, a lot of people saw no need to buy a computer. A small calculator was enough for budgets and taxes, and a typewriter for letters. Only when they saw how much fun video games were did they decide to splurge on a computer.

Fred Savage and Peter Falk in *The Princess Bride* (1987).

▶ IS IT COMMUNICATION?

Video game speed of play, their graphics, and the amount of data needed for the different paths a storyline can take are behind the demand for better computers. Professor James Paul Gee of Stanford calls the games "a new form of art. They will not replace books, they will sit beside them, interact with them, and change them and their role in society in various ways, as, indeed, they are already doing strongly with movies." He added, "When people learn to play video games, they are learning a new literacy."[5] Games juxtapose symbols and images with text for players to decode as they move through the challenges. Unless they overdo it, players are not wasting time.

It would seem reasonable to wonder why a discussion of video games belongs in a book about communication. Several reasons brought it here:

1 Tens of millions of players from all over the world, most of them young, use computers and other communication devices to play these games. Many of the games are played online.
2 Some "games," like *Second Life*, are not games at all, but are a fantasy social network, a means to communicate with others far away.
3 Other video games such as *FarmVille* and *CityVille* are a part of social networks like Facebook and can be played with friends. They are means of communication.

4 Many games have an educational function. They communicate such knowledge as math lessons. Unfortunately, some games teach violence.

5 Recognizing the hold that games have on so many younger people, educators are turning to them as a way to communicate information and skills. The University of Minnesota School of Journalism and Mass Communication is just one of the institutions where research in this field is conducted. The U.S. Army has even used video games for training.

▶ GAMES ARE UNIVERSAL

Every society on Earth plays games of one kind or another. It is doubtful that a school or community exists anywhere without them. Did cave dwellers play games to sharpen their skills at bringing down hoofed food? Did quieter games in every century help pass the evening hours and long stormy days? Bet on it.

We also enjoy *watching* games of every sort, and we engage in all manner of personal competition from cards and chess to running and wrestling, just as we like team competition ranging from debates to football. The list is endless. Or we play by ourselves against a machine or against our previous "personal best."

Inserted into this world of games is modern mediated communication in the form of video games. They are all about choice. The *Oregon Trail* blazer must choose the longer river path or the shorter but more dangerous mountain path. Ms. Pac-Man must instantly go left or right to evade the gobbling monsters. The making of decisions never ends until the game does. The challenge is addicting, and doubly so against human opponents who face the same choices. We play video games against family members or friends or classmates. We carry on conversations with strangers in faraway lands as we try to "kill" them or partner with them without knowing who they are except what they tell us, and that may be as true as what we tell them. Video games are played in homes, business offices, arcades, on game consoles, on cellphones, on television sets, and in places you might not expect to find electronic games.

It has been said that our storytellers determine our culture. Radio, television, and movies have been our latter day storytellers. Television airs programs that are talked about at the office water cooler and on the phone the next day. If storytellers do indeed determine our culture, we must consider the cultural impact of storytelling video games.

▶ LEANING FORWARD OR BACK?

Steve Jobs offered this prediction: "I don't really believe that televisions and computers are going to merge. I've spent enough time in entertainment to know that storytelling is linear. It's not interactive. You go to your TV when you want to turn your brain off. You go to your computer when you want to turn your brain on. Those are not the same thing."[6] His comments created the concepts of *leaning forward* and *leaning back*. Video games are not just child's play. Nearly three-quarters of all American households played video games. The average age of players in 2013 was 30, and 58 percent of Americans play video games. Nearly half—45 percent—were women. Reasons given for buying a game included quality of graphics, an interesting story line, a sequel to a favorite game, or a word-of-mouth recommendation. Players say they are spending less time playing card games, going to the movies, watching television, or watching movies at home.[7]

Games are played on office computers by employees who should be working, on home computers by "screenagers" who should be studying, and by their parents. They are played quietly using software sold in stores or downloaded from the Internet, or noisily in clubs and tournaments. Many games are played online against unseen opponents.

Maybe board games draw in competitors whose enthusiasm for Scrabble or Monopoly has evolved into addiction, but nothing that came before matches the mass hypnosis of video games. "I don't believe anyone ever expected video games to have such a fundamental impact on our society in so many areas," said Dr. Christopher Geist, chair of the department of Popular Culture at Bowling Green University and a member of the Videotopia Advisory Panel.[8] "[They] have become an integral part of the fabric of American life, changing the way we think, the way we learn, and the way we see the future."

Game designer and author Jane McGonigal has given public talks to argue that game playing can add to life's happiness and can actually extend life. "When we play a game, we tackle tough challenges with more creativity, more determination, more optimism, and we're more likely to reach out to others for help," she said.[9]

▶ HOW VIDEO GAMES BEGAN

Like computers and the Internet, video games were born in academia. A game was played a few years after the first computers were built, assembled in the engineering department of a famous university. In 1952, the room-sized EDSAC at Harvard, depending on thousands of vacuum tubes, was programmed to play tic-tac-toe. A. S. Douglas wrote the program as part of his doctoral dissertation, just to show that it was possible. Douglas and his professors may have been the only players.

In 1958, when computers still filled entire rooms, William Higinbotham, at the Brookhaven National Laboratory in New York, a nuclear research lab, created *Tennis for Two* using an analog computer and two hand-held control boxes. The screen was a five inch oscilloscope. Higinbotham wrote the game program to entertain visitors to the National Laboratory. Lab staffers waited for hours to play, but Higinbotham did not think enough of his little invention, the first interactive video game, to bother getting a patent.

Empire was the popular game at Cal Tech. To get around a no-nonsense systems operator, one student changed the name of his game to "Test." No one objected to a student running a test program. With millions of government dollars being spent on equipment and research time, IBM tried to ban games from their buildings, but so many employees complained that IBM executives backed off.

The first commercial games went into arcades. An important difference between arcade games and handheld or console games was based on how their manufacturers made money. Arcade games make money when people plunk in quarters, so the most commercially successful games have no endings. The aliens keep coming as long as you have quarters. Manufacturers of games played on computers and hand-held devices make money when buyers finish a game and head to the store for another. So the popular games played at home have stories that end. You can win.

A goal of every game maker is to keep the player at it. Psychologist B. F. Skinner devised the "Skinner box" at Harvard in 1930 to show how rats can be conditioned to keep at a task for the reward of a crunchy food pellet. The smart rat learned to keep pressing the lever. A nice reinforcement, but it did not go on like this forever. After a while the device no longer handed out a pellet with each press, only an occasional pellet. This "partial reinforcement" kept the rats at it. Now consider the game player who is rewarded by higher and higher scores for hitting a button. The player discovers that the game grows harder with time and success, awarding fewer points. This partial reinforcement makes the activity even more addictive. The player has to try harder to build up a score. The goal—the pellet equivalent—is the higher score. The computer makes it easy to program a game to be addictive.

Excessive playing of video games is not unusual, with players logging on for 24 hours or longer at a session. For some online game players it becomes the most important activity in their lives. It is the most important social pursuit some youngsters and adults have, and when they are alone at the computer, exchanging messages with other players is their only social interaction. It has led to both marriage and suicide.

Describing *SimCity*, Communications Professor Ted Friedman wrote, "It's easy to slide into a routine with absolutely no down time, no interruptions from complete communion with the computer. The game can grow so absorbing, in fact, your subjective sense of time is distorted. You look up, and all of a sudden it's morning. It's very hard to describe what it feels like when you're 'lost' inside a computer game, precisely because at that moment your sense of self has been fundamentally transformed."[10]

▶ WHAT CAN WE LEARN?

Parents and teachers have complained that game players are so much into their games that they move with little awareness of what is immediately around them. That raises a useful question: what can society learn from an activity that is so attractive? That question was asked years ago about television programs. Now it is video games. What can teachers learn from game designers? For example, adults are nervous when they go into surgery, but a youngster can be terrified. In 2005, anesthesiologist Anu Patel noticed that a friend's seven-year-old son was so busy playing his Game Boy that he wouldn't eat or talk to anyone. Dr. Patel did an experiment with 72 children, ages 4 to 12. She found that children who were given a Game Boy to play before anesthesia showed the least anxiety and often no anxiety at all. They did much better than children who were given tranquilizers or children whose only comfort was their parents.[11]

Video games can encourage fantasy lives, where we can do dangerous or illegal things that no reasonable person would actually do. In a fantasy game, these reservations do not matter and playing well raises self-esteem. Get a high score, surpass your personal best, or slay large numbers of the enemy, and you feel good about what you have accomplished. Gaming can also be a conduit for social activity. Particularly in Asia, teenagers like to play video games in crowded rooms while carrying on conversations with old friends and striking up new acquaintances.[12] Some youths develop such dexterity that they earn prizes in competition. Las Vegas sponsors the annual Evo Championship Series.[13] E-sports events are played in several American cities. In South Korea, the best video gamers are treated like rock stars.

▶ PHYSICAL ACTIVITY

Obviously, excessive game play limits physical movement. While the monsters run and jump, the players do not. They sit still, except for busy fingers making repetitive movements. Staring at screens doesn't help their bodies either, nor do sudden spurts of game-infused adrenaline. Physical problems have been blamed on heavy video game play. Joints, skin, thumbs, and muscles have suffered from repeatedly hitting buttons. Players have complained of neck stiffness, wrist pain, finger numbness, blisters, calluses, sore tendons (that some doctors have jokingly called "Nintendinitis"), and sore elbows (sometimes called "Pac-Man's elbow"). In rare cases, epileptic seizures were reported among players who were photosensitive. In terms of health, some critics think the best thing that can be said about video games is that they are a step up from staring at TV.[14]

Nintendo's Wii system gets players up and moving. The motion control gaming system has been a runaway best seller, attracting seniors as well as the youth market. Depending on the game, the player swings a virtual baseball bat, a tennis racquet, a golf club, a bowling ball, a fishing pole, a sword, or a fist. Despite their value as a spur to exercise, the games have caused some injuries and property damage in the hands of overzealous players.

In PlayStation Eye games for PlayStation 4, a camera and microphone (accompanied by voice recognition software in 20 languages) that is pointed at the player converts body movements into movements onscreen. Crouch and your character starts to move. Lean to the right and your character moves right. Roll your arms in circles and your character does a back flip. If you want to stop, hold your arms out to the side. And so on. Your body moves. After doing this for a while, the player has acquired a day's ration of exercise but can still get sore or may even dislocate something.

On a positive note, Dr. James Rosser, director of the Advanced Medical Technologies Institute at Beth Israel Medical Center in New York, headed a study showing that surgeons who played video games three hours weekly had 37 percent fewer errors and accomplish tasks 27 percent faster in doing laparoscopic surgery, where the surgeon's movements are guided by watching a television screen.[15] (However, it won't help your chances of getting into medical school.)

THE SIMS

Another favorite of female players, *The Sims* series, deals with ordinary people living ordinary lives. The player controls the characters and navigates them through human situations. Said writer John Seabrook, "As my fourteen-year-old niece exclaimed recently, when I asked her what she liked about playing *The Sims*, 'You've got one Sim who you've got to get to school and another who needs to get to his job and their kid has been up all night and is in a bad mood and the house is dirty—I guess there's a ton of things to do!'"[16]

▶ GENDER DIFFERENCES

Women prefer to solve puzzles, test their dexterity (Wii is popular), help their comrades put dragons in their place, and heal their fallen friends. They play *Angry Birds* on smartphones; by the end of 2012, 1.7 billion copies of the *Angry Birds* family of games were downloaded.[17] As noted in the previous chapter, the online social network *Second Life* is a favorite. If disturbances to the daily pattern of real life are too upsetting, *Second Life* lets players live out perfect dream lives. In 2013 Candy Crush Saga reported a monthly worldwide average of 46 million users.[18] To get a sense of its appeal to women, just look around to see who is playing the game on hand-helds.

Game hardware manufacturers and game software makers put a lot of thought into how to hang on to customers as they grow older. Teenage boys remain the most important market for many games, especially the first-person shooters known also as "twitch" games. But young consumers are a shifting market. Today's teenager is tomorrow's adult. Boys who grow up to discover that girls are not so annoying after all become less concerned about blasting monsters, so the market has adjusted for changing interests. Video game makers discovered that girls wanted to play too, so they created the Nancy Drew mysteries. Girls' heart rates increased more than boys' rates. That was true for both playing and just watching.[19]

Women and younger girls particularly like non-violent games that require sharp eye-hand coordination, sometimes called "muscle memory." You need quick reflexes to play *Angry Birds*, *Pac-Man*, *Donkey Kong*, *Frogger*, and *Prince of Persia*. An Entertainment Software Association study in 2012 reported that nearly half of all game players are women. In fact, women over 18 were more likely to play games than boys 17 or younger (30 to 18 percent).[20]

Looking at the blockbuster game of *Tetris*, the author of *Joystick Nation*, J. C. Herz observed, "*Tetris* . . . is more popular with women than any other game and notoriously addictive among female professionals . . . It's about detritus raining down on your head, trash falling into messy piles and piling up until it finally suffocates you. The psychological payoff for the player is a state of rapturous relief. 'Yes,' she thinks. 'Yes! The mess is vanishing! I can make the mess disappear.'"[21] The game is, of course, popular with men also. An Oxford University study concluded that *Tetris* helps block the mind from storing painful memories.[22]

Testosterone continues to get the game designers' attention. In 1996, from Britain came *Lara Croft, Tomb Raider*. Despite being a female hero, her busty, leggy appearance was designed to appeal to young males. The original script called for the main character to be a man, but the designers feared that the game looked like an Indiana Jones rip-off. Instead, Lara was born. By *Tomb Raider III*, the player who reached a higher level sent Lara into a new virtual reality in some exotic corner of the world. What seemed just a game combined a geography lesson with a male fantasy. A later version of *Tomb Raider* shows a more believably proportioned Lara Croft in less revealing clothing, perhaps in recognition of all the female players.

TOMB RAIDER

Lara Croft in the 2013 re-boot
of the *Tomb Raider* series.

Electronic games have a way of getting under the skin of some players. A study of how players referred to games reported that most people referred to a game as the impersonal pronoun "it," as in "It hates me." Next most common was the personal pronoun "he," as in, "He's trying to get me." Also common was "you" ("You dumb machine!") and "they" ("They think they're so smart; I'll show them"). No one referred to a game as "she."[23]

A GOD GAME

In the role-playing god game *Black & White* (2000), the player is considered a god and decides the kind of god to be: either cruel or gentle. As a god you will be worshipped, you can uproot trees with your bare hands and you can raise fierce animals to enforce your will and expand the empire you control. What you get is up to you. If you pet an animal each time it eats a villager, guess what kind of animal you will have?

GAME TYPES

Games are divided into types, but some games fit into more than one category. Here is one of several lists:

Adventure: reach a goal by solving puzzles.

God games (also called "simulation"): manage a community, an empire, or a war.

Scroll: run and jump and avoid the nasties.

Sports: play tennis, golf, hockey, football, race cars.

First-person shooters: slaughter the endless numbers of the enemy.

One-on-one: hit, kick, do whatever it takes to put an opponent down.

Brain and finger busters: match your skills against the machine.

Learning: solve math, language, and other school subject problems.

Role-playing: adopt an identity, wander through other worlds.

▶ VIOLENT GAMES

The effect of violent video games may be greater than that of other media because they are interactive and more involving. In some games the player identifies with the aggressor, participates in crime, learns by repeating violent acts, and is rewarded for doing so. Two students obsessed with the ultra-violent *Doom* and *Duke Nukem* committed the Columbine High School killings in Colorado in 1999. News reports have piled up of many school shootings committed by angry boys, some of them stimulated by violent video games. Adam Lanza, who killed his mother and then 26 others at Sandy Hook Elementary School in Newtown, Connecticut, liked to play *Call of Duty*.

A 2006 study of brain activity among players of the shooter game *Medal of Honor* compared with players of a non-violent game showed greater activation in the amygdala, the portion of the brain involved in emotional arousal, and less activity in the prefrontal portions of the brain involved with control, focus, and concentration.[24]

The industry response to complaints about violence has been disingenuous, but that is scarcely unexpected. It is not difficult to find in most industries the argument that customers should get what they want, not what is best for them, or for society as a whole. As usual in the world of mediated communication, the users determine its direction. Among the best-selling games are those that appeal to some of the worst of human impulses.

Despite a rating system, it is easy for a ten-year-old to buy a game in which scantily dressed prostitutes, begging the player to kill them, are murdered by chain saws. Filthy language spews from cartoon mouths. Cannibalism is treated casually in *F.E.A.R.* and *Fallout 3*.[25] *Blitz: The League* has scenes of football players hiring prostitutes and engaging in drug deals.

Nor is it difficult for kids to get *Grand Theft Auto*, which presents drive-by shootings and drug dealing as cool, and awards points for killing innocent people and for having sex with prostitutes.

In *Clock Tower 3* a little girl has her head smashed with a sledgehammer and a screaming old woman is lowered into a vat of acid. In *Carmageddon*

First-person shooter *Call of Duty: Ghosts* (2013), the tenth installment in the *Call of Duty* franchise.

and *Twisted Metal* the player scores points for running over pedestrians. Similar brutality runs through other games as game designers vie for viciousness. *Quake* lets the players digitally superimpose images of people and places they know to customize the game. As video games become the storytellers for the younger generation, the cry for government regulation grows louder from many camps.

Some games are damned as sexist and racist. In one game, *Ethnic Cleansing* (2002), points are awarded for killing African American, Latino, and Jewish characters. Another game, *Border Patrol* (2002), awards points for killing Mexican children and pregnant women.[26] We are confronted with more than the familiar question of whether fictional violence leads to real violence. Do such blatantly racist video games serve to undo the efforts of schools and governments to foster a more tolerant society? And what can be done about it in a democracy that prizes freedom of expression?

▶ CRITICISM AND PRAISE

Doom and *Grand Theft Auto* have been denounced again and again for glorifying acts that in real life earn long prison sentences. The protests have had negligible effects. Criticized as lacking morals and being "ethically reprehensible," the games won praise for the quality of their graphics and game play. Such praise is reminiscent of the uproar that greeted the films *Birth of a Nation* and *Triumph of the Will*, movies that were also praised for their artistry and condemned for their content.

RATING GAMES

Complaints against offensive games led eventually to a self-protective, industry-designed rating system. Hollywood had taken the same step with its G, PG, R and NC-17 ratings in hopes of avoiding government censorship. The AAMA (American Amusement Machine Association) and the Entertainment Software Rating Board representing the video game industry created this ratings system in the hope that its own controls would avoid government laws:

EC: for children

E: for everyone

E10+: for everyone ages 10 and up

T: for teens

M: for mature

AO: for adults only

In 2011 the Federal Trade Commission sent teenagers into stores to try to buy games rated Mature. They were able to do so 13 percent of the time. They could buy R-rated DVDs 20 percent of the time.[27]

The U.S. Supreme Court in 2011 struck down a California law to limit violent games, saying the ban went too far to limit free speech. Senators Joseph Lieberman and Sam Brownback have asked this: "Defenders of these games say that they are mere fantasy and harmless role-playing, but is it really in the best interest of a child to play the role of a murderous psychopath? Is it all just good fun to positively reinforce virtual slaughter? Is it truly harmless to simulate mass murder?" The senators led hearings that industry executives chose to avoid.[28]

▶ VIOLENT GAMES AND BEHAVIOR

A number of studies have shown a correlation between playing violent games and violent behavior by children.[29] The more time spent playing electronic games, the lower the school performance. Teens who played violent games did worse in school than teens who did not. Boys and girls who preferred violent video games were more likely to get into arguments with their teachers. They were also more likely to get into physical fistfights.[30] Eugene Provenzo, a University of Kentucky professor of education who called video games "a teaching machine," added, "When violence is stylized, romanticized and choreographed, it can be stunningly beautiful and seductive. At the same time, it encourages children and adolescents to assume a rhetorical stance that equates violence with style and personal empowerment."[31]

Military games, such as the wartime-focused *Call of Duty* series, with intense, realistic, and brutal action, are best sellers. The U.S. Army has used video games as training material for recruits. For example, *Full Spectrum Warrior* teaches maneuvers in an urban environment along with hand-eye coordination and "muscle memory." Skill at the joystick may aid future pilots as well as assassins. *America's Army*, a training and recruiting game supported by the U.S. Army, had more than 6 million registered players in 2006. *Time* magazine, referring to the potential of this cross between *The Sims* and *Doom*, called it a "killer app."[32] The British army trained troops with a version of another military game, *Half-Life*. One of its developers noted that the commercial version of the game had to be altered for military use to remove some of its fantasy. In combat, the soldier who is shot doesn't simply get up and continue to fight.

Some games have modern political connections, and they reflect the emotionally charged political climates where they are sold. For example, particularly after the 9/11 attacks, some games such as *America's Army* had Arabs as villains, just as some films did. On the other hand, *Under Ash* and its sequel, *Under Siege*, are just the opposite. Their hero is a young Arab who shoots and throws stones at Israeli soldiers and civilian settlers. The game makers recognize it as a first person shooter game, but contend it is a call for dialogue, coexistence, and peace.[33]

▶ ONLINE MULTIPLAYER GAMES

Multiplayer gamers send text or voice messages to each other while they battle assorted demons or other players, or try to avoid battle altogether. Friends and fellow workers take supporting online roles in team play. For them, cooperation is more important than conflict, and that attracts women to the game. If your character meets another character in the game, you can just sit around and chat while other players look for players to exterminate.

One way or another, players can reach out and touch someone without actually touching. Yet social get-togethers online have sometimes expanded to get-togethers in real life. People in the same community have established clubs and luncheon groups. Some players have met for dates. A few who met in game play have married. It has been said that the players have taken the game over from the designers.[34]

As of 2013, choosing among more than four dozen languages, an estimated 7 million players worldwide of *World of Warcraft* surrounded themselves with reference books, maps, and one or two computers for daily or all-night adventures in a medieval fantasy world where a player's avatar can make friends or slay enemies. The game combines sexy images plus dragons and sword fights with player teamwork. To participate in such online games, each player pays about U.S.$15 a month. This has led to friendships being created and solidified, to relationships that bloom into marriages.[35]

A survey reported that the average age of players of another large multiplayer game, *EverQuest*, was 25. About one in six players was a woman, two out of three were single, and one player in five had children. One person in three said making friends was the most important reason for playing.[36]

While conservative Christian groups have argued that the Dungeons & Dragons games encourage worship of the occult, violent behavior, and suicides, Christian-themed games are commonly sold.[37] *Left Behind: Eternal Forces* was in the genre of the *Left Behind* books that imagine a world in which the elect are lifted into Heaven and the rest suffer the eternal penalties of the damned. The game has fighting, suspense, and romance, along with Biblical references. Critics say it promotes intolerance and religious warfare.[38] In 2008, the game was given away free, a kind of Gideon Bible for the new century.

A different complaint about all online games comes from social scientists who think it is not healthy for a nation that so many of its citizens—and voters—are so wrapped up in an ideal but artificial environment that they neglect our messy real world.[39]

▶ REAL MONEY CHANGES HANDS

Players advertise on game websites that they own certain virtual (not real) game items that are hard to win in the game. These are for sale for real dollars—in some cases, thousands of dollars. Starting with an investment of U.S.$9.95, Ailin Graef, born in China and living in Germany, earned more than U.S.$1 million buying, building, selling, and trading virtual property in *Second Life*.[40] She is not alone in playing to accumulate an online treasure to sell for real money. *EverQuest* hosts a site, "Station Exchange," where players can buy or sell—for real money—weapons, play money, or entire characters. After learning that the game generates several million dollars each month—real dollars—in game economic activity, a Congressional subcommittee met to considered taxing those who have prospered from the sale of these fantasy assets.

Before its new owner, Electronic Arts, shut it down in 2013 because of waning public interest, Playfish, a maker of online games, reported selling 90 million virtual items a day to players of its games on Facebook, MySpace, and other social websites, and on iGoogle and iPhone Platforms.[41] These players tend virtual farms, look after pets, or enjoy being virtual gangsters with virtual guns. Game play is free. The virtual products demand real cash.

Why would people pay real money for imaginary property? One reason is that it takes many hours of game play to accumulate the virtual goods; paying cash is a shortcut. As for how much something is truly worth, the law of supply and demand operates.

An industry has sprung up to help frustrated players negotiate their way through games. The player who cannot figure out how to cross a bridge, enter a room, or get past a troll can find the answers in books that supply either hints, which many players prefer, or actual directions. These guidebooks are known as "hint books," "walkthroughs," or strategy "cheat sheets." They are the *SparkNotes* and *CliffsNotes* of the video game world. Some games contain their own "cheats," built-in codes that give the players a boost. The cheats can also be found on the Internet.

▶ GAMES AND LIFE

Are these games? If you think of a game as a contest that has an ending, a winner and a loser, perhaps the online virtual worlds are not quite games. Some games feature their attached chat rooms. Several sites, such as Games Chat, G4, and Kidzworld, are chat rooms mostly about video games. Some of the newest games allow modification by the players, building choice as players let their imaginations flow about the persons they would like to be and what they would like to own. Something of the same motivation is true for video games of professional sports and the assembling of dream teams.

Wherever you look, video games have entered into the activities of ordinary life. We are adapting ourselves to the video game tool, changing how learning and so much else have traditionally been done. Military forces and corporations use them for training. Educators design them for teaching at the college level. Kids learn math and vocabulary from *Reader Rabbit* and geography from *Carmen Sandiego*. Faith-based games impart religious values. The Wii games and *Dance Dance Revolution* provide physical exercise. Surgeons and pilots have even reported improved hand-eye coordination.

In development as this book edition was written, the Oculus Rift, a headset device, promises to eliminate image frames and provide a totally surrounding 3-D experience for game playing and such other experiences as *Magic School Bus* field trips.

Along with a number of educators, James Paul Gee has argued that a study of game psychology can improve educational methods. "I have first wanted to argue that good video games build into their very designs good learning principles and that we should use these principles, with or without games, in schools, workplaces, and other learning sites . . . Through good game design we can leverage deeper and deeper learning as a form of pleasure in people's everyday lives, without any hint of school or schooling."[42]

Meanwhile, dreamers encounter other dreamers at online communities. Once again, by their choices the users dictate the direction that a communication medium takes.[43] From these choices has arisen a culture.

▶ TIMELINE

1952   Game written for Harvard doctoral dissertation played on EDSAC computer.

1958   At Brookhaven Lab, nuclear physicist designs a video game, *Tennis for Two*.

1960   PLATO educational system looks for ways that video games can teach.

1961   *Spacewar* at MIT is first interactive computer game.

1968   Ralph Baer produces games played on television sets.

1971   *Computer Space* is the first video arcade game.

1972   Atari's *Pong*, a hit in arcades, taverns, starts video games as major industry.

1974   Arcade video game *Tank* uses ROM chips to store graphics.

1975   100,000 coin-operated video games are played in the United States alone.

        Gunfight uses a microprocessor instead of hardwired circuits.

1980   *Zork* attracts players to adventure games.

1981   *Pac-Man* and *Donkey Kong* dominate the arcade video game world.

        Some games use holograms.

1982   Disney's *Tron* game earns more than *Tron* movie.

        U.S. Surgeon General calls video games evil.

1985   Kids can't get enough of *Super Mario Brothers*.

        Tetris is developed by a Russian programmer.

1986	*Gauntlet* is a multi-user dungeon (MUD) game for up to four players.
1989	Research blames video games for poor physical fitness of U.S. schoolchildren.
	Nintendo's hand-held Game Boy sells for U.S.$109.
1994	Total annual sales of video games: U.S.$3 billion.
	Senate probe of video game violence results in rating board, rating system.
	Sony PlayStation is released in the United States, a huge hit.
1998	Sony's *EverQuest* multiplayer online game attracts tens of thousands worldwide.
1999	Video games bring in more money than movie box offices do.
	Columbine High School killings blamed partly on *Doom*, *Duke Nukem* fixation.
2000	*The Sims* is a big hit with families.
2001	From Microsoft: Xbox game player.
	From Nintendo: the GameCube.
2004	More than half of all Americans play video games.
	*Grand Theft Auto: San Andrea*s sells 2 million plus copies in first week.
2006	*World of Warcraft* has 6 million online players worldwide.
	Nintendo game controller Wii responds to hand, body movements.
2007	China combats online game addiction; cuts points in half after three hours' play.
	More than 6 million "residents" of *Second Life*, but not all are active.
2009	*Wii Sports* breaks video game records with more than 40 million sales.
2010	New motion-sensing video games compete with Wii.
2011	*Call of Duty: Modern Warfare 3* grosses U.S.$1 billion in 16 days.
2012	Of video game players, more are adult women (30 percent) than boys under 18.
2013	*Call of Duty: Ghosts* grosses U.S.$1 billion in one day.

▶ NOTES

1 "Modern Warfare 3 Sells 6.5M On Launch Day In North America, UK," *Gamasutra*, November 11, 2011, http://www.gamasutra.com/view/news/38530/Modern_Warfare_3_Sells_65M_On_Launch_Day_In_North_America_UK.php.

2 Kevin Lynch, "Confirmed: Grand Theft Auto Breaks 6 Sales World Records," *GuinnessWorldRecords.com*, October 8, 2013, http://www.guinnessworldrecords.com/news/2013/10/confirmed-grand-theft-auto-breaks-six-sales-world-records-51900/.

3 Stephen Rex Brown, "'Call of Duty: Ghosts' Crosses $1B in Single-Day Video Game Sales Record," *Daily News*, November 6, 2013, http://www.nydailynews.com/entertainment/games/call-duty-ghosts-crosses-1b-single-day-video-game-sales-record-article-1.1508704.

4 *The Economist* presented a broad analysis of the video game industry in a special report, December 10, 2011, 1–12.

5 James Paul Gee, *What Video Games Have to Teach Us About Learning and Literacy* (New York: Palgrave Macmillan, 2004) 13, 204.

6 Speech delivered by Steve Jobs, 1998, http://www.imore.com/steve-jobs-tvs-computers-merge.

7 *Entertainment Software Association Report, 2013*, http://www.theesa.com/facts/pdfs/esa_ef_2013.pdf.

8 See http://www.videotopia.com/intro.htm.

9 TED talk with Jane McGonigal, March 2010, http://www.ted.com/speakers/jane_mcgonigal.

10 Ted Friedman, "Making Sense of Software: Computer Games and Interactive Textuality," in Steven G. Jones, ed. *Cybersociety* (Thousand Oaks, CA: Sage Publications, 1995).

11 *Nursing Spectrum*, January 3, 2005.

12 See "Asia Is Still the Hotbed for Gaming," no. 9, in Lisa Galarneau, "2014 Global Gaming Stats: Who's Playing What, and Why?," *Big Fish*, January 16, 2014, http://www.bigfishgames.com/blog/2014-global-gaming-stats-whos-playing-what-and-why/.

13 Learn more at http://evo.shoryuken.com.

14 Some of the more common ailments related to video game play may be found in Bahar Gholipour, "Nintendinitis, Playstation Rash and Other Odd Technology-Related Injuries," *Mother Nature Network*, April 13, 2013, http://www.mnn.com/green-tech/gadgets-electronics/stories/nintendinitis-playstation-rash-and-other-odd-technology.

15 James C. Rosser, Jr. et al., "The Impact of Video Games on Training Surgeons in the 21st Century," *Archives of Surgery*, vol. 142, no. 2, February 2007: 181–186.

16 John Seabrook, "Game Master," *The New Yorker*, November 6, 2006, http://www.newyorker.com/archive/2006/11/06/061106fa_fact?currentPage=all.

17 Ingrid Lunden, "Angry Birds Maker Rovio Says 2012 Sales Up 101% to $195M with Merchandising, IP 45% of That; Net Profit $71M," *TC*, April 3, 2013,

http://techcrunch.com/2013/04/03/rovios-revenues-up-101-to-195m-non-games-45-of-that-net-profit-71m/.

18 Andrew Webster, "Half a Billion People Have Installed 'Candy Crush Saga,'" *The Verge*, November 15, 2013, http://www.theverge.com/2013/11/15/5107794/candy-crush-saga-500-million-downloads.

19 B. De Waal, "Motivations for Video Game Play," MA thesis, School of Communication, Simon Fraser University, 1995.

20 *2012 Sales, Demographic and Usage Data*, Entertainment Software Association, p4, http://www.theesa.com/facts/pdfs/ESA_EF_2012.pdf.

21 J. C. Herz, *Joystick Nation* (Boston: Little, Brown and Company, 1997) 172.

22 Richard Alleyne, "Playing the Video Game 'Tetris' Could Reduce Trauma, Claim Oxford University," *The Telegraph*, January 6, 2009, http://www.telegraph.co.uk/science/science-news/4142908/Playing-the-video-game-Tetris-could-reduce-trauma-claim-Oxford-University.html.

23 K. E. Scheibe and M. Erwin, "The Computer as Altar," *Journal of Social Psychology*, vol. 108, 1979: 103–109.

24 Study headed by Dr. Vincent Mathews, Indiana University School of Medicine, reported November 29, 2006, http://www.medicalnewstoday.com/articles/57771.php and *Newsweek*, November 28, 2006.

25 Holly Green, "Press X to Eat Flesh," *Gameranx*, December 12, 2012, http://www.gameranx.com/features/id/11408/article/press-x-to-eat-flesh-10-examples-of-cannibalism-in-games.

26 "Outrage over Racist Online Video Game Targeting Mexicans," *National Latina Institute for Reproductive Health*, http://latinainstitute.wordpress.com/2009/05/19/outrage-over-racist-online-video-game-targeting-mexicans/.

27 Christopher Rick, "Games Industry Tops Retail Enforcement of Age-Rated Material Says FTC," *Gamers Daily News*, April 21, 2011, www.gamersdailynews.com/story-23276-Games-Industry-Tops-Retail-Enforcement-of-Agerated-Material-Says-FTC.html.

28 Congressional hearings held or planned were summarized in an opinionated article by Anthony L. Fisher, "Sex, Violence and Satan: 6 Unbelievably Dumb Congressional Hearings," *Reason.com*, January 18, 2013, http://reason.com/reasontv/2013/01/18/a-brief-history-of-dumb-censorship.

29 For example, read the discussion in Soledad Liliana Escobar-Chaves and Craig A. Anderson, "Media and Risky Behaviors," *Children and Electronic Media*, vol. 18, no. 1, Spring 2008, http://futureofchildren.org/publications/journals/article/index.xml?journalid=32&articleid=60&sectionid=291.

30 Steven Kent, *Minneapolis Star Tribune*, November 6, 2004: E1.

31 Testimony at the 1993 Congressional Committee hearing reported in Kent, 471ff.

32 *Time*, February 28, 2005: 43.

33 Gee, 156, and underash.com.

34 Brad King and John Borland, *Dungeons and Dreamers: The Rise of Computer Game Culture from Geek to Chic* (New York: McGraw-Hill/Osborne, 2003) 170.

35 Luke Karmali, "World of Warcraft Down to 7.7 Million Subscribers," *IGN*, July 26, 2013, http://www.ign.com/articles/2013/07/26/world-of-warcraft-down-to-77-million-subscribers.

36 King and Borland, 224–225.

37 King and Borland, 72.

38 Cathy Lynn Grossman, "Critics: 'Left Behind' Game Glorifies Violence," *USA Today*, December 14, 2006, http://usatoday30.usatoday.com/tech/gaming/2006-12-13-left-behind-controversy_x.htm?POE=TECISVA.

39 For example, see Garry Crawford *Video Gamers* (New York: Routledge, 2012).

40 Rob Hof, "Second Life's First Millionaire," *Business Week*, May 1, 2006, cover story.

41 Daniel Lyons, "Money for Nothing," *Newsweek*, March 29, 2010: 22.

42 Gee, 215.

43 Will Wright, "Dream Machines," *Wired*, April, 2006: 112.

16 Persuasion: The Push Never Stops

What in human interaction is so common as the effort to convince? If nothing else is consistent in history, you can count on the desire of almost everyone to try to persuade someone else of something. The push to win over others has traveled across the centuries on a parallel track with informing others. It operates through essays, drawings, photos, slogans, editorials, advertising, public relations, government propaganda, and blogs. The media that are used to inform and entertain you are also used to convince you of something. So is this paragraph.

Teaching the art of persuasion dates back at least to the ancient Greek and Roman rhetoricians who sought not only to convince but lectured and wrote about the means of doing so. The classical rhetoricians identified the appeals to *ethos* (ideals), *pathos* (emotion) and *logos* (reason). Rhetoric was taught from ancient times through the Middle Ages and well into the 19th century as one of the *trivium*, along with grammar and logic, the foundation of a liberal education. Among the most famous ancient writers on rhetoric were Gorgias, Isocrates, Plato, Aristotle, Cicero, and Quintilian. Persuasion has always mattered.

▶ THE START OF ADVERTISING

In ancient Greece and Carthage a whitewashed board announced a gladiatorial contest. The ruins of Pompeii reveal a terra cotta image taking the place of words for an illiterate population. In the Roman world, a sign of a goat signified a dairy. A boy being whipped signified a school.

Advertising signs and street criers grew more common as medieval town populations increased. Like the ancient ads, these fall in the category of information rather than persuasion. The spread of printing in Europe brought the posting of printed handbills listing books for sale, a logical activity because printers of handbills also printed books. A few 16th-century posters survive, again basically informational. The 17th century saw the start in England and France of public registers, government publications where buyers and sellers could post notices. It was also the century of the first newspapers and the first newspaper ads.

Shakespeare and the King James Bible used the word "advertisement" to mean "warning" or "notification." The term "*siquis*" from the Latin *si quis* ("if anyone" desires) meant a notice. It was replaced when the words "advices" and then "advert' and "advertising" gained currency. Also used were the pejorative terms "puff" and "puffers," from which "puffery" derives.[1]

Handbills became fancier, with woodcut illustrations, hand lettering, and border designs. The 18th century introduced the billboard.

The governments that controlled newspapers also controlled advertising. Britain imposed a tax on each page of a newspaper and a heavier tax on each advertisement. Censors were ever present to look for anything smelling of sedition or blasphemy. The powerful guilds watched for any sales effort that might encroach on their control of trade. Nevertheless, as trade grew so did notices of goods for sale. In Paris, *Les Petites Affiches* (*Little Notices*) reported the sale of property and goods, currency exchange rates, and new books. Germany, England, and the American colonies developed their own newspapers devoted to commerce and notices for auctions, houses for rent, spices for sale, and other merchandise just arrived by ship, plus rewards for runaway horses or runaway apprentices. Before the Civil War, notices of slaves for sale were common.

Persuasion crept more forcefully into 19th-century advertising with notices of patent medicines guaranteed to cure a long list of ailments. These ads followed what advertising leader Rosser Reeves argued was a basis of advertising: if you buy *this* product, you will get *that* specific benefit.[2] Since the patent medicines failed to cure anything except the thickness of wallets, a certain skepticism arose. The conjoined twins of advertising claims and public skepticism have been together ever since.

A PRICE FOR OPINIONS

Expressing political opinions via mediated communication in the hope of swaying opinion has a long history. The first broadsheets, newsbooks, and newspapers in Europe did not differentiate between news and opinion, but most did not stray from what the government would approve, for the printer's freedom and perhaps his neck were at risk.

Printers were forbidden to publish without permission, evidence that even in the age of the divine right of kings those in power were aware of the potential for mischief of political expression in print. Yet, a few printers dared to defy authorities. At least one printer in Protestant-controlled Elizabethan England, William Carter, was hanged, drawn, and quartered in 1584 for printing pamphlets that supported the Catholic cause.

▶ ADVERTISING AGENCIES

Mass advertising began during the Industrial Revolution. For mass *production* of goods there must be mass *demand*. This requires mass *information* and *persuasion*. Newspapers offered advertisers such improvements as rotary presses, paper from trees, and mass mailing to spread their messages.[3] Factories turned out goods and needed customers. Workers received cash wages that they could spend on what the factories produced. As production of a variety of goods and mass distribution grew, it was inevitable that mass marketing would become part of the process, for the goods had to be sold. Advertising did more than keeping factories running and stocking home larders with food and closets with clothes. It affected our morals, manners, customs, and the other elements of our culture.[4]

Marketing meant advertising beyond simple notices to *meet* demand. Advertising was needed to *create* demand. At the beginning of the 20th century, the national magazine was the natural vehicle for national advertising of factory goods, starting with a campaign for the Columbia brand of a new means of transportation, the bicycle. Its success led the way to national ads for a newer wheeled conveyance, the automobile.

The advertising agent as a wholesale buyer of newspaper space began in France. Entrepreneurs bought space in bulk from newspapers and magazines, then sold it retail to the manufacturers, offering advice as needed at first, but no extra service. Their role took on added value when they could offer cut rates to national businesses to advertise in several dozen newspapers at a time with the same ad. They also revealed actual circulation figures, which differed from the inflated numbers that publishers claimed. They found a typical niche as middleman in a wholesale-retail operation.

Eventually space brokers became full-service advertising agencies. The practice spread to the United States and evolved into the advertising agency that could offer the sellers of goods a range of services such as ad layout and copy writing, as well as space brokering for both newspapers and magazines. They designed the ads, wrote the copy, drew or photographed the illustrations, and handled ad budgets. Advertising expanded into campaigns managed by agencies. Out of this came slogans, branding, trademarks, and, in the early 20th century, the Audit Bureau of Circulation that produced verifiable circulation figures instead of publishers' myths.

Curiously, some publishers regarded the acceptance of ads directly from advertisers as beneath their dignity. They sold ad space as a kind of *noblesse oblige*, the moral obligation of powerful people to treat weaker people with kindness. Asked by an advertising agent for circulation figures, *Harper's Magazine* executives responded by rejecting his advertising. This attitude certainly did not stand the test of time.

Competition to newspaper and magazine advertising came from direct-mail catalogues that contained nothing but ads, especially those of Montgomery Ward and Sears Roebuck. Most Americans lived out in the country, far from stores. These "wish books" were treasured, despite their reputation of being the wherewithal of outhouses.

The combination of mail order catalogues and brand names led to the decline of an American tradition, the traveling salesman or "drummer" who carried his battered case to small towns around the country, giving a personal touch and a human face to selling. A writer for the Lord & Thomas agency said that ad agencies were not selling space or slogans, but salesmanship in print. It wasn't the same.

▶ USING PSYCHOLOGY

As advertising agency pioneer J. Walter Thompson noted, "The purpose of advertising is to sell goods to people living at a distance." That raised issues of trust, for buyer and seller could not look each other in the eye or shake hands in the time-honored way of closing a deal. Historian Richard Ohmann observed that in transactions generated only from advertising no one could say, "'My word is my bond.' The seller is a stranger; buyers are masses; anonymity prevails."[5] Here in the early years of mass communication, the separation from what was close at hand was at work, replaced by a preference for what was at a distance. It was a communication with unknown others.

Before advertising campaigns in magazines and newspapers, customers did not ask for a brand. Soap flakes were ladled out of a grocer's barrel. To sell a pickle, the grocer rolled up his sleeve and plunged his arm into a barrel of brine. Butter and lard were scooped from large tubs. The druggist squirted soft-drink syrup from a bottle and mixed it with carbonated water. Customers bought what the grocer had in stock without wondering who manufactured it.

Advertising of brand names changed all that and introduced packaging for food and household staples. Flour was just flour until it became Gold Medal Flour or Pillsbury Flour. Tea and coffee were just that until it mattered that they were Lipton's and Maxwell House. The cracker barrel around which men sat to talk really existed until the National Biscuit Company began its advertising campaign for Uneeda Biscuits. This campaign convinced housewives that crackers were better for their families if they arrived wrapped in wax paper inside a cardboard box than if they were pulled out by the grocer's unwashed hand from a barrel or a bin.

To create a human face for printed ads, agencies invented icons to symbolize products, such as the Morton Salt girl with an umbrella, the sleepy boy holding a Fisk tire, Aunt Jemima, Betty Crocker, and Nipper, the dog listening to a Victor record. Today it might be a real elephant, an animated gecko, chipmunks, a monkey galloping on a dog, and the ageless Betty Crocker. Product testimonials now given by baseball players and movie stars were once sought from opera singers, boxers, and explorers.

▶ BRAND LOYALTY

Advertisers tried to build "brand loyalty" in consumer purchasing decisions. *Printers' Ink*, published for the advertising industry, said in an 1895 editorial that the ad writers would have to study psychology because "The advertising writer and the teacher have one great object in common—to influence the human mind."[6]

Research grew in scope and included studies of human behavior managed by psychologists with PhD degrees who examined subtle differences in motivation and consumer activity. For instance, pursuing the psychology of fear, advertisers created campaigns that ran for years promising protection against such previously overlooked bodily demons as halitosis, gingivitis and "BO" (body odor).

The growing advertising industry managed to survive a reputation for fraudulent practices during scandals revolving around rigged lottery schemes and worthless patent medicines. *The Ladies' Home Journal* took the lead in publishing chemical analyses of widely advertised nostrums, revealing that alcohol and cocaine were added. Morphine was an ingredient in a soothing syrup for babies. Truth-in-advertising was codified into law, starting with New York State. The pharmaceutical industry itself tried with mixed success to set ethical standards. The government stepped in by passing the Federal Food and Drugs Act in 1906.

The early 20th century brought more ads based on a naked appeal to emotions. For example, at the start of World War I, the British government needed soldiers for the brutal trench warfare that would take so many lives. Its advertising included such questions as, "What will you answer when your children grow up, and say, 'Father, why weren't you a soldier, too?'"

Radio broadcasting added slogans and singing commercials to rattle around inside people's heads. Hearing a jingle sung innumerable times led some people to sing or hum it themselves at odd times. Anglo-Saxon males dominated ad agencies from the start, a condition recalled by the *Mad Men* television series. It was reflected in advertising images that too often showed women as appendages to men, and almost never featured darker-skinned people or those without conventional Anglo-Saxon features.

Slogans in both radio and television commercials became so familiar that they identified a fellow American in other parts of the world. Among them: "Where's the beef?," "Don't leave home without it," "Be all you can be," "Breakfast of champions," "You deserve a break today," and "Strong enough for a man, but made for a woman."

In the cities and along the sides of the roads, billboards appeared. Signs advertising tobacco and patent medicine went up on fences, barns, bridges, large rocks, and even curbstones. Vacation destinations, roads, and railroad pathways have been favored locations for billboards, to the point that a few communities have passed laws limiting such signage; later, some laws faced First Amendment challenges. Serial signs along highways, notably the Burma Shave rhymes, became part of the American culture, changing the look of the landscape. In 1891, the first electric sign was installed on Broadway, and later the street would come to be called "The Great White Way." Shortly after the Wright brothers took to the air, advertising did as well, and soon the skies were filled with skywriting, banner towing, and ads on the sides of blimps.

Today, outdoor (or "out of home") advertising has expanded to taxi roofs, gasoline pumps, and the sides of buses. Meanwhile, the billboard industry has embraced digital technology, offering signs that switch messages every few seconds.

▶ ADVERTISING SPREADS

During the Depression of the 1930s, advertising was an obvious target for a nation's discontent. Yet it survived, expanded, and embedded itself not only in the United States but in every country of the world, including those that had nothing good to say about capitalism. The outcome? Advertising today is everywhere in the world, including the government-run media of the communist countries that damned it.

Winston Churchill once wrote enthusiastically of advertising, "It sets before a man the goal of a better home, better clothing, better food for himself and his family. It spurs individual exertion and greater production. It brings together in fertile union those things which otherwise would never have met."[7]

During much of the 20th century newspapers dominated mass communication. First radio then television chipped away at their financial base. In the new century Internet ads have cut deeply into newspaper revenue. Craigslist, a network of classified ad websites, has been partially depriving metropolitan newspapers of a main income source.

We are little more aware of most ads than we are of the air around us. One researcher estimated that the average American sees or hears 3,000 ads a day.[8] The inevitable result of such an assault is a numbness to ads that advertisers try to break through. Another result of this saturation, critics allege, is that an increasingly materialistic public has learned to define happiness in terms of ownership: never satisfied, always wanting.

All of advertising has formed the basis of the consumer culture that is so pervasive in American society and has spread to cultures around the world, based on the premises that buying something solves emotional problems and that worth can be measured by ownership. Advertising has stirred emotions, changed attitudes, created appetites, made people want what they do not have, dissatisfied with what they do have. However, when something is added, such as a hankering for certain advertised products, it replaces something else, such as a yearning for simplicity. Advertising has given values to the public but these values, such as a standardization of judgment and taste or the belief that purchasing certain goods will bring happiness, are not always in accord with the values taught in the home, in the school, or in the pulpit. Mountains of credit card debt and the notorious American paucity of saving for old age may indicate that advertising has been more successful than is healthy for the nation.[9]

ADVERTISING FOR A MATE

The advantages of advertising were not lost on those seeking to improve their romantic relationships. Long before Facebook, the personal ad offered a break from the tradition of arranged marriages, introductions by friends, and other conventional ways of connecting with prospective mates.

Starting in the 19th century, potential suitors advertised themselves. A man suspiciously regarded as an "adventurer" wrote that he wanted to meet a younger woman with property. A woman was more likely to appeal for a potential mate by identifying herself as "upstanding, virtuous," adding that no adventurers need apply. Match.com and the lovelorn ad continue that tradition of longing for romance and finding unblushing exaggeration.

Advertising for love and companionship through the media has grown exponentially. In the most personal way, mediated communication has replaced the tradition of centuries of family involvement in marriage selection. The traditional marriage broker, the matchmaker, has moved online or on television.

PAYING TO RUN FOR OFFICE

In a perfect world, advertising would be an example of how mediated communication signals a democratic, egalitarian society, for everyone could advertise to everyone else. Yet, we live in an imperfect world, where some people are more able than others to spread their opinions.

The advantage to political candidates who can afford to advertise is frequently commented upon, overshadowing fitness for office. In politics, candidates with deep pockets can buy more advertising than candidates with small budgets.

Despite the accepted doctrine that money buys political power, the former CEO of eBay, Meg Whitman, lost in 2010 after spending U.S.$142 million of her own money ($46.91 per vote) in the race for governor of California. In Connecticut, professional wrestling executive Linda McMahon spent $100.07 of her own fortune per vote and suffered the same fate.

▶ PUBLIC RELATIONS

Keeping pace with advertising, public relations via mediated communication tries to persuade us on business matters of public interest and on political issues, especially the demerits of opposition candidates. Negative advertising is increasingly damned as counter-productive public relations, but increasingly used because negativity, in a word, works.

Publicity, a far-reaching part of public relations, was developed into a raucous art form by the circus impresario P. T. Barnum during the post-Civil

This 1888 advertisement for P. T. Barnum's "Greatest Show on Earth" promises "a strange and amazing show without parallel."

War years. Using trickery and exaggeration with gusto, Barnum planted newspaper stories to get the public excited about Buffalo Bill, Tom Thumb, and the "Swedish Nightingale" Jenny Lind.

When Theodore Roosevelt and the "muckrakers" (Roosevelt's derogatory term) exposés in magazines of big business and big finance, a public relations industry arose in their defense. Over time the industry expanded to include government and other corporate and private organizations. Edward L. Bernays, who styled himself the "father" of public relations, laid out the goal in frank terms. It was, he said, "manipulation."[10]

Since that pejorative assessment, public relations has advanced to something more. Public relations executive Ivy Lee explained its necessity, "The crowd is now in the saddle. The people now rule. We have substituted for the divine right of kings the divine right of the multitude."[11] Lee argued forcefully and usually successfully that public relations should be candid in presenting facts, not hiding them.

The 1930s saw political polls and marketing surveys to examine public opinion as tools of public relations advisors. The Public Relations Society of America was created in 1948. University schools of journalism began to teach PR methods. Today, public relations is a craft taught widely in universities alongside journalism, advertising, and other forms of mediated communication.

The modern philosopher Jürgen Habermas analyzed the rise of publicity and public opinion in his influential book, *The Structural Transformation of the Public Sphere.*[12] He held that a public space existed outside of government, but the growth of commercial mass media turned a critical public into passive consumers.

▶ POLITICAL PERSUASION

William Randolph Hearst's jingoism in the run-up to the Spanish–American War is well documented. Through his newspapers he pushed for American involvement in Cuba and the Philippines. By the advent of World War I, a huge reading public had come into existence. Propaganda led Americans into drum-beating patriotism and the conviction that their armies would quickly carry the day against the wickedest enemy the world had ever known. Government censorship was hardly necessary when publishers considered it more of a duty to raise public morale than dispassionately informing the public.[13] That attitude has carried on in war after war.

The wish to persuade readers to a point of view that will make itself felt at the ballot box continues to be a part of newspaper journalism. Newspapers were joined during the 1930s by radio journalism and commentary, later by television journalism and, at times, situation comedies, and now, in the 21st century, by Internet blogs. People naturally gravitate to others who share their views. That certainly holds for those with extreme views.

Even before the appearance of mass media during the Industrial Revolution, mediated persuasion at a relatively simple level was used to foment revolution, peaceful and otherwise. That was true when Martin Luther's theses were translated into the German vernacular, printed and distributed during the early 16th century. It continued to be true when Thomas Paine published his pamphlets in American colonial times. Today the small media of blogs are making serious inroads into the information monopoly of established large media.

Before the blogosphere, to share your views with like-minded thinkers you had to at least get dressed and go out to where they were. Now you can stay home in your pajamas while you share your thoughts, vicious or benign. One research study concluded that putting together people who think alike polarizes them even more. Hawks become more hawkish, doves more dovish, and racists more racist.[14] Accepting that this is valid for the general population, the study points to a more polarized electorate and less communication between groups with opposing viewpoints. Recent elections bear this out.

Because of modern methods of communication, anti-intellectualism thrives. Ill-informed communicators are able to reach out through media channels to large numbers of people who seem predisposed to being ill informed. In addition, the blogosphere and other tools give everyone a voice; knowledge doesn't matter. In a more genteel past only a small percentage of people ever engaged in intellectual public discourse. The change currently evident comes from the powerful communication tools that are now widely available.

EDWARD R. MURROW

Of the journalists in the past century, no one stood taller than the broadcaster who convinced without hammering his argument. He let his surroundings convey his message.

Reporting from London during the early days of World War II, Edward R. Murrow made it clear that England needed America's support. He did so indirectly because CBS did not allow him a more direct option.

Murrow's baritone spanned the Atlantic Ocean night after night through the "Blitz," but he spoke like the neighbor next door. He let American listeners hear German bombers over the city each night and the footsteps of Londoners resolutely trudging to work the next morning.

For his listeners, the world shrank. No voice may have done so much to bring ordinary American people to sympathize with ordinary British people and ultimately support America's involvement on Britain's side, no sure thing one generation removed from World War I in a nation with millions who took pride in their German heritage.

▶ PERSUADING BY RADIO

The history of the United States is peppered with political violence. Yet during the "golden age" of radio in the 1930s and 1940s, the streets were comparatively quiet. Part of the reason: most Americans chose to listen. They stayed home close to the radio and looked forward each evening to news and opinion from a favorite commentator, a span of 15 minutes that put an exclamation point on the day.

These were the times of the Depression, then gathering war clouds followed by World War II. Radio delivered the ready answers from left and right. Whether or not you agreed with what you heard, the explanations from a familiar voice may have had a "we're-in-this-together" effect even when this was not what the commentator intended to convey. The best of these "excess prophets"[15] had a folksy manner, taking advantage of the apparent intimacy of the radio medium.

CBS television anchor Bob Schieffer observed that successful presidents knew how to use the dominant medium of their times. Theodore Roosevelt developed personal friendships with a number of well-known magazine journalists. As president, Franklin Delano Roosevelt recognized the intimacy of radio with considerable success in his "fireside chats." John F. Kennedy was elected because he understood television in 1960 and Richard Nixon did not.[16] In 2008 and again in 2012 Barack Obama displayed a feeling for the Internet that the campaigns for John McCain and later Mitt Romney failed to grasp fully.

▶ FAIRNESS DOCTRINE

Expressing a station's political opinions during broadcasting's first two decades was routine. In fact, the right to air opinions was not given much thought until a challenge to a station's license, which included the charge that it editorialized, led to the Federal Communication Commission's (FCC's) Mayflower Decision in 1941 that broadcasts must not take political positions. Broadcasters who wanted a newspaper's freedom of choice to say anything, as embodied in the First Amendment, rebelled. They pressed the FCC to reverse the ruling.

Eight years later, the FCC did just that, but went further than the broadcasters intended. In 1949, in its Fairness Doctrine, the FCC said not only that stations *may* offer political opinions, but also that they *must* do so, seeking out matters of importance to a community. This hardly satisfied broadcasters. They wanted the same freedom of choice that newspapers enjoyed.

Meanwhile, the Fairness Doctrine was a catalyst in ending tobacco advertising on television. A successful petition to allow anti-smoking commercials as a counter to cigarette commercials frightened the tobacco industry into calling for a law that banned all broadcast advertising related to tobacco. Broadcasters bridled at the hypocrisy of support for this law by magazines and newspapers that continued to reap millions from tobacco ads. After strong criticism from broadcasters who argued that the Fairness Doctrine chilled free speech, the FCC abandoned most of the Fairness Doctrine's provisions in 1987 and wiped out the rest in 2011.

▶ POLITICAL CARTOONING

Drawn images also persuade. Drawing or sculpting figures for lampooning, which led to political cartooning, traces back to the ancient Chinese, Egyptians, Greeks, and Romans. We can't know for sure if the pot-bellied Chinese gentlemen who survive in carvings were being ridiculed. Nor is it known if any of the foxes, lions, dogs, and monkeys behaving like humans in Egyptian carvings represented actual people. Nevertheless, the comic touches are undeniable. Did tweaking the powerful with these ancient images have an effect? Human nature being what it is, a smirk or two would not be out of the question.

Greek caricaturists seemed to be poking fun at the gods in images on pottery. Graffiti artists drew and carved satirical sketches on a variety of media that survive in Rome and Pompeii. During the Middle Ages, when cathedral windows told Biblical stories to the illiterate faithful, sketch artists chose religious images such as the devil and the grim reaper. Their work in prayer books displays a high degree of artistic skill.[17]

The late Middle Ages, the Age of Enlightenment, and the Victorian Age brought forth artists willing to risk official displeasure. In England during the 18th century, the brilliant William Hogarth's sketches showed the moral decay of the city. In the 19th century George Cruikshank exposed the foibles of society and, in a pamphlet that went through 40 printings in six months, attacked government corruption, and James Gilray did not hesitate to caricature leading political figures. In France, Honoré Daumier took aim at government incompetence. In 1832 he went to prison for six months for his caricature of King Louis-Philippe.

In the United States, Thomas Nast's cartoons helped to bring down the corrupt Tweed Ring in New York. One cartoon that found its way to Spain led to the recognition and arrest of the fugitive Boss Tweed, who would die in prison. Nast used his artist's pen to support the abolition of slavery and to protest the plight of Native Americans and Chinese immigrants. But he also used his artistry to express bias against Irish Americans and the Catholic Church. One of Nast's cartoons was credited with the reelection of Abraham Lincoln. He has been called the father of American political cartooning, although some historians bestow that credit on Benjamin Franklin, whose pre-Revolutionary War sketches stirred patriotic fervor.

One of Thomas Nast's final Boss Tweed cartoons. Published in 1886, eight years after Tweed's death, the cartoon points out that though Tweed was dead, bribery and corruption lived on.

▶ NO SIMPLE LIFE

Persuading has marched arm-in-arm with informing throughout recorded history. Both add richness and complexity, not simplicity, to our lives. Our comfort with persuasion and information, and our dependence upon them in mediated communication have become almost as intrinsic as breathing and eating.

Our attachment to media and what it delivers is, in many ways, a reward for labor because we work to pay for our newest media devices and subscriptions, and it is more central to human lives today than ever before. How a particular kind of mediated communication has made a difference in life is not always clear, but we sense that it has altered the human experience.

Whether simplicity once had value to us, we should recognize that a simpler life went out the door when the first radio or television set was carried in, or when going out to the movies became a weekly ritual. It was not long ago that people lived in a narrower world. Some people still do, but the benefits of mediated communication, exchanged for that simpler life, overwhelm any awareness that we have surrendered something. Persuasion with all its complexity cannot be separated from life today. And few of us would truly prefer the simpler life.

▶ TIMELINE

1477   In England, an advertising poster.

1666   After the Great Fire in London, merchants advertise to win back customers.

1704   In the American colonial city of Boston, newspaper ads.

1742   Benjamin Franklin's *General Magazine* prints ads.

1832   Honoré Daumier imprisoned for caricatures of France's king.

1842   Barnum opens the American Museum in New York City; shameless fraud works.

1849   The term "advertising agency" is used by Volney B. Palmer.

1867   Double column advertising appears in newspapers.

1868   Thomas Nast begins cartoon attacks on corrupt Boss Tweed ring.

In Philadelphia, N. W. Ayer & Son begins a full-service advertising agency.

1873   Advertising agents convene in New York.

1880   "Advertising copywriter" becomes an occupation.

1893   *Munsey's Magazine* sells for 10 cents, below production cost; depends on advertising.

1898	Uneeda Biscuits seeks brand loyalty with million dollar ad campaign.
1904	Advertising discovers hard-sell.
1905	Popular actors are used to advertise a product, Murad Cigarettes.
1906	Pure Food and Drug Act requires listing ingredients on product labels.
1911	Sex appeal appears in an ad for Woodbury Soap. The concept works.
1917	The American Association of Advertising Agencies, a trade association, is formed.
1920	Stanley and Helen Resor introduce psychological advertising research.
1922	A commercial is broadcast on radio for real estate near New York City.
	Walter Lippmann's *Public Opinion* is a seminal study of opinion formation.
1923	A sponsored radio program, *The Eveready Hour.*
1928	Edward Bernays, "father" of public relations, writes book about it, *Propaganda.*
1932	George Gallup's opinion poll learns what Americans are thinking.
1941	First television ads; a Bulova watch ticks for a full minute.
1947	American television viewers watch commercials.
1948	The Public Relations Society of America is created.
1949	The Fairness Doctrine requires broadcast advocacy expression.
1957	Vance Packard's best-selling *The Hidden Persuaders* attacks advertising.
1958	The National Association of Broadcasters bans subliminal ads.
1965	British ban televised cigarette advertising.
1971	U.S. Congress bans radio and television cigarette commercials.
1976	The Supreme Court grants advertising First Amendment protection.
1987	The Fairness Doctrine is repealed.
1990	World Wide Web opens a new universe of persuasion opportunities.
1991	Gulf War TV reports show that government learned Vietnam War propaganda lessons.

2006   Arab street riots in response to Danish newspaper cartoons.

2010   U.S. Supreme Court blocks a ban on corporate political spending.

2011   "Arab Spring" shows that social networks can compete with government propaganda.

▶ NOTES

1 Philippe Schuwer, *History of Advertising* (London: Leisure Arts, 1966) 42.

2 ContentEqualsMoney.com, "Conversion Writing Tips from 'Mad Men' Model Rosser Reeves," July 11, 2013, https://contentequalsmoney.com/rosser-reeves-tips/.

3 James R. Beniger, *The Control Revolution* (Cambridge, MA: Harvard University Press, 1986) 18.

4 James Playsted Wood, *The Story of Advertising* (New York: Ronald Press, 1958) 342.

5 Richard Ohmann, *Selling Culture: Magazines, Markets, and Class at the Turn of the Century* (London: Verso, 1996) 106.

6 *Printers' Ink*, October 1895, cited in Wood, 6–7.

7 Wood, 13.

8 Barry Schwartz, *The Paradox of Choice: Why More Is Less* (New York: Harper-Collins, 2004) 53.

9 For a fuller discussion, see C. Edwin Baker, *Advertising and a Democratic Press* (Princeton: Princeton University Press, 1994) 4 ff.

10 He wrote: "The conscious and intelligent manipulation of the organized habits and opinions of the masses is an important element in democratic society. Those who manipulate this unseen mechanism of society constitute an invisible government which is the true ruling power of our country . . . It is they who pull the wires which control the public mind." Edward L. Bernays, *Propaganda* (New York: Horace Liveright, 1928) 9–10.

11 Stuart Ewen, *PR!: A Social History of Spin* (New York: Basic Books, 1996). The author repeats the phrase "The crowd is in the saddle" throughout the book, and makes it the title of Part 2.

12 Translated from the German (1962) and published by the MIT Press, 1989.

13 G. J. Meyer, *A World Undone: The Story of the Great War, 1914 to 1918* (New York: Delacorte Press, 2006) 434.

14 Elizabeth Kolbert, "The Things People Say," *The New Yorker*, November 2, 2009, 110–114. This topic is considered more extensively by Cass R. Sunstein, head of the White House Office of Information and Regulatory Affairs, in five

books: *Republic.com* (2001), *Infotopia* (2006), *Republic.com 2.0* (2007), *Going to Extremes: How Like Minds Unite and Divide* (2009), and *On Rumors: How Falsehoods Spread, Why We Believe Them, What Can Be Done* (2009).

15 A term coined by one of their own, Quincy Howe.

16 Jonathan Alter made this point in a column: *Newsweek*, June , 2006: 35.

17 See Syd Hoff, *Editorial and Political Cartooning* (New York: Stravon Educational Press, 1976) 16–26.

17

Media Matter: Entwined in Human Life

These chapters have taken note of the communication media that have come along since humans decided to keep records. Do we see common factors among them? Or common trends? Are there commonalities among such advances as the adoption of a phonetic alphabet, the inventions of photography and the telegraph, and today's mobile phones, web pages, and blogs? Let us recognize and review some common effects of mediated communication both old and new:

"We're not hibernating this year.
Too much cultural change to keep up with."

- Because of <u>mediated communication</u>, everyone's <u>potential knowledge base has expanded from what one person can be expected to know.</u> It is now <u>boundless.</u> The most educated scholars a few years ago could not have dreamed of the amount of information so readily at hand everywhere.
- <u>Mediated communication has led to new means of education and to libraries holding ever more information remote from the here and now.</u> If we can store information, we can reflect upon the past and <u>build upon that information.</u> We can <u>share</u> it systematically. This happens every day.
- We use mediated communication to take our attention from the *here* to connect to the *there*. The *there* now can be anywhere on Earth at any time in history. The philosopher Martin Heidegger observed that "<u>everything is equally near and equally far.</u>"[1] This can affect not only the information

and entertainment we choose to receive, but where we choose to live and other factors central to our lives.

- The more we use media, the more we separate ourselves from those physically close to us and from our surroundings. In this way mediated communication separates as it connects. McLuhan also spoke of "the isolation of the visual sense by means of alphabet and typography."[2]

- Information, misinformation, and opinions come from people we don't know. From its ancient beginnings, mediated communication has enabled individuals to access information that they came to deeply believe from people they would never meet, people separated by distance, by generation, and by culture and experience.

- Time and attention spent with mediated communication are not spent in other ways. There is always a trade-off. Words, pictures, and sounds occupy our attention. They often drive out silence and any deep thought that accompanies silence.

- Respect for the knowledge of elders, a vital part of every traditional society, diminishes with the arrival of competing, distant standards. In a heavily mediated world, the accumulated wisdom of family and community elders loses value and may become superfluous. Nothing new here. Early printed books brought knowledge that competed with the acquired wisdom of parents and the local elders.

- As new inventions and new methods diffuse into our lives, the number and variety of our choices of information and entertainment grow. Interest grows in what is distant. Life becomes more complex. McLuhan wrote, "We may yet yearn for the simple days of the automobile and the superhighway."[3] And as Postman noted, "The world has never before been confronted with information glut and has hardly had time to reflect on its consequences."[4]

- The experts are not always right. McLuhan spoke of the "bulldog opacity" of scholastic philosophers who ignored the impact of printing. Hollywood executives dragged their feet about sound and color. The popularity of drive-ins should have alerted them to home rentals of movies. The Telefon Hirmondo anticipated broadcasting by decades, but who predicted the role that broadcasting would play in everyday life? Again, when the technology was available, people adapted their lives to the communication tools.

- *Personal* communication uses the expanded tools of *mass* communication. Email users, for example, are certainly aware that *mass* communication intrudes into a means of *personal* communication. As noted, the truly descriptive term is *mediated communication*.

- The expansion of the personal into the mass has weakened the economic underpinnings of traditional mass communication.[5] In the several ways that we read, hear, and view information, the industrial model of mass communication is breaking apart. And national borders matter less.

- Beyond population growth, the number of information *producers* expands as media choices expand. They reach more and more information *consumers.* This was true in the 15th century when Gutenberg began printing. It is true today. When available to everyone, mediated communication has a leveling, democratic effect even if real equality remains out of reach.

- In a mediated world, talent trumps individual expression. We are provided with professional entertainment at the expense of family closeness. Before the phonograph and certainly before broadcasting took hold, enjoyment in the home often came from family members reading, telling stories, playing a musical instrument, or singing to one another. Little of those old pleasures remain in a heavily mediated household.

- Today we never have to separate ourselves from media. As our portable communication tools shrink, thin, add functions and power and capacity, they attach to us like the shirt we put on each day. What cannot walk down the street with us now: songs? news? novels? games? work files? blogs? phone and even visual contacts? All of that can, and more. We never need to be parted from our distant connections.

- Owning or using media takes time and money. Media require not only the hours to use them but also the working hours to pay for them. Those who can afford media often have an important advantage.

- The more educated we are, the more we rely on mediated communication. It is an essential part of becoming a specialist. The content that we choose, of course, determines what we know.

- The effort to convince others continues to increase. With the transmission of knowledge has come persuasion, using every means of communication to that end. One of the commonalities of all media is their use to convince message receivers to buy what the senders sell, not only goods but also opinions.

- Mediated communication of every type is used by rulers to maintain their power and by specialists to retain their influence. Those who gain added power and influence by holding the levers of mediated communication frequently withhold them from those who want to share power or influence. This pattern has ancient roots.

- The entire history of communication has been spotted with efforts to limit, censor, or punish those who would say what those in power did not want them to say. Efforts at control never flag. Yet, even in dictatorships more information is sent and received than ever before. Witness the killing of journalists in a number of dictatorships amid the continued flow of news.

We should consider why, century by century, and now year by year, media have increasingly become enmeshed in our lives, and if anything is wrong with that. Whether it is reading, watching television, listening to music, working on the computer, or Internet surfing, a significant part of our attention each day is spent apart from other people. The more time spent with mediated communication, the less time remains for the direct contact that was once a social dynamic. We have made a trade.

Whether it is talking on the telephone, writing email, using a pen to send a greeting card, connecting via Facebook, or Skyping, we are still not in direct contact. What we are doing satisfies our needs and gives us some degree of pleasure, but there are differences. For all their benefits, media bring unintended consequences. We employ media instead of living the simpler life that is frequently praised, but infrequently chosen. Few of us since Henry David Thoreau would truly prefer the simple life of Walden.

Mediated communication has been entwined in human life through recorded history, now more than ever. As noted in the Introduction, the tools of communication have accompanied us in our journey across the centuries. One does not have to be a technological determinist to recognize how the media of communication—from the alphabet to the Internet—have altered human life, and what societies would be without them. The media matter to us. The more educated we are, the more media matter. That has been true since ancient Greece. Mediated communication is not something we can easily take or leave alone, and leaving media alone is not really an option in a modern world. We will not allow ourselves to be deprived of mediated communication. We would vigorously resist any attempt to reduce what we have. If nothing else, that is worth our attention and our study.

▶ NOTES

1 Jeff Malpes, *Heidegger's Topology: Being, Place, World* (Cambridge, MA: MIT Press, 2007) 279.

2 Marshall McLuhan, *The Gutenberg Galaxy* (Toronto: University of Toronto Press, 1962) 254.

3 Marshall McLuhan, *Understanding Media: The Extensions of Man* (New York: McGraw-Hill, 1964) 105.

4 Neil Postman, *Technopoly: The Surrender of Culture to Technology* (New York: Vintage Books, 1993) 61.

5 See John B. Thompson, *The Media and Modernity: A Social Theory of the Media* (Stanford: Stanford University Press, 1995) 24–31. Thompson offers a number of reasons to argue that "mass communication" is now a misleading term. Like the author, Thompson prefers "mediated communication."

Further Reading

▶ **INTRODUCTION: ADAPTING TO OUR MEDIA ENVIRONMENT**

Beniger, James R., *The Control Revolution*. Cambridge, MA: Harvard University Press, 1986.

Canton, Norman and Michael Werthman, *The History of Popular Culture*. New York: Macmillan, 1968.

De Sola Pool, Ithiel, *Technologies of Freedom*. Boston: Harvard University Press, 1983.

Fang, Irving, *A History of Mass Communication: Six Information Revolutions*. Newton, MA: Butterworth-Heinemann, 1997.

Freud, Sigmund, *Civilization and Its Discontents*. New York: W.W. Norton, 1961.

Friedman, Thomas L., *The World Is Flat*. New York: Farrar, Straus, and Giroux, 2005.

Levy, Steven, *The Perfect Thing*. New York: Simon & Schuster, 2006.

McLuhan, Marshall, *Understanding Media: The Extensions of Man*. New York: McGraw-Hill Book Co., 1964.

McLuhan, Marshall and Bruce R. Powers, *The Global Village: Transformations in World Life and Media in the 21st Century*. New York: Oxford University Press, 1989.

Morris, Ian, *Why the West Rules—For Now*. New York: Farrar, Straus and Giroux, 2010.

Popcorn, Faith, *The Popcorn Report: The Future of Your Company, Your World, Your Life*. New York: Doubleday, 1991.

Postman, Neil, *Amusing Ourselves to Death*. New York: Viking Penguin, 1985.

Postman, Neil, *Technopoly: The Surrender of Culture to Technology*. New York: Knopf, 1992.

Putnam, Robert, *Bowling Alone: The Collapse and Revival of American Community*. New York: Simon & Schuster, 2000.

Seavoy, Ronald E., *An Economic History of the United States: From 1607 to the Present*. New York: Routledge, 2006.

Thompson, John B., *The Media and Modernity: A Social Theory of the Media*. Stanford: Stanford University Press, 1995.

▶ 1. WRITING: GATHERING THOUGHT

Allen, Marti Lu, *The Beginning of Understanding: Writing in the Ancient World*. Ann Arbor: Kelsey Museum of Archaeology, 1991.

Daniels, Peter T. and William Bright, eds., *The World's Writing Systems*. New York: Oxford University Press, 1996.

Delaporte, L., *Mesopotamia: The Babylonian and Assyrian Civilization*. New York: Columbia University Press, 2004.

Durant, Will, *Our Oriental Heritage*. New York: Simon & Schuster, 1936.

Eisenstein, Elizabeth, *The Printing Press as an Agent of Change*, vol. 1. Cambridge, UK: Cambridge University Press, 1979.

Febvre, Lucien and Henri-Jean Martin, *The Coming of the Book: The Impact of Printing 1450–1800*. Trans. French edition 1958. London: Verso Editions, 1984.

Fischer, Steven Roger, *A History of Writing*. London: Reaktion Books, 2001.

Gnanadesikan, Amalia E., *The Writing Revolution: Cuneiform to the Internet* Oxford: Wiley-Blackwell, 2009.

Goody, Jack, *Literacy in Traditional Societies*. Cambridge, UK: Cambridge University Press, 1968.

Graff, Harvey J., *Literacy and Historical Development*. Carbondale: Southern Illinois University Press, 2007.

Havelock, Eric, *A Preface to Plato*. Cambridge, MA: Belknap Press of Harvard University Press, 1963.

Hooker, J. T., ed., *Reading the Past: Ancient Writings from Cuneiform to the Alphabet*. Berkeley: University of California Press, 1990.

Houston, Stephen, ed., *The First Writing: Script Invention as History and Process*. Cambridge, MA: Cambridge University Press, 2004.

Innis, Harold A., *The Bias of Communication*. Toronto: University of Toronto Press, 1951, 2007.

Innis, Harold A., *Empire and Communication*. Toronto: Dundurn Press, 2007.

Jacoby, Susan, *The Age of American Unreason*. New York: Pantheon Books, 2008.

Martin, Henri-Jean, *The History and Power of Writing*. Trans. Lydia G. Cochrane. Chicago: University of Chicago Press, 1994.

McLuhan, Marshall, *The Gutenberg Galaxy: The Making of Typographic Man.* Toronto: University of Toronto Press, 1962.

McLuhan, Marshall and Bruce R. Powers, *The Global Village: Transformations in World Life and Media in the 21st Century.* New York: Oxford University Press, 1989.

Morris, Ian, *Why the West Rules—For Now.* New York: Farrar, Straus and Giroux, 2010.

National History Publication Committee, *The Political Structure of Early Chosun: Korean History*, vol. XXVII. Seoul: Tamgudang, 1994.

Ong, Walter J., *Cognitive Development: Its Cultural and Social Foundations.* Cambridge, MA: Harvard University Press, 1976.

Ong, Walter J., *Orality and Literacy: The Technologizing of the Word.* London: Methuen, 1982.

Plakins Thornton, Tamara, *Handwriting in America: A Cultural History.* New Haven: Yale University Press, 1996.

Robinson, Andrew, *The Story of Writing.* London: Thames & Hudson, 2007.

Sacks, David, *Letter Perfect: The Marvelous History of Our Alphabet from A to Z.* New York: Broadway Books, 2003.

Schmandt-Besserat, Denise, *Before Writing.* Austin: University of Texas Press, 1992.

Seavoy, Ronald E. *An Economic History of the United States: From 1607 to the Present.* New York: Routledge, 2006.

Thornton, Tamara Plakins, *Handwriting in America: A Cultural History.* New Haven: Yale University Press, 1996.

▶ 2. EARLY PRINTING: REACHING MORE OF US

Anderson, Benedict, *Imagined Communities: Reflections on the Origin and Spread of Nationalism.* London: Verso, 1991.

Ariès, Philippe, *Centuries of Childhood: A Social History of Family Life.* New York: Random House, 1962.

Briggs, Asa and Peter Burke, *A Social History of the Media: from Gutenberg to the Internet.* Cambridge, UK: Polity Press, 2002.

Cantor, Norman and Michael Werthman, *The History of Popular Culture.* New York: Macmillan, 1968.

Carter, Thomas F., *The Invention of Printing in China and Its Spread Westward*, 2nd ed. New York: Ronald Press, 1955.

De Tocqueville, Alexis, *Democracy in America*, 1831. New York: Penguin Books, 2003.

Einstein, Alfred, *Short History of Music*. New York: Vintage Books, 1954.

Eisenstein, Elizabeth, *The Printing Press as an Agent of Change*. Cambridge, UK: Cambridge University Press, 1979.

Eisenstein, Elizabeth, *The Printing Revolution in Early Modern Europe*. Cambridge, UK: Cambridge University Press, 1983.

Finkelstein, David and Alistair McCleery, *An Introduction to Book History*. New York: Routledge, 2005.

Graff, Harvey J. ed, *Literacy and Historical Development*. Carbondale: Southern Illinois University Press, 2007.

Howard, Philip N., *The Digital Origins of Dictatorship and Democracy: Information Technology and Political Islam*. New York: Oxford University Press, 2010.

Innis, Harold A., *The Bias of Communication*. Toronto: University of Toronto Press, 1951, 2007.

Jensen, De Lamar, *Renaissance Europe: Age of Recovery and Reconciliation*, 2nd ed. Lexington, MA: D. C. Heath and Company, 1992.

Kapr, Albert, *Johann Gutenberg: The Man and His Invention*, tr. by Douglas Martin. Aldershot, UK: Scolar Press, 1996.

Manchester, William, *A World Lit Only by Fire: The Medieval Mind and the Renaissance*. Boston: Little, Brown and Company, 1992.

Martin, Henri-Jean, *The History and Power of Writing*. Trans. Lydia G. Cochrane. Chicago: University of Chicago Press, 1994.

McLuhan, Marshall, *The Gutenberg Galaxy*. Toronto: University of Toronto Press, 1962.

Nicolson, Adam, *God's Secretaries: The Making of the King James Bible*. New York: HarperCollins, 2003.

Pan, Jixing, *History of Chinese Science and Technology: Papermaking and Printing*. Beijing: Kexue, 1998.

Postman, Neil, *Technopoly: The Surrender of Culture to Technology*. New York: Knopf, 1992.

Stephens, Mitchell, *A History of News: From the Drum to the Satellite*, 3rd ed. New York: Oxford University Press, 2006.

▶ **3. MASS PRINTING: REACHING STILL MORE**

Blanchard, Margaret, ed., *History of Mass Media in the United States*. Chicago: Fitzroy Dearborn Publishers, 1998.

Emery, Michael, Edwin Emery, and Nancy Roberts, *The Press and America: An Interpretive History of the Mass Media*, 9th ed. Boston: Allyn & Bacon, 2000.

Goodwin, Doris Kearns, *The Bully Pulpit: Theodore Roosevelt, William Howard Taft, and the Golden Age of Journalism*. New York: Simon & Schuster, 2013.

Gray, William, and Ruth Munroe, *The Reading Interests and Habits of Adults*. New York: Macmillan, 1929.

Greenspan, Ezra and Jonathan Rose, eds., *Book History*, vol. 3. University Park: Pennsylvania State University Press, 2000.

Howsam, Leslie, *Old Books and New Histories: An Orientation to Studies in Book and Print Culture*. Toronto: University of Toronto Press, 2007.

Kozol, Jonathan, *Illiterate America*. Garden City, NY: Anchor Press, 1985.

McLuhan, Marshall, *The Gutenberg Galaxy*. Toronto: University of Toronto Press, 1962.

Nasaw, David, *The Chief: The Life of William Randolph Hearst*. New York: Houghton Mifflin, 2000.

Ohmann, Richard, *Selling Culture: Magazines, Markets, and Class at the Turn of the Century*. London: Verso, 1996.

Ravitch, Diane, *The Language Police: How Pressure Groups Restrict What Students Learn*. New York: Alfred Knopf, 2003.

Serrin, Judith and William, eds., *Muckraking: The Journalism That Changed America*. New York: The New Press, 2002.

Vaidhyanathan, Siva, *The Anarchist in the Library*. New York: Basic Books, 2004.

Vincent, David, *Literacy and Popular Culture*. New York: Cambridge University Press, 1989.

Winship, Michael, *American Literary Publishing in the Nineteenth Century*. New York: Cambridge University Press, 2003.

Wood, James P., *The Story of Advertising*. New York: Ronald Press, 1958.

▶ 4. MAIL: THE SNAIL THAT COULD

Blanchard, Margaret, ed., *History of Mass Media in the United States*. Chicago: Fitzroy Dearborn Publishers, 1998.

Boorstin, Daniel, *The Americans: The Democratic Experience*. New York: Random House, 1973.

Bowyer, Matthew J., *They Carried the Mail: A Survey of Postal History & Hobbies*. Lincoln, NE: iUniverse. com, 2000.

Bruns, James H., *Mail on the Move*. Polo, IL: Transportation Trails, 1992.

Cullinan, Gerald, *The United States Postal Service*. New York: Praeger Publishers, 1968.

Fuller, Wayne E., *The American Mail*. Chicago: University of Chicago Press, 1972.

Fuller, Wayne E., *Morality and the Mail in Nineteenth-Century America*. Champaign, IL: University of Illinois Press, 2003.

Hallgren, Mauritz, *All about Stamps*. New York: Alfred A. Knopf, 1940.

Harlow, Alvin F., *Old Post Bags*. New York: D. Appleton, 1938.

Henken, David M., *The Postal Age: The Emergence of Modern Communications in Nineteenth Century America*. Chicago: University of Chicago Press, 2006.

John, Richard R., *Spreading the News: The American Postal System from Franklin to Morse*. Cambridge, MA: Harvard University Press, 1995.

Kielbowicz, Richard B., *News in the Mail: The Press, Post Office, and Public Information, 1700–1860s*. New York: Greenwood Press, 1989.

Manchester, William, *A World Lit Only by Fire: the Medieval Mind*. Boston: Little, Brown, 1992.

McLuhan, Marshall, *Understanding Media: The Extensions of Man*. New York: McGraw-Hill, 1964.

Menke, Richard, *Telegraphic Realism: Victorian Fiction and Other Information Systems*. Stanford: Stanford University Press, 2008.

Starr, Paul, *The Creation of the Media: Political Origins of Modern Communications*. New York: Basic Books, 2004.

Van Doren, Carl, *Benjamin Franklin*. New York: Viking, 1938.

Walker, George, *Haste, Post, Haste*. New York: Dodd, Mead & Co., 1939.

Zilliacus, Laurin, *Mail for the World*. New York: John Day Co., 1953.

▶ 5. TELEGRAPH: UNITING THE UNITED STATES

Beniger, James R., *The Control Revolution*. Cambridge, MA: Harvard University Press, 1986.

Boorstin, Daniel, *The Americans: The Democratic Experience*. New York: Random House, 1973.

Boorstin, Daniel, *Hidden History: Exploring Our Secret Past*. New York: Harper & Row, 1987.

Coe, Lewis, *Telegraph: A History of Morse's Invention and Its Predecessors in the United States*. Jefferson, NC: McFarland & Co, 2003.

Czitrom, Daniel J., *Media and the American Mind*. Chapel Hill, NC: University of North Carolina Press, 1982.

Dilts, Marion May, *The Telephone in a Changing World*. New York: Longmans, Green, 1941.

Harlow, Alvin F., *Old Wires and New Waves: The History of the Telegraph, Telephone, and Wireless*. New York: D. Appleton-Century, 1936.

Marvin, Carolyn, *When Old Technologies Were New: Thinking About Electric Communication in the Late Nineteenth Century*. New York: Oxford University Press, 1988.

Oslin, George P., *The Story of Telecommunications*. Macon, GA: Mercer University Press, 1992.

Postman, Neil, *Technopoly: The Surrender of Culture to Technology*. New York: Knopf, 1992.

Sloan, William, James Stovall, and James Startt, *The Media in America*. Worthington, OH: Publishing Horizons, 1989.

Standage, Tom, *The Victorian Internet: The Remarkable Story of the Telegraph and the Nineteenth Century's On-line Pioneers*. New York: Walker Publishing Co., 1998.

Williams, Francis, *Transmitting World News*. Paris: UNESCO, 1953.

▶ 6. TELEPHONE: REACHING WITHOUT TOUCHING

Basalla, George, *The Evolution of Technology*. Cambridge, MA: Cambridge University Press, 1988.

Brooks, John, *Telephone: The First 100 Years*. New York: Harper & Row, 1976.

Czitrom, Daniel J., *Media and the American Mind*. Chapel Hill, NC: University of North Carolina Press, 1982.

Dilts, Marion May, *The Telephone in a Changing World*. New York: Longman's Green, 1941.

Fischer, Claude, *America Calling: A Social History of the Telephone to 1940*. Berkeley: University of California Press, 1992.

Friedman, Thomas L., *The World Is Flat*. New York: Farrar, Straus, and Giroux, 2005.

Harlow, Alvin F., *Old Wires and New Waves: The History of the Telegraph, Telephone, and Wireless*. New York: D. Appleton-Century, 1936.

Marvin, Carolyn, *When Old Technologies Were New: Thinking About Electric Communication in the Late Nineteenth Century*. New York: Oxford University Press, 1988.

Oslin, George P., *The Story of Telecommunications*. Macon, GA: Mercer University Press, 1992.

Prescott, George B., *Bell's Speaking Telephone: Its Invention, Construction*. New York: Arno Press, 1972.

Shirer, George, *The Telephone: An Historical Anthology*. New York: Arno Press, 1977.

Shulman, Seth: *The Telephone Gambit: Chasing Alexander Graham Bell's Secret*. New York: W. W. Norton, 2009.

Sloan, William, James Stovall, and James Startt, *The Media in America*. Worthington, OH: Publishing Horizons, 1989.

▶ 7. RECORDING: BEYONCÉ SINGS BETTER THAN OUR SISTER

Aldridge, B. L., *The Victor Talking Machine Company*. Camden, NJ: RCA Sales Corp., 1964.

Butterworth, William E., *Hi Fi: From Edison's Phonograph to Quad Sound*. New York: Four Winds Press, 1977.

Chanan, Michael, *Repeated Takes: A Short History of Recording and Its Effects on Music*. New York: Verso, 1995.

Gronow, Pekka and Ilpo Saunio, *International History of the Recording Industry*. Tr. Christopher Moseley. London: Cassell, 1999.

Gumpert, Gary, *Talking Tombstones and Other Tales of the Media Age*. New York: Oxford University Press, 1987.

Hollander, Richard S., *Video Democracy*. Mt. Airy, MD: Lomond Publications, 1985.

Inglis, Andrew F., *Behind the Tube: A History of Broadcast Technology and Business*. New York: Focal Press, 1990.

Levy, Steven, *The Perfect Thing: How the iPod Shuffles Commerce, Culture, and Coolness*. New York: Simon & Schuster, 2006.

Litman, Jessica, *Digital Copyright: Protecting Intellectual Property on the Internet*. Amherst, NY: Prometheus, 2001.

Marty, Daniel, *An Illustrated History of Phonographs*. New York: Dorset Press, 1981.

Marvin, Carolyn. *When Old Technologies Were New*. New York: Oxford University Press, 1988.

McLuhan, Marshall, *Understanding Media: The Extensions of Man*. New York: McGraw-Hill, 1964.

Oslin, George P., *The Story of Telecommunications*. Macon, GA: Mercer University Press, 1992.

Sterling, Christopher H. and John M. Kittross, *Stay Tuned: A Concise History of American Broadcasting*. Belmont, CA: Wadsworth Publishing Co., 2nd ed., 1990.

▶ 8. PHOTOGRAPHY: PERSONAL AND SO MUCH MORE

100 Photographs That Changed the World. New York: Life Books, 2003.

Batchen, Geoffrey, *Each Wild Idea*. Cambridge, MA: MIT Press, 2001.

Boorstin, Daniel J., *The Image, or What Happened to the American Dream*. New York: Atheneum, 1961.

Boorstin, Daniel J., *The Americans: The Democratic Experience*. New York: Random House, 1973.

Broecker, William L., ed., *Encyclopedia of Photography*. New York: Crown Publishers, 1984.

Buckland, Gail, *Fox Talbot and The Invention of Photography*. Boston: D. R. Godine, 1980.

Ellul, Jacques, *The Technological Bluff*. Grand Rapids, MI: Wm. B. Eerdmans Publishing Co., 1990.

Gernsheim, Helmut, *The Origins of Photography*. New York: Thames and Hudson, 1982.

Hofstadter, Richard, *The Progressive Movement, 1900–1915*. New York: Simon & Schuster, 1963.

Jeffrey, Ian, *Photography: A Concise History*. New York: Oxford University Press.1981.

Newhall, Beaumont, *The History of Photography*. New York: Museum of Modern Art, 1982.

Rosenblum, Naomi, *A World History of Photography*. New York: Abbeville Press, 1989.

Sontag, Susan, ed., *A Barthes Reader*. New York: Hill and Wang, 1982.

Spira, S. F., *The History of Photography: As Seen Through the Spira Collection*. New York: Aperture Foundation, 2001.

Turner, Peter, *History of Photography*. New York: Exeter Books, 1987.

Wells, Liz, ed., *The Photography Reader*. New York, Routledge, 2003.

▶ 9. SILENT FILM: THE AUDIENCE WAITS

Boorstin, Daniel J., *The Image, or What Happened to the American Dream*. New York: Atheneum, 1961.

Bowser, Eileen, *The Transformation of Cinema, 1907–1915*. Berkeley: University of California Press, 1994.

Coe, Brian, *History of Motion Picture Photography*. New York: Zoetrope, Inc., 1981.

Gabler, Neal, *An Empire of Their Own: How the Jews Invented Hollywood*. New York: Anchor Books, 1989.

Geldud, Harry M., *The Birth of the Talkies: From Edison to Jolson*. Bloomington: Indiana University Press, 1975.

Hansen, Miriam, *Babel and Babylon: Spectatorship in American Silent Film*. Cambridge, MA: Harvard University Press, 1991.

Jarvie, Ian C., *Hollywood's Overseas Campaign: The North Atlantic Movie Trade, 1920–1950*. Cambridge, UK: Cambridge University Press, 1992.

Koszarski, Richard, *An Evening's Entertainment: The Age of the Silent Feature Picture, 1915–1928*. Berkeley: University of California Press, 1994.

May, Lary, *Screening Out the Past: The Birth of Mass Culture and the Motion Picture Industry*. Chicago: University of Chicago Press, 1980.

Morris, Lloyd R., Not So Long Ago. New York: Random House, 1949.

Musser, Charles, *The Emergence of Cinema: The American Screen to 1907*. Berkeley: University of California Press, 1994.

Nasaw, David, *Going Out: The Rise and Fall of Public Amusements*. New York: Basic Books, 1993.

Rosten, Leo, *Hollywood, the Movie Colony and the Movie Makers*. New York: Harcourt Brace & Co., 1941.

Shipman, David, *The Story of Cinema*. Englewood Cliffs: Prentice-Hall, 1982.

Thompson, Kristin, and David Bordwell, *Film History: an Introduction*, 3rd ed. New York: McGraw-Hill, 2010.

▶ 10. A MOVIE CENTURY: MOVING US

Cameron, E. W., ed, *Sound and the Cinema*. New York: Redgrave Publishing Co., 1980.

Ellis, Jack C., *A History of Film*, 2nd ed. Englewood Cliffs: Prentice-Hall, 1985.

Jarvie, Ian C. *Hollywood's Overseas Campaign: The North Atlantic Movie Trade, 1920–1950*. New York: Cambridge University Press, 1992.

Lardner, James, *Fast Forward*. New York: W. W. Norton, 1987.

Manovich, Lev, *The Language of New Media*. Cambridge, MA: MIT Press, 2001.

McKeon, Elizabeth and Linda Everett. *Cinema under the Stars: America's Love Affair with the Drive-In Movie Theater*. Nashville: Cumberland House, 1998.

McLuhan, Marshall and Bruce R. Powers, *The Global Village: Transformations in World Life and Media in the 21st Century*. New York: Oxford University Press, 1989.

Popcorn, Faith, *The Popcorn Report: The Future of Your Company, Your World, Your Life*. New York: Doubleday, 1991.

Putnam, Robert. *Bowling Alone: The Collapse and Revival of American Community.* New York: Simon & Schuster, 2000.

Rosten, Leo, *Hollywood, the Movie Colony and the Movie Makers.* New York: Harcourt Brace & Co., 1941.

Thompson, Kristin, and David Bordwell, *Film History*, 3rd ed. New York: McGraw-Hill, 2010.

Thomson, David, *The Whole Equation: A History of Hollywood.* New York: Vintage Books, 2006.

Thomson, David, *The Big Screen: The Story of the Movies.* New York: Farrar, Straus and Giroux, 2012.

Walsh, Frank, *Sin and Censorship: The Catholic Church and the Motion Picture Industry.* New Haven: Yale University Press, 1996.

▶ 11. RADIO: HELPING US THROUGH THE ROUGH YEARS

Barnouw, Erik, *The Sponsor.* New York: Oxford University Press, 1978.

Beniger, James R., *The Control Revolution.* Cambridge: Harvard University Press, 1986.

De Sola Pool, Ithiel, *Technologies of Freedom.* Cambridge: Harvard University Press, 1983.

Douglas, Susan J., *Inventing American Broadcasting, 1899–1922.* Baltimore: Johns Hopkins University Press, 1987.

Fang, Irving, *Those Radio Commentators!* Ames: Iowa State University Press, 1977.

Halper, Donna L., *Invisible Stars: A Social History of Women in American Broadcasting.* Armonk, NY: M. E. Sharpe, 2001.

Hilliard, Robert L. and Michael C. Keith, *The Broadcast Century and Beyond: A Biography of American Broadcasting.* Woburn, MA: Focal Press, 2001.

Inglis, Andrew F., *Behind the Tube: A History of Broadcast Technology and Business.* New York: Focal Press, 1990.

Keith, Michael C., *The Radio Station: Broadcast, Satellite, and Internet*, 7th ed. Boston: Focal Press, 2007.

Lenthall, Bruce, *Radio's America: The Great Depression and the Rise of Modern Mass Culture.* Chicago: University of Chicago Press, 2007.

Lewis, Tom, *Empire of the Air: The Men Who Made Radio.* New York: HarperCollins, 1991.

Pease, Edward C., ed., *Radio: The Forgotten Medium.* New York: Columbia University, 1993.

Razlogova, Elena, *The Listener's Voice: Early Radio and the American Public*. Philadelphia: University of Pennsylvania Press, 2011.

Schiffer, Michael Brian, *The Portable Radio in American Life*. Tucson: University of Arizona Press, 1991.

Sterling, Christopher H. and John M. Kittross, *Stay Tuned: A Concise History of American Broadcasting*, 3rd ed. Belmont, CA: Wadsworth Publishing Co., 2002.

Weightman, Gavin, *Signor Marconi's Magic Box*. London: HarperCollins Publishers, 2003.

▶ 12. TELEVISION: PICTURES IN OUR PARLORS

Abramson, Albert, *The History of Television, 1942 to 2000*. Jefferson, NC: McFarland & Company, 2003.

Barnouw, Erik, *The Golden Web: 1933–1953*. New York: Oxford University Press, 2001.

Barnouw, Erik, *The Image Empire: A History of Broadcasting in the United States: From 1953*. New York: Oxford University Press, 2001.

Baughman, James, *Same Time, Same Station: Creating American Television, 1948--1961*. Baltimore: Johns Hopkins University Press, 2007.

Briggs, Asa and Peter Burke, *A Social History of the Media: From Gutenberg to the Internet*. Cambridge, UK: Polity Press, 2002.

Downie Leonard Jr. and Robert G. Kaiser, *The News About the News*. New York: Alfred A. Knopf, 2002.

Edgerton, Gary, *The Columbia History of American Television*. New York: Columbia University Press, 2007.

Ellul, Jacques, *The Technological Bluff*. Grand Rapids, MI: Wm. B. Eerdmans Publishing Co., 1990.

Inglis, Andrew F., *Behind the Tube: A History of Broadcast Technology and Business*. New York: Focal Press, 1990.

Lenthall, Bruce, *Radio's America: The Great Depression and the Rise of Modern Mass Culture*. Chicago: University of Chicago Press, 2007.

Magoun, Alexander, *Television: The Life Story of a Technology*. Westport, CT: Greenwood Press, 2007.

McLuhan, Marshall, *Understanding Media: The Extensions of Man*. New York: McGraw-Hill, 1964.

Postman, Neil, *Amusing Ourselves to Death*. New York: Viking Penguin, 1985.

Postman, Neil, *Technopoly: The Surrender of Culture to Technology*. New York: Knopf, 1992.

Roman, James, *From Daytime to Primetime: The History of American Television Programs*. Westport, CT: Greenwood Press, 2005.

Sterling, Christopher H., and John M. Kittross, *Stay Tuned: A Concise History of American Broadcasting*, 3rd ed. Belmont, CA: Wadsworth Publishing Co., 2002.

▶ 13. COMPUTERS: BEYOND CALCULATION

Berners-Lee, Tim, *Weaving the Web*. San Francisco: Harper, 1999.

Campbell-Kelly, Martin, and William Aspray, *Computer: A History Of The Information Machine*, 2nd ed. New York: Basic Books, 1996.

Castells, Manuel, *The Information Age: Economy, Society, and Culture*. New York: Oxford University Press, three volumes, 1996–1998.

Ceruzzi, Paul, E., *A History of Modern Computing*, 2nd ed. Cambridge, MA: MIT Press, 2003.

Ellul, Jacques, *The Technological Bluff*. Grand Rapids, MI: Wm. B. Eerdmans Publishing Co., 1990.

Greenberger, Martin, ed., *Management and Computers of the Future*. Cambridge, MA: MIT Press, 1962.

Ifrah, Georges, *The Universal History of Computing: From the Abacus to the Quantum Computer*. New York: John Wiley & Sons, 2001.

Levy, Steven, *Hackers: Heroes of the Computer Revolution*. Sebastapol, CA: O'Reilly Media, 2010.

Manovich, Lev, *The Language of New Media*. Cambridge, MA: MIT Press, 2001.

Okin, J. B., *The Information Revolution: The Not-for-Dummies Guide to the History, Technology, And Use of the World Wide Web*. Winter Harbor, ME: Ironbound Press, 2005.

O'Regan, Gerard, *A Brief History of Computing*. London: Springer-Verlag, 2008.

Sellen, Abigail and Richard Harper, *The Myth of the Paperless Office*. Cambridge, MA: MIT Press, 2002.

Swedin, Eric and David Ferro, *Computers: The Life Story of a Technology*. Westport, CT: Greenwood Press, 2005.

Standage, Tom, *Writing in the Wall: Social Media, the First 2,000 Years*. New York: Bloomsbury, 2013.

Toffler, Alvin, *The Third Wave*. New York: William Morrow, 1980.

Wren, Daniel A. and Arthur G. Bedeian, *The Evolution of Management Thought*. New York: John Wiley and Sons, 2009.

▶ 14. THE INTERNET: THE WORLD AT OUR FINGERTIPS

Abbate, Janet, *Inventing the Internet*. Cambridge, MA: MIT Press, 1999.

Banks, Michael, *On the Way to the Web: The Secret History of the Internet and Its Founders*. New York: Springer-Verlag, 2008.

Berners-Lee, Tim, *Weaving the Web*. San Francisco: Harper, 1999.

Haffner, Katie and Matthew Lyon, *Where Wizards Stay Up Late: The Origins of The Internet*. New York: Simon & Schuster, 1996.

Hauben, Michael, *Netizens*. Los Alamitos, CA: IEEE Computer Society Press, 1997.

Johnson, Steven, *Everything Bad Is Good for You*. New York: Riverhead Books, 2005.

Levy, Steven, *Crypto*. New York: Penguin Books, 2001.

Naughton, John, *A Brief History of the Future: From Radio Days to Internet Years in a Lifetime*. Woodstock, NY: Overlook Press, 2000.

Okin, J. R., *The Information Revolution: The Not-for-Dummies Guide to the History, Technology, and Use of the World Wide Web*. Winter Harbor, ME: Ironbound Press, 2005.

Ryan, Johnny, *A History of the Internet and the Digital Future*. London: Reaktion Books, 2010.

Standage, Tom, *Writing in the Wall: Social Media, the First 2,000 Years*. New York: Bloomsbury, 2013.

Van Schewick, Barbara, *Internet Architecture and Innovation*. Cambridge, MA: MIT Press, 2010.

▶ 15. VIDEO GAMES: LEANING FORWARD

Anderson, Craig A. et al., *Violent Video Game Effects on Children and Adolescents: Theory, Research, and Public Policy*. New York: Oxford University Press, 2007.

Bissell, Tom, *Extra Lives: Why Video Games Matter*. New York: Pantheon Books, 2010.

Calvert, Sandra, Amy Jordan, and Rodney Cocking, eds. *Children in the Digital Age: Influences of Electronic Media on Development*. New York: Praeger, 2002.

Donovan, Tristan, *Replay: The History of Video Games*. Lewes, UK: Yellow Ant, 2010.

Egenfeldt-Nielson, Simon et al., *Understanding Video Games: The Essential Introduction*. New York: Routledge, 2008.

Gee, James Paul, *What Video Games Have to Teach Us About Learning and Literacy*. New York: Palgrave Macmillan, 2004.

Greenfield, Patricia Marks, *Mind and Media: The Effects of Television, Video games, and Computers*. Cambridge, MA: Harvard University Press, 1984.

Herz, J. C., *Joystick Nation*. Boston: Little, Brown and Company, 1997.

Jones, Steven G., ed. *Cybersociety*. Thousand Oaks, CA: Sage Publications, 1995.

Kent, Steven L., *The Ultimate History of Video Games*. New York: Three Rivers Press, 2001.

King, Brad and John Borland. *Dungeons and Dreamers: The Rise of Computer Game Culture from Geek to Chic*. New York: McGraw-Hill/Osborne, 2003.

Poole, Steven, *Trigger Happy: The Inner Life of Video Games*. London: Fourth Estate, 2000.

Wolf, Mark J. P., ed., *Video Game Explosion: A History from PONG to PlayStation and Beyond*. Westport, CT: Greenwood Press, 2008.

▶ 16. PERSUASION: THE PUSH NEVER STOPS

Baker, C. Edwin, *Advertising and a Democratic Press*. Princeton: Princeton University Press, 1994.

Beniger, James R., *The Control Revolution*. Cambridge, MA: Harvard University Press, 1986.

Bernays, Edward L., *Propaganda*. New York: Horace Liveright, 1928.

Cutlip, Scott, *Public Relations History: From the 17th to the 20th Century: The Antecedents*. Hillsdale, NJ: Lawrence Erlbaum Associates, 1995.

Emery, Michael, Edwin Emery, and Nancy Roberts, *The Press and America: An Interpretive History of the Mass Media*, 9th ed. Boston: Allyn and Bacon, 2000.

Ewen, Stuart, *PR!: A Social History of Spin*. New York: Basic Books, 1996.

Fox, Stephen, *The Mirror Makers: A History of American Advertising and Its Creators*. New York: Morrow, 1984.

Friedman, Thomas L., *The World Is Flat*. New York: Farrar, Straus, and Giroux, 2005.

Fukuyama, Francis, *The End of History and the Last Man*, 2nd ed. New York: Free Press, 1993.

Hoff, Syd, *Editorial and Political Cartooning*. New York: Stravon Educational Press, 1976.

Lears, Jackson, *Fables Of Abundance: A Cultural History of Advertising in America*. New York: Basic Books, 1994.

Lewis, Bernard, *What Went Wrong: Western Impact and Middle Eastern Response*. New York: Oxford University Press, 2002.

Meyer, G. J., *A World Undone: The Story of the Great War, 1914 to 1918*. New York: Delacorte Press, 2006.

Pearse, Meic, *Why the Rest Hates the West: Understanding the Roots of Global Rage*. Downers Grove, IL: InterVarsity Press, 2004.

Pincus, Stephane and Marc Loiseau, *A History of Advertising*. Cologne, Germany: Taschen, 2008.

Roy, Olivier, *Globalized Islam: The Search for a New Ummah*. New York: Columbia University Press, 2004.

Schuwer, Philippe, *History of Advertising*. London: Leisure Arts, 1966.

Schwartz, Barry, *The Paradox of Choice: Why More Is Less*. New York: HarperCollins, 2004.

Sivulka, Juliann, *Soap, Sex, and Cigarettes: A Cultural History of American Advertising*. Belmont, CA: Wadsworth Publishing, 1997.

Tungate, Mark, *Adland: A Global History of Advertising*. New York: Kogan Page, 2007.

Tye, Larry, *The Father of Spin: Edward L. Bernays and The Birth of Public Relations*. New York: Henry Holt, 1998.

Wood, James Playsted, *The Story of Advertising*. New York: Ronald Press, 1958.

▶ 17. MEDIA MATTER: ENTWINED IN HUMAN LIFE

Briggs, Asa and Peter Burke, *A Social History of the Media: From Gutenberg to the Internet*, 3rd ed. Cambridge, UK: Polity Press, 2009.

Easterbrook, Gregg, *Progress Paradox: How Life Gets Better While People Feel Worse*. New York: Random House, 2003.

Hallowell, Edward M., and John J. Ratey, *Delivered from Distraction*. New York: Ballantine Books, 2005.

Johnson, Steven, *Everything Bad Is Good for You*. New York: Riverhead Books, 2005.

Malpes, Jeff, *Heidegger's Topology: Being, Place, World*. Cambridge, MA: MIT Press, 2007.

McLuhan, Marshall, *The Gutenberg Galaxy*. Toronto: University of Toronto Press, 1962.

McLuhan, Marshall, *Understanding Media: The Extensions of Man*. New York: McGraw-Hill Book Co., 1964.

Postman, Neil, *Technopoly: The Surrender of Culture to Technology*. New York: Knopf, 1992.

Putnam, Robert, *Bowling Alone: The Collapse and Revival of American Community*. New York: Simon & Schuster, 2000.

Qualman, Erik, *Socialnomics: How Social Media Transforms the Way We Live and Do Business*. Hoboken, NJ: John Wiley, 2009.

Schwartz, Barry, *The Paradox of Choice: Why More Is Less*. New York: HarperCollins, 2004.

Thompson, John B., *The Media and Modernity: A Social Theory of the Media*. Stanford: Stanford University Press, 1995.

Image Credits

Page 2, by K. J. Lamb, courtesy of *The Spectator* (http://www.spectator.co.uk/) © The Spectator / K. J. Lamb

Page 24, Medieval manuscript: courtesy of Shutterstock, Inc.

Page 29, *The Reader*: courtesy of Weinstein Co/Photofest © The Weinstein Company; Photographer: Melinda Sue Gordon

Page 136, Tahrir Square: courtesy of Shutterstock, Inc.

Page 155, Bing Crosby: courtesy of Ampex, reprinted with permission

Page 189, Mutoscope: courtesy of Shutterstock, Inc.

Page 205, *Gone with the Wind*: courtesy of MGM/Photofest ©MGM

Page 208, *Midnight Cowboy*: United Artists/Photofest © United Artists

Page 215, Drive-in: courtesy of Shutterstock, Inc.

Page 234, Radio: courtesy of Shutterstock, Inc.

Page 256, Zenith remote: courtesy of Shutterstock, Inc.

Page 280, ENIAC: courtesy of US Army Photo.

Page 282, *Desk Set*: Courtesy of 20th Century Fox/Photofest © 20th Century Fox

Page 309, *Lonelygirl15*: courtesy of EQAL.

Page 316, *The Princess Bride*: courtesy of 20th Century Fox/Photofest © 20th Century Fox.

Page 351, Cultural change cartoon: courtesy of Shutterstock, Inc.

Index

Page numbers in **bold** refer to text boxes and figures

abstraction 14
Academy Awards 197, 204, 207, **208**, 210, **212**, 220–221
Adams, Ansel 174
Adams, John 52
Adams, Samuel 51
adaptation 3, 9, 14, 141, 153, **256**
addiction to media 1, 6, 11n1, 260–261, 298, 308, 310, 319
advertising 11, 39, 53, 59–60, 62, 64–65, 71–73, 79–81, 84, 103, 106, 131, 133, 139, **149**, 150, **152**, 207, 217, 232–233, 237, 239, 257, 260, 262, 335, 337–340, 342, 345, 347–348. *See also* classified ads; personal ads
African Americans 28–30, 60–62, 65, 68–69, 72, 148, 151, 153, 184–185, 192, **194–195**, 242, **262**, 264, 336
Agnew, Spiro 265
Albrecht VII 92
Alexanderson, E.F.W. 229, 246
Alexandrian Library 22, 32. *See also* libraries
Alger, Horatio **75**, 268
Alhazen 164
alphabet 4–5, 15–20, 31, 34n36, 42, 90, 112, 351, 352, 354
American Revolution, the 28, 48, 50–52, 94–95
Andreessen, Marc 297
animation 177, 199, 210–211, 286. *See also* cartoons
apps 6, 138, 144, 145n29, 283
Archer, Frederick 168, 179
Aristotle 20, **21**, 45, 164, 335
Armstrong, E. Howard 228–229, 235, 243
Arnold, H.D. 132
Assange, Julian 304

audio 30, 148–155, 157, 158, 159, 161
audio books 5, 64, 76, 150, 158
automobile 3, 69, 174, 184, 206, 214, 236, 324–325, 352
Autry, Gene 206

Babbage, Charles 278, **279**, 288–289
Bacon, Francis 42
Bain, Alexander 252
Baird, John Logie 252
Baran, Paul 295
Barnum, P.T. 70, 341–342, **342**, 347
Barraud, Francis **152**, 160
Barry, Dave 299
Barrymore, Lionel 190
Barthes, Roland 193
Barton, Clara 130
Battleship Potemkin, the 199, 209
BBC (British Broadcasting Corporation) 233, 257, 272
Beato, Felice 169
Bell, Alexander Graham 120, **126**, 127–128, 132–133, 141, 149–150, 227
Bennett, James Gordon 65
Berg, Michael **29**
Berliner, Emile 128, 142, 150–151, 160
Bernays, Edward 71, 342, 348
Berners-Lee, Tim 297
Berzelius, Jöns 252, 272
Bible, the **19**, **23**, 28, 31–32, 38, 40, 43–44, 47, 54–55, 88, 114, 163, 229, 313n34, 336
bigotry 185, 309, 326, 343, 349–350n14. *See also* racism
Bill of Rights, the 52, 55. *See also* Constitution (United States); First Amendment
billboards 79–80, 139, 336
Bina, Eric 297

Birth of a Nation, the **194–196**, 199, 325

BlackBerry 137, 139, 283, 290

Blair, Montgomery 102

blogs 5, 14, 77, 79, 135, 183, 244, 300, 304–307, **309**, 311, 335, 343, 351

"Bly, Nellie" (Elizabeth Cochrane) 67

books 27, 30, 32, 37–39, 41, 43–47, **48**, 60, 62, 64, 68, 71, 75–77, 80–82, 169, 171, 184, 188, 191, 216–217, 293, 301, 303, 316, 327, 335, 336

Boorstin, Daniel J. 113, 117

Bordwell, David 197, 204, 219

Bowling Alone 6, 217–218, 223n19

Bozak, Rudolph 152

Bradford, Andrew 48, 72

Brady, Matthew 169, **170**, 179

Braille, Louis 77–78, 82, 149

Brainerd, Paul 285

Branly, Édouard 226, 245

Braun, Karl Ferdinand 246, 252, 272

Briggs, Joseph 102

Bristol, Horace 171

broadcasting 80, 131–132, 160, 204, 225–249, 251–273, 287, 339, 345, 352

Browder, Earl 176

Brownback, Sam **326**

Bunyon, John 68

bureaucracy 26, 140

Bush, George W. 304

cable 59, 67, 114, 120, 122, 132, **134**, 142–143, 148, 219, 251, 268–273

Calhoun, John C. 176

Calvin, John 44

camcorders 156, 184, **219**

cameras 59, 79, 135, 138, 141, 156, 165, 173, 174–175, 178–179, 184, 199, 283, 304, 309, 320

capitalism 17, 19, 37–38, 50, 70, 100–101, 104, 106, 112, 299, 327–328, 330, 336–340

Carey, Philip 252

Carnegie, Andrew **129**

Carpenter, Edmund 261

Carter, William **336**

Cartier-Bresson, Henri 174

cartoons 177, 199, 206, 210, 211, 345–346. *See also* animation

Caselli, Abbé 252

catalog/ues 4, 54, 62, 103–104, 106, 337

Cather, Willa 68

CBS (Columbia Broadcasting System) 6, 8, 150, 152, **235**, 237, **239**, 247, 253–255, 258, 263, 272, **281**, 304, 344

CDs 156, 159, 161, 244

celebrities 190, 195, 196, 197, 199, 211, 214, 237, 239, 348

cellphones 1, 6, 11n1, 134–139, 140, 143, 145n30, 179, 184, 219, **245**, 259, 271, 283, 299, 307, 310, 351

censorship 28, 32, 38, 39, 42, 46–47, **48**, 51–52, **52**, 53, 80–81, 86n24, 95, 105, 135, 136, 153–154, 178, 197–199, 212–214, 230, 233–234, **235**, 237, 240, 257, 267, 302, 306–308, 318–319, 336, **336**, 339, 343, 345, 348, 353

Chaplin, Charlie 194–195, 199, 204, 207, 221n3

Charlemagne 90, 92

Chauvet Cave 15

Chavez, Cesar 82

children 3, 4, 7, 9, 19, 26, 28–29, 35n51, 43, 62–63, 69, **75**, 81–82, 125, 130, 153, 163–164, 167, 171, **172**, 178, 260–263, 275n20, 282, 288, 298, 308–309, 319–322, 329–330, 332n29, 339

Churchill, Winston 340

Cicero 89, 335

cinemas 5, 189, 190, 192–193, 199, 206, 216–218, 220, 251, 255

city-states 13, 20

Civil War (American), the 30, 53–54, 60–61, 63, 71, 102, 111, 115, 122, 168, 169, **170**, 172, 179, **194–195**, 336, 341–342

classified ads 340. *See also* advertising; personal ads

clergy, the 25, 43, 44, 47, 65, 114, 198. *See also* monks; priests

Clooney, George 197

cloud computing 157, 290

CNN (Cable News Network) 4, 270, 273

Cochrane, Elizabeth 67

cocooning 6–7, 215

collaboration 303–304, 316–317, 327–328, 351–352

comics 71, 82, 84, 139, 177–178

commercials 6, 232–233, 239, 244, 248n14, 261, 339, 345, 348

computers 3, 5–6, 10, 30, 60, 63, 76–78, 105–106, 114, 128, 130, 132–133, 159, 163, 175–177, 184, 210–211, 218, 259, 271, 277–290, **280**, **282**,

294, 298, 307, 309, 315, 317–318, 327, 329, 353
Comstock, Anthony **47–48**
Confucius 26
Conrad, Frank 231
Constitution (United States), the **52**, 95. *See also* Bill of Rights; First Amendment.
Cooke, William 114
Cooper, Martin 138, 143
Copernicus, Nicolaus 42
copyright 157, 159
Coughlin, Charles 242–243
Counter-Reformation, the 44
    See also Protestantism; Reformation (Protestant)
courier 87–92, **93**, 98, 107, 127, **129**
Crane, Stephen 68
Cronkite, Walter 263, **264**, 266
Crookes, William 252, 272
Cros, Charles 148–149, 160
Crosby, Bing 155, **155**, 161
Crossley, Archibald 236
Cruikshank, George 345
cuneiform **16**, 31
Curtis, Cyrus 73

da Vinci, Leonardo 164, 278
Daguerre, Louis 166–167, 179
dance 70, 151, 183, 188, 197, 210
Darwin, Charles 2, 9
Daumier, Honoré 346, 347
Day, Benjamin 64
de Forest, Lee 132, 228–230, 233, 235, 246
de Tocqueville, Alexis 53, 55, 96
Debs, Eugene V. 72
Defoe, Daniel 72, 75
DeMille, Cecil B. 199, 217
democracy 20, 22, 38, 50, 55, 90, 95–96, 107, 135, 140, 191–192, 353
Depression, the 70, 76, 171, 209, 214, 233, 237–239, 253, 340, 344
Dewey, John 60, 112
Dickens, Charles 53, 54, 62, 75
Dickinson, John 51
Dickson, W.K.L. 186–187, 198
digital files 79, 143, 157, 159, 183, 210, 211, 218, **219**, 220–221, 267, 279, 283, 301, 304
Dilts, Marion May 112
Diocletian 89
disc jockeys 153–154, 160–161, 226

Disney, Walt 70, 152, 210, 214, 329
distraction 134, 137, 158–159
documentaries 171–172, 184, 194, 198, 206, 212, **212**
documentary photographs 164, 167, 169, 170–173, 178, 180n7, 184, 266
Dolby, Ray M. 156
Douglas, A.S. 318
Douglass, Frederick 61
downloading 5, 147–148, 157, 159, 161, 216, 217, 218, 290
Doyle, Arthur Conan 176
Dreiser, Theodore 68
DuMont Television Company 253, **254**, 255
Durant, Will 19–20
DVDs 104, 148, 156, 161, 216, 217–219, 221, 256, 271

Earl of Warwick 92
earphones 156, 158–159, 235, 236
Eastman, George 174–175, 179, 184, 186, 190
eBay 299, **341**
e-books 64, 67, 76–77, 83, 285. *See also* iPads; Kindles; Nooks
Edison, Thomas 120, 128, 142, 148–150, 160, 183, 186–188, 190, 193–194, 198–199, 203
education 10, 17, 22–23, 25, 28, 30, 37–38, 41–43, 59, 60, 62–63, 75, 104, 178, 207, 257, 273, 301–302, 311, 317, 319–320, 326, 328–329, 343, 351, 353
Edwards, Jonathan 47
Einstein, Alfred **46**
Eisenhower, Dwight D. 105
Eisenstein, Elizabeth 14, 38, 44
Eisenstein, Sergei 209
Elizabeth I 44
Ellis, Jim 296
Ellul, Jacques 175, 251, 277
email 4, 121, 133–135, 138–139, 144, 144n11, 244, 293, 299, 301, 309–311, 352, 354
Emerson, Ralph 87
English 32, 46, 53, 72, 75, 185, 200n5, 203, 221n2
Enlightenment, the 38, 45, 345
Entertainment Weekly 6
e-readers. *See* e-books, iPads, Kindles, Nooks
escapism 191, 238
Evans, Walker 171

Facebook 4, 126, 134, 135–136, 159,
    161, 164, 175, 294, 298, 301–303, 307,
    309, 311, 312n11, 316, 328, **341**, 354
FaceTime 7
Fairbanks, Richard 93
fake events 176–177, 180n16, 181n17,
    193, 211, **239**, **259**, 342, **342**, 347. *See
    also* photography, manipulation of;
    virtual events
Faraday, Michael 226, 252
Farben, I.G. 154
Farkas, Sandor Bölöni 53
Farnsworth, Philo 252, 272
fax (facsimile) 70, 121–122, 252
FCC (Federal Communications
    Commission) 234, **235**, 253, 255, 257,
    260, 263, 268, 345
Fenton, Roger 169
Fessenden, Reginald 228–229, 246
feudalism 38, 41–42, 90
fiction 30, **43**, 47, 74, 77, 158, 184, 193–
    194, 206–208, 210, 237, 238
file swapping 157
film 6, 156, 183, 185–186, 188–199,
    203–204, 208–220, 221n2, 255, 315
Fiore, Marilyn 154
First Amendment, the 52, **52**, 53, 55, 80,
    94–95, 198, 220, 228, 237, 339, 345.
    See also Constitution (United States);
    Bill of Rights
Flaherty, Robert 199, **212**
flash mobs 10, 135, 136, 311
Fleming, John Ambrose 229
Flickr 175, 301
Fonda, Jane 176
Fox, William 189
Franklin, Benjamin 4, 5, 48, **49**, 50, 52,
    93–95, 285, 346, 347
Franklin, James 48
Franklin, John 94
Franklin, William 50
free press 52, 53, 54, 95
Freed, Alan 153, 161
Freneau, Philip 51
Freud, Sigmund 2, 125
Friedman, Ted 319
Friedman, Thomas 133
Friese-Greene, William 186
Fulton, Robert **97**

Galen 45
Galileo 42
Garbo, Greta 193
Garrison, William Lloyd 60, **61**

Gee, James Paul 316, 329
Geist, Christopher 318
Gertie the Dinosaur 199, 210
Gessner, Patricia 7
Gilray, James 346
Gish, Lillian 190
globalization 133, 159, 267–268, 303,
    316
Gnanadesikan, Amalia 18, 26
Goldmark, Peter 152, 272
Goldwyn, Samuel 189, 207
Gone with the Wind **205**, 213–214, 220
Google 4, 6. 64, 83, 141, 144, 298, 302,
    307, 311, 328
Gore, Al 153
Gore, Tipper 153
Gorgias 335
Graef, Ailin 327–328
Grant, Cary 117
Grant, Ulysses S. 115
Gray, Elisha 126, 128, 141, 149
Great Depression, the 70, 76, 171, 209,
    214, 233, 237–239, 253, 340, 344
Greeley, Horace 60, 62, 65
Grierson, John 209
Griffith, D.W. 190, **194–195**, **196**, 199
Gutenberg, Johannes 15, 26, 38, 39, **40**,
    41, 42, 43, 44, 47, 54, 59, 285, 293,
    353
Gutenberg Galaxy, the 46, 60

Habermas, Jürgen 342–343
Hamilton, Alexander 50, 52
Hansen, Miriam 192
Harding, Warren G. 231
Harlow, Alvin 126
Harris, Joel Chandler 62
Haüy, Valentin 77–78
Havas, Charles 115
Havelock, Eric 20, 21
Hayes, Rutherford B. 61
Hays, Will 198, 220
Hearst, William Randolph 66, 68, 70,
    177, 343
Heidegger, Martin 351–352
Henry, Joseph 114, 226
Henry VIII 44
Heraclitus 82
heresy 42, 44, 46, 47
Herodotus 89
Herrold, Charles ("Doc"), 229–230
Herschel, John 166, 179
Hertz, Heinrich 226, 245
Herz, J.C. 322

hieroglyphs 17–19, 31
Higinbotham, William 318
Hill, Rowland 99–101, 107
Hine, Lewis 171, **172**, 178
Hitchcock, Alfred 209
Hogarth, William 177, 345
Hollander, Richard S. 158–159
Hollerith, Herman 279, 289
Hollingshead, Richard 214
Hollywood 184, 190, 194, 197, 199,
    204–210, 212–214, **219**, 220–221,
    258–259, 286
Homer 20–21
Hooke, Robert 114
Hoover, Herbert 232
Hopalong Cassidy 206
Hulu 6, 216, 271
humanism 21, 22, 37, 45

iBook 64
Iliad, the 20, 31
Industrial Revolution, the 8, 29, 53–54,
    61–65, 77, 79, 115, 126, 285, 337, 343
Innis, Harold 13, 17, 20, 25, 46
Instagram 5, 175
interactivity 5
Internet 5–7, 10, 14, 30, 71, 78–79, 82,
    87, 104, 108, 115, 120–121, 135, 138–
    141, 148, 157, 177, 215, 218–219, 235,
    245, 251, 258, 260, 269, 270, 283, **286**,
    293–311, 318, 328, 340, 343–344,
    352–354; defined, 311n1
Intolerance **195–196**
iPads 5, 64, 71, 290. *See also* e-books;
    Kindles; Nooks
iPhones 121, 138, 144, 158, 245, 283,
    328
iPods 147, 157–158, 161, 216, 259, 271
Isocrates 335
isolation 4, 5, 7, 14, 16, 42, 68, 76, 80,
    87, 90, 104, 111–112, 125, 126, 130,
    137, 158–159, 188, 191, 215, 217–
    218, 223n21, 242, 308, 319, 338, 343,
    349–350n14, 352–353, 354
Ives, Herbert 253

Jackson, Andrew 54
Jackson, William Henry 170
James, William 298
James I 44
Janssen, Pierre 186
Jazz Singer, the 204, 220
Jefferson, Thomas 40, 52–53, 95
Jenkins, Charles Francis 253

Jensen, De Lamar 42
Jixing, Pan 39
Jobs, Steve 284, 302, 317
John of Plano Carpini 39
Johnson, Eldridge 151
Johnson, Lyndon B. 266
Johnson, Samuel 23
Jolie, Angelina 197
Jolson, Al, 204 220
Jones, Buck 206
Joplin, Scott 151
journalism 22, 48, 50–54, 61, 64–70, 72,
    79, 80–82, 113, 115, 117–120, 136,
    139, 164, 169, 170–173, 178, 184,
    193–194, 198, 211, 266–267, 284,
    287, 304–306, 342–343, 353

Keaton, Buster 194
Kennedy, John F. 264, 265, 273, 344
Kerry, John 176
Kindles 5, 64, 77. *See also* e-books;
    iPads; Nooks
King, Rodney 184
King Jr., Martin Luther 264
Klipsch, Paul 152
Kloss, Henry 152
Kurasawa, Akira 210

labeling 153
Laemmle, Carl 189
Lamb, K.J. **2**
Land, Edwin 175
Lange, Dorothea 171
Lansing, James 152
Lanza, Adam 324
laptop. *See* computer
Latin 23, 26, 32, 41, 43–44, 46, 89
Lee, Ivy 70, 342
Leibniz, Gottfried 278
Levy, Steven 158, 309
Leyden, Peter 287
librarians 20
libraries 14, **21**, 39, 43, 44, 48, 60,
    62–63, 77, 159, 214, 301, 303–304,
    351. *See also* Alexandrian Library
Lichfield, Lord 100
Lichtenstein, Roy 178
Licklider, J.C.R. 294, 310
Lieberman, Joseph 326
Lincoln, Abraham 63, 70, 115, 176, 346
Lippmann, Walter 70, 70–71, 348
literacy, 3–4, 10, 13–20, **21**, 30–31,
    33–34n25, 37, 41, 43, 44–47, 54, 63,
    70, 90–91, 107, 203–204, 213, 214,

244, 245, 259, 316, 335, 336; and
gender 25–29, 35n46, 42, **43;** and
race 28–29, 60–62; and social class
22–23, 25–27, 29–30, 33–34n25, **45,**
62–63, 99–100, 191, 209
literature 18, 22, 44–45, 75, 207
Lloyd, Harold 194
Lodge, Oliver 226, 228
Loew, Marcus 189, 193
Logan, Robert K. **19**
London, Jack 68
Lord, Daniel 198
Louis XI 92
Lovejoy, Elijah 60
Lovelace, Ada 278–279, 289
LPs 152, 154, 157, 161. *See also* records
(phonograph albums)
Ludd, Ned 77
Lumière brothers (Louis and Auguste)
186–187, 193, 199
Lunsford, Andrea 30
Luther, Martin 15, 43, 44, 55, 89, 343

magazines 2, 8, 41, 48, 50, 60, 62, 68,
72–75, **75**, 77, 80–81, 105–106, 117,
139, 169, 171, 173–174, 184, 188, 191,
197, 203, 217, 236, 251, 284–285, 293,
303, 315, 337, 345, 347
mail 4, 9, 39, 40, **47**, 48, 60, 66, 70,
73–74, 80, 87–108, 112, 115, 140,
217, 293, 311
Manovich, Lev 277
Mao Tse Tung 26
Marco Polo 39, 54, 88
Marconi, Anne Jameson 227
Marconi, Guglielmo 59, 60, 226–227,
227, 245, 246
Marey, Etienne Jules 186, 198
Marhsall, Thurgood 82
Maxwell, James Clerk 126, 226, 245
May, Joseph 252, 272
Mayer, Louis B. 189
McCain, John 344
McCarthy, Joseph 82, 176, 207, 264, 272
McClure, S.S. 73
McCormick, Robert 68
McGonigal, Jane 318
McGuffey, William **75**
McLuhan, Marshall 3, 8, 14, 17, 37, 39,
41, 46, 60, 90, 148, 213, 258, 274n14,
299, 352
McPherson, Aimee Semple, **231**
mediated communication, defined, 1,
3–4, 354n5; effects of, 2–4, 6–9, 11,

11n1, 17, 30, 42, 76, 100–101, 107,
130, 147–148, 151, 158, 163–164,
184, 190–191, 216–217, 225, 287,
309, 320–321, 329, 347,
351–354
Méliès, George 193
memory 10, 14–15, 20–21, 33–34n25,
178, 200n11, 220, 282, 319, 352
mercantilism 50, 90, 91
microphones 128, 150–151, 204, 320
middle class 38, 42, 54, 59, 62–65,
75–76, 167, 187, 192, 198
Mill, Henry 77
millennials, 2
Milton, John **51–52**
Minow, Newton 260
mobile phones. *See* cell phones;
smartphones
monasteries 23, **23**, 25, 32, 39, 90
monks **23**, 40, 41, 47. *See also* priests;
clergy
monopoly 131, 139
Montgolfier, Jean 40
Montgomery Ward, Aaron 103–104
MOOCs (Massive Open Online
Courses) 301
morality 43, **47–48**, 75, **75**, **129**, 130,
150–151, 153, 177–178, 187,
197–198, 212–213, 323–326,
325–326
Morita, Akio 156, 158
Morris, Lloyd 191
Morse, Samuel F.B. 70, **91**, 111, 114,
115, 120, 122, 131, 167
Morse Code 59, 113, 117, 118, 131, 225,
228, 229, **229**, 230
motion pictures. *See* movies
movable type 37–38, 47, 54
movie ratings **208**, 213, 221. *See also*
video game ratings
movie theaters 5, 189, 190, 192–193,
199, 206, 216–218, 220, 251, 255
movies 6, 10, 30, 60, 70, 104, 114, 128,
139, 151, 155–156, 171–172, 178,
183–199, 200n5, 203–223, 221n2,
222n7, 239, 252, 258, 286, **286**,
315–318, **316**
Muir, John 68
Müllensiefen, Daniel 11n1
Mullin, John 155
Munsey, Frank 73
Murphy, George 197
Murrow, Edward R. 80, 240, 264, 272,
344

music 5, **46**, 126, 144, 147–148, 151–
    161, 191, 217, 226, 229–231, **236**,
    240, 244, 315, 353
Muybridge, Eadweard 185–186, **186**,
    198
Mydans, Carl 171
MySpace 328

Nanook of the North 199, **212**
Napster 159, 161
Nasaw, David 185, 192
Nast, Thomas 346, **346**, 347
nationalism 38, 46, 70, 112, 120,
    207–209, 227, 233–234, **344**
Native Americans 13, **28**, 68, 69, 82, 93,
    170, 346
Negroponte, Nicholas 141
Netflix 87, 184, 216, 219, 271, 303
news 5–7, 53, 59, 61, 64–71, 73, 77–79,
    80, 112–121, 132–133, 135–136,
    139–140, 156, 194, 206, 211–212,
    230–231, 236, 238–241, 245–247,
    263–270, 272, 284, 297, 299, 301–
    302, 304–307, 311
newspapers 8, 14, 41, 48, 50–55, 59–64,
    66–74, 77, 78–80, 83, 94–96, 100,
    103–106, 113–115, 117, 119, 169,
    172–173, 176–177, 184, 191, 193,
    203, 231, 237, 240–241, 251, 254, 265,
    284–285, 293, 301–302, 305, 307,
    336–337, 340, 342–343, 345
Newton, Isaac 42
Niépce, Joseph Nicéphore 166,
    178–179
Nightingale, Florence 130
Nipkow, Paul 252, 272
Nixon, Richard 106, 264, 265, 344
nonfiction 30, 158, 184, 207, 211, 240
Nooks 64. *See also* e-books; iPads;
    Kindles
novels 5, 8, 32, **43**, 47, 63, 72, 75–76,
    158, 178

Obama, Barak 139
objectivity 22, 118–120. *See also*
    rationality
obscenity **235**, 237. *See also*
    pornography
Odyssey, the 20, 31
Oersted, Hans Christian 114
Ohmann, Richard 338
Omidyar, Pierre 299–300
Ong, Walter 14
online libraries 77

oral tradition 13, 15, 20–21, 33–34n25,
    37, 41, 64, 71, 88, 90–91, 125,
    147–148, 150–151, 153, 183, 185,
    187, 204, 217, 226, 238–239, 259, 335,
    352
Oscars. *See* Academy Awards
Ottinger, George M. **98**
Oxford English Dictionary 304

Paine, Thomas 51, 52, 137, 343
paper 4–5, 15, 17, 25, 32, 39, 40, 50, 54,
    59, 63–64, 82–83, 173, 337
papyrus 20, **21**, 22, **23**, 31, 88, 90
parchment 20, 22, 25, 40, 90
Parks, Gordon 164
Parsons, Richard 159
Pascal, Blaise 278
Patel, Anu 319
patents 78, 115, 122, 126, 141, 148, 150,
    187, 190, 226, 228, 252
Patten, Simon 192
Patterson, Joseph Medill 68
personal ads **341**. *See also* advertising;
    classified ads
Pfleumer, Fritz 154
Phaedrus 20–21, 33–34n25
phone. *See* cellphones; smartphones;
    telephone
phonetics 15
photography, 5, 10, 59, 69–71, 83, 114,
    128, 133, 135, 138–139, 141, 144,
    145n28, 148, **149**, 150–151, 155–156,
    160, 163–179, 180n13, 183, 185, 187,
    191, 203, 206, 229, 231–232, 294, 300,
    335, 351; manipulation of, 176–177,
    180n16, 181n17, 193, 211. *See also*
    fake events; virtual events
photojournalism 139, 164, 169,
    170–173, 178, 193–194, 211
Pickford, Mary 190, 196, 199
piracy 157, 159, 307, 311
Plato 20, 21, 335
politics 50–51, 61, 64–66, 71, 74, 79,
    104, 111, 113–114, 117–119, 135,
    164, 176–177, 197–198, 206–208,
    212, 220, 237, 240, 242–243, **262**,
    264–265, 267, 299, 301, 326, **336**,
    341, 343–346, **344**, 349
Popcorn, Faith 6, 7, 215
Popov, Alexander 226
pornography **47–48**, 178, 308–309.
    See also obscenity
Porter, Edwin 193–194
postal service. *See* mail

Postman, Neil 3, 6, 7, 52, 112, 251, 273–274n4, 352
postmaster 92–96, 100, 102–103, 105, 131
Poulsen, Valdemar 154
Powers, Bruce R. 213
Preece, William 126–127, 227
Presley, Elvis 153
priests 14, 16–18, 23, 25, 37, 39, 47, 90, 198. *See also* clergy; monks
printers 121
printing 3, 9, 15, 27–28, 37 55, 59 84, 172–173, 335–336
printing press 5, 37–39, 40, 42–44, 59, 63, **69**, 82, 84, 113, 337
privacy 42, 130, 134, 137, 139, 158, 303, 309
proletariat. *See* working class
propaganda 11, 38, 44, 80, 132, 176, 193, 207, 209, 243, 335, 343, 348–349, 349n10
Protestant Reformation. *See* Reformation (Protestant), the
Protestantism 43, 44, **52**. *See also* Counter-Reformation; Reformation (Protestant), the
Ptolemy 45
Ptolemy II 88
public administration 17, 22, 23, 26–27, 88
public relations 66, 335, 341–343
publishing 48, 52, 66, 68–69, 72, 74, 76, 80, 82, 118, 172, 239
Pulitzer, Joseph 66, 67, 68
Putnam, Robert 6, 217–218, 223n19
Pyle, Ernie 81–82

Quindlen, Anna 137
Quintilian 335
quipu **27**, 88

racism 28–30, 60, 62, 65, 67–69, 71–72, 81, 131, 153, 170, 184–185, 192, **194–195**, 207, 242, 264, 326, 343, 346, 349–350n14. *See also* bigotry
radio 7, 10, 37, 60, 70–71, 78, 80, 87, 115, 119, 120, 131–133, 137–139, 148, 152, 154, **155**, 156, 160, 200n5, 203, 212, 221n2, 225–249, 251, 253–254, 257–261, 284, 293, 305, 315, 317, 339–340, 343–344, 347–348. *See also* wireless
Rather, Dan 304
ratings **208**, 213, 221, **325–326**.

rationality 22, 38, 45, 277. See also objectivity
RCA (Radio Corporation of America) 152, 155, 227, 232, 237
Reader, The **29**
reading **21**, 37, 41–43, 75–77, 148, 241, 301, 353
Reagan, Ronald 197
recording (audio) 5, 10, 30, 60, 147–155, 157–159, 161, 304
records (phonograph albums) 16, 150, **152**, 154, **154**, 232. *See also* LPs
records (documentation) 16, 18, 22, 39, 351
Reeves, Rosser 336
Reformation (Protestant), the 15, 37, 43, 44, 45. See also Counter-Reformation; Protestantism
religion 17, **19**, 23, 25, 28, 30, 32, 37, 42–47, **52**, 67, 71–72, 74, 90, 92, 114, 163, 197–198, 121, **231**, 309, **323**, 327–328, 345–346
Remington, Frederic 68
Renaissance, the 32, 37, 44–45, 47
reporters 65–66, 69–70, 80, 82, 117–118, 155, 171, 197, 266, 284, 287, 304, 306, 342, 353
Reuter, Paul Julius **91**, 115–116
Reuter(s) 70, 91, 116, 123n15
Revolution (American), the 28, 48, 50–52, 94, 95
Richardson, Samuel 75
Righi, Auguste 227
Riis, Jacob 69
Rivington, James 51
Robert, Nicholas-Louis 63
Robertson, James 169
Rockefeller, John D. 68
Roget, Peter 185
Romney, Mitt (Willard) 344
Roosevelt, Franklin Delano 68, 240–242, **241**, 246, 344
Roosevelt, Theodore 68, 344
Rosing, Boris 252–253, 272
Rosser, James 321

Sacks, David 19
Said, Salma 135
Sargon 88
Sarnoff, David 243, 253–254
satellite 6, 87, 128, 132–133, 135, 141, 143, 145n19, 219, 244, 247, 251, 255, 263, 269, 273
Savonarola 47
Schickard, Wilhelm 278

Schieffer, Bob (Robert) 344
scholarship (writing) 27, 46
Schulze, Johann 165, 178
Scott, Leon 148
scribes 17, 18, 20, 22, 23, 25, 41, 44
scriptoria **23**, 41
Second Life **305**–306, 316, 321, 330
secularism 17, 21, 22, 37, 44, 45
Sejong the Great 26
Seneca 22
Sennett, Mack 194
Sequoyah **28**
Serrin, Judith 69
Serrin, William 69
sewing machine 3
Shahn, Ben 171
Shakespeare, William 92, 336
Shannon, Claude 142, 279, 289
Shepard, Horatio 64
Sholes, Christopher 78, 83
shortwave 155
Shumate, Jane **28**
silent film 183–199, 204, 212, 221,
    221n3
Sinclair, Upton 68–69, 198
Skinner, B.F. 319
Skype 4, 7, 126, 141, 143, 354
smartphones 1, 6, 11n1, 134, 137–138,
    140, 144, 159–160, 184, 218, 283, 321
Smith, Alfred E. 190
Smith, Oberlin 154, 160
Smith, Trixie 153
Snow, Charles Percy 281
Snowden, Edward 304
social change 17, 44, 46, 50–51, 60–77,
    100–101, 130–140, 151–158, 164–
    178, 184–188, 197–198, 204–208,
    213, 217–220, 226, 236–237, 242–
    268, 273, 287–288, 299–302, 307–
    300, 323–327, 337, 343, 345–346,
    352–353
social class 17, 22–23, 25, 26–30, 34n29,
    38, 41–46, **45**, 50–51, 60, 62, 63, 67,
    75, 99, 100, 131, 153, 183–184, 187–
    192, 204, 209, 237, 260, 273, 288, 337
social networks. *See* listings
Socrates 14, 20, 21, 33–34n25
Sontag, Susan 178
Sony 156, 161
Sousa, John Philip 150
specialization 42, 45, 47, 71–74, 77–78,
    81, 102, 214, 244, 247, 255, 260, 270,
    303, 305, 353
Spectator, the **2**
Spiegelman, Art 178

Spielberg, Steven 184, 203
Spotify 11n1, 159, 160, 161, 244
stamps 50, 99, 100, 101, 102, 106, 107,
    108, 112, 113
Standage, Tom 303
Stanford, Leland 185
Steffens, Lincoln 68
Steichen, Edward 174
Stein, Joel 2
Stewart, James, 214
Stewart, Martha 176, 181n17
Stibitz, George 280–281, 289
Stieglitz, Alfred 174, 179
Stone, John 228
Stowe, Harriet Beecher, 137
Strowger, Almon 129–130, 142
subscriptions 48, 64–65, 73, 76, 103,
    113, 131, 160, 237, 240
Sukarno 184
Summerfield, Arthur 105
Surveys 1, 11n1, 30, 143, 236–237, 310,
    342, 348

tablets. *See e* books, iPads, Kindles,
    Nooks
Talbot, William Fox 166–168, 179
"talkies" 203–204
tape (audio) 148, 154–155, 159
tape (video) 155–156, 161, 184, 213–
    214, 216–221, 267–268, 273
Tarbell, Ida 68
telegraph 5, 9, 59, 67, 70, 78, 87, 111–
    122, 131, 133, 149, 203, 227, 252, 351
telephone cable 59, 67, 114, 120, 122,
    132, **134**, 142–143, 148, 219, 251,
    268–273
telephone 2–3, 5, 10, 87, 112, 115, **116**,
    121, 125–144, 144n11, 144n14, 148,
    159, 163, 203, 217, 225, 227, 229, 237,
    293–294, 296, 300, 310, 354
television 2, 4–8 10, 14, 30, 60, 70–71,
    74, 78, 80–81, 87, 104, 115, 119–120,
    128, 133, 136–37, 148, 151, 156, 174,
    184, 212–220, 233, 236, 238, 243,
    251–273, **281**, 284, 293, 302, 305,
    310, 317–318, 329, 339, 340, 343, 345,
    347–348, 353
texting 134, 300
Thomas, Isaiah 51
Thompson, Fred 197
Thompson, J. Walter 338
Thompson, Kristin 197, 204, 219
Thomson, David 213
Thomson, J.J. 252
Thomson, John 170

Thomson, Lord 255
Thoreau, Henry David 354
Time magazine 2
Toffler, Alvin 288
Tomlinson, Ray 300
Torres, Della 91
transcontinental telephone line. *See* cable
translation 44, 45, 290n10
Truscott, Tom 296
Tumblr 136, 301
Turing, Alan 279, 289
Twitter 4–5, 10, 14, 134–137, 144n11, 294, 300, 303, 307
Tydings, Millard 176
typewriters, 59, 77–78, 121, 283–284, 315

universities, 23, 39, 48, 63, 90, 107, 234, 294, 296, 301, 310, 318, 328

Vail, Alfred 114, 131
Vail, Theodore 131
Victoria I (Alexandrina) 132
video 144, 148, 155–157, 175, 180n13, 183, 210–211, 213–214, 218–219, **219**, 252, 271, 283, 285–286, 296–297, 300–301
video game ratings **325–326**. *See also* movie ratings
video games 5–7, 11, 30, 81, 217–218, 258, 300, **305–306**, 315–330
videotape 155, 156, 161, 184, 213, 216, 217, 218, 219, 220, 221, 267, 268, 273
Vine 5
violence 308, 317, 323–326, 344, 349
virtual events **305–306**, 316, 320–321, 330. *See also* fake events; photography, manipulation of
von Henneberg, Berthold 38
von Neumann, John 279

Walker, John 73
Walkman 148, 156, 157, 161
Wanamaker, John 103
Wang, An 284
War of the Worlds, the **239**, 246
Warner brothers (Aaron, Hirsz, Itzhak, Szmul) 189, 193
Washington, George, 51, 70
Watson, Thomas 127
Weaver, Warren 279, 289
websites 139, 309, 327, 351
Webster, Noah 117

Wedgewood, Thomas 165–166, 178
Weiner, Norbert 279
Welles, Orson 207, 209, **239**, 246
Wells, H.G. **239**
Wells, Ida B. 72
Wertham, Fredric 177–178
Weston, Edward 174
Wheatstone, Charles 114
White, E.B. 271, 272
White, William Allen 68
Wigman, Charles 169
WikiLeaks 304
Wikipedia 303–304, 307, 311
Wiley, George 261
Wilson, Jackie 153
Winslet, Kate **29**
wireless 5, 59, 132, 141, 225–230. *See also* radio
Wizard of Oz, the 133, 220
Wolff, Bernard 115
women 25–30, 35n54, 38, **43**, 65–68, 72–77, 80, 94, **129**, 130, 142, 145n29, 153, 176, 180n16, 181n17, 192, 197, 221, 275n20, 298, 299, 318, 321–322, **321**, 324–325, 339, 348
word processing 283–285
working class 28, **43**, 62–63, 65, 73, 99, 183, 187–192, 209, 237, 260
World War I 53, 69, 70, 80, 105, 132, 151, 176, 208–209, 225, 227, 229, **229**, 230, 234, 253, 339, 343
World War II 68, 70, 73, 80, 105, **121**, 138, 152–153, 155, 174, 206–207, 209–210, 213, 238, 240–241, 243, 253–254, 270, 277, 279–281, 344
World Wide Web 245, 293, 297, 298, 310, 311, 348; defined, 311n1
writing 9, 13–18, 20–31, 37, 40, 46, 101, 104, 130, 300, 335, 354; and empire 13, 16–17, 20, **23**, 67, 88, 106

Young, Thomas 148
Younger, Cole **127**
YouTube 4–5, 135–136, 139, 164, 175, 183, **235**, 267, 301, 303, **309**

Zenger, John Peter 50, 52, 55
zip codes 105, 108
Zuckerberg, Mark 303
Zukor, Adolph 189
Zuse, Konrad 281, 289
Zwingli, Ulrich 44
Zworykin, Vladimir 253, 272